"With direct, encouraging, and heartfelt advice,
Lythcott-Haims covers a lot of sensitive, relevant, and
crucial territory."—*Booklist* (starred review)

In the twentieth century, psychologists came up with five markers of adulthood: finish your education, get a job, leave home, marry, and have children. Since then, every generation has been held to those same markers. Yet so much has changed about the world around us. Those markers are choices, and they're all valid, but any one person's choices do not make them more or less of an adult.

A former Stanford dean of freshman and undergraduate advising and author of the perennial bestseller *How to Raise an Adult* as well as the lauded memoir *Real American*, Julie Lythcott-Haims has encountered hundreds of twentysomethings (and thirtysomethings, too), who, faced with those markers, feel they're just playing the part of "adult" while struggling with anxiety, stress, and general unease. *Your Turn* offers compassion, personal experience, and practical strategies for living a more authentic adulthood, as well as inspiration through interviews with dozens of voices from the rich diversity of the human population who have successfully launched their lives.

Being an adult is not about a particular checklist; it is, instead, a process, one you get progressively better at over time—becoming comfortable with uncertainty and gaining the know-how to keep going. Once you begin to practice it, being an adult becomes the most complicated yet also the most abundantly rewarding thing. And Julie Lythcott-Haims is here to help readers take their turn.

wise older friend whose wisdom will benefit anyone who's trying to figure out this thing we call life—which is to say, everyone."

—Lori Gottlieb, *New York Times* bestselling author of *Maybe You Should Talk to Someone*

"This is the one book you need to read if you're ready to take up the challenge of becoming your true and vital adult self. It is filled with great stories of people just like you, told by a master storyteller. We need more adults in the world and it really is *Your Turn*."

—Bill Burnett, #1 *New York Times* bestselling coauthor of *Designing Your Life* and *Designing Your Work Life*

"As a wise person once said, 'Prepare the child for the road, not the road for the child.' In all the discussions and debates about the challenges faced by young people today, too little effort has been spent helping them feel empowered, excited, and ready for the challenges of adult life. Julie Lythcott-Haims, after her parenting masterpiece *How to Raise an Adult*, has turned her skill and wisdom into a guide for living a fulfilling, rich, and meaningful life."

—Greg Lukianoff, *New York Times* bestselling coauthor of *The Coddling of the American Mind*

YOUR

HOW TO BE AN ADULT

TURN

JULIE LYTHCOTT-HAIMS

A HOLT PAPERBACK   HENRY HOLT AND COMPANY   NEW YORK

Holt Paperbacks
Henry Holt and Company
Publishers since 1866
120 Broadway
New York, New York 10271
www.henryholt.com

A Holt Paperback® and ⓗ® are registered trademarks of
Macmillan Publishing Group, LLC.

The Library of Congress has cataloged the hardcover edition as follows:

Names: Lythcott-Haims, Julie, author.
Title: Your Turn : how to be an adult / Julie Lythcott-Haims.
Description: First edition. | New York, New York : Henry Holt and Company, 2021. | Includes index.
Identifiers: LCCN 2020051626 (print) | LCCN 2020051627 (ebook) | ISBN 9781250137777 (hardcover) |
    ISBN 9781250137784 (ebook)
Subjects: LCSH: Adulthood. | Adult children—Psychology. | Parent and adult child.
Classification: LCC HQ799.95 .L97 2021 (print) | LCC HQ799.95 (ebook) | DDC 305.24—dc23
LC record available at https://lccn.loc.gov/2020051626
LC ebook record available at https://lccn.loc.gov/2020051627

ISBN 9781250838414 (trade paperback)

Our books may be purchased in bulk for promotional, educational, or business use. Please contact
your local bookseller or the Macmillan Corporate and Premium Sales Department at (800) 221-7945,
extension 5442, or by e-mail at MacmillanSpecialMarkets@macmillan.com.

Originally published in hardcover in 2021 by Henry Holt and Company

First Holt Paperbacks Edition 2022

Designed by Kelly S. Too

Interior illustrations by Clarice Cho © 2021

Printed in the United States of America

1   3   5   7   9   10   8   6   4   2

CONTENTS

YOUR TURN

INTRODUCTION

We're adults. When did that happen? And how do
we make it stop?

—Meredith Grey, *Grey's Anatomy*

Fresh off a book about how we parents can inadvertently rob our children of agency and resilience when we do too much for them, I got a call from my publisher suggesting I write a book about adulting for young adults. I agreed. I got a nice contract that would help pay my bills. And even better than the money was knowing that my publisher believed in me.

Over the last ten years, a whole lot's been said about young adults who are unready for adulthood. For everyone, from the media, to influencers, to relatives, to you yourselves with your adulting memes, your hesitance to become adults has been a constant subject. I read everyone else's stuff. I tried to enter the world of all that writing and joking to see if I could offer something new and useful. But repeatedly, and maddeningly, I came up short. I was stuck at the front door of this subject, wondering, *Who the hell am I to try to tell anyone else how to live their life?* And *How do I write about a broad topic while honoring the needs of each individual?* For three years I kept failing to write the book you're now reading. And while I continued to fail, the stereotypes and memes about you grew even more popular.

After a ton of thinking about adulthood and its vast and various pieces; after considering, through a lens of humility and curiosity, you, the young adult in question, and your generation more broadly; and after searching myself for what I, as the author, could bring, I decided the only way I could write this book was to drop any pretense of authority about this all-important and universal subject and, instead, lead with vulnerability. So, here goes:

I am not wiser than you.

I have been broken, sad, scared, bewildered, worried, and ashamed.

I try to help humans make their way in life.

I'm rooting for all of us to be okay.

This book comes from that place.

This isn't a generic adulthood we're talking about. It's yours. I'm going to try to cut through the noise, the judgment, and the bullshit, and offer you thoughts from my own experience that I think might be useful. I'll pretend you're one of my former students who met me over coffee for a bit of life advice, or a younger relative who decided to take a chance that I might be a good listener. Whatever I have to offer you, equally valid are your own hopes, fears, plans, and dreams. I want you to bring those to the reading of this book. I want you to bring it all.

There's a lot here and you might get the most out of it if you talk it through with friends, elders, and mentors. That way, beyond whatever you get from me, you also get love and support from those who know you best and who are going through it all with you, more or less, or who have been through it themselves. Tackle a chapter together once a week, or once a month. Share the stuff you feel you've got a handle on. Listen well to others and see what you can learn from them. Maybe take a bit of a risk and open up about your fears and concerns and watch how that vulnerability builds connection and understanding. It's a lot. Commit to supporting each other. Commit to holding each other accountable for whatever growth everyone wants to experience. None of us is meant to go it alone.

If that sounds cool, then let's get started. Note, this book is embedded with valuable questions, considerations, advice, and lessons. Get a journal or some other way to track your thoughts. As you read, notice and be curious about what resonates with you from the main text, the lists, and the stories. You'll decide which pieces are relevant to your journey and which are not. Each chapter concludes with four questions which I encourage you to unpack and reflect upon within yourself and maybe also with friends, family, mentors, and your therapist/coach (if you have one). These questions are designed to help you become more familiar with your own self. There are no "right" answers.

1

ADULTING

(WHAT EXACTLY *IS* IT?)

my whole life is on the tip of my tongue
empty pages for the no longer young
—Indigo Girls, "Virginia Woolf"

As you read this I'm past the halfway point of my life, and my young adulthood waves at me in the rearview mirror. The wrinkles I thought I'd somehow avoid stand out in every photo. The gray hairs I started plucking when they first arrived are overtaking the brown. My college sweatshirt feels even softer than it did back in the day, but it has a lot of holes. My dying days are nearer, I know. Is that weird to say? Maybe. But, it's true. Yet even so, I am still becoming me. And you are becoming you. This I also know.

What a cool thing.

You may think that adulting is all about paying your taxes and trying to make sense of the benefits package at work (assuming you're lucky enough to have a benefits package, or steady work for that matter). But you would be wrong to think it's all about that stuff. It *is* about that stuff. But that's like saying high school is about registering for classes and finding your locker.

Think bigger. Adulting can't be boiled down to ten tips or even a thousand. Being an adult is a state of mind that ignites the "doing" that ends up forging your adult self. It's part wanting to, part having to, and part learning how. The hardest part is that because it's happening in your own mind you pretty much do it by yourself. Yet you have all the adult humans around you going through it, too. They get it.

I wish I could tell you why adulting seems so complicated or unattractive these days. Maybe your parents' generation gave off a lot of stress and anxiety and you looked at them and thought, *Blech! Who would want to do that?* Or maybe all the basic life skills just aren't learned at home or taught in school anymore, and you feel like an idiot for not knowing how to do what older people think you should already know how to do by now. Maybe your parents were like superheroes who stepped in to help with everything right in the nick of time, so you didn't get a lot of practice handling messy situations or tough feelings. Maybe it's your friends who seem like superheroes, out there on the right "track" in Adult Land, and you're judging yourself for not being as far along as they are. Maybe it all just feels like *a lot.*

Just gonna pause here to say that the "right track" concept is bullshit. I swear to you there is no track, no path, no lockstep plan that equals adulting that you're somehow failing to adhere to. Life is too grand and mysterious for any track to keep up with. It's a wide-open landscape like the Pacific Ocean, the Rocky Mountains, the high plateaus of Montana, the sweeping fields of Iowa or Louisiana, the intricate grid of a major city like Chicago, Atlanta, or New York. You get to decide where to be out there, what you're doing, and how to navigate toward it. You'll have others with you—the people you choose to spend your life with. But you'll chart your particular path on your own. And if you want to feel really alive you'll examine your choices continually and make adjustments every now and then.

Adulting is a relatively new verb (thank you, Millennials) but the concept is as natural as breathing. In the twentieth century, psychologists came up with five markers of adulthood, which were, in this order: finish your education, get a job, leave home, marry, and have children. This old idea is the definition your generation has been held to. Yet so much has changed about life and living since that definition was formulated:

Finish your education. Why finish your education at eighteen or twenty-two when you're probably going to live to a hundred? Today we know that going back to school throughout the later decades of your life is a great thing, whether it's to gain a new skill set or to soak up the enrichment that comes from lifelong learning.

Get a job. You need to pay your bills somehow. Yes, that's true. But you will have multiple jobs in your lifetime, unlike your great-grandfather who may have had precisely one job all his life, or your great-grandmother whose job was likely to stay home. Work looks so different today—the possibilities are almost endless. Conceptually, it belongs in the adulting definition, but it would be better phrased as "Support yourself somehow."

Leave home. Even if you want to, you may not be able to leave home anytime soon, because macroeconomic forces have made it impossible for you to afford to live independently in the town in which you grew up. Multigenerational living works perfectly well in many cultures as long as everyone is doing their fair share. And that's the key. It may not be realistic to expect you'll *leave* home; being an adult is about behaving responsibly and accountably and having freedom and independence in whatever dwelling you call your home.

Marry and have children. Okay, sure, if you feel like it. Or you may remain both single and childless. Or maybe you'll have a lifelong partner without a religion or state sanctifying your union. And maybe you and your partner will have children, or maybe you won't. Or you may have children without having a partner. Neither marrying nor having children is any longer a requirement of adulthood.

All of these are choices, and they're all valid and up to you, and your choices along these lines do not make you any more or less an adult. Except you *must* have a way to support yourself. That's not negotiable. But it's hardly all there is to adulting.

For a more up-to-date take on the topic of adulting, I turned to my kids and their friends—then eighteen- and twenty-year-olds—for their definition. Sitting on the front patio of our house after feeding them brunch, here's what I got out of them about #adulting:

- It's up to *you*.

- It's realizing you can do whatever you want, and then dealing with the consequences.

- It's independence more than anything.

- It's walking down a street and getting that feeling that you're in charge of where you go.

- Making your own decisions.

- Cooking.

- The shopping is a big part of it. Actually going to the store, picking out food, choosing what you want to eat. Just having to actually worry about your nutrition instead of having someone worrying about that for you. You can eat caramel for the rest of your life. But it would be a very short and miserable life. You can eat "whatever the fuck," but you will suffer from whatever the fuck.

- It's knowing you don't *have* to. The first day I was at college, I knew we had the school orientation the next day, which was BS, and I was like, *I don't WANT to do that.* So, I went to the radio station with a bunch of punk rock dudes, and said, "I don't want to wake up at eight a.m. and make a dumb poster," and they were all, "Then don't." And I was all, "Cool, yeah, I don't *have* to."

- It's a certain level of if not *actual competency*, if not *faking competency*, then a certain level of *projecting competency*.

My house used to be filled with these kids and their hilarious laughter, and it became way too quiet after they'd all gone their separate ways toward what's next. Even though I'm so happy for them to be headed wherever they're going, I miss them. A lot. I offer to cook for them whenever they pay us a visit, even though they can eat "whatever the fuck." Maybe because.

There are other markers—the somewhat incongruous, age-based adulting stuff we've enacted into law and policy in this country. A brief snapshot:

18: Fight and die for your country
Create an Airbnb account
Vote

Marry without your parents' consent

Be accountable for yourself in the eyes of the law

21: Drink alcohol and smoke tobacco and cannabis

25: Rent a car (This is when your brain has fully developed. Coincidence?)

Run for Congress

30: Run for Senate

35: Run for President

In spite of these markers, William Kamkwamba built a wind turbine to generate power to save his Malawian village from famine at age fourteen. Malala Yousafzai dared to attend school in the Swat Valley in northwest Pakistan and actively promoted the right of girls to do so, and when she was fifteen, a member of the Taliban shot her in the head for it, but she survived and continued her activism. Greta Thunberg sailed across the Atlantic Ocean at age sixteen to force indifferent elders to pay attention to the climate crisis. Are these not examples of #adulting? A sixteen-year-old high school student at the Groton School in Massachusetts cited Greta's example and said he felt like he was wasting his life by being away at school in the woods. I told him not to compare himself to Greta or to anybody else. "Thoreau went off to the woods to learn," I reminded him. "At some point you will come out of the woods and figure out what you want to make of your life."

This book isn't about the absurdity of some of the above legal distinctions or about the few examples of humans who defy the odds at a young age. It's a compassionate beckoning into the freedoms and responsibilities of adulthood whatever your task at hand may be. The definition of adulting should be one that applies to everyone, throughout time, and that withstands changing societal norms and macroeconomic forces. The best I can come up with is this: You begin as an infant, completely cared for by others, and at the end of life you're completely cared for by others before you die. It's those sweet, sweet years in between that are the adult years. A vast set of years (if we're lucky) in which, barring having a significant disability, we are capable of caring for ourselves. That's pretty much it.

I know you want to succeed at it. But you may have been misled about what that means. A successful life is not about getting into a certain school, or having a certain job or career, or about how much money you have. It's not about perfection, making a singular noteworthy achievement, or having the most followers. People will hold these things out as the finish line for you to cross. But forget that. There is no finish line. Your work will feel most fulfilling if you've spent some time figuring out your unique interests and talents and you go out there and get better and better at doing that stuff. And much more important than the work you do is how you behave with humans. Research proves you'll feel happiest—during life and at its end—if you find some small set of humans who know the real you and who love and support you no matter what, and whom you love and support in return.

In terms of actually doing the adult thing, it's less a checklist and more a process that you'll get progressively better at over time. It requires balancing a lot of competing things. By the time this book is done we'll have covered a lot. But there will still be a lot you don't know. Part of the adulting mindset is about getting much more comfortable with not knowing, with figuring things out, and with keeping going. Being an adult will become the most complicated and yet the most natural thing you've ever done.

Sometimes you might long to be a kid again. (Not to be the actual diapered or play-dating child, but at least to feel taken care of.) Is it scary out there in the wide-open landscape of life where you fend for yourself and where anything is possible? Yeah.

But you have to. And you must want to. And you need to learn how. It's your turn.

I'm the latest person to try to tell this story. You're the latest to listen. The reason we keep telling these stories is that all of us have to learn it to survive. Nobody before you knew how to do this, either. We're all winging it, full of shit and fear. Sometimes I am still terrified, too. Cue the baby animal video.

But you (and I) can conquer that fear. And when you feel the fear again, you'll conquer it again.

You'll be okay.

And while we're speaking fundamental truths, let me also say that adulting is at times delicious. Believe it or not, this adulting thing? You'll *want* to.

Unpack and Reflect

- What does adulting mean to me?
- Who were my role models for adulting when I was growing up, and to what extent do I emulate those people now? Do I want to emulate them or do I not? Regardless of my answer, what's that about?
- When I look at the three components of adulting (wanting to, having to, and learning how), to what extent am I further along, and why, and where do I need a nudge?
- What, if anything, is holding me back from wanting to, having to, and learning how to be an adult? What steps can I take to do something about that? If I need help in doing so, where might I find that help?

2

TAG, YOU'RE IT

(THE TERROR AND JOY OF
FENDING FOR YOURSELF)

You just watch a season of *Girls* and do the opposite
of what they do.

—David, *Schitt's Creek*

In the waning summer of 1994 I got one of those phone calls you don't
ever forget.

I'd graduated from law school at Harvard in early June. Studied for
the hardest test of my life, the California Bar Exam, for the next seven
weeks straight. And in August, with the exam behind me, my husband,
Dan, and I packed the contents of our Cambridge apartment into dozens of boxes to be shipped to California, where I'd be starting up at a
law firm in October. Packing was tedious. I mean, who enjoys packing?
Even so, we felt giddy as we did it. The Boston area had never felt welcoming to us and we couldn't wait to return to California. We'd met
there, and as we were falling in love with each other, we were falling in
love with California, too.

The Cambridge apartment was the first place we'd lived in as a "married couple," a concept that didn't hold a lot of meaning for us because we'd
lived together for a few years before the wedding. But it was something
the older generation *said* in those days—"You're married now!"—as if
the marriage ceremony had *changed* things between us. In our eyes, all
that had changed was that people were forced to treat us as a unit, as

inseparable, which, as a Black and white pair in the early 1990s, was something we did not take for granted. It meant I could say, "Excuse me, he's my fucking *husband*." And Dan could say, in his more mild-mannered way, "Yes, please, it'll be the *two* of us. This is my *wife*." It also meant my mom would finally have to allow us to sleep in the same bedroom when we visited my parents' house. (This *really* cheesed me—she'd had sex before marriage, and I had the sibling to prove it.)

Then that August in 1994, Dan and I waved goodbye to the driver of the enormous Bekins moving van, spent one last night living out of suitcases in the bare apartment, and boarded a tiny plane from Boston to the island off Cape Cod called Martha's Vineyard where my parents had just decided to retire. They'd been living busy lives in New York when, in 1990, my then seventy-two-year-old dad got a diagnosis of metastatic prostate cancer (which meant it was terminal). He was well for another couple of years, but by 1994 his commute to and from the big city every day was starting to wear him out. Not knowing how much time he had left, he and my mom decided to leave the important jobs and hectic schedule behind. They sold their place in New York and bought a modest house in the woods on the northern end of Martha's Vineyard near Lake Tashmoo. Tucked into a grove of trees off a dirt road, they planted flowers and vegetables, fed the birds, and spent their evenings in their recliners, with Daddy watching whatever team was playing, and Mom doing the crossword. (I'm paying attention to this lesson of theirs: when your partner is terminally ill, drop everything and be together—though I hope to God I never "need" to do it.)

This grotto of sorts was where Dan and I hid out while our huge moving truck made its slow roll across the country. In the daytime we'd go out on errands with my folks and mooch around Oak Bluffs, Chilmark, and the island's other quaint towns. Each day ended with one of my mom's wonderful home-cooked meals and some television together. Then we'd turn in. Those days weren't just quality time with my parents; they forced me to confront the reality that Daddy was dying.

Holed up in my parents' guest room, Dan and I folded our bodies into each other as quietly as possible, and then sleep inevitably came. One night, we dreamed out loud about living a slower-paced life on this island. Dan could easily be a handyman. He understands how things work, likes to be helpful, and loves to make things. Being more of a people-person, maybe I would work selling fried clams near the beach, or T-shirts. Then we started really fantasizing. Maybe we could open a little inn to serve the tourists who make this their summertime mecca, and relax into a much slower-paced life during the other eight months of the year. But we'd always end these conversations with a wistful sigh. We were twenty-five (Dan) and twenty-six (me), and I'd just graduated from a powerhouse law school. Slower-paced didn't seem the right speed for our age and stage of life.

Looking back, I will say that to be moving away from the Boston area just as my folks had landed there was rather unfortunate timing. We were the proverbial ships passing in the night. But law school back east had been just a detour. The life Dan and I envisioned for ourselves had started in California and was destined to continue in California, we were certain. We were twentysomethings heading out into the wide-open landscape of the rest of our lives. What was going on with Daddy's health didn't have to change the course of our lives, right?

If you think you detect a twinge of regret in my rememberings, you may be correct. Nowadays parents and their grown children are more likely to have close relationships. To be intimates who stay in constant touch. But back when I was coming up, it was common for young people to move away from home. In fact, both of my parents and all of my siblings had done so. Besides, my parents had moved me seven times during my childhood, then they moved again while I was in college, and they had moved yet again to Martha's Vineyard. Maybe I was looking to plant roots for once in my life in California and didn't want to be part of an itinerant lifestyle any longer.

With a few nights to go before flying out to California, and dinner about to be on the table, I decided to check our voice mail. There was a message from the moving company asking us to call, so I did. I gave my name to the operator, and as she transferred me to someone else I pondered the clunky, new hyphenated last name that Dan Haims and I had invented for ourselves—"Lythcott-Haims"—which still felt like a pile of rocks in my mouth. Two years into married life I still felt like I was mostly just playing the part of the grown-up married woman.

I swallowed hard and hung up the phone. Turned around to face Dan and my parents. "Bekins called," I announced to the dining room. "A fire started in our truck somewhere near the border of Texas and Oklahoma? It's bad. We won't know how bad until it gets to some warehouse in a town called San Leandro near Oakland where they'll unload all our stuff. We have to call this number again in a few days to find out when to go there." My voice trailed off as I pictured our belongings all burned up. Then I tightened my lips and raised my eyebrows in a look of *Well that's the way it is*. I wanted so badly to act like this was not scary as fuck. I wanted to be brave. Dan came over to me with the same look on his face and we hugged really tight, but briefly. My parents came over and hugged us, too. Then we sat down, and my mother began serving dinner.

The news was shitty. My law firm had insured the move, so we'd likely be able to replace our clothes, furniture, and appliances. We were middle- and upper-middle-class people with parents who could provide a safety net if disaster happened—so, this is not a story of tragedy or suffering. But we still felt like newlyweds, and all the irreplaceable stuff—like the love letters we'd written to each other whenever we'd been apart—was in that truck.

Getting the news about the fire in our moving truck turns out to have been my first adulting moment. I mean the wedding wasn't it—that was just a big party where I wore a poufy dress. The bar exam wasn't it—that was just another standardized test. Even the job at the law firm would still be somehow *playing the part* of the grown-up. But this unexpected snafu where I knew I had to fend for myself turned out to be the moment I unambiguously *knew* I was an adult. What I mean is, while yes, my parents *felt* for us, and in the moments following the phone call they expressed compassion and reassurance, nothing in their eyes said that this was on them to handle. Nothing in me felt that way, either. I mean, sure, I would have loved for someone to step up and handle it, and yet, you know what? That's not true. The four of us knew that this was mine and Dan's to handle. And I knew we *could* do it, or that we would do our damnedest to try. We weren't kids anymore and we didn't want to be treated as kids. It actually felt good knowing, *Yup, this is some shit and it is OUR shit.*

Your "I know I'm an adult" fending-for-yourself moment is coming (if it hasn't happened already). And it will be shitty and scary and you will want to be a child who gets to turn away and be held in someone's arms as somebody else takes over. But you won't. As my friend Janet likes to say, "You'll say to yourself, 'Crap, where are the adults?' And then you'll realize 'Aw shit. It's me.'" And you'll step up to face it. Which will turn out to feel terrifying on the way to feeling very empowering. And once it is all behind you, you, like me, will turn out to be fine. Better than fine, actually, because whatever you've just survived will make you stronger.

WHAT EXACTLY IS "FENDING"?

Fending is knowing it's on you to handle something and you're pretty sure you can at least give it a try. If, when we're teens and young adults, we don't know how to fend for ourselves, life can feel like a perpetual game of dodgeball against five opponents where you just want to cower in the corner and cover your head with your hands. Or, if someone is managing our life for us, life is like sitting in the bleachers watching someone else play *for* us, while we just sit there observing. And hey, yeah, it is kind of a relief to see someone else dodging the ball or throwing it back really well on our behalf, but at some point, psychologically, our mind goes, *Hey, wait. Aren't I the one playing this game?* When we're successfully fending for ourselves, life is more like a game with an evenly matched opponent. You win some points, you lose some, you keep going.

Fending means being responsible and accountable. It means *you* seek the thing—the job opportunity, the apartment to rent, the medication refill, the groceries to make a meal, the jack for the flat tire, the info on how to pay your taxes—and *you* find it and make something of it, rather than waiting around to have the thing handed to you or handled for you by someone else. Fending is also about assessing options. It's asking yourself, *Well, what should I do, and what am I capable of, and what resources and tools are around me?* And you assemble some solution out of that. It's usually not a perfect solution, but at least it's a way forward.

NINE BASICS OF FENDING

Here's a list of some of the basic things you want to be doing for yourself now that you're an adult. (People have written entire books about just these subjects but I'm not doing that because you can learn most of this stuff on YouTube. You can also ask your family, mentors, and friends to teach you these things. My point here is that adulting isn't just about learning how to do these things, it's also about *appreciating* what's expected of you, *wanting* to learn to do this stuff, and *motivating* yourself to do so.)

1. *Attend to the care and maintenance of your body.* Everything from personal hygiene, to buying and cooking food, to making doctor's, dental, and counseling appointments (and listening to their advice while also interrogating whether it's right for you), to renting, buying, or constructing a safe and suitable shelter, these are the baseline things you want to be taking care of for yourself no matter how much time your mom has on her hands.

2. *Find work that pays your bills.* If you're going to rent, buy, or build that shelter (let alone support your Netflix and Hulu habits), you're going to need a job of some kind. You'll earn money from that job and at the end of the year you'll file your tax returns. If you don't do the former you won't be able to pay your bills. If you don't do the latter the government will come for you at some point. Don't be that person.

3. *Try hard.* Sometimes we parents say to our kids, "Just do your best." But if you think about it that basically means "Only/always do your best," which is a standard few people I know can meet (not me, for example). What we actually mean is that the real world requires hard work and your *effort* is the critical variable. You will stumble a lot and sometimes you will royally screw up. And when those things happen you need to nurse your wounds and get back up and try again. That's how you learn and grow, and that's also how you learn to be stronger in the face of the inevitable next setback.

4. *Make your own decisions.* How to dress for the weather; whether you can take the bus or need to grab a Lyft; how much to spend on shampoo or takeout; asking yourself, "Is today the day for that errand or can it wait?" or "Is this data charge too high?" All of these everyday questions are now on you to figure out (and are not

for your ever-loving parent who may have always been there to tell you what to do and how to do it). These issues are not the same as life-changing questions. Know the difference. Expect that you can handle everyday questions. Get advice and guidance when you're mulling over the bigger stuff.

5. *Get along with others.* Like it or not, human beings are everywhere. In my experience, 90 percent of them are perfectly reasonable—okay, 30 percent of them are *perfectly* reasonable, but the other 60 percent can be reasoned with—and being able to interact with humans in a manner that is courteous and respectful *while* advocating for what you need is the key to your survival. (Because unless you choose to be all by your lonesome in the outback somewhere, you will actually find yourself needing the cooperation of humans more often than you may think. Besides, some of them are cute.)

6. *Keep track of your stuff.* From coats and bags and phones, to deadlines and obligations, now it's on you to keep track of it all. If you were rescued a lot in childhood—if someone brought your schoolwork, instrument, or sporting equipment when you forgot it, or if someone made all your appointments and filled out all your forms and applications—handling ordinary life obligations may be more challenging for you. But taking care of this stuff is a huge part of fending for yourself. It's key to #adulting. So, don't avoid it, embrace it. Pro tip: If you have ADHD and find scheduling and tracking stuff next to impossible, work with an executive function coach who can help you develop a few systems that will start to make this easier in time. (Note: Experts say the coach cannot be a parent because the parent/child dynamic interferes with the coaching. My offspring and I can attest that this is true.)

7. *Reply and show up.* Literally as I'm typing this I get a tweet from a college professor that says, "Can you tell your readers that if they schedule a meeting they need to show up for it." However formal or informal, whether in the context of work, school, or your

personal life, requests for your time deserve a response. Even a "maybe" is better than silence, but it's not a whole lot better because people are trying to gauge if this date works for all, or if they've already picked a date they are now buying food and drinks or tickets or whatever, and they rightfully want to know if they should expect your participation or not. Don't insult people by saying, "It's open at the moment," because that implies that if something better than their invitation comes along you might ditch them! (You may secretly be hoping for that, but it's a real jerk move to act on that feeling.) It's perfectly okay to say no (in fact, getting better at saying no is a way to protect your time and mental health). But when you've said yes, put it in your iCal or GCal or some other kind of calendar and SHOW UP. (Again, super hard for people with ADHD, I know, and also for those with social anxiety, but this is something to make a point of trying to get better at. And if you can't show up for some reason, text an apology in advance, if possible, and if not then as soon as you are able.)

8. *Find your people and care for them.* At some point you will likely form a group, a squad, a fam—a small collection of people who matter to you, regardless of whether they know one another or not, and who are genuinely good for and to you. You may even decide to commit and conjoin your life with others. These people, whoever they are, need you to have their backs (just as they will have yours). This means setting self-interest aside sometimes and taking an interest in what *they* need in order to feel safe and whole. You may decide to bring smaller humans into the world, known as babies, and they will 100 percent need you to have their backs while being wholly incapable of reciprocating for quite some time. Pro tip: If this is your plan, maybe get a pet first, preferably a dog— dogs teach you to be responsible for another living being and are preferable to most other pets in this regard (only) because other pets can poop without you needing to be there.

9. *Plan for your future.* Unlike my generation (Gen X), a lot of people in your generation are expected to live to the ripe old age of one

hundred. That's a lot of years of spending, and if you don't want to have to be working until you're ninety-nine, then you're going to need to know how to save your money and how to have that saved money grow for your use later. Most basic would be contributing to a retirement plan at work, known as a 401(k), for the portion of the tax code it comes from, which allows you to stash money for later in a manner that is favorable tax-wise, and buying insurance to ward off financial catastrophe (you can get health, dental, vision, and life coverage and insurance for your home, car, and belongings). If you're a gig worker, don't worry; you have access to a 401(k) and other investment accounts, too. More advanced is putting money into things like stocks and bonds, real estate, and other investments that can grow your money faster than happens in a regular savings account.

Wait, is that it? No, actually there's more; most of those topics are fleshed out in subsequent chapters.

WHEN YOU HAVE SOME "ADULT AWARENESS" AND WHEN YOU DON'T

As I said earlier, for three years I struggled with whether I could even *write* this book. Then, one day in the midst of that angst, I was sifting through the mail and saw a hand-addressed letter among the magazines, catalogues, and bills. At first I worried that it was one of those YOU SUCK AND SHOULD DIE letters (authors get such things, and as a matter of self-care I am not interested in reading them). So, I asked Dan to read the letter for me and I watched with trepidation as he ripped open the envelope and pulled out a piece of notebook paper crammed with cursive writing on both sides. (The look of the letter made me even more scared.) Dan scanned his eyes back and forth over the first few paragraphs and handed the letter back to me with a smile.

Turns out the letter was not from a troll. It was more like a message in a bottle. The author, Kristine, was writing to say that my first book, *How to Raise an Adult* (on the harm of overparenting), had really resonated with her. "The stories you told have helped me see the places where I am not necessarily an adult yet. A little 'underbaked' as my friend likes to say," she wrote. She included this detail about her mother's continued overparenting, "This morning I almost had to fight (more like 'aggressively posture') my mom to allow my brother to cut salami for himself. (He's sixteen.)" And then Kristine asked me a question: "As I get older, I suppose I could blame my parents for not really letting me crash and burn, or even drive in heavy snow (or until recently, on the highway), but how do I regain agency and raise myself to become a better adult? What can I do as a sibling to foster that for my brother?"

By the time I was done reading Kristine's handwritten letter, I was pumping my fists and shouting at Dan, "THIS IS WHY I'M WRITING THE NEXT BOOK." Then I screenshotted Kristine's letter and sent it to my editor and my research assistant. "HEY Y'ALL WE'RE WRITING THIS BOOK FOR KRISTINE!" Needless to say, Kristine became a huge motivator for me. Her letter gave me a much-needed kick in the pants.

The following summer, I get on the phone with Kristine. She tells me a little about herself. She's Chinese American. She's twenty. She's just finished her freshman year at Washington University in St. Louis, where she's majoring in economics. She's home in Naperville, Illinois, where she's doing a summer internship in finance. I ask her why she wrote me. She goes, "For a while it felt really good for my parents to be doing most tasks for me—but there came a point where it stopped, and I was left with many regrets after the good feeling was gone."

One of Kristine's biggest frustrations is that before she left home, her mom never taught her to cook, which kinda smacked her in the face when she got to college. It wasn't for lack of trying; she'd go up to her mother at the stove and beg to be taught but her mother would wave her off, not thinking it important that Kristine learn that skill in that moment. Kristine worries about her little brother not learning the basics either, like budgeting for groceries or knowing which ingredients expire quickest. She worries that when he lives alone for the first time, he'll eat frozen pizza every night and ruin more than a few dinners trying to figure out how to cook for himself. I love how much she cares about her little bro.

Although Kristine says she wouldn't call herself an adult yet, she says she finds herself waking up to what she calls an "adult awareness," and notices little changes as they happen. "When I'm in 'adult mode,' I'm making presentations at work and packing lunch for myself." She even got her mom to pass on one household responsibility: cleaning toilets. "It's so nice not to have to do everything around here," her mother told her. "Yes, isn't it?" Kristine replied.

I know toilets isn't where most people want to start. But I'm here with a loud amen to Kristine for that one.

BECOMING AN ADULT TOO EARLY? A REALITY CHECK

I want to pause here and say that, unlike Kristine, many people have to fend for themselves much earlier in life due to tougher circumstances—things like economic hardship in childhood, having to care for younger siblings, a parent losing their job, severe illness or death of a parent, becoming a parent as a teen, surviving a catastrophic accident, recovering from a life-threatening illness. These situations tend to grow you up real fast—too fast sometimes (which feels unfair, and in the grand scheme, *is* unfair, but sadly, pro tip: There is no referee out there blowing the whistle on all of life's unfairness). But the secret embedded in these really challenging circumstances is that, chances are, you'll emerge from them much more capable in at least some respects: Fending! Then you'll look around at all your friends who can't do half of what you can do for yourself, and you'll think, *Come on, y'all, grow up!*

The thing is, none of us should wait for the unexpected, terrifying, awful thing to happen in order to get off our butts and take charge of our life. And that's because not only is fending a key component of adulting (i.e., necessary), but it actually ends up *feeling really good*. Young adults can feel a bit confused about their own ability to take care of business—something psychologists call "learned helplessness" if most of the fending tasks of life have been handled by a parent or other caretaker.

A lot of us are going to have to snatch our right to fend for ourselves away from those who protectively keep us from it. When, for example, we have a diagnosis that might require the support of others (perhaps Type 1 diabetes or autism spectrum disorder), it can be super hard to assert our ability and right to make our own decisions and do increasingly more for ourselves. And those around us—though loving and well intentioned— can exhibit low expectations for us because they're trying to protect us. But it is really essential to our psychological and physical well-being that we do *as much as we can* for ourselves. No matter what our challenges, *all* humans are hardwired to want to make, tackle, handle, and accomplish stuff. This is all shorthand for *live our own lives*.

An episode of the TV show *The Good Doctor* portrayed this really well. Here's the setup: A teen on the autism spectrum named Liam is in the hospital for abdominal pain. He's not very verbal. We've seen his discomfort at lights and noises, and at being touched, and we've seen his parents instinctively jump up to mitigate or handle those discomforts. Our hero—the doctor Shaun Murphy, who is also on the spectrum—mystifies Liam's parents. "It's amazing how accomplished you are for someone with autism spectrum disorder," Mom says. As the episode unfolds, Dr. Shaun Murphy makes an important diagnosis: the kava root herbal supplements Liam's parents give him have caused a bowel obstruction, yet the parents refuse to let Dr. Murphy participate in the surgery fearing he cannot handle a stressful situation because he is autistic. Dr. Murphy's colleagues stand by him and tell the parents they'll have to seek care at a different hospital. Liam overhears this and speaks up. "I want. I want. He said I could do it. I want Dr. Shaun." The parents capitulate and let Dr. Shaun Murphy participate. The surgery goes well, thanks to Dr. Murphy's having detected a further complication of the kava root. It's now post-surgery. Liam's parents are by his bedside as he wakes, and Dr. Murphy announces to Liam that the surgery was a success. Liam looks up at the ceiling and his eyes blink a few times. Dad follows Liam's gaze, says, "Lights," then goes over to the switch on the wall. But it's late in the episode and by now Dad has learned that he and his wife have been doing way too much of the thinking for Liam. Dad pauses, turns around, and finally, looks at Liam. "Are the lights okay? Do you want them dimmed?" Liam hesitates for a moment, and then responds, "They're . . . okay."

Regardless of our abilities and health circumstances, it doesn't feel good when others step in and make decisions for us or handle things on our behalf that we could handle for ourselves. It makes us feel like a dog on a leash, or like a robot perfectly executing someone else's instructions, or like a puppet where someone else is manipulating the strings. Fending is unabashedly going *off* leash, where nobody tells you what to do, and you get to make choices and experience the results (which are sometimes great, and, yes, are also sometimes not great). But being in charge of you is an existentially and anthropologically fantastic feeling. Picture a toddler insisting on tying their own shoes, yelling, "I DO IT!" while helpful parents try to intervene. Fending is the grown-up equivalent of that. It's *Get out of my fucking way and let me do this, people. It's MY life.*

I hope you feel this beckoning. Like, *Come on in. Yes, you. It's your turn.* You deserve to feel good about #adulting.

<hr>

DON'T JUST TAKE MY WORD FOR IT

When you're new at fending for yourself you're going to have these memorable signature moments that show you you're doing it—like me and Dan dealing with the whole moving truck situation. Then, over time, as you fend for yourself more and more, these small moments are less important because fending for yourself has simply become your normal life. It goes from feeling like *Oh my gosh, I have to fend for myself* to *Yup, I've got this.* Because of the work that I do, I often interact with young adults who share examples of how they're fending (or not!). Here are three who *are.*

MEET KYLE—Fending When Parents Flounder

One day I got an email from a kid named Kyle who felt the need to reach out after watching my TED Talk about how to raise successful kids without over-parenting them. Kyle tells me he's a twenty-year-old who worked three different jobs during high school while his younger sister cooked for the family, all because their widowed mother was addicted to opioids. "That required me to roll up my sleeves and get to work," he tells me, "and I developed the mindset that has led to where I am today. Today I'm the founder and CEO of a small nonprofit looking to inspire youth in the Appalachian region to develop that same mindset and use it to change their world and ours."

Well, you know I just had to get Kyle on the phone to hear more about his story.

So, Kyle has become an undergraduate at Berea College, in Berea, Kentucky, which he tells me was founded in 1855 and is the "first interracial and coeducational college in the antebellum South." He's a white man who grew up in Appalachia and is proud to be attending a school with such a deeply embedded mission around equity and justice. I can hear this pride in his voice. I like him already.

But college was not the obvious trajectory for Kyle. "It was more like a dream," he tells me. Enter the guidance counselor at his high school, who pulled all the poor kids into a room one day and said, "There's a college you can go to for free." Kyle and his classmates thought it was a scam. But he just had to find out for himself, so he visited. Sure enough, no scam. (Pro tip: Berea College does in fact offer free education for all, and is considered a top liberal arts college in the country, featuring some of the very best teaching.) Kyle wouldn't have to pay a dime for housing, tuition, or food, and like every student accepted to Berea he would also get a free laptop. But when Berea admitted him, whether to go was a harder decision than you might appreciate, because it would mean leaving behind his little sister. "Home would be three hours away. I felt guilty. Selfish. To say the least."

Kyle and his sister are tight. Their father died of melanoma when Kyle was twelve, which was just one in a string of traumatic events that resulted in his mother's opioid addiction. Prior to that, they were an intact family of four living in Florida and life was good. "She was a damn good mother back in Florida. On *American Idol* night, back when that was a thing, she'd get my dad, sister, and me on the couch and we'd laugh at the auditions. She made my sister and me hug each other when we were fighting. She taught me to stand up for myself and not to let people pick on me." But after his father's death, Kyle's mom couldn't afford the payments on their house; she relocated the three of them to the small Virginia town where both she and her husband had grown up. Shortly after that, her *own* father died. She became depressed. "She was still on painkillers from a bad car accident a few years earlier, and had no husband and two kids to take care of, in a place she hardly knew anymore."

Whenever Kyle's father had had to leave the house he always told Kyle, "You're the man of the house." This mandate rang in Kyle's young ears. He bagged groceries at Food City to make ends meet. Did construction with his uncles. Mowed lawns whenever he could. And it wasn't only to help pay for food and rent—his sister is a Type 1 diabetic and needed medical supplies.

Kyle also had a diagnosis for which he'd been taking meds, ADHD, but he decided to go off his meds in order to save money.

Kyle and his sister responded differently to their mother's addiction. "For my sister, Mom was her best friend when she was sober and her worst enemy when she wasn't. For me—I just wanted her to make it to the next day because I couldn't stand the thought of losing both my parents. When I would take her car keys and her pills I would put on this real formal face and say, 'Ma'am, I will be taking your car keys for the night. You're in a state where if you were to drive you would be a danger to yourself and others. I will give you your car keys back in the morning when you are sober.' She'd say, 'Go to hell. You kids make me want to kill myself.'" When Kyle was sixteen, he and an aunt paid for his mom to go to rehab. "It was money I'd saved to go to college but we needed to use it for Mom." By the time he was eighteen, he was paying half his family's bills.

I wonder out loud about how Kyle decided he could or even should go to college given the key role he played in keeping his family afloat. "Everyone was telling me to go," he tells me. "Guidance counselor, family." Everyone but his sister. A week before leaving for Berea, she met him in the hallway between their bedrooms, wrapped her arms around him, and said, "Please don't go. You're abandoning me." Kyle pauses his story. I pause, too, and just hold this young stranger through the silence. I can hear him holding back his emotion. "That broke me," he continues. "My sister was the person who always asked if I was hungry and who would make me dinner if I was. Feeling guilty about going away can be a real thing for kids growing up like I did. Especially with the 'man of the house' idea. I knew I had to take care of my mom and my sister. And my sister would take care of me."

Yet Kyle decided he had to go to college. "It was fear. Fear of getting stuck in my mom's situation. I was scared, young, and selfish in that moment. It was a failure of my moral compass but ultimately a decision that changed my life for the better and allowed me to do more than I would have been able to do if I hadn't gone. I told myself I'd make a damn good worth out of it." I'm struck by Kyle's word choice. He speaks like a person from a different era. He sounds so old for someone so young.

Kyle graduated high school in 2017. Even though his mom had gone to rehab toward the end of his junior year, recovery would not be that simple. She relapsed a few times, including the day before his graduation. "I could just tell. She behaved kind of weird. She'd get angry, depressive, threaten to kill herself." This time, his mother's behavior pushed this preternaturally optimistic young man over the edge. "I was just young and angry. I finally was going to graduate, and my mom wasn't in the right state. She was scared I was growing up. I was mad at my situation. I packed my things and went over to my grandma's house and ended up staying there for a while after I graduated. It was a decision of anger that I regret."

Kyle's mom has been in recovery for some time now. "Rehab worked. She relapsed twice and we weren't really sure whether she would ever be better. But I'm really, really happy to say she's clean and has a job. I'm really, really proud of her. I like to tell my mom's story as one of overcoming obstacles, how people offering support can help. The opioid epidemic is real and a lot of parents are going to jail. There are more single mothers going through this than I can count. Kids are growing up working their butts off just to make it. She really came through."

Kyle is a business administration and finance major at Berea. His approach is, "Go to the tool shop and buy the right tool for the job." His major is "a tool in my tool belt, a hammer with which I can build a house. I intend to use that major so I can start several enterprises that will help kids who grew up like I did." Kyle is fully fending, helping his family fend, and he's on a path toward doing great things for others.

MEET LEVI—Fending Instead of Depending

I met Levi a couple summers ago in a Lyft. (Heads up: This book contains lots of examples of me chatting up strangers! Not only that, but in chapter 7, "Start Talking to Strangers," I encourage you to do the same.) Anyway, Levi: Our family (Dan, me, and our two kids, Sawyer and Avery, then both in their late teens) had just spent an amazing week vacationing in the Lake Tahoe area and we were midway through the four-and-a-half-hour drive home when the engine in our Prius conked out outside Sacramento. Dan called AAA to come and tow the car back to our mechanic, but the driver wouldn't be able to fit the four of us in the tow truck cab. So, I googled rental car agencies and found one about thirty minutes away, then hailed a Lyft to take me and the kids from the side of the road to Avis. (This story isn't about me, but I will point out that dealing with a broken-down car, including fixing it yourself, is a great example of "fending," whereas calling a parent to handle it all for you is *not* fending. You *are* fending if *you're* able to fix it yourself, or if you're the one calling AAA, the mechanic, or a friend all by yourself—and that's what Dan and I did, which you'd expect us to be able to do because we are in our fifties, but anyone licensed to operate a motor vehicle should be able to do this.)

So, the Lyft driver was this twenty-three-year-old white guy named Levi, and I tell him the story of what just happened to our car and my plan to rent a car to get us home to Palo Alto. He goes, "You know, I could just drive you home. It'll probably be about the same price as the rental. It's a long way, but it's fine. I need the money." TBH, I'd never dreamed you could take a two-and-a-half-hour Lyft, but after verifying the validity of Levi's suggestion with a quick Google search, it was clearly the best option.

Levi does a U-turn and then makes a big right-hand turn to begin our trek west to the Bay Area. The kids and I chat with him about this and that, and after a while I realize my teenagers haven't said anything in some time, and I look back and see them both fast asleep with their mouths gaping open like when they were little ones. Levi and I smile at each other and continue talking, and we end up talking the entire way home. He tells me that when he was growing up his parents had made clear to him that he needed to be "out at eighteen"—meaning fending for himself. And that he's finishing community college intending to start his bachelor's degree next semester. So, I ask him if I can follow up to interview him for this book. And a few months later we are on the phone chatting, and this time I am taking notes!

Levi grew up with serious financial hardship. His parents divorced when he was four and shared custody of Levi. His dad had the means to provide financial support for Levi but didn't. He also had an alcohol problem and could be very difficult to be around. Levi's mom was loving and kind, but could barely make ends meet. She and Levi would move from house to house to make rent, and sometimes Levi didn't know whether there'd be food to eat when he was at her house.

"I've seen struggle, yet my dad has been very prosperous. He's an official with the state of California where he makes about one hundred and twenty thousand dollars after taxes. So, he has the resources to help me—even said he would buy me a house in Texas later on, if I want him to—but he won't help me through school. He never went to school. Mom didn't go to school, either; she worked to support the two of them while he went through an intense training and certification program for his job. She always just worked hard. There were times when I was in middle school and all we've got is cereal in my mom's house, so we're eating breakfast for dinner. Then I'd go to my dad's and we'd have steaks. He didn't pay child support until I was in high school—after my mom had finally gone after him legally and he was forced to pay nine hundred dollars a month. I was always happier at my mom's though. Always. Showed me money doesn't really matter; it's just a tool in our society that everybody needs. Being able to see both sides has helped me shape who I am and has shaped my vision of what I want."

Levi went back and forth between his parents' houses every week right up until Christmas break senior year of high school, when he was with his dad and left because they had a bad fight. "I'm a quiet person," Levi tells me. "I couldn't handle the chaos. I went back and got my clothes when he wasn't home."

"By now my mom was finally making decent money. She could afford to buy a house and make dinner every night, but she couldn't afford to put money away for a college fund, or pay for tuition. And my dad *could* help, but he never even helped me pay for books. The other day we had lunch and I mentioned that the parking pass at Sacramento State is going to be two hundred dollars and tuition is like four *thousand* per semester and that's a lot of money for me, and he's just like, 'Oh. Yeah.' I see other parents with less money and more children helping their kids. But I'm so used to it at this point that it doesn't bother me. I'm glad I'm not like him."

I ask Levi about the expectation that he be "out at eighteen" and how that actually played out. "As soon as I graduated high school my mom was all, 'You need a job. If you want to go to school I'm not going to be able to help you that much. You need money.' I was like, okay. Made sense. I went to a community college in Sacramento called American River College (ARC). Started working at Chick-fil-A and worked there almost two years. Made a lot of good friends, and it was a good first experience for work."

Levi didn't have enough money to live on his own that first year at ARC, so he continued to live with his mom. But the next year, he moved into an apartment with two friends. "It felt really good. I was working, paying rent, all that stuff. When I moved out I felt very confident in my ability to take care of myself. Sometimes you want to rely on your parents so you don't have to spend money, but it's also a good experience to move out and give yourself that self-confidence. Literally as soon as I moved out, the first night I was in the apartment lying in my bed I was all, 'Wow, like, this is happening.' It was a moment. The fact that I can even move out means that I can do this, I have the confidence in myself now. I know I can work, go to school, pay rent, all that stuff. It was just a matter of proving to myself that I didn't need help from my dad, or anybody to help me. I'm now in charge of me. I felt safe—an emotional safeness and a physical safeness. If anything happens to me now, it's my fault. I think being an adult is when you start making decisions for yourself. Moving out was a decision for myself. Nobody else except me."

Levi was fending. But that's not to say it was easy. "It took me five years to finish ARC because first semester I took four classes and dropped two, failed one, and got an A in the other. I just wasn't ready. I don't necessarily regret how things played out in that first year cuz I think I needed that experience, but it prolonged my schooling. I didn't know what I wanted to major in my first two years. I was just taking general ed classes to get through school. I stopped working at Chick-fil-A cuz I just hated, HATED, working in food service. I liked the people that I worked with, but dealing with customers and the overall stress was too much. I was always closing, which meant working until one a.m. and then I'd wake up and go to school at ten a.m. I got so worn out. After two years I started applying anywhere that was offering part-time jobs that were not about food. Landed at a NAPA Auto Parts distribution center where my job was to get the parts and put them in my delivery car and take them to shops around Sacramento. So, basically I was driving. I worked there two years but quit because they were scheduling me for holidays even though I told them not to. Lyft was the same money, if not more, for working less, and I could make my own schedule. Once I started to work for Lyft I did better in school because I had more time to focus on it."

I ask him what matters to him now. "It's my last semester at ARC and I'm about to transfer to Sacramento State University for my bachelor's. I need to focus when I get there because I don't want to make the same mistakes I made at community college. In today's world you need a degree to live comfortably or even just to pay your bills and to not have to worry where your next meal and things like that are coming from. My thing is just to be an overall nice person that wants the best for everyone. That's literally as simple as it can get for me. I don't like chaos—I had too much of it in my childhood. I like tranquility. I like calmness. At this point in life, getting a bachelor's degree, getting a job, getting my own place, building my life from there—that's what's most important for me. Focusing on myself. That's what I care about right now."

I ask him what he's going to major in and am surprised by his answer. "My first couple years at ARC, my dad was like, "You should do nursing. You'll make a lot of money, blah blah blah." So, I put nursing down as my goal on the freaking orientation whatever, but I ended up changing, first to psychology, then to business. You know what? None of those are things I truly care about or am good at or enjoy. One day, it came to me; I was super good in history growing up, and my Grandpa Richard was a writer and had given me a lot of history books to read over the years, which I loved. I started thinking, 'What can I do with history? I can be a teacher. I like to help people and am a very patient person. I can DEFINITELY be a teacher.' Once I told myself, 'Do history,' that was the moment."

I'm so happy for Levi because he's found his way forward despite a lot of obstacles in his path, and because his way forward is going to entail work he loves. (When you find work that is at the intersection of what you're good at and what you love that's the *sweet spot*. But I'm getting ahead of myself—we'll cover that and more in chapter 5, "Stop Pleasing Others.")

I ask Levi if he has any words of advice. "My parents have never helped me," he says. "I mean, they did a bit but not to the point where I could just focus on my schoolwork. I always had to work, buy my own car, fix my own car. It's all been on my own. The fact that I've done things for myself is satisfying to me. It shows me I'm a strong person overall, whether emotionally, financially, or in terms of responsibility. I don't need anyone to hold my hand. When I graduate and get a job, it'll be all that more special to me. I'm kind of a loner, too," he adds. "Being able to do it on my own is just how I am." Everyone needs other people in this life. But the satisfaction of knowing how much you can achieve on your own is a really good feeling, one that Levi knows well.

MEET ZURI—Standing Up for Your Right to Fend

I bumped into a former colleague, Elaine, at a party one weekend, and when I told her I was trying to write this book and what it was about, she said, "Oh, you *need* to talk to Zuri. She's really in the swing of that now." Zuri is Elaine's daughter, and me being me I reached out to see if Zuri was willing to talk. To my delight, she was.

Zuri Adele is a thirty-one-year-old African American woman with a bachelor's degree from Spelman College and an MFA in acting from UCLA. At the time I speak with her, she is making a living as an actor on the show *Good Trouble*, a spinoff of *The Fosters*, now in its third season. But before all of that took shape, Zuri had to do a ton of that somewhat uncomfortable fending. I get on the phone with her to learn what that stage was like.

Zuri may be a masterful actor, but she has had some horrible auditions. When she first moved to Los Angeles, she showed up late for auditions partly because the freeway traffic was even worse than normal. Once she arrived on time but hadn't been informed of the tight security she would have to walk through just to get to the holding area—so she was late. There were screen auditions at which she was afraid her theater training would make her acting too unsubtle—and she pulled back too far, giving a performance so subdued there seemed to be nothing there. At the next auditions, she "course-corrected" and went over the top in the casting room. The rejections kept coming. She worked as a nanny and taught yoga, but even those two jobs weren't enough to make ends meet in an expensive city. She went on food stamps for additional support. "That was a difficult chapter," Zuri tells me warmly, "but from all that failure, I learned how to always be a beginner. I realize now that if I had booked one of those earlier acting jobs I wanted so bad, maybe I wouldn't have the job I have now."

When her big break with Freeform/*Good Trouble* came, Zuri had to keep the news a secret for months as is the norm in Hollywood. She did share it with her closest friends—part of the Spelman sisterhood that Zuri cites as the foundation of her strongest relationships—and they were ecstatic for her. But once the news was out, plenty of other people started coming out of the woodwork, wanting to hang out with her, and their intentions were unclear.

One of these peripheral friends who reached out once Zuri had the great gig was a coworker with a tough demeanor who gives feedback on everything, qualities Zuri appreciates in a teacher but sometimes finds stressful in a friend. Zuri wanted to say no to their lunch proposal but felt like she couldn't. "Maybe I was intimidated." I listen to Zuri, thinking, *Was she feeling intimidated or was she feeling obligated?* When we make it onto that next rung on the ladder of success, we can feel like we really have to make time for that person who reaches out, even if we aren't close to them or it's not what we want to do.

Her friend picked an expensive restaurant. Zuri stared at the menu. She'd just started filming and wouldn't start getting paid for a few weeks. Her rent was soon due. The Department of Social Services was still mailing her reminders to renew her food stamps. She just ordered a wine and a salad. Her friend ordered a significant amount of food. When the bill came there was a loaded silence, as if her friend expected Zuri, with her newfound Hollywood success, to pick up the check. Zuri awkwardly asked if they could split it, but as Zuri crunched the numbers in her head, she realized that paying for even a portion of her friend's larger lunch would mean that she wouldn't have enough money for rent. Infuriating, right? Zuri was doing her best to keep her finances in order, but her friend assumed that because Zuri had now "made it," she could treat the other person to a fancy lunch.

The lesson I take from this is that fending includes *de*fending yourself from those who would impede your choice-making and maybe even violate your boundaries. Thanks to that lunch, Zuri, too, had this aha moment. But before the "Aha!" was the "Oh no!"

"I was like, 'Oh, my God, I'm filming episode two of *Good Trouble* but I don't know when I'm going to get paid or how I'm going to get paid,'" she remembers. She made rent that month by borrowing money from her mom, and that didn't feel very good.

"All of a sudden, I realized it's time for us young adults to speak up for ourselves," she tells me. "It's time for us to get clear on our expectations and intentions ahead of time. Back when I was constantly trying to impress authority, I'd be really perfect and cheery on the outside but I would break down as soon as I was by myself. As an adult, I'm not doing things to impress my parents, my directors, casting agents, or people in authority. I had to learn to set healthy boundaries so I wouldn't put myself in a place of breakdown. Making pros and cons lists for hard decisions helped me do this. Now I'm standing up for my 'no.' I trust my instincts and my body; I get tension in my body if something isn't right for me. I have to trust my instincts without knowing the full picture. 'No' is a complete answer. 'No' means, 'I appreciate how much you want this, but I have to say no to you and say yes to myself.'" Fending is indeed standing up for your "no." It also entails letting others know that you are capable of fending for yourself.

"As an adult, my dad and I are just, like, fellow adults. I speak up more. I don't look for his approval in the same way. I'll be texting him while I'm on break on the show, and he'll be like, 'Stop. Do your work. Don't text me. Focus.' And I'll be like, 'I *am* doing my work, I *am* focusing. I'm on break right now and I want to celebrate these moments with you because nothing will ever be new like this again.'

"Thanks to *Good Trouble* I was able to end my time on food stamps. I'm still getting mail from the Department of Social Services saying, 'It's time for you to renew,' and I'm like, *I'm not on that anymore.* Not that I wasn't enjoying that chapter. Maybe this is the yoga in me speaking, but all parts of the journey really do serve."

I ask Zuri what else she's learned. "The main things are to keep going, stay for the miracle, and set up healthy boundaries. I'm intentional about setting up boundaries from a place of love because there can be a thin line between healthy boundaries and harmful barriers. I grew up with a lot of fear about disappointment, especially regarding my dad, and I would be harder on myself because I knew other people had high expectations of me."

"Maybe this is a small thing," she says as we're nearing the end of our call. "I want to be a badass. I've started to do boxing and I like punching really, really fast. One day, I hope to own a home with a view of the mountains where my parents can come visit me and I can cook for them and they can write. I'd like to have a partner who'd host them alongside me. All of it, all of it—the only thing is, I don't want to be hating Mondays."

I tell her it doesn't seem like a small thing to me at all.

IN SHORT: FENDING IS FUNDAMENTAL

Fending boils down to knowing *you* are the person who is in charge of things in your life. You develop what's called a "horizontal" relationship with your parents with whom you may be quite close yet who no longer have the primary responsibility for making sure your needs are met and your obligations are taken care of. Fending means it's on you. And oh. Did I mention? It feels GOOD.

Unpack and Reflect

- What does fending mean to me?
- What emotions arise when I think about having to fend for myself?
- Looking at the "Nine Basics of Fending," which things am I able to handle? In which areas am I less skilled?
- Where do I want to grow in this area? What help do I need?

3

YOU'RE NOT PERFECT

(YOU'RE HERE TO LEARN AND GROW)

Let it go.

—Queen Elsa, *Frozen*

If this book's quest is to beckon you into your adulthood, then we have to slay any monsters of childhood that are lingering at the door. Contemporary American parenting has an unhealthy attachment to the word *perfect*, and I'm not here for it. I'll go so far as to say that, yes, that one word might have harmed you. You need to get rid of it. Let it go.

Hearing your parent or caregiver chirp "Perfect" in response to every little thing you did (you slid down a slide, took out the trash, finished your homework) can convey to you that perfection is required—which, I promise you, it isn't. And it can make you feel that everything you accomplished *was* in fact perfect—which, I promise you, it wasn't. (Classic example: "Perfect. You didn't hit Billy!" *Really?*) It can also train you to expect that other authority figures in your life, such as teachers and bosses, will tell you you're perfect all the time. They won't. Because you aren't. Am I making my point?

Perfection shimmers like a mirage way out there in the desert. Seeking it is fucking misery because it's a place you will never reach, and you'll stress out yourself and everyone around you as you desperately try to crawl to it. (You may be thinking, *I'll get there, lady, just you watch me.* And hey, that's fine. I'm not here to laugh at you when it happens.)

Let this chapter be the antidote to all the "perfects" you ever heard or wanted. The life of your dreams results not from being perfect but from your efforts to learn and grow. Lean into that, and your life will become deeply satisfying, which is a much more delicious feeling than perfect. Of course, just reading that promise here on the page won't make it so. Kicking perfection to the curb takes intentionality, effort at practicing it, maybe even some therapy. But you can decide today that you want to let go of "I need to be perfect" as your goal and replace it with "I'm here to learn and grow." And that's a strong start.

THE FALSE ALLURE OF THE LOCKSTEP PLAN

If you are somewhat of a perfectionist, you come by it honestly. We parents create (or buy into) a perfect lockstep plan for our children because it makes us feel safe. (I say "us" because I'll admit that I was at times a perfectionist control freak with my two kids, Sawyer and Avery. And sometimes I still am.) Childhood can easily become "Do this, then that, then this other thing," all in a certain order—a scheme designed by others to impress even more others who are sizing you up to see if you are good enough to move on to the next thing. It stresses me out just to write about it.

When kids don't seem to be achieving according to plan, it can frighten us, your parents. It can make us afraid that you're ruining the future we have in mind for you. TBH, it also makes us worry about *our* future. As in what we're going to tell *our* friends, colleagues, and the extended family, and what we're going to post on *our* Instagram.

The thought that our kid's life might not proceed according to the "perfect" plan freaks us out so much that we sometimes feel the need to intervene to a small extent (or maybe a large extent) to help you achieve what *we* want for you. This intervention can lead to a lot of handling, fixing, managing, reminding, nudging, and nagging from parents. Paradoxically, such intervention *can* assist you in the immediate moment, and maybe it even gets you closer to the thing we think of as the perfect end goal. But this kind of help is *not* a magical elixir. In fact, it's actually more like poison, because it sends your developing brain some terrible messages that can make you feel inadequate, incapable, even helpless. Messages like:

"Hey kid, this life of yours is about doing what other people expect."

"Hey kid, you're loved according to how perfect you are in our eyes."

"Hey kid, everything goes to hell if you don't get this right."

"Hey kid, getting this right means getting it the way your parents want it."

"Hey kid, you actually aren't good enough on your own, so I'm going to do some of it for you."

Ingest enough of these messages, and your sense of who you are, what you're capable of, and what you want out of life will be completely fucked up. I don't want that to happen to you, and if it has happened to you, I want to help you overcome it. (Yes, you can!)

You're on an adventure now that bears no resemblance to childhood. You're fending. And it's time to cast aside simple platitudes like "perfect!," to engage in broader thinking, and to grow more comfortable dwelling in the uncertain gray areas of life, of which there are multitudes. You're going to take steps forward, but also some steps backward and even some steps sideways. You'll decide when to accelerate and when to slow it down. You'll need to allow for whimsy and the clarion call of a dream, which may mean you need to go off in a completely different direction. You'll need to catch your breath when you can't even look yourself in the mirror because you are so embarrassed, scared, or ashamed. Adulting is perpetual trial and error, all of which contributes to your growth. In fact, your bad experiences will teach you far more than the good ones do. (Think about Zuri, whom we met in chapter 2, "Tag, You're It!"; it was when she didn't get the audition, it's when she didn't have money for both the restaurant bill and her rent, that she learned.) Only through trial and error do you become better able to face the next challenge.

You want that.

Believe me.

GOD LAUGHS

When I was a university dean, one of my favorite students came to my office hours during his sophomore year to go over his plan for his future.

(The topic of this meeting was *his* idea.) As he took out his laptop and pulled up a spreadsheet, I could see from the look on his face that he was very proud of what he was about to show me. I'll admit I felt bemused by the whole idea of counting on any particular postgraduate future during the second year of college, but I was curious to see what he had in mind.

"At twenty-two, I'll go to a top-ten med school. Graduate at twenty-six and start my residency at UCSF. Residency will last between three and five years depending on what I decide to specialize in. I'll meet my girlfriend during my first year. We'll get married in my third year, have the first baby when I'm thirty, then a second one at thirty-two when I'll either be starting or completing my fellowship!" He closed his laptop. He was beaming.

I suppressed an exasperated gasp. I knew he was waiting for the approval he'd received countless times in life ("Perfect!") but I couldn't give it. I thought, *How could someone so smart be so unaware of the ways of the world?* His attitude also felt very cis-gender straight male, very patriarchal. His plan literally involved someone else's body yet sounded very "It shall be so." I retreated into my head and replayed my late twenties and early thirties when it took me and Dan two and a half years to conceive our first child, our son, Sawyer; that was a time when sex went from fun to a job to a disappointment. I also asked myself, *Does this kid even want to be a doctor, or is he doing what he thinks he's supposed to do?*

Sooooo, I chuckled softly. Told him that sounded *amazing*, and I hope it all worked out. Then with a gentle smile I said, "You know, you actually don't *plan* to meet the love of your life; you meet the love of your life when you're doing things you love because that's when you're at your most attractive. Hopefully your residency will be *it*." I said, "While you most certainly *will* get pregnant if you have sex in the back of your parents' car at sixteen (ha ha), when you're thirty, conception doesn't necessarily just happen because your spreadsheet says it's time." When I proceeded to ask, "Now, tell me why you're headed toward medicine," he looked like he was going to cry. Like I was ripping the screenplay of his life to shreds.

I'm not against making plans. (Pro tip: Making concrete plans is the only way you'll reach your biggest goals.) And I wasn't trying to be mean to my student. But, you see, this student came to me for approval, yet the lesson I was there to teach that day was that it helps to be humble in the face of life's mysteries and to be prepared for the possibility that sometimes plans go completely awry.

I was channeling a centuries-old Yiddish saying that goes: "Der mentsh trakht un Got lakht," or "Man plans and God laughs." If you're not religious, think of it as, "Shit happens."

There's so much that lies beyond the control of even the most privileged among us. Shit will most definitely happen. (And I'll say a ton more about this in chapter 10, "How to Cope.") When shit happens, it's natural to curl up in a ball for a while, particularly if the shit is big. But you're here to *live* this life, not just curl up in a ball until it is over, and living requires action. So, you don't want to wallow in the face of it forever. Adulting means sitting with your feelings of imperfection or fear or inadequacy or shame or disappointment, and then accepting those feelings as valid, thinking over what happened to lead you to this point, figuring out what you want to do next, getting back up, and *doing something* to move yourself forward. Shit will at some point happen again. And you'll be more ready for it. At some point you'll be like, *Ha! Take that, shit! I'm ready for you. This sucks right now but I've learned something and I'm going to be okay.*

My hope was that all of this would sound amazing to my student, and I hope it sounds amazing now to you. But maybe it doesn't? If you've been primed to follow a checklist and to execute that checklist flawlessly, your checklist likely did not allow for mistakes or detours or even a periodic rest on a small bench by the road. And it gave you zero preparation for how to navigate the wide-openness of life with its boundless opportunity and infinite uncertainty. So, maybe the challenge to discard the idea of "perfect" (and the lockstep plan associated with it, and the effort to control people and situations in order to achieve it) makes you feel lost. Or afraid.

That's to be expected.

So, let's go further.

LIFE'S BEAUTIFUL F-WORDS

We're taught to avoid *failing*, and its siblings: *falling, faltering, flailing, floundering, fumbling.* (I call these life's beautiful F-words.) But we'd all have an easier time if we accepted that these seemingly disastrous experiences are not only a normal part of life but are actually our greatest teachers in disguise. The right mentors encourage it even. Take this from *Game of Thrones*:

> JON SNOW: "I failed."
> SER DAVOS: "Good. Now go fail again."

We mentors, teachers, and parents are not sadists eager to see you outright screw up or feel pain. Not at all. In fact, we wince when these things happen to you, and our hearts ache for you always. When you were tiny, we watched you struggle a dozen times before you were able to pull yourself into a standing position, and we watched you fall on your butt a dozen more times before you could actually walk, because we knew that your chubby little legs would only grow stronger and your balance would only grow more sure *if we let you fall and get yourself back up.* We weren't rooting for you to fall or fail. We were rooting for you to have those essential tough experiences because without them you would never make it. See the difference?

Point being these experiences are scary, yet you *want* to have them. To do this you gotta leave your comfort zone and move into your "stretch zone," as they call it at Global Citizen Year, the organization using the gap year to launch next-generation leaders. They send diverse cohorts of fellows to communities around the world, where they live with a family and apprentice to local efforts. (Stretch zone, for sure!) I know it sounds incongruous to leave the safe and comfortable. Why would we want to venture out only to have a potentially risky experience? Here's why. By definition you can't learn in your comfort zone because it's all cozy and familiar there. (Think of your couch. How much learning and growing are you doing there?)

We parents, guardians, teachers, and mentors, *do* want to help you avoid the "panic zone," where you literally have no preparation for what awaits and could possibly die. But in this twenty-first-century existence, unlike in the wild world of *Game of Thrones*, most undertakings don't threaten your very life.

What *does* threaten your life, actually, is staying forever in your comfort zone. If you dwell there for too long you'll end up bored, dissatisfied, and listless. You will grow to be complacent about life being comfy but *meh*. Then you will become mentally and physically stagnant. And from there you will slowly shrivel up, wither, and die. Probably in your parents' basement.

THE ULTIMATE GROWTH HORMONE

Another one of life's beautiful F-words is *feedback*, which is the ultimate growth hormone if you're willing to take it. I've gotten my share of tough feedback over the years, so believe me when I say I know how hard it is to hear that you're not perfect. But in the long term I learned that feedback is good for you.

About four years into a fourteen-year career at Stanford, I became the university's first dean of freshmen after a dear mentor had come up with the idea and suggested it would be a good role for me. I put together a proposal and pitched it to the powers that be, who said, "Okay, yeah, go for it."

I moved quickly. Found discarded office space. Got the guy who designs Apple Stores to donate computers and renovate the office in that sleek Apple-ish vein. Began developing new approaches to working with the first-year students focused on creating a sense of belonging, both in terms of systems (how we interacted with them and how they interacted with the university) and of programs. Eighteen months in, we were a success. First and foremost my team and I were visible, relevant, and credible in the eyes of the students. Their parents appreciated our efforts. Even colleagues in the alumni and development offices praised our new approach because they thought it would yield tighter bonds to the university that would serve the university's interests down the road. I was firing on all cylinders.

A fellow staff member and I went out to lunch off campus one day. I drove. As I pulled up to her building to drop her off, she sat in the car, turned to look at me, and confided that she had overheard many of our colleagues in Student Affairs talking about me. They felt I was:

1. Unqualified for the role. "She never would have gotten the job if it had been posted."

2. Taking opportunity that had been theirs. "She sat down on the park bench and bumped us off of it."

3. Too ambitious. "A ladder climber who doesn't care who she steps on on her way to the top."

I sat there blinking back tears. I loved my job, and up until that moment, I'd thought I was absolutely freakin' perfect at it. I was stunned by the news I was hearing and felt humiliated to be a person who needed this feedback. I could see that my friend was having a hard time looking me in the eye as she told me all of this.

This wasn't about a memo I'd written, or a meeting I'd held, or a budget line item that had gone awry. I wasn't going to be able to just show up at work the next day and fix it. The ideas I'd thought were innovative and exciting were irrelevant—I'd done it without being collaborative or respectful of those who had gone before me. This was about how I was showing up in the workplace over a span of months and years. How I was perceived by my colleagues. What I wanted most of all in life was other people's approval. Yet it seemed I was utterly failing to gain it from people who mattered a lot to me. Worse, it seemed I was actually hurting other people.

I didn't yet know the term "growth mindset"—Carol Dweck's ground-breaking work *Mindset: The New Psychology of Success* would not come out for two years—but I knew the only thing within my power to change any of this was to make a better effort at being a good colleague. I knew that was the work in front of me. Doesn't mean I had a damn clue about how. And TBH, part of me just wanted to convince those naysayers that they were flat-out wrong.

My inability or unwillingness to collaborate seemed to be the main issue to focus on. I'd actually already sensed that that mattered on our campus. No matter how good ideas were, some people would strike them down or flat out dismiss them if they, the naysayers, weren't part of the process. This wasn't a Stanford thing per se; academia tends to be a very collaborative organism (that is, slow to move and reliant on consensus-building). So I said to myself, *Fine. I'll go and have meetings with people about my ideas.* But I did so with a shrug and a sigh. Collaboration was the hurdle to get over on the way to the outcome I wanted: my great idea!

After a few years of this forced collaboration I'd had more than a few experiences where collaborating actually led to better ideas. *What?* I was probably thirty-seven years old. And that's about when I learned that my ideas were not inherently the best ones. (I can't believe I'm putting this in writing because it is so absurd, and painful, and shameful. But hey, it's a huge part of my adulting journey.) Yes, I *needed* to be the smartest person in the room, and it was really getting in the way of my being able to see and hear the wisdom inside other people.

Once I took in the painful information that I needed to become someone who collaborated much better, my growth accelerated. I even began collaborating not because I *had* to but because I *wanted* to. Because I knew it was not only the right process for effecting change on our campus but because I valued the way others could help shape things. It required shutting up sometimes to make room for other voices.

But sometimes my voice was still too much. At thirty-eight, I was told that while the speech I gave regularly to parents about the importance of letting go of their college student was terrific, I was upstaging more senior people, and I needed to stop. I reeled from this. Public speaking was something I knew I did well, and I enjoyed it, too. But I had to learn you can't bite the hand that feeds you. I also started to appreciate that it's best to work for someone who will mentor you and seek opportunities to further your career rather than tell you to sit down.

Then, when I was forty-one, my boss and her boss took me out for dinner at my favorite restaurant and gave me the harshest feedback of my life to date: that I was too big for my britches in choosing to hold my fortieth birthday at the Stanford Faculty Club (where I was a member), complete with the Stanford Band, and that I was egotistical in having brought back trinkets from a work-related trip to many African countries and distributing them to my team as a prize to those who had read the details in the blog I'd posted along the way. Yet again I was offending people—this time by the fun I was having and by the way I chose to distribute gifts. Another wrecking ball to my ego. We were in public—did I mention this had been my favorite restaurant? Somehow I managed not to bawl at the table.

But this time, the blow (the feedback) came with a silver lining.

I made it clear to my colleagues that I was listening and that I wanted their feedback, and that I was going to do everything in my power to learn and grow—and minutes later they told me I was getting a huge promotion. They wanted to merge my tiny freshman dean's office staff of six with two other teams totaling about thirty-five people and put me in charge of it all. This promotion didn't come with more money—this was late in 2008 and the Great Recession was just starting to unfold—but it was an unabashed vote of confidence that I could unify and lead. And that's exactly what I set out to do.

These three teams were disparate and wary of one another. I decided we couldn't do great work on behalf of Stanford students unless we all loved coming in to the office every day to work with one another. Working with my senior team (senior members from across what had originally been three teams), we created a climate of sharing at staff meetings in which everyone had a chance to teach others about their work, to be seen and heard and understood. Then, I told the entire group that we were not a hierarchical org chart, but rather a circle of humans gathered to do important work. That no one was inherently more valued or less valued, and that at every given moment "the wisdom was in the room." This meant that any one of us could step into the circle and offer an idea that would be the right next step forward. I'd gone from collaborating because I *had* to, to embracing a management style that recognized the inherent value of each and every person on the team. It was joyful to watch humans come to believe more in themselves and in each other. The camaraderie brought tears to my eyes. And the work we were able to achieve together was profound.

But that's not the end. In the inevitable continual effort to learn and grow I would go on to do some good things in that job and I would do bad things as well. Sometimes when I think about the things I'm ashamed of from my past I gasp out loud. Like present me just cannot believe what past me did. Then I tell myself, *Okay, you can't go back and change that, but you are learning from it*. I want that. I want to learn and grow until I take my last breath.

I want that for you, too.

PRACTICE VULNERABILITY

Did you notice that I was super vulnerable with you on the page just now? We're taught not to do that—particularly those of us who are male-identified, which I am not, but I just want to put a pin in that. I told you some shit I'd rather everyone not know. I'd rather you think I'm perfect and amazing and kind (and while we're at it, beautiful, thin, and rich). But the work of author and researcher Brené Brown teaches us that vulnerability isn't something to be ashamed of, it's a power. And if we can own up to what hurts or sucks or shames us, tell the truth of it to our own consciousness and maybe to a few people we love, and then talk through what we might do next, we emerge stronger and more ready to handle the (inevitable) next blow that comes. And we can connect more beautifully with each other. My life is a testament to that truth. I'm a person with a lot more growing to do through my own efforts. Just like you.

Earlier, I alluded to Professor Carol Dweck's work on "growth mindset." Her research teaches us that if we focus on how perfect or smart we are, those ideas about ourselves actually hinder our opportunity to grow. We fear bigger challenges or risk-taking because those ventures/next steps might not go well, which will be evidence that we are in fact *not* perfect or smart. Focusing on being perfect or smart is called having a "fixed mindset." Instead, her research shows, we should focus on our effort, which is largely under our control. This is called having a "growth mindset."

FIVE HACKS THAT CHANGE FIXED MINDSETS TO GROWTH MINDSETS

There are tons of resources out there about how to develop a growth mindset but here are a few starter concepts:

1. Change "I am perfect" to "I am trying to get better at this."
2. Change "I am smart" to "When I work hard at things, it pays off."
3. Change "This is hard" to "I do hard things."
4. Change "I can't" to "I can take the first step, and see what happens."
5. Change "I suck" to "I haven't learned how to do this yet."

THAT'S WHY THEY CALL IT WORK

Since you're at a stage of life where how you show up and conduct your-self at work is one of the things that matters most, where your boss and coworkers have opinions and needs related to you, and because who you are in the workplace is going to play a big role in whether you advance or fall behind when it comes to achieving your goals, the remainder of this chapter offers feedback on how to do the hard work of learning and growing in the workplace.

To set the stage: At a minimum, your boss wants you to do as you're told. This boils down to showing up on time, wearing clothes that are appropriate for the type of organization employing you, doing the work that is assigned to you, being a positive not a negative force in the lives of everyone else, and staying at work until your shift or day or the project is done. That's pretty basic. What bosses *really* want is for you to make their lives easier and that's going to require some learning and growing on your part.

What you want and need matters, too, of course. You want an oppor-tunity to demonstrate your capabilities, a chance to become more skilled, to be given more trust and responsibility, to be compensated fairly for your contributions, and to enjoy your work experience. So, drawing upon the prior conversation about learning and growing, failure, feed-back, and growth mindset, here's how those things tend to come into play in the workplace:

THIRTEEN WAYS TO LEARN AND GROW AT WORK

1. *Prepare.* This advice comes from a senior partner at a private equity firm in Silicon Valley (the sort of place that invests huge sums of money for wealthy clients) who is also a father of four. This is the advice he gives his kids about preparing for a job interview: "First, know the organization, know the person who is interviewing you, know their role and their background, where they're com-ing from, what perspective they bring, and what they care about, and speak to them as a person. It's a conversation and you have to engage them as a person. Second, don't *tell* them you have the

skills; *show them how you got* those skills. For example, don't say, 'I'm a really hard worker.' Show them by saying, 'I think I'd be good at this because last summer I had to carry two million bricks from one place to another place and it was really hard work.' Don't say, 'I'm an expert at Excel.' It's better to say, 'In my Econ class we had to model this and that and I used Excel and I had to create these tables, and macros.' It's so much more convincing and memorable to show your qualifications through stories."

2. *Play well with others.* Once you get the job, no matter what it is, other humans will likely be involved. According to the psychotherapist and bestselling author of *Maybe You Should Talk to Someone*, Lori Gottlieb, the number one thing that matters in the workplace is relationships. She says, "Do people like you? Can they rely on you? Do you have a good attitude?" To work well with others you want to demonstrate respect and kindness to all, and you ought to offer deference to those who are senior to you in experience and/or years of life. Sometimes people say, "To give respect you first have to get respect." But I'm here to say, that's backward. (If that's the way we all behaved, then no one would give respect at all and we'd all be waiting around to be respected by others.) The right way to think about respect is "To get respect you first have to give respect." Gottlieb also says, "If you are this neurotic ball of anxiety and you bring that energy into the workplace, or you're perfectionistic and you aren't able to complete anything unless it's perfect, you'll drive everyone around you crazy." Now, I'm not trying to gloss over anxiety. (We'll talk about that in chapter 9, "Take Good Care.") Just making the point that how you self-regulate at work matters.

3. *"Even Awesome has to get coffee," (i.e., Pay your dues).* This line about coffee belongs to the brilliant Rachel Simmons, an educator, coach, and author (*Odd Girl Out* and *Enough as She Is*) whose work focuses on adolescent girls. She writes that many young adults (of all genders) are showing up in the workplace thinking

their smarts and credentials mean they should only be given the most interesting and important work to do. Nope. You sat at the kids' table once upon a time at Thanksgiving and now you have to sit at the equivalent of the kids' table at work. This means doing the boring and seemingly unimportant stuff the underlings do. To put a more positive spin on it, it means pitching in to make things easier, cleaner, safer, and more satisfying for those around you. You'll get points for this. And once you're there long enough, someone else will have to get the coffee for . . . you! (And when you become a higher-up and don't *have* to get the coffee, your team will love it when occasionally you do!)

4. *Learn the ropes.* Lori Gottlieb advises that yes, you need to learn how to make coffee, but also how to make *copies*. She says if you are responsible for external correspondence, you need to know the format for formal correspondence between adults. Don't think, "I don't need to know that, I'm not going to need that, this isn't relevant to me." If you feel like you know more than you actually do, she says, it suggests to your boss an impulse to show how talented you are instead of actually listening to what is needed. Try not to be impatient with learning to do what is needed. Don't take an "Is this going to be on the test?" mentality. There is no test in adulthood. You will never stop learning.

5. *Join the ecosystem.* Every workplace is a bureaucracy, an ecosystem, a network of intertwined humans. You may think the most important person is the big boss (whoever that may be), and that their underlings are the next most important and so on all the way down to you. And as I've said, it is important to demonstrate some deference to those who are higher than you on the org chart. But all humans deserve respect and dignity—don't ever forget that. Most of us are really hungry to be seen and heard, to know we matter, and the best way to make a person feel that they matter (whether in the workplace, at a cocktail party, or at a family reunion) is to ask them about THEM. Don't ask them where they went to school or what job they have. Ask them what's good

in their life these days. And finally, sometimes the person with a seemingly less important job actually has the most information and insight to offer because everybody talks to them. These are important people to meet, show deference to, and befriend. They will know how you're perceived well before you do, and if you've worked on developing a good relationship with them, they just might have your back if others start squawking about you. (Like my friend who took me to lunch back at Stanford that day and told it to me straight.)

6. *Find a mentor.* Every one of us needs people who believe in us *who are not our parents.* Picture that person who is a lot wiser, a lot more experienced, a lot more able to shine a light on your path and illuminate things you otherwise would not see. Figure out who that person is, and cultivate an increasingly strong connection with them. Work closely with them. Figure out what matters most to them in this job. Become not just dependable but indispensable. Then, ask them to coffee where you ask about how things are going in *their* life. At some point they will ask you about yours, and then you can share. Afterward, send a thank-you note. As the years go by, drop a text every now and then to say you were thinking of them. Update them on your successes and struggles and don't forget to keep asking them about their lives, too. When you are frustrated at work, stuck, wondering whether it's time to move on, seek them out for advice and guidance. Listen well. A good mentor isn't going to tell you what to do, but they'll ask you good questions that will open you up further to what you really want. The reciprocal thing here, of course, is that the older you get the more you need to BE a mentor, too.

7. *Work your ass off.* Roll up your sleeves. Do the assignment well. Ask yourself, *Have I anticipated every possible expectation they have for this project, every question they might want answered?* Really work at it. Make it shine. Get it done a little earlier than required. You're trying to demonstrate not only that you can DO the work correctly but that you can be TRUSTED to understand

what is required and why it all matters. Even if you hate the place and are eager to move on, don't take your job for granted or do the bare minimum. (You will want and need a good reference from them, so don't burn those bridges—you owe it to yourself and to the people who raised you to maintain a good work ethic no matter what.) Speaking of work ethic, I've heard it said that some people consider Cornell University to be at the "bottom" of the eight schools in the Ivy League. (I think college rankings are absolute bullshit so I'm not here for that, nor am I trying to perpetuate that, but there's an interesting story here.) Okay, so, I've also heard from corporate recruiters that Cornell grads are aware of this stereotype and seem to feel that they have something to prove because of it. As a result, they end up working harder—they come in earlier, stay later, go the extra mile on assignments—and they're hungrier for feedback that will help them improve. So, while in some people's eyes they may be at the so-called bottom of the Ivy League, *they turn out to be the better employees.* Boom. Take that, Harvard, Yale, Princeton, Dartmouth, Columbia, Brown, and Penn. (Pro tip: A brand-name college might land you the first job, but beyond that it's your ability to work hard and respond to feedback that will garner folks' respect, get you promoted, and get you that *next* job.)

8. *Ask for help.* This advice comes from my dear friend Donnovan Somera Yisrael, who is senior health educator for mental health and well-being at Stanford's Vaden Health Center. (We'll hear more from him in chapter 9, "Take Good Care," where I share Donnovan's work more deeply.) When Donnovan gives student workshops he goes, "How many of you are happy to help someone else out, but won't ask for the same thing from others?" Then he goes, "Do you know that Michael Phelps had a swim coach, Simone Biles a gym coach, and Serena Williams a swing coach?" Then he goes, "What are YOU so good at that you don't need help?" Point being, they didn't hire you because you're the be-all and end-all perfect most amazing person who ever lived. They hired you because you can work hard, get back up when you

fall, and get along well with others. Ask for help when you need it, so you can solve problems more quickly! It's much better to find out how to use a thing rather than break it, and to appreciate the nuances of a situation rather than have to apologize for your blunder. That said, the importance of asking for help is balanced by the need to demonstrate progressive independence (see below).

9. *Become progressively responsible and independent.* While on the one hand you want to be getting help and advice, the higher-ups will be very annoyed if you seem to literally be able to figure out nothing for yourself. There's a theory in the business world about five stages of employee maturity that I heard about from that same senior partner at a private equity firm in Silicon Valley who advised earlier on how to prepare to get the job in the first place:

STAGE ONE: Sitting and waiting for assignments

STAGE TWO: Proactively seeking out assignments

STAGE THREE: Recognizing that something needs to be done, thinking what the likely task or solution needs to be, and proposing it

STAGE FOUR: Just doing it and promptly updating your boss or team on your actions

STAGE FIVE: Just doing it and only bringing it up at a regularly scheduled quarterly review

The higher-ups will get frustrated if you get stuck at the first stage—sitting around waiting for work. The senior partner tells me, "I feel that some of our young employees have been told what to do so many times that they don't have the know-how to scan the landscape to see what needs to be done. And they certainly wouldn't risk doing that without getting specific instructions ahead of time. But the scrappier kids have more self-confidence because they've gone through life doing more on their own, so they are much more comfortable saying, 'Hey, I think this needs to be done,' or 'Hey, I see you're struggling with this. Can I help?' Or, 'The client called with this question and here's what I think.

Do you agree?'" So, if you're stuck in stage one, you need to get off your butt and seek stuff out (it's called *taking initiative*), just don't go overboard and take on *too too* much without checking in with a higher-up. You don't run the place . . . yet!

10. *Don't shy away from challenging situations.* At some point you will likely be managing others if you're not already. Maybe the group of interns reports to you. Or an executive assistant is your direct report. Or you manage an entire team. Your purpose as a manager is not to beat people with a stick but to help those folks learn and grow. And that means that as they experience life's beautiful F-words you will have the uncomfortable job of giving them feedback. I'll be vulnerable again and tell you that at times in my career I've been so afraid of giving people feedback that I've avoided it entirely. Then the situation with them gets more acute, and my not having given timely feedback becomes part of the problem! Humans need feedback in order to learn and grow. Do it kindly—use words, tone, and body language that demonstrate you truly care about their growth. But do it cleanly—don't hem and haw, beat around the bush, or fail to be clear. (A colleague of mine in the president's office at Stanford liked to say, "The ax is kinder than the file." By which she meant just DO IT. Most of the time you're not literally axing someone—the point is that the feedback, whatever it is, needs to be communicated clearly.) You're not judging THEM, you're giving feedback on a behavior. You can still very much care about THEM and it helps them take the feedback if they feel seen and valued as a human even as you're delivering tough news. One of my proudest moments from my professional life is when I've had to fire someone yet they thanked me for treating them with dignity and respect in the process.

11. *Apologize for your mistakes and keep on going.* This advice is from the same senior partner at the private equity firm. "When they screw up, what you want them to do is apologize. The best thing a young person can do is walk into my office and say, 'I feel

really badly. It looks like you're busy. If you'd like to talk about it more, or if you have advice for me, please know that I would love your feedback.'" Boom. Note the subtlety here: *You* may want to debrief the whole thing down to the minutiae in order to feel better about things and in order to learn and grow, but the person you work for may not have the time for that right now. An in-person apology with eye contact, if you're able, tells them you get it and you're not going to let it happen again. Indicating you would love their feedback is also reassuring to them, yet allows them to do it on their timeframe. Note, what we've got above is one guy's preference for how to effectively apologize. (In the next chapter, chapter 4, "Be Good," I detail the five types of apology, so skip ahead to read up on that now if it feels particularly relevant to you.) With keen observation, and some trial and error, you will figure out which type of apology your boss needs in order to feel confident about you again. Once you hit on it you'll find you can develop a much more comfortable and trusting relationship in the workplace. (Pro tip: Your colleagues all have preferred apology languages, as do you!)

12. *Best to assume your parents have no formal role to play in your workplace.* I feel the need to point this out because this has become a concern for many employers. You (and/or your parents) may want them to sit in on a job interview, help you negotiate a salary, benefits, or bonus, or to join you when you know you're about to have a difficult conversation with your boss. Even if you want/don't mind them there, think of the optics—it looks like you're not grown-up enough to have the job in the first place. So, *do not bring your parents.* Consult with them prior if you like, and debrief after. That's fine, and even a good idea when you're just getting started in the working world and have few instincts of your own to go on.

13. *Constantly work your network.* Even if you love your job, you're probably going to want a different one someday, which is going to require activating your network. Don't think of "networking"

as a bad thing. Your network is merely the set of humans whom you know, even perhaps just tangentially, with whom you need to interact if you're to make your way toward new opportunities in the world. (If you're worried about whether you really have such people in your life, have no fear, I'm confident you have *some*, and we'll cover that in chapter 5, "Stop Pleasing Others".) Networking is not rocket science. It's much more delicate than that.

For guidance on networking I turned to Christina Blacken, founder and chief narrative strategist at the leadership development and communication consultancy TheNewQuo.com. Christina shared the following advice on effective networking with me and said I could also share it with you. (Thank you, Christina!)

- **Don't pray and spray**—go into networking with the goal of making a few deeper connections rather than of throwing your business card at everyone and their mama. You're likely to find more reciprocal long-term benefits by making a genuine connection with a few people.

- **Ask interesting questions**—the questions you ask shape the conversation, help you to figure out what you have in common past the surface/work, and create better bonds. Don't just ask people what they do. Some of my favorite questions: 1) What did you enjoy about the event/speaker/organization we're at? 2) What inspired you to go into your project/job/industry? 3) What's something you're creating right now that you're excited about? 4) How long have you lived in (city) and what motivated you to live here?

- **Don't let business cards crust up in your bag**—try not to let potential connections dry up and move nowhere or collect cards that end up being cute coasters for dust in your bag and around your house. Follow up with people within *the next day*, continuing whatever conversation you had, with a simple line, etc. Even better, use digital if cards aren't available or you don't carry them and take an email or LinkedIn on the spot so following up is easy.

- **Don't just be the friend who calls when you need something**— when keeping up with people, don't just ONLY hit them up when you need a favor or an ask. Give a congrats when you see they get a new gig, share their work online and give them a shout-out, check in just to check in and give each other updates—just generally be a curious supportive human rather than the sort of opportunistic person who sends out random communications that are thinly veiled asks. When you build a genuine relationship with someone you admire and like, the reciprocity for helping each other out will naturally unfold.

- **Give thanks and gratitude**—one thing that I like to do is give quick notes of thanks to people who have had an impact on my career/ideas and just let them know I'm thinking of them—high school teachers, professors, old bosses, previous coworkers, friends. A simple quick email letting someone know that you were thinking about them, how they impacted or inspired your journey and what you're up to now, and asking for updates on their end is a great way to keep in touch with contacts who are easy to lose due to distance and time. Doing this even just once a year can make a difference and feels good for you and for the people you're rekindling a connection with.

DON'T JUST TAKE MY WORD FOR IT

So, I've just given you some pretty specific instructions about how to learn and grow in the workplace, which will make you a strong employee, and these tips will also strengthen you as a person. However, don't sweat this list too much right now. Try to remember the main point, which is that you aren't perfect and you're going to fail as well as succeed and that is okay. In fact, it's great. And you don't need to take my word for it. Here are two people who exemplify that learning and growing is the name of the game.

MEET JAMIE—Failing, Falling Back, Then Learning and Growing Forever

I'm on the board of the San Francisco–based nonprofit Common Sense Media, which "provides education and advocacy to families to promote safe technology and media for children," and they invited me to do a reading from my memoir on race as part of their retreat about diversity and inclusion. While chatting with some of the employees afterward, this guy locked eyes with me and smiled one of the kindest smiles I've ever seen. He wanted to talk further. We decided to get lunch and I settled in for a good long story.

Jamie is a forty-two-year-old Latino man, and a star on the Common Sense education team, the arm of the organization that teaches educators and parents how to understand what kids are going through developmentally, and how the information they have access to online interacts with the complex soups known as the child brain and the adolescent brain. This means that when cyberbullying, sexting, or fake news incidents arise in the classroom, Jamie can help school administrators, educators, and parents diffuse and mitigate the impact while creating empathy for what the children are going through. "Instead of judging and punishing kids, can we take a step back and understand that it's all a part of their normal development?" Jamie's empathy for kids is a mile wide and a lifetime deep.

With his gentle voice he asks me if I've ever worked on a farm. I tell him, yes, I'd had a corn-detasseling job in Wisconsin the summer after my freshman year of college, but I lasted a total of two whole days so it probably doesn't count. Farming turns out to be a huge piece of this guy's story and it'll help him tell the story to me if I can feel the sun on his shoulders and see the endless row of a crop in front of him. He smiles, puts his hand on my wrist, and says my two days in a Wisconsin field do count.

Jamie's parents were born in Mexico, where his dad finished fourth grade and his mom left school after third grade to care for her siblings. They migrated to Southern California near the town of Ojai, where his dad became a gardener and his mom became a seamstress. Jamie is the youngest of their ten children, nine of whom lived. He describes his childhood as impoverished. With nine mouths to feed, Jamie's dad made it clear that everyone was expected to support the family. The boys would work in his landscaping business. The girls would learn to cook, clean, and take care of the younger siblings. At seven, Jamie started delivering newspapers and helping with his dad's business.

When Jamie was nine and in third grade, his dad decided it was time to level up the lesson on hard work, which led to what Jamie calls "the most pain-in-the-ass experience I've ever had."

One day, toward the end of the school year, his dad came into his classroom after school. Jamie translated. His dad informed Jamie's teacher that Jamie would be leaving school a few weeks early and going down to work on his grandfather's farm in Mexico. As he translated his father's Spanish into English, Jamie could hardly believe his ears. While his father pressed the teacher for any homework Jamie would be missing and for additional homework that would allow Jamie to advance to the forefront of the class, all Jamie could think was, *Wait, I'm going to do . . . what?* Jamie's teacher, an "amazing man," asked what this was all about. Jamie's dad responded, "I'm going to teach my son the other life skills, the ones found outside of the classroom." "I didn't quite understand," Jamie tells me. "I do remember translating 'La manera de la vida'—which means the way of life, how to sustain yourself. My teacher gave me a massive packet of work. In early May, a few weeks before school ended, Dad and I got on a plane to Guadalajara and drove two hours to Grandfather's farm."

Grandfather made his living selling peanuts, known as "the poor man's protein," and owned a modest peanut farm on the outskirts of Mexticacán, a small town in the state of Jalisco. "We rode on a mule with giant sacks on either side. I had to pick the peanuts and put them in the sacks. When we got back, I'd have to water the peanuts down, then make peanut butter or dry them out and salt them. Grandfather would make his living selling his peanut products in plastic bags in the social center of town, called *el jardín*." One very hot night at the end of July, Jamie's father announced that he was returning to California alone. "He told me, 'What I need you to do is continue to stay here and support your grandfather. This is the amount of money you'll need in order to get back home. You can fly back or take a bus back.' Through my tears I asked why he was leaving me. 'Nobody is leaving you,' he said. 'You're working. You're going to work your way back up. I need you to understand how to make a living. How difficult it is to make a living unless you use all the parts of your body: your brain and your hands.' I didn't really understand. I remember my grandfather giving me my pay that particular week—it was like three or four dollars. I remember thinking, *My God, am I really going to have to work and work this hard in order to be back home with my family?* Keep in mind, I was nine years old."

Jamie didn't meet expectations. His dad ended up coming back to get him. When they got to the bus depot his father deliberately counted out the money he'd earned for the teller to see. "He made me use my earned pesos to pay for the bus ticket. I remember that. It upset me that I couldn't use the money I'd earned to buy what I wanted." Jamie started fourth grade a week behind everyone else.

I'll pause and say that I grew up middle to upper middle class, which means I had absolutely zero of this kind of experience in my childhood. While Jamie rode a donkey to harvest peanuts, I had a Shetland pony (roughly the same size as a donkey) that I rode in horse shows, and I put green ribbons in his mane and on his tail to match my green hat and green cowboy boots. I got a lot of great things out of my childhood, but outside of an academic setting I don't think I learned how to work hard until the summer I was eighteen when I had a job as a busgirl at a twenty-four-hour restaurant called Perkins where I had to clean and set tables and mop bathrooms. (This was the job I got after quitting my corn-detasseling job.) So, I want to take care here not to romanticize poverty and struggle as I share and then respond to Jamie's story.

In the fourth grade, Jamie's parents had thought he had a learning disability. Teachers said he wasn't paying attention. He constantly sketched everything around him with stick figures, diagrams, arrows, and circles. His parents thought he was being defiant. He tried to explain to all of those adults in his life that he was just trying to understand what was going on in the classroom. He knows now that "information comes in the form of images, that everything I learn has an associated visual reference point." But back then he himself barely understood what was going on inside him. Many more years of working with and observing his grandfather helped Jamie sort it all out.

"Because my grandfather was starting to go blind, there had to be unique ways for him to communicate the worth of his product, its market value, and how it differed from what others were selling. My skill set of visual diagramming— a trait where you can use imagery as a way to understand information—was reinforced through my grandfather's ability to buy and sell something while being partially then totally blind. He would pick up on a person's voice, laughter, the handshake. He could tell if the person was a man or woman based on how rough their index finger was. Learning about different kinds of abilities, important non-academic abilities, plays out in my life today. Last Monday I gave a presentation to a number of educators and the first thing I did in the room was I had the adults identify their own learning style. 'Introverted types,' I said to some of the group, 'these are things I'm going to do to keep you connected in this space.' Grandfather gave me that scope of understanding."

In subsequent summers, Jamie's father made good on his threat and didn't come back for him. "He became very serious that I could not come back unless there was enough money. That I would have to work harder and figure out how to sell peanuts in different communities in order to earn my way back." In the five or six summers he worked on his grandfather's peanut farm in Mexico, Jamie learned to hustle, talk to people, and deal with feeling uncomfortable in different situations. "Grandfather would chuckle and say, 'You've earned your money today. Do you want a little bit of tequila?' To this day whenever I have tequila I remember that."

Jamie's relationship with his grandfather grew quite strong. Yet back at home he was becoming a defiant teen. "I fell in love with the water, bleached my hair, and became a Latino surfer. One summer I made some friends down in Mexico and consequently didn't make enough money to get back and my father hung up the phone on me. 'You're not coming home,' he told me. 'Good luck.' At the time I couldn't understand he was modeling how to be an adult—how to conduct yourself in a public space where you feel uncomfortable, how to persevere. But now I respect and admire what he did and I take those lessons with me. I actually enjoy feeling uncomfortable. It allows different parts of me to activate."

Jamie stopped working on his grandfather's peanut farm altogether midway through high school and instead worked at the local gas station year-round. Most of his peers were white and conservative. His lived experience was a stereotype to them and he started to feel alienated. "High school made me feel very rebellious. I was being tokenized being the only Latino in my classes, being maybe one of four Latinos out of fifteen hundred students, or one of eleven to fifteen Latinos if you include the farmworker kids who were only there for one semester each year. But I was academically successful. I could compete. I really enjoyed surfing, but it was a very white male thing and I didn't want to associate with everything else that was related to that. I would often be asked, 'Why can't Latino communities get their act together? Why are the women always pregnant?' It dawned on me early that I was having to be the spokesperson for Latinos, and that the majority white population seemed unaware of so much of the cultural fabric that I was raised with. I couldn't stand it when teachers wouldn't stand up for me; I didn't have the voice to express myself early on. Inside I was thinking, 'That's not who I am. I'm going to prove you all wrong. And I'm going to make you feel foolish.'"

In high school, a teacher took him aside and said, "With writing like that, all you're going to get is a McJob." Jamie took the teacher's concern to heart and enrolled in a college writing course the summer after junior year; when he came back to school that fall, he asked that same teacher to read some of the writing he'd done. She was impressed. "I wanted to rebel with these small gestures. Show that you can't put me in a box because I'm from a particular race or culture. As an adult, I'm constantly having to challenge the presumptions and preconceived ideas about people like me. I have to humble myself, prove I can do this work through the lens of being kind. It would eat me up if I didn't have the perspective my father taught me, which was that you can be sad that you don't have shoes until you meet a man who has no legs."

Jamie graduated from college at the University of California–Santa Barbara in 2001 and entered the Peace Corps to work on community development in El Salvador. One of the many projects Jamie worked on involved helping gang members rehabilitate themselves. "I have a drive to understand the way others are learning and why. And to help." While there, he suffered a brutal knife wound and had to return home for treatment and recovery, which traumatized him for years. Once back on his feet, he spent his twenties in a relentless pursuit of the credentials and work experience that would prepare him to better serve young people. He got a teaching degree. Taught in the classroom. Became a school administrator. But there, he tells me, "I was so frustrated with an educational system that didn't speak to people who look like me." He went on to earn a second master's, in trauma and post-conflict education. In his thirties he spent five years as director of the Boys and Girls Club in the Mission District of San Francisco, where he and his team strengthened the relationships between schools, parents, the police department, and health providers in order to better serve kids. "It was an amazing experience that gave me a chance to understand my own people, and the socioeconomic dynamics that impact lifelong learning." He started a consulting business to help nonprofits work more effectively with families of color.

And in 2018, at age thirty-nine, he joined the team at Common Sense, one of the most trusted brands in education nationwide, where his role is to promote appropriate and responsible technology use by and with children. "Whether and how children are accessing the Internet and other tools matters. I teach administrators, educators, and parents, whether it's migrant communities, families of color who struggle with media use, or white families who don't want to have those deep conversations with their kids. My life's mission is to provide kids with an experience that will make them feel connected with themselves and with others, because once you have your voice and understand who you are in the presence of others, you can really thrive."

Back in 2004, while attending grad school for his master's in trauma education, Jamie was standing in the financial aid line awaiting an appointment with a counselor and encountered the woman who would become his life partner. They couldn't take their eyes off each other. She passed him her number. They married seven years later. A few years after that, their daughter arrived. "We live very passionately. We salsa dance. It's a beautiful presence. She is every ounce of detail I am not." His partner also works for a nonprofit, so they keep their eye on their finances. "We live a simple life. Our worth looks different. I know what to spend on. Growing up poor you realize you can make so much out of a basic tortilla. My wife and I love to reinvent ourselves using the resources we have." To hear him speak, though, there are no deficits, only joy and gratitude. They entertain in their home regularly (pre-COVID) and they spend their money on international travel, where they delight in learning from humans who walk completely different paths in life.

"I think about how our choices in life impact our values. There's an ever-present tension between valuing professional achievements and staying grounded to the foundational values on which I base my life. I'm exploring ways to challenge my narrative. If I feel myself reacting to some comment or social trigger, I try to shift my narrative to see it through the lens of someone who has not lived my life—a perspective I've gained through my travels and awkward moments selling peanuts in the plaza. In doing so, I'm able to humble myself by looking through the lens of others. Those subtle moments of stress often bring me back to what's real and authentic about life. Whatever's eating you up inside, think about a different perspective. 'Challenge your *cuento*,' my father would say, because that's where you find kindness and gratitude. Perhaps that's why I rarely sweat the small stuff." For Jamie's family the goal was never perfection—the goal was and is perspective.

MEET ANANDA—Free from the Stranglehold of "Perfect"

Ananda is a thirty-year-old white woman originally from Livingston, Montana, about a half hour east of Bozeman. She is the youngest of four, and was just two years old when her parents divorced. Her father won custody of all four kids, and supported them by selling insurance. "Montana was about playing out on the hills and probably getting into too much trouble. Sitting on cactuses. Roaming wild. I think because I was raised by a single parent and was the youngest of four I likely had too much liberty for a little kid. There was a lot of trial and error. If I wanted to do something I had to figure it out myself."

When Ananda was seven, her father moved them to Raleigh, North Carolina, to be closer to a good friend of his. He continued to sell insurance. "Because my dad was raising four kids and didn't have a lucrative job, he had a lot of financial struggles. He had his car repo'd the day after Christmas. It was a brutal thing to see. He'd gotten my siblings and me gifts for Christmas, and he is one of the sweetest people out there, but it wasn't the most fiscally responsible move. Like, hey, that felt good but maybe it wasn't the right decision? I felt responsible in some way. Throughout my childhood, I was constantly thinking about divorced parent dynamics, and money, and about how I could be less of a burden."

School became Ananda's obsession. "It looked like a magical portal into a different way of living. I threw all of my effort into *I'm going to go to college and life is going to be different*. It was a way to focus my energy. A way out. I read a lot of fiction because it transports you, but it also teaches you different foils about what type of person you could be or should be. You get to see courage in action and then figure out what that means for yourself." Her other passion was soccer. She was a competitive player who earned scholarships to cover the various fees associated with the sport. She also reffed soccer on weekends, which paid $34 an hour and gave her great exercise. She used that money to fund some of her own expenses, such as gas money or new clothes, and she saved whatever she could.

Her main goal was to get into college. "I was completely trashed and burned out by high school." She had learned about the Morehead-Cain program right up the road at UNC–Chapel Hill, a fully funded four-year college scholarship that included travel abroad each summer. "I applied but wasn't even considered. I get it. I don't have the crazy experiences to write about—music lessons, travel abroad, stories that make for a good applicant—because my dad didn't have the means." But what stuck with her was that she really wanted to do something like that. She realized, "I wanted to go away to find my why."

Her godparents were a well-off family in town who offered Ananda a second home of sorts. She ate dinner there, occasionally slept there, and they were the ones who talked through the college admission process with her, read through her applications, and gave her overall guidance. Their own daughter, also a high school senior, was planning to do a fifth year of high school in Scotland. Between learning about her friend's gap year and the Morehead-Cain program, finding a way to travel beckoned Ananda hard. She says she knew she needed to get away to figure herself out. She felt sure she'd apply herself better and more wisely in college if she could go away first. Why was she *so certain* that going to a different country was the right next step for her?

"I grew up with all of this baggage," she tells me. "When I was young, I was introverted, had a super quick temper, and a lot of me was very numb. If you blame yourself for everything, you are always in control, and you don't have to rely on others, so you're not disappointed by them; if you don't feel things deeply, then you can't be hurt deeply. So, I lived a good life, but because I was so closed off I wasn't opening myself to feeling a lot of experiences. I didn't have deep connections with people. I didn't really *love* people. Yet intellectually I knew love is the reason we exist."

"When I was sixteen, I was reading some book that posited the question, 'How could you imagine yourself as an older person?' And I thought, *You know those old grandmas with the BEST stories? That is what I want to be. When people can wrap others up in their stories and it feels like magic, that is the person I want to be.* And I had this terrible realization then that I didn't have the capacity to tell those stories because I wasn't living in a way that would let me take the chances to live those stories. I wanted to start having experiences you can tell stories about. I started to ask, *If I open myself up to people, what is the worst that can happen? Nothing is going to be worse than being left by your mother and having negative interactions with her. There are great things about life—soccer, school—so even if there is pain, whatever you experience by opening yourself up will make you feel alive, which is way better than not caring about what you're doing.* The author was like—just do something. Start small. So, that's what I did. The next day I went to a science museum and I bought a lollipop with a cricket inside. A cricket sucker could be my first story."

Later in college a systems professor would tell her class, "The problem with your generation is they had no time to daydream." Looking back, she realizes, "Yes, that's it. All I had done was work tirelessly. In middle school I was on a super advanced math track and they were like, 'Alright, what college do you want to go to?' I was only in middle school. So, I began to understand that I desperately needed time to daydream. To have the space to ask the right questions. I thought it'd be a helluva lot easier to redefine myself if there was nothing familiar around me. I wanted a shock to the system. I wanted to be convicted about the person I wanted to be. It doesn't happen overnight. But if you know your why you can always figure out your how.

"Going far away would be a chance at something so drastically different that it would make me sort through my baggage. A forcing mechanism. It wasn't about which country I ended up in, it was all on me. The details of which program or where weren't necessarily relevant."

In the midst of college application season, Ananda's godfather mentioned a startup called Global Citizen Year that planned to reinvent the gap-year concept and might be getting off the ground that very year. *Might be.* "And I was like, hell yeah, whatever it takes. This is going to happen. I started hounding the staff. *When is the application opening? What more can I do to show you I want to do this?* I knew there would be at least *some* financial aid. I'd gotten into a couple colleges by this point (Barnard, UNC, Tulane, Clemson)." Because Ananda's cohort was going to be Global Citizen Year's first year, they still didn't really know if it was even happening. There were no testimonials to go on. She didn't know what country they might send her to. But Ananda was set on making her gap year a reality.

In May of her senior year, she is at a poetry open mic night in Raleigh supporting friends. A call comes in from a California area code. She steps outside. Global Citizen Year director Abby Falik tells Ananda she's gotten in. Ananda throws her cell phone in the air. "Don't hang up!" Abby yells through the phone. She then tells Ananda that the program will be fully funded. "I tell her, 'Ma'am, you've just changed my life.'"

In the fall of 2009, Ananda went to Senegal, a country in West Africa. She lived with a host family in a tiny ecotourism village where French, Wolof, and a Creole mixture of those languages were spoken, and while she'd had some French in high school she was effectively learning all three languages at the same time. "I'm a super sarcastic, jovial, joking kind of person. But early on when I was learning the languages you're just limited in how you can express yourself. So, I had a lot of time to think. And I wrote a lot. A lot of my time was spent learning and writing about my experiences. I started to become familiar with the voice in my head. When you put it on the page you can't hide from yourself. I would ask myself if I really believed what I had just written.

"My site leader was a soon-to-be professor who had us read over a thousand pages of scholarly work on Senegalese and African history. Those writings gave me a deep context and a questioning mentality about what was going on around me in terms of ecotourism and international development. Two really big things sat with me: Learning to let myself question, and daydream. That's how you figure out how to start asking these questions in yourself. You can get anywhere you want in Senegal—there are buses to everywhere. But it might take two days or it might take two hours. There's a lot of waiting. You have to figure out how to *be*. That downtime lets you daydream and think about more complicated questions. All that waiting also allowed me to be light and joyous."

After about five months into her seven-month stay in Senegal, Ananda went on an eight-mile hike to the beach on a hot, hot day with a couple of people from her office. "Two of us were near the water; one was staying behind near the forest edge to watch our bags. From the beach we see these two guys come out from the tree line and take the bags right behind our friend. Going into it I'd thought this was not a big deal—just a day trip with people from my work. I'd thought it would be fine. But here I was with nothing besides a bathing suit, a pair of pants, and a half-filled water bottle. First I'm like, *Holy shit, how am I going to get home, I have no money, no phone.* Second I'm like, *I am in so much trouble. My site director is going to kick me out of GCY because I didn't talk to her about this day trip. How did I let this happen?* I felt like I'm fucked, the people I'm with are French. It's an eight-mile walk back. It's hot. I have half a bottle of water, no money, no phone, no sunscreen. That's why it was, *Oh shit.*

"We start to walk back through the forest and come upon a person who was chopping a tree down and starting to burn it to make charcoal. In Wolof, I convey that we'd been robbed. He brings us to a nearby village where some researchers from the local university in Dakar were researching salinity levels in the water. They said they'd take us home in the back of their truck. The whole ride home I was thinking GCY was going to kick me out. I tell my program manager what happened, and she's like, 'We'll talk about it later, just take care of yourself.'

"She comes over the next day. I'm destroyed. Cuz if you look back to my childhood it's all, 'This is all my fault.' I was sitting there with all of this guilt. At the same time, I get swine flu. I feel absolutely terrible. I end up sweating out gallons and gallons of water over days. My site director says they're not going to kick me out because the guilt I feel from putting myself in this situation and my stuff being stolen is way worse than anything they could do to me. 'Figure out what you're going to learn from it,' she says. I realized I could beat myself up, not forgive myself, and have a miserable last couple of months. Or I could forgive myself and then redefine the couple of months I had left in Senegal. So, I forgave myself. I didn't have a watch anymore because it had been stolen but I didn't care about time anymore. This failure I was beating myself up for turned into a super liberating moment."

Ananda realizes that as a young kid, at some subconscious level she blamed herself for her parents' divorce. In deciding to forgive herself for the beach trip snafu she began to learn how to forgive herself generally, take control over the things she was truly responsible for, and let go of what she was not. "I learned how to forgive myself. I learned that I can control what I can—my reactions, my approach—and to let go of trying to control anything else. That understanding is incredibly important because it refocuses what you actually put your effort on and allows you to move through the world better. You're not micromanaging every detail of your life but instead are creating the right kinds of circumstances so that life can work in your favor."

Ananda figures out that her "why" is learning how to ask really good questions and not accepting a superficial answer. She goes off to UNC–Chapel Hill, where she changes her major ten times before settling on public policy, focusing on international development and public health with a minor in entrepreneurship. "I started taking the courses that seemed right. Followed the courses that were answering the questions that were important to me. Learning how to ask questions served me immeasurably in university. If you can learn how to ask a question and admit that you don't know, you can get a hell of a lot quicker to the right answer or the next question you need to ask. Critical thinking, whether for writing papers or answering a complex supply-chain problem, is key. You gotta have the right information to make a decision.

"In Senegal I was considered relatively rich. After I got robbed I was like, you need more data. You need to ask more questions. My best friend in Senegal had a lung disease and her school had asbestos, so she had to quit school. Whereas I have a heart condition, but the randomness of where we were born meant I ended up in a completely different situation. I was interested in the why behind that. In my final months there I end up talking with a guy on a bus who'd created this startup that raised algae, which is a superfood like kale. He dried it, ground it into powder, and would bake it into bread, which made a very nutritious meal and drastically changed the health outcomes of the youth in the test village. The locally driven, entrepreneurial approach had the capacity to effect large changes.

"When I graduated from college, I thought I could go back to Senegal but my big hack on people in international development was that so many have really good intentions but no idea what they're doing. I decided I need to learn how to make stuff, so I can go back there with a skill to offer." So, Ananda worked at Carbon in San Francisco—a maker of industrial 3D printers—where she helped design a sneaker for Adidas and a new bike seat for Specialized. She recently moved to a stealth startup called Syng, a "future of sound" company in Los Angeles.

"I've just been learning how to make stuff," she tells me. "My next step after this will be figuring out the spaces where I want to apply my expertise. I don't see sub-Saharan Africa as a place for development; I see it as a place for opportunity. My role isn't to go in and save people. I need to bring some kind of skill set and then go in and work with the people who have the ideas and create epic companies that actually solve problems. I want to be good enough to have earned a seat at the table."

IN SHORT: GOOD NEWS—YOU'RE GOING TO MAKE MISTAKES

Take some deep breaths. Tell yourself you don't need to hear the word *perfect* and to need to always feel "comfortable" to know you're okay. Do this over and over again until the thought begins to come naturally to you. (It will.) Remember that this life you're leading is a process of learning. Look for the teachers who can help you grow. They are everywhere.

Your own actions and your own reactions are the only things you can be in control of. Let go of the rest. Seek to become more capable at the things you're good at. Seek to get better at bouncing back after something goes wrong. Ask better questions, not just of others but of yourself. And of all the things to work on, try to be a good person, because in addition to being "the right thing to do" in a morals sense, it'll make you happier and it'll open the most doors to you in life. As for what it means to be a good person, and how to be one, well, that's where we're headed next.

Unpack and Reflect

- What is my relationship with perfectionism? What do I feel the need to prove to others? What am I afraid of? What do I feel the need to control?
- How do I feel when "Life's Beautiful F-Words" (failing, falling, faltering, feedback, flailing, floundering, fumbling) happen to me?
- When have I taken a learner's mentality and readily focused on my growth? How did it feel? Can I point to a lesson learned or a strength gained after messing something up?
- Looking at the "Thirteen Ways to Learn and Grow at Work," in what respects am I doing well and where can I grow further?

4

BE GOOD

(UNLOCK A MAJOR ACHIEVEMENT)

> Principles aren't principles when you pick and
> choose when you're gonna follow them.
>
> —Chidi, *The Good Place*

I'll risk your eye-roll because this needs to sink in: Life is not about getting to some perfect destination that gives everyone else FOMO. When your death comes, and you're sized up by your family, friends, God, and the universe, or whatever you believe in and wish happens at the end, the small moments of you just being you will form your final video. Whether you're a good person or a bad person in the tiny little moments along the way is E.V.E.R.Y.T.H.I.N.G. What we're talking about here is your *character*.

That should feel like a relief. Because you actually have control over your character. But what is it? It's the outward manifestation of your personality and behavioral traits, which others can observe and experience from interacting with you. You wouldn't need to worry much about your character if you lived on an island alone. But we are a social species, so your character matters because it matters to others. Character can make or break you. You want to make your character good.

THOU SHALT BE A GOOD PERSON—HOW TO GROW YOUR CHARACTER

Our son, Sawyer, was born in the early summer of 1999 and our daughter, Avery, was born in 2001 almost exactly two years later. With our new parenting hats on Dan and I told people that to us, parenting was about taking sandpaper and sanding off whatever rough edges our kids were born with (whether thanks to DNA or personality), so that they would be able to go out into the world and interact kindly and effectively with other humans. Like any parents, we expected and hoped that our children would be good people.

These twenty-two years later it's interesting to me that our philosophy was about changing our kids (by sanding off the rough edges) as opposed to giving them their first little tool kit equipped with the tools they would need in order to make it in the world. In hindsight, the tool kit is probably a kinder metaphor than sandpaper! Regardless, our intentions were spot on. Character matters big time. And the cool thing about good character is that it benefits those with whom you interact *and* it means the doors of life are more likely to open wide for you. Good character is a win/win. It benefits everybody. And although you may feel you're beyond needing to learn this stuff since you're already grown, I've found I personally need a refresher from time to time as an adult so I'm thinking you may benefit from one, too.

WISDOM FROM THE ELDERS

For thoughts on cultivating a good character, I want to set the stage with a bit of folklore my mother likes to recite. Mom is an eighty-two-year-old white British lady from a region in the north of England called Yorkshire, near the border with Scotland. That's where folks including my great-grandfather mined the earth and spoke (and still speak) a dialect that the more wealthy and educated Brits almost literally can't understand and make fun of. So, while she tells this story in her "Broad Yorkshire" dialect, I've put it into American English for you.

The setting is an old man sitting in a chair on the outskirts of his village whose job is to monitor who is coming and going and interrogate any strangers who approach.

The old man sat on a roadside seat, solemn and deep in thought.

Thinking on the ways of man with man, and changes time had wrought.

When up comes a stranger chap, a man who'd come to town.

An outsider, it was plain to see, taking his first look around.

"What sort of folks live here?" asked he. And the old man replied,

"What sort of folks are you from?" Said the stranger with a sigh,

"Suspicious, narrow, mean as muck, and most unfair, I fear."

"Then friend you'll find . . ." was his reply, "same type of folks live here."

The stranger left. The old man sat that day and then some more.

When up there came another man, just like the time before.

"What sort of folks live here?" asked he. And the old man says again:

"What sort of folks are you from?" And the stranger then began,

"Glad you asked, I miss them so, it's been so far I've come

"Finest in world, a champion lot, good neighbors every one."

Beamed the old man's face like the risen sun, and stole to his eye a tear.

"Then friend you'll find . . ." was his reply, "same type of folks live here."

As I type this wisdom from my elders, tears spring to my eyes. I can hear their dialect and I can travel back in time to sit in the lap of my Grandma Snookes—my mom's mom, who is long gone—who treated me, her only Black grandchild, with unconditional love. And in addition to the personal memories it evokes, this story just gets me because it's so damn on point. Aside from the prejudice of others—which is a very real thing, I wrote a whole book about my experiences with it—our experiences in life are largely influenced by our behavior and outlook. Our character determines our perception, and how the world will respond to us. We receive what we give. It is so fucking simple.

And here's another piece of inspiration from someone else whose voice resounds in my head, yet who died just six months after I was born: Dr. Martin Luther King Jr. Two months before he would be assassinated, King was preaching at the Ebenezer Baptist Church in Atlanta, where he told a story about character based on a New Testament story about Jesus and two of his disciples. The disciples were ambitious and wanted to be, as King puts it, "great." But Jesus taught them that while ambition is a good thing and striving for excellence is a fine goal, what we should be ambitious about is having a strong character. King makes two points about Jesus' teachings. First, he notices (as we noticed, too, in chapter 3!), that greatness isn't just about being someone's favorite; it's about skills. It's not about someone saying you're perfect; it's about you doing things well. But then King points out that Jesus is making another point here, which is that greatness is actually about goodness, it's not about being the top dog. "[T]he greatest among you shall be your servant" is how King quotes Jesus. King's definition of greatness is about someone who wants to be of good use.

> And so Jesus gave us a new norm of greatness. If you want to be important—wonderful. If you want to be recognized—wonderful. If you want to be great—wonderful. But recognize that he who is greatest among you shall be your servant. That's a new definition of greatness.

> And this morning, the thing that I like about it: by giving that definition of greatness, it means that everybody can be great, because everybody can serve. You don't have to have a college degree to serve. You don't have to make your subject and your verb agree to serve. You don't have to know about Plato and Aristotle to serve. You don't have to know Einstein's theory of relativity to serve. You don't have to know the second theory of thermodynamics in physics to serve. You only need a heart full of grace, a soul generated by love. And you can be that servant.

The third description of character I want to share with you is from professor Emma Seppälä, who is the science director at Stanford's Center for Compassion and Altruism Research and Education. Professor Seppälä and I are in an authors' group, and she recently opined in an email to all of us that in needing to achieve some external definition of success her students were missing the larger point of life:

> I asked my undergraduates a question the other day: *What are the characteristics of the most wonderful people you know? The WONDERFUL ones?*

> They said, *Loving. Caring. Kind.*

> And so I asked them, *Is that not what success actually is? To be a wonderful person who touches someone else's life?*

From Dr. Seppälä, to Dr. Martin Luther King Jr., to Dr. Jean Lythcott (my mother!), these are beautiful reminders of what good character looks like. Looking back over the years of my life, it was hardest for me to exhibit good character when I was struggling, angry, or sad. Once, when I was in fifth grade, a classmate named Suzie was going to get a special surgery for problems she was having with her knees and she got all kinds of attention for that. I was jealous. And one day when everyone was at recess I went into Suzie's desk and broke her ruler. When she saw it and told the teacher, and the teacher asked our class who had done it, I didn't say a word. In fact I've never told anyone about it until right now as I share it with you on this page. Why does something from so long ago stay with me? Because my soul still knows it was wrong and I haven't asked for forgiveness. My soul is keeping track of my character. Even though it's been forty-three years, I think I'd better reach out to Suzie.

MY PRACTICE

I've been an asshole at times. Maybe you've been one, too. (I'm using "asshole" as a catchall term for all the things that comprise bad character—including lying, cheating, stealing, being mean, hurting others, misusing authority, and seeking revenge.) As we discussed in chapter 3, none of us pops out of the womb perfect, and perfection itself is not even the point. The point of our lives is to learn and grow, and that concept applies to character, too. So, I can accept that I have all kinds of character flaws; but now that I'm a certified adult, the thing I cannot accept is being complacent about my assholery. I can say to you in all honesty that I am working at being a better person over time. That is, even at my wizened age, I am still a work in progress. Maybe you are, too.

For example, I've had a hard time accepting some aspects of having chosen to conjoin my life with my mom's, which happened when I was thirty-four and she was sixty-three. She, Dan, and I moved into a house together, and became co-equal owners, for the sole purpose of getting our kids into the "right" public school district. While the upsides were enormous and included free childcare of the highest quality, the downsides included less privacy for me and Dan as a couple and me feeling like she was judging me (and perhaps my parenting) and telling me what to do, as if I was still a child. When, after eleven years of three-generations-under-one-roof, Dan and I had enough money to build an attached cottage for my mom, we did. It benefitted everyone.

As I finally grew to love and accept myself regardless of how others (including my mother) may or may not have been judging me, I found myself wanting to finally get back at my mother for all the times when I was growing up that she was strict and opinionated and offered little leeway; all these years later, something deep inside me needed to put my mom in her place. Like I could finally say, *See, you have your flaws, too.* I wasn't outright mean—just more like impatient and eager to correct. Her correcting me and me correcting her became our dynamic. As she got to be in her late seventies I thought to myself, *Why can't I be as nice to my mother as I am to the elderly neighbors on our street?* Of course I realized, DUH, BECAUSE SHE'S YOUR MOTHER. But still. I was curious. Could I de-escalate stressful moments between us by simply pretending she was just a regular person, and not the woman who had raised me with whom I had a lot of baggage? Turns out, I could.

In the summer of 2017 I put three goals in my journal for the remainder of the year: 1) My new memoir on race would be a *New York Times* bestseller; 2) Oprah would endorse it; and 3) I would improve my relationship with my mother. I'm happy to say that only the most important of these three goals was achieved: I began a practice of treating my mother not just with the kindness with which I would treat an elderly neighbor, but with the same kindness I wanted in return. My mindfulness practice (which I'll say more about in chapter 12, "Unleash Your Superpowers") allows me to notice how I'm feeling in the moment when conversations are happening, and allows me to regulate my emotions and decide if and how I want to respond. In conversations with my mom where I might in the past have gotten triggered, then acted out, I can now let it go, not necessarily forever, but long enough to think through and decide, *What's the best way for me to respond if I'm trying to improve our relationship instead of just be RIGHT.*

An opportunity to further improve our relationship appeared early in the pandemic. It was late March 2020. We were two weeks into our practice of not going out of the house except for necessities, and so on. Dan, Avery, and I were on the front patio when my mom came by with her purse slung over her shoulder and announced to us that she was going to the grocery store because "I've only seen you all three times in the last two weeks." I flat out knew she had seen me at least twenty times in the last two weeks, not three times. Why? Because every damn day I'd made it a point that no matter what else I was doing—serving food to Sawyer, who was quarantined upstairs; wiping the entire house down with Clorox daily; spending time with Avery, who was at times really struggling emotionally; working on this book; writing newsletters that I hoped would support other people who were struggling with the lockdown; spending precious minutes with Dan—I would stop by my mom's cottage and say hi to her or just check in about something. Now here she was outright lying about not seeing us. Either that or her memory was really starting to go. I was mad. I felt completely unseen in my efforts. I also felt a little scared that maybe this was a sign of her having memory loss. And feeling defensive and scared can make you act like an asshole.

Dan, Avery, and I tried to dissuade my mom from leaving. We reminded her that we were always available to go get anything that she might need at the store. We reminded her about the local government regulations that clearly stated that people her age should not leave the house, period. And I in my assholery made the point of forewarning her that if she got the virus we would not be allowed to visit her in the hospital. All of this was to no avail. She kept saying how much she needed to see people. She strode to her car, her eighty-one-year-old, five-foot-and-shrinking frame filled with strength and righteousness, and shouted over her shoulder, "If it's crowded I'll turn around and come home."

We watched her drive off. Avery, who was then eighteen, pulled me aside and said, "Mom, I think maybe both you and Gaga are right." (My kids call my mom Gaga.) There was nothing in me that held open even the possibility that my mother was right, so I was pretty skeptical about what my kid was about to say next. But she's my kid. So I listened. She said, "Mom, you KNOW you check in with Gaga daily. You make the effort every single time. I see that. But to Gaga, it's not a real visit unless you come inside and sit down for at least forty-five minutes and she offers you a beverage."

POW! Crystal clear. Gol darn if this kid wasn't 100 percent right. I felt relieved and was able to cool down almost instantly. When my mom got back I hustled over to her cottage to tell her about Avery's analysis of the situation. Mom agreed. And she'd also cooled down, so she was able to apologize for her prior frenzied state and chalked it up to her frustration over all the text notifications she was getting now that our entire extended Lythcott family had set up a text chat, which can be a lot for an octogenarian to handle. I showed her how to turn off the notifications. And from that day forward, I've tried to show up to be what my mother needs and deserves—quality time—which means I've had an 8 a.m. coffee date with my mom on her front stoop every weekday (I sleep in on weekends). My soul—which I really do believe tells you how your own character is doing—makes sure of it. I also pulled Avery aside later that day and reiterated how much I appreciated her insight. When someone teaches you a lesson—as my kid had just done—you need to acknowledge and thank them. That's good character!

So, I've personally experienced the inroads we can make to improve our character when we try, and I like to try to engage others in thinking about it, too. We have a fire pit in our backyard surrounded by an array of eight or ten wooden chairs. (It's a gas fire with fake logs because we're no longer allowed to burn wood where we live, which is hard for me as a fire-lover but I appreciate the why.) On some summer nights Dan and I gather with friends or colleagues for dinner and then retreat out back with some beverages and maybe some dessert. I sit in my favorite chair, the one that puts me at due west, where the sun has set, which for some reason makes me feel more centered and at peace. When everyone is settled I tell everyone something along the lines of, "I hope to learn and grow until I draw my last breath. So, I'm interested in what I need to work on. Who I am becoming—not in a position, rank, or salary kind of way but what am I working on in order to be a better person? If the same holds true for you, if you're willing, please share what you are working on. Who are you becoming?" Usually this goes incredibly well. People open up and share some shit. Once I got a handwritten thank-you note from a friend's husband, a guy I barely knew, who made clear that he would never forget that conversation.

But sometimes it doesn't go well. Once I had members of a board on which I serve over for drinks. There we were, gathered around the fire pit drinks in hand, I gave my preamble statement and question, and one of my board colleagues responded by shaking her head and protesting that this was a navel-gazing, privileged, even narcissistic question. I smiled, took a deep breath, thanked her for the pushback and opportunity to clarify, and said that yes, it's a privilege to be living a life where you have the space and wherewithal to even entertain such a question, but doesn't such a life require us to ask how we can continue to grow to be a better person so as to be of more use to others in our work and our communities? She just shook her head again. She 100 percent did not get it. I chalked this up to her being an economist :) But I do believe that asking this question of ourselves—who am I becoming—is a profoundly valuable way to continually keep ourselves in check, set intentions for our own character growth, and not let our success or station in life make us complacent.

As of this writing, I'm working on these two things on a daily and constant basis:

1. Make room for others in conversation. I'm an extrovert, so I find it easy to speak up and share my thoughts. In fact, I enjoy it! But I know from the work of Susan Cain (author of *Quiet: The Power of Introverts in a World That Can't Stop Talking*) that introversion is a thing, and that introverts need the quiet spaces to remain quiet for a bit because only in the quiet spaces do they feel ready to speak up. If we extroverts constantly fill the silence, we literally make no room for the introverts. I work on this. A.L.L.T.H.E.T.I.M.E.

Dan is an introvert, so whenever we go out with another couple and they ask us a question either of us could answer, I smile, close my mouth, and maybe look away. I might raise my eyebrows in a smile. These are all the behavioral things I try to deploy to keep myself from consuming the silence with my ever-ready voice. Don't get me wrong—I'm not silencing myself *at all*; I'm just practicing not being the first and most frequent voice in the room.

2. Overcome my prejudices. With the help of my executive coach way back at Stanford over a decade ago, I learned that I can have a lot of control over my actions and behaviors if I pay close attention to the feelings that arise in my body in response to what's going on around me. (This is a shorthand way of referencing "mindfulness," a concept I'll discuss more in chapter 12, "Unleash Your Superpowers.") Through mindfulness, I can notice a feeling coming, and talk to myself about what I'm feeling and why I'm feeling it, and decide whether I need to do something in response to it or not while the conversation around me keeps going. I work really hard to notice my stereotyping, prejudice, and bias. Am I going to treat this person differently because they are wearing a symbol of a religion I don't really understand? Because they have a different skin color than me? Because they are differently abled? Because they are unkempt? These are just some of the biases I've noticed creeping into my mind, and thanks to Jennifer Eberhardt's work on implicit bias (readily available in her terrific book *Biased: Uncovering the Hidden Prejudice That Shapes What We See, Think, and Do*) I know that society made me (and you) this way starting pretty young. So, I don't feel bad about the fact that those biases are there—I just try to name them. Because I've learned that if you can name it you can tame it. It's mental magic as far as I'm concerned. And my practice is to deploy it whenever needed.

And I guess my third practice is to share my growth with others. Both to model the importance of continually working on our character, and to share some specific areas of my growth that others may resonate with and want to incorporate into their work. (I see you, fellow extroverts!)

THE "SWEET SIXTEEN" OF GOOD CHARACTER

So, with the caveat that I'm a flawed human being and do not have all the answers, which I hope by now is obvious, here are sixteen principles I've been taught or learned about good character over the years. They're mine, my guiding principles of character, but they're not terribly different than the penal code in any jurisdiction around the world. They're also a distillation of the non-religious aspects of the Ten Commandments. If we could all develop and hone these character traits, we just might be able to prevent our society from dissolving into violent shards of self-interest, which looms like an ominous possibility in these times. I hope you'll take them to heart and be curious about which of them are hardest for you.

1. *Know that there is more than you.* You are but one of billions. Your needs and wants matter, but that is true for all. If you're able to read this book, that means that you likely enjoy a quality of life that is better/higher than the vast majority of other humans on the planet. Take a deep breath and as you exhale be humble for a moment and for moments more. Most of what is happening is not about you at all. Let that fill you with relief instead of sadness. Use the privilege you've got to make life kinder and safer for others.

2. *Embrace that your purpose in life is to learn and grow.* What a wonderful thing that is. There's so much to learn and explore. Be curious about your own sharp edges and dull sides. Be interested in growing to be the kind of person others feel safe and seen around.

3. *Put a smile on your face and let it warm your heart.* I want to acknowledge that this may be the hardest principle for some because it's about mood, which is not entirely under our control, to say the least. Research shows that we all have different mood or attitudinal set points. Some of us are more naturally optimistic and others are more naturally neutral or pessimistic. This is

our hardwiring. On top of our hardwiring we also experience things that pump us up or get us down. Sometimes we are situationally depressed or anxious, or even clinically depressed or anxious. All of that is valid. Yet, when we can manage to bring a positive attitude to our interactions with other humans, it's like a balm that makes our interaction smoother. So, it's helpful to us (and to the others with whom we interact) if we can up our set point at least when we have to interact with others. Taking a few breaths from deep in the belly can help us have this reset.

4. *Be well mannered.* Although I was being raised in the "anything goes" era of the 1970s, my strict British mom wasn't having any of it. My friends would call her by her first name but I had to call adults by some kind of title. My friends didn't say please and thank you all the time but those words were hardwired into my brain. Having to observe all these niceties chafed when I was little (particularly when I saw other kids get away with stuff) but as I grew older I came to appreciate that manners are like a red carpet: they usher you in to whatever place it is you want to go. So, when Dan and I became parents, the first thing we wanted to establish in Sawyer and Avery behaviorally was manners. Well before they had friends with whom to learn to share, well before they were old enough to be helpful, they were asking for things they wanted. And our feeling was, if they could say the word *cookie*, they could say the word *please*. If they could say the name of a toy, they could say thank you. Strangers at playgrounds and restaurants would tell me and Dan how "lucky" we were that our kids were so polite. We wanted to shout, *It ain't luck, people!* But shouting this would not have been good character! (Pro tip: People with good character tend not to brag about themselves.)

5. *Have patience and grace.* There's a whole lot going on that has nothing to do with you. Make room for people to do what they need to do, particularly if things are getting stressful or tense. Patience looks like you nodding slowly with a gentle smile on your face like, *It's all good, no worries.* Patience becomes a nice,

warm, weighted blanket that just settles everything down. As Pastor Kaloma Smith of University AME Zion Church in Palo Alto says, "Don't respond to every dog that barks at you."

6. *Take turns, compromise, share.* My mom was pretty strict about this one, too! She taught me that when I had a friend over and there was an uneven number of cookies I was to offer the extra cookie to my guest. No prob. I got it. I'd get the same courtesy at their house, right? Not necessarily. When I went out into the world and the rules were different, it really messed with me. I was known to be the four-year-old who would proclaim at someone else's house, "No, *I'm* the guest so I get the extra cookie. When you're at *my* house then *you'll* get the extra cookie." Cookies are delicious and life continually offers them in uneven numbers. (Of course, while cookies can be split, many other things we covet cannot be cut in half.) Our capitalistic society reduces worth to money. Imagine a society where we instead considered circumstances, labor, effort, and intentions. What if we all knew how to value others based on what they were able to offer? What if we all knew to take turns, compromise, and share instead of just grabbing everything for ourselves without giving thought to the impact on others? Look for ways to be creative about sharing, whether it's bartering goods and services or innovating your roles in the workplace or in relationship. There is enough for us all if we articulate that as a value.

7. *Work hard.* I'm chuckling at how often my mother is coming up here, but what are parents for if not to instill these maxims that stay with us forever? I can hear her saying, "If a job's worth doing, it's worth doing well." Again, something that kind of annoyed me as a child (because it often felt like judgment) but as an adult I totally get what she meant. If you do something in a half-assed way, the outcome won't be as good as it might have been, and people who happen to observe or be impacted by your meh effort—whether your boss, coworkers, employees, family, friends, or even strangers—will feel annoyed and demoralized.

Whereas going for it with true effort and commitment inspires and motivates others. An added bonus is that working hard makes you feel good inside of you. In his bestselling book *Drive: The Surprising Truth About What Motivates Us*, behavioral scientist Daniel Pink says a deep sense of engagement in your work "is the oxygen of the soul." Woo!

8. *Pitch in, and be of use to others.* There's work to be done all around us that isn't necessarily our responsibility yet our help could be so beneficial. Tasks to be completed. Things to be fixed. Situations to be handled. A person of good character asks themselves, "Hmmm, how can I help?" then acts accordingly. Such persons immediately endear themselves to whomever owns the problem, although, may I add that as with kindness, it's great if you can come from a place where you don't need recognition for it and instead have confidence that the behavior itself yields its own reward to you in the form of helping others and in growing your character. It's the people who can pitch in without a need for recognition who are most appreciated by others.

9. *Be compassionate toward others.* Sawyer was the kind of two-year-old who was excited to have a baby sibling. He was loving and patient with Avery from the very first day of her life, and for years they were close and exhibited no sibling rivalry issues. But by the time they were seven and five he would sometimes pick on her. Avery would entreat, "Punish him!" It was never quite that simple for me and Dan. Why was Sawyer, normally kind and easygoing, acting out? In the coming years, after I'd done some reading on the subject, I came to appreciate that if someone is acting out it's often because they themselves have been hurt. (The classic example from the research is that of the kid who bullies other kids or hurts animals—they are likely being hurt by someone, too.) One day when Sawyer was eleven, and he was being mean to Avery, I comforted Avery, and then instead of just punishing Sawyer, I turned to him with a kind voice and asked, "Was someone mean to you today?" He looked at me like

I'd just read his mind and proceeded to tell us what had gone wrong for him that day. I told him that that's probably why he was being mean to his sister. He was able to apologize to her, and she was able to accept it. It felt like a parenting WIN. A couple years later the bigger win would come. I arrived home after a rough day of work at Stanford and began being snippy with Dan and the kids as we got dinner onto the table. Sawyer came up to me and said kindly, "Mom, was someone mean to you today?" I just stared at him, the truth of his question kneading me like a good massage, the wisdom of this kid blowing my mind. (Pro tip: Children can be quite wise.) I drew him to me for a tight hug and kissed the top of his head. The answer was yes. But I didn't need to take it out on my family. I apologized, and they forgave me.

10. *Be aware of prejudices that arise, and acknowledge them to yourself.* As I mentioned earlier, this is one of my regular practices and I'm grateful to Professor Jennifer Eberhardt's research on the subject (again, check out her book, *Biased: Uncovering the Hidden Prejudice That Shapes What We See, Think, and Do*). When you notice within you a prejudice (or even just a stereotype) due to someone's appearance or behavior, tell yourself, *Hey, I'm about to stereotype that person. How about I just treat them like they're my best friend.* The act of noticing releases the hold the stereotype tried to clamp on your mind and heart. Then you can put a smile on your face, which warms your heart, and you end up being able to interact with that person with kindness and treat them with the love you want shown to you. It is deceptively simple. You get better and better at it the more you practice it. Imagine the world we can create if we could all behave this way for just one day.

11. *Tell the truth.* The truth can be scary as fuck. When something awful is happening or when we ourselves have made a mistake or outright done something awful, we don't want to face it. But lies and cover-ups are just a temporary relief—in the long run

they can suck you down like quicksand, and draw you under, and now you're living life in an underworld, which feels complicated and frightening. The ability to know the truth about what's happening and the ability to cop to the truth if we've played a part in the problem are such liberating parts of adulthood. When you've done something wrong or bad, you can come to feel that the wrong or bad thing defines you, like it's all that will ever matter about you. Here's the rub—it WILL define you in your own mind as long as it stays hidden in your psyche, where it will lurk like a scary shadow; if you speak up about it, that's when the sunlight comes in and takes the shadow away. You may fear you won't survive the truth once it's out there—yet the opposite is true. Your conscience feels strangled by lies and the cover-ups but the truth sets your conscience free. Now, all of that said, it's not always an *opportune time* for the truth, because there are times when the truth would hurt others. And you don't have to type up your truth for all to see. Use your good judgment about whether your truth should come out *now and to whom you will tell it*. And even if it's not the right time to share it for all kinds of good reasons, have a conversation with yourself about what you're keeping silent, and why, and until when you're going to hold it in. When you can say to the pertinent people, *This is what I did, I'm sorry, I'm learning from it, I'm trying to be better*, that's really all anyone can ask of you. And you will feel free.

12. *Ask for help when you need it, and accept it graciously.* In chapter 3, we discussed why asking for help matters in the workplace, but it applies broadly to life. The stoic rugged individualist who thinks they're an island and doesn't need help can be a bit of a pain in the ass. I'm thinking about various episodes of *Survivor* when one person just has to build the shelter the way they think is best and everyone else stands around just going, *um, OKAY.* This person has something to prove and often ends up wasting everyone else's time and resources in an effort to do it themselves. My advice is: work that shit out in therapy. When others are repeatedly offering to step in and help, it usually means you've gone past the point of

comfort for the folks you're with. Don't fall into the trap of thinking your way is the only way. Step back and say, "Okay yeah, you probably have some thoughts here." Often our ideas and solutions are not the best ones! (Remember my story in chapter 3, "You're Not Perfect," about how I learned this the hard way?) Often we can't go it alone. Ask for help and accept it graciously, not begrudgingly.

13. *Apologize and learn from your mistakes.* We all fuck up. It's usually obvious when we do. Far less obvious is when someone's feelings are hurt by something we said or did. (This is one of the grayest areas of human interaction. What you intended is one thing. How the person experienced it is another. Both are valid.) Yet when the other person says that your behavior negatively impacted them, you should seek to understand, apologize, and learn from that, regardless of what you may have intended. Don't be that person who says, "I'm sorry *IF you were offended.*" That's not an apology. The apology is, "I'm sorry that I offended you. I didn't mean to. But I understand that you were offended. I'm so sorry. I'd like to do better." In his book *Five Languages of Apology: How to Experience Healing in All Your Relationships*, Dr. Gary Chapman explains that depending on how we were raised, our personality, and our fears, there's a specific variant of apology each of us most "needs" to hear in order to be able to move on from whatever happened. The five variants are:

- Expressing regret ("I am sorry.")
- Accepting responsibility ("I was wrong.")
- Making restitution ("What can I do to make it right?")
- Genuinely repenting ("I'll try not to do that again.")
- Requesting forgiveness ("Will you please forgive me?")

The better you know people the more you'll be able to intuit (or ask) which variant works best for them. But if you don't know and can't figure it out just go with "I am sorry."

14. *Debate and disagree courteously.* Too often today we label someone we disagree with as "backward" or a "libtard." We refuse to

hear people out. Instead we shut people down, and sometimes outright "cancel" them. This is ruining us. It's fracturing our communities and families, and it hurts inside when we're on the receiving end. None of us wants to be forever judged by a bad thing we did, so why do we do this to others? We can be bigger than this. Take a deep breath. Listen to the person. Ask them questions so you can get a better grip on where they're coming from. Truly seek to understand. It's hard for one person to do this all by themselves within a sea of oppositional hate. But when a group, or a team, or a friend group, or a family, or a classroom, or a grade, or a school, or a workplace can all agree to a practice of setting ego to the side and listening to the other side with respect, well, maybe we can get somewhere. You'll get some real guidance on this when you "Meet Irshad" in the "Don't Just Take My Word for It" part of this chapter.

15. *Forgive.* This is the one I'm just beginning to learn. I've held grudges for years because I was so upset or angry with the person and desperately needed them to understand the harm I felt they had done. But as I've aged and worked with therapists I've come to really *get* that I can't change anyone else's behavior or opinions. That is, whether the person is going to come to see the situation from my point of view is entirely up to them. Psychologists say that when we harbor anger and resentment toward others, it lodges like a tumor in *our* mind and heart. So, I can't *make* the other person see it my way but I can waste a lot of my mental energy on being angry with them, and holding onto that grudge will start to impact my quality of life and maybe even the duration of my life. (There's science to back this up!) Even if you think you can't or shouldn't psychologically let go of what they did or said (or didn't do or didn't say), for your sake, I encourage you to find a way to let it go.

16. *Behave right even if nobody is watching.* It's easy to exhibit these principles when you're in the company of others. But how about when you're alone? Do you do the right thing? Or, because no

one can see you, do you do something you know you shouldn't? The truest measure of good character is that you practice these principles even when nobody is watching. Otherwise you're two-faced: one person to the outside world and a different person with yourself. You want to be one person. You want to always know who you are and how you behave and why, and you want to consistently and continually practice at being that person. You want to have as much respect for yourself as you do anyone else. Otherwise you'll find yourself regretfully saying, *Man, I can't believe I behaved that way, that's not really who I am.*

So, there you have it. The secret sauce for good character. If these sixteen principles are just too much to remember (or you don't want to carry this book around at all times), it all boils down to this: be loving.

In many respects, humans are astonishingly evolved. We've decoded some of the human genome, and we have sent machines to Mars. Yet we cannot seem to escape the us/them mentality playing out in all realms of life, be it rivalries between countries, sports teams, social clubs, cultures, and stations in life. Research shows that it comes from our ancient ancestors' need to form "in-groups" as a way to protect them from others, the outsiders. Today, even something as totally inconsequential as the color shirt you're wearing can lead to an in-group/out-group association (when prompted in a laboratory setting). The lizard part of our brain seems hardwired to know which team we're on, and to create a rather sizable hostility to those on the other team.

We are so advanced as a species and yet our ability, willingness, even desire to locate an "other" we can demonize, sometimes painfully, sometimes violently, is very much still with us. As a Black person in America, I've lived this up close. If I could change just one thing about humans it would be that we would stop judging and harming each other on the basis of our immutable characteristics, like race. This is the very purpose of the Black Lives Matter movement. Sometimes I think that maybe catastrophic climate change is the ultimate "them" that will bring "us" together once and for all. Then again, I also thought that about the pandemic.

Imagine one single day on Planet Earth when every human alive exhibited these sixteen character traits, and expressed only love to themselves and to all others. We would be forever changed—we'd make a quantum leap forward in our existence as a species. We are capable of that. This I know. But this book isn't about everyone, it is about you. And for now I want to keep the lens there.

MEET IRSHAD—Being Good by Having the Tough Conversations

One evening when she was about ten years old, Irshad's father was ranting that he was going to kill her mother when she got home from her evening shift at her job cleaning airplanes. "I can't remember what he was angry about. But I do remember reminding him that we live in a country where he is not allowed to do that, and that if he did, I could go to the police. He responded in the only way he knew how. He pulled a knife out of the kitchen drawer and ran after me with it, threatening to slice off my ear. I flew up the stairs, into my bedroom, and out the bedroom window, where I sat on the roof for much of the night. And as I surveyed the neighborhood, I made a pact with myself that I would never as an adult allow myself to be stuck in the situation that my mother found herself in."

Irshad Manji is a queer Muslim woman who is now fifty-two years old. She's the child of an Egyptian mother and an Indian father who were living in the East African country of Uganda when she was born. When she was four, Uganda's President Idi Amin called for the removal of all Asians and other non-Africans from Uganda, so she and her parents became refugees. They fled to Canada's west coast, and made their home in a community outside Vancouver, where Irshad would spend the rest of her childhood.

You might say Irshad's entire life trajectory was launched out on the roof that night when she was ten. "This notion that either you do as your father orders or you have your ear sliced off struck me as a profoundly limited and limiting way to live. I decided to use my education to ensure to the best of my ability that nobody else—women, men, children, adults—would be trapped in an either/or situation like that. I think that is part of what motivates me to continue reconciling seeming opposites." If her first example of being trapped in irreconcilable either/or situations was at home, the second was at religious school. Her parents supplemented Irshad's public school education by sending her to a madrasa—Islamic religious school—for eight hours a day each Saturday. "Every single week it was thrust into me that I was not to ask questions of the Koran. And that if I did, I was not a true Muslim." But ask questions she did. And when she was fourteen, the teacher at the madrasa grew tired of her questions and kicked her out.

Irshad's theory of how we can reconcile seeming opposites is to develop "moral courage," which she defines as "having conversations about difficult things, then doing the right thing in the face of our fears," and this is the focus of her remarkable career. In our era of profound political, cultural, and ideological polarization, and of a hardened unwillingness to try to communicate across differences, Irshad speaks of this moral courage not just as a right of all humans but as a *responsibility*. I agree. I believe that at the core of good character is seeking to better understand our fellow humans and being able to communicate with others amicably and with integrity, i.e., while retaining your wholeness. Which is not to say it's easy—it's not! So, I called Irshad up to learn more about who she is, and how she manages to have difficult, important, and effective conversations with others.

By the time fourteen-year-old Irshad got home from the madrasa that fateful Saturday, her mother had already received a phone call from the teacher explaining what had just gone down. "They told my mother that I was being kicked out for 'repeatedly disrupting.' Mom said to me, 'Look, you're a clever girl. I'm not going to try to convince you to grovel for forgiveness. I'm sure you don't think you've done anything wrong. I'm going to ask one thing of you. Now that you're no longer welcome at the madrasa, ask yourself, where *are* you going to go? What's next for you on Saturdays?'" Irshad explains that because her mother had faith in Irshad's capacity to be thoughtful, she wanted to live up to that expectation. "That's why I didn't become a mall rat or hang out at the arcade. I did what the closest thing to Google was at the time—I went to the public library, where eight hours every Saturday I read everything I could about not just my religion but other religions. Not just about my culture but about other cultures. Not just the ideas I was raised with but many other ideas. It's because of that period of self-study that I discovered something I would never have been taught at the madrasa, namely that my religion has a tradition of discovery called *ijtihad*, which promotes struggling with our minds to comprehend the wider world out there."

Discovering ijtihad was a turning point for Irshad. She now knew that the absolutes with which she was being presented (be a faithful Muslim OR question Islam; respect your father OR protect yourself) are actually things Islam wants you to question through the concept of ijtihad, which permits us to hold two warring truths in our minds at once. Reconciling doesn't mean one is right and the other is wrong; reconciling is saying, *Okay, both of these can be true.* "Thanks to ijtihad I realized, *Nope, you don't have to choose.*" This turning point led Irshad toward her calling—helping humans maintain a harmony within the self, when in a group, and between groups in the face of seemingly irreconcilable differences.

Irshad would come face-to-face with another seemingly irreconcilable difference at the age of twenty-two when she woke up one day and realized she was in love with her female colleague. This woman had come out to Irshad weeks earlier, and Irshad's first thought was, *Wait, but you're not ugly!* She explains to me that the message she'd received from both her religion and from society writ large was that only ugly women were lesbians. Here was proof that this was simply not the case! "Over the course of several weeks I wound up falling in love with her. I realized at that time that I was happier than I had been in many years. I felt the kind of wholeness that leads to peace of mind." On paper, Irshad's sexual orientation and her faith were said to be irreconcilable. Yet this young woman, who'd fled a violent father and been kicked out of a madrasa, wasn't going to turn her back on either her religion or herself.

"I wanted my mother to know how happy I was. I called her and I said, 'Mom, I'm coming home to tell you some news. And don't worry, it's not cancer.'" Her sisters later confided to Irshad that when they heard this from their mom, they knew Irshad was going to come out. "Over toast and tea, my mother had all of the questions: 'Is this a phase?' I said, 'Maybe. I don't think so. But I don't know for sure.' 'Did your father's violence turn you into this?' I said, 'Mom, I'm pretty sure it didn't. After all, so many girls and people have abusive parents and many of those people remain straight.' After that conversation my mom told me to remember that I will always be her daughter and that she will always love me unconditionally. What I loved about how she put it was she wasn't being histrionic—it wasn't, *Now I love you more than EVER because you were honest.* No. She loves me no less and no more than she ever has."

As Irshad grew older she began to realize that "occupying a complicated space is the work of all humans who want to live honestly." And with that she began to try to shatter this dispiriting notion that we can only be one thing and not another, that we must adhere to the dogma of our religions and groups, and that we must shut down those with whom we disagree. It was time to try to tackle some problems she was having with the way Islam was widely practiced.

Three years after 9/11, against the backdrop of so many non-Muslims in the Western world asking themselves, *What is this religion called Islam?* and *What is up with Muslim extremists?*, Irshad set out to get her fellow Muslims to ask some really hard questions of themselves. In 2004 she published the book *The Trouble with Islam Today*, in which she aimed to say to her fellow Muslims, "It's we Muslims who have to change our defensiveness within ourselves." She notes, as an aside to me, that defensiveness and the need for self-questioning are hardly just a Muslim thing. "In the book I say we Muslims need to interrogate our reflexive anti-Semitism, the inferior treatment that we give to women, and this completely unfounded notion that human rights are Western concoctions. I say we need to appreciate that thinking is not a sin, therefore questions are not sinful, and that asking questions opens the door to the delicious complexity that is the creation of God. And I love to remind my fellow Muslims that curiosity and ingenuity are in our nature. That when Europe was in the Dark Ages, Islamic civilizations led the world in curiosity and ingenuity. That coffee and the guitar came from Islamic civilizations. That even the Spanish-language chant 'Ole!' came from the exuberant chant 'Allah!' That we can become Muslim reformers in part by reminding ourselves of our roots and history."

During the decade in which Irshad toured the book *The Trouble with Islam Today* she was met with at least some anger and derision in almost every community. After all, she was a Westerner, a woman, and queer. What could she know about Islam and what right did she have, as a person with those identities, to speak about Islam at all? "Not surprisingly, I was pelted with accusations by both Muslims and non-Muslims that I'm wrong, that I'm simply not authentic as a Muslim, and that even if I'm right I'm feeding Islamophobia." It made her very defensive, and at every stop she'd steel herself for battle. "We human beings crave power and control, and are therefore highly insecure whenever we feel threatened and we will lash back, which is just impulse." She was about to get a big lesson from students.

"Amid the various challenges that I encountered on my book tour, I had appreciative students—college students, high school students—who would come up to me afterward, which was wonderful. And they'd say, 'Thank you so much for doing what you're doing. This is really important work.' But then they'd always add a *But*... For example, the young Christian in the South would go on to say, '...but if you want to talk about religious dogma let me tell you about the dogma that is coming from *my* religious community.' The young Jew would say, '...but let me tell you about the intolerance I receive when I try to stand up for Palestinian rights.' The young atheist would say, '... but in my community we have a real hate on religious people like you; we say that we practice rationality, but hate is irrational. And so what am I supposed to do with that?'" You'd think Irshad would be nodding her head in agreement with these young people and saying, *Yes, exactly, I get you.* Instead, because of where Irshad was on her journey in feeling powerless and defensive all the time, she thought these students were criticizing her. "What I heard from these young people was, *You are wrong. It is NOT the trouble with Islam today. After all, we're also experiencing the kind of closed-mindedness that you tell us you feel as a Muslim.* My EGO flared and I would start debates with these kids! Only later would I come to understand what they were *really* trying to tell me, which is, *Your message is so much bigger than Islam, that every human community needs individuals to stand up and hold the community accountable for the values that it preaches instead of constantly and exclusively pointing fingers at the other.* It was on reflection that I decided I needed to take the cues that I was being given by a new generation and start the Moral Courage Project."

And in 2008 that's what she did. She began the Moral Courage Project at New York University (NYU), where she was a professor of leadership at the school of public service. She was directing and teaching others in this work but her own growth was very much still underway. Five years later she was still touring *The Trouble with Islam Today* and unfortunately still triggered at almost every turn. "I allowed myself to become defensive far too often, because I felt under assault. What I didn't realize was that my defensive crouch only made other people defensive in turn. And what could have been productive discussions often became destructive debates." These destructive debates were beginning to wear her out.

In 2013, nine years into being the author of *The Trouble with Islam Today*, she was about to do what she calls "the most important debate of my life as a Muslim reformer." It was a one-hour television show on Al Jazeera called *Head to Head*, implicitly a debate. "But I was so tired of feeling like I needed to have my guard up that I decided to do something different. I made an emotional pact with myself that rather than go into this thing with my guard up, I would be vulnerable. When my opponent (notice I'm not saying 'enemy,' that was important) made a good point, I told myself, *I'm going to acknowledge it as a good point*. When I am asked a question to which I don't have a ready and legitimate answer, I'm going to say, *I don't know*. When I need time to think, I'm going to take it and not feel weirded out by the dead air. I did all of those things and it turned out to be the most transformative discussion I've ever had about these issues—both for me and for the religious authorities who were in the audience and watching the debate on television and online. To this day (more than seven years after the episode aired) I get emails from young imams who say, 'I was fully expecting you to be rigid and dogmatic in your own point of view, even as you criticized dogma, because that is what I was told you are. But when I watched this and I saw you take the slings and arrows with grace, I came to realize that you're actually speaking to me. I saw a way of being that I didn't think was possible. And I want you to know that your ideas represent me more than I would have wanted to acknowledge.'"

She had learned that destructive debate, with its posture of lashing back, is the easy, lazy thing to do (even if emotionally draining). "What takes a lot more power and control—self-control—is to engage." Now she was ready to fully integrate her Moral Courage Project wisdom into her own life, and was on her way to becoming the face of moral courage in the world.

She explains to me why letting down your defenses and listening to your opponent works. "There's an ironclad law of human psychology that if you wish to be heard you must be willing to hear. This does not mean that every conversation using this approach will go swimmingly. Sometimes you'll realize the person or persons with whom you're engaging are not engaging with you in good faith, in which case you have permission to thank them for their time and walk away. But the bottom line is: you will never know who is worth engaging until you first give it a shot. The labels we stick on one another: ignorant, evil, stupid, backward, white, black, libtard, racist, these are all labels that conveniently let us off the hook for doing the real work of getting to know people for who they are rather than merely knowing of them because of *what we assume* they are. I want to really emphasize that seeing the humanity of your 'Other' is not about being *nice*. It's not even about being *civil*—we know that much harm has been done in the name of civility. This is about being EFFECTIVE. I came to realize how effective grace can be. I wish I had known that nine years before!"

In teaching about moral courage, Irshad explains that while communication would seem to be about interacting with others, it's actually rooted in how in charge you are of your own self. "Leadership doesn't start when you have followers. Leadership begins by governing yourself." She explains that we *all* have fears and we will have them for the rest of our lives, but that we can tame our fears simply by noticing them, and "by telling your fears that *you're not the boss, I'm the boss.*" She calls it "taming the civil war within you." By taming our fears—not tamping down, silencing, or ignoring our fears, but simply by being aware of them and talking ourselves through them—we actually become more powerful, and more capable of being able to effectively interact with others.

"For young people who have conviction, who want to change something about their world—something in which they passionately believe—it is easy to take up the cudgel and damn whomever gets in the way. But the other person isn't likely to buy it, and it's just going to raise their defenses. You may think that just because you've made a compelling argument or succeeded at imposing your solution you've won, but it's a temporary victory because what you've actually done is sown the seed of blowback. The noise amplifies and the cynicism you feel toward one another deepens. How is that solving any-thing? If you wish to be heard, you must first be willing to hear. If we want to win over the holdouts, we have to lower their defenses, not raise them. Instead of seeking to win, seek to understand what matters to *them.* So, step up and go first in the *listening* department. The more you learn what matters to them the more you can reframe your points in a way that they can hear. It's often assumed that if you listen to somebody you disagree with, you're ceding your power. Nothing could be further from the truth. It's exactly the opposite. You're claiming your power. You're setting an example. You're shaping the culture of the conversation. You're signaling to the other, *What I am role modeling here is what I also expect of you.* This is in fact the most compassionate way possible of asserting your power."

Upholding these ideals feels incredibly daunting in the face of the rela-tively new concept of "cancel culture," which can make it all but impossible to have any kind of meaningful dialogue about a concerning situation or reach any kind of détente or understanding. Who among us wants to be judged by E.V.E.R.Y.O.N.E. based on the worst thing we've ever done? Not me! When

Irshad visits schools, cancel culture is one of the first things young people come up to her afterward to talk about. "I hear, 'I'm afraid of being canceled. When I try to be a good ally, I am so scared that I'll say or do the wrong thing and my sincere intention to be a good ally will be lost, vaporized, by what other people might take as my racism or misogyny or homophobia.' I find that a lot of really good kids who have the potential to be empathetic leaders wind up refusing to lead, period. They would prefer to defer for fear of being disappeared by the very people whose causes they support."

Irshad also hears from young people who may disagree with a belief popularly held within their own group—they relate to her story of being Muslim and having questions about practices within Islam. "I'll remind them that even when they feel comfortable in any particular group, community, or tribe, it doesn't mean that you can't keep asking questions of those inside the tribe. There will be people within the tribe who will want you to conform. Who will want you to believe that there is only one right way to BE part of the tribe. You need to remember that you are as much an individual as you are a member of one or more communities. Belonging is a beautiful thing and we are social creatures—we crave belonging. But don't let belonging lead you to accept being bullied by those who want you to believe that there is only one right way to belong. You're not just a mascot of this or that tribe." For Irshad, this imperative to question what your own group is teaching you about yourself and others is the only way to truly *choose* to be a member of that group. "I was born into the Muslim faith but that didn't mean that I had to stick with it. Like so many immigrant children who question for their own sanity the traditions and customs elders tell them they must adhere to, I knew that to belong sincerely—not through coercion but through choice—I had to give Islam a chance. And the only way I could do that was to keep asking questions and keep pursuing answers not from one perspective but from multiple perspectives."

After founding the Moral Courage Project at NYU in 2008, Irshad went on to create, in 2013, *Moral Courage TV* on YouTube with race scholar Dr. Cornel West, and, in 2016, a second Moral Courage Project, at the University of Southern California (USC). High school students began writing to her asking, "What about us?" So, she launched Moral Courage College, a space within high schools to engage honestly and learn the skills of honestly engaging in what would otherwise be polarizing conversations. You can learn about all of this at moralcourage.com.

"Young people will need to create enduring solutions for the existential challenges that we're all facing today. But if they can't communicate across lines of disagreement, then whatever solutions they come up with will not endure, and they will make the same mistakes we've been taught to make." Irshad is offering a new identity to you young folks: "Instead of merely thinking of yourself along racial lines or sexuality or gender or religion, I'm suggesting that you are part of a tribe that I would call 'Plurals.' You are a Plural. I am a Plural. If you can appreciate that you belong to a tribe of Plurals, people who recognize that they themselves are multifaceted and out of self-respect treat other people as multifaceted as well, then you always have somewhere to belong. You always have a home."

MEET KIRSTIN—Being Good by Engineering Her Own Self

If you walk into Kirstin Milks's high school science classroom, you'll see a wall display she calls "What's in our heads?" It's a bunch of life-sized silhouetted faces cut out of paper, each filled with pictures and words that inspire her students and give them hope. "Band names, stick figures of horses, misshapen footballs, phrases like *mechanical engineering*, and *the child I gave up for adoption*. The words *college* and *my future* appear inside many heads, sometimes so small you can't see unless you get close." In 2020, Kirstin received the Presidential Award for Excellence in Mathematics and Science Teaching, said to be the highest honor a K–12 science teacher in the U.S. can receive. (I'm pretty sure she would say that the highest honor would be the trust of a student. But we'll get to that.) Her trajectory to this point of excellence in teaching is as much a function of who her own teachers *weren't* as who they *were*. She doesn't blame them. But she does hold herself to a much higher standard.

Kirstin is a forty-year-old white genderqueer vegan survivor of childhood trauma who teaches science at a large public high school in Bloomington, Indiana. In a recent podcast she says, "I can unwind the person I am today back to that moment...." The moment to which she refers is a snowy afternoon in high school in upstate New York, when practice for the school musical was over and she'd waited outside in the cold for over an hour until her mother finally drove the mile from their house to come pick her up. Kirstin had called home like all the other kids and had reached her mom. And Kirstin's drama teacher had stood with her and watched as every other student got picked up. But when Kirstin called home her mom had had a familiar tone in her voice, which Kirstin knew meant unreliability. Kirstin would have loved nothing more than to just walk the mile home alone. But the drama teacher informed her that because she had already called home, "We have to wait together."

Retelling this tale, Kirstin says she'd thought to herself, *I should just tell someone, you know? Like this drama teacher here, with the snow in his beard.* "But I am young, and things are bad, and my mother has not yet received an evaluation, and I find myself deciding to manifest the reliability I crave in my life." So, after forty-five minutes of waiting for her mother Kirstin does her best to casually explain to her teacher that this is just a totally normal delay for a totally normal reliable parent. "'Happens all the time,'" she tells the drama teacher "with a sudden grin and a dismissive wave of my mittened hand that I hope will be particularly convincing." Then she can't stop talking. "I keep gesturing and talking about my 'normal reliable mom taking care of us and our house and our dog and our cats, and starting to look for a teaching position.'" The drama teacher "murmured politely for ten or so minutes." Kirstin was sure he must "smell trouble" based on her attempts to explain. But the teacher never stepped up. Never stopped her from spewing her explanations. Never asked her if things were okay. Kirstin says that this is when she learned "that people don't necessarily want to hear the truth." She became a teacher because she wants to be the teacher who wants to hear what kids need to say.

In the months following that awkward snowy day, the quality of life in Kirstin's home deteriorated. This was upstate New York outside Albany in the mid-1990s. Everybody in her town was Italian Catholic, Irish Catholic, or from what people on her street called a "mixed-marriage," which meant Irish-Italian Catholic. Many families were affluent and there was a sense of ease and community among them. "But mental illness meant that my family's social circle was very circumscribed and there weren't many other grown-ups around." Her dad started "working late," i.e., not coming home. The family became food insecure. Kirstin and her younger sibling shared knowing glances and comforted each other in quiet spaces. Her mom was eventually diagnosed with schizophrenia. "When I applied to college, my mom was institutionalized and then homeless, Papa was basically not working, we were not on aid; it was a mess."

But high school had been a place of stability and opportunity for Kirstin where, despite all that was going wrong at home, she had managed to do very well academically. She received a full-ride merit scholarship to Penn State

University, where she double majored in chemistry and biochemistry. She went to Denmark on a Fulbright Scholarship to pursue research in solar biotechnology. She became a PhD student in biochemistry at Stanford—the most elite level of study available in the subject she loved, which would position her to be a faculty member at a university or a research scientist. She had also met an amazing guy in her PhD program, named Frank, who is now her partner. To many, it looked like she had transcended the challenges of her upbringing and "made it." But as her PhD graduation neared and those next steps in her career came into view, something started to feel off.

"I call much of the work of academia—sitting and reading an article or putting together a paper, reading the data—'armchair science,' and I like the intellectual work of it. But during the second half of my PhD I was feeling lost and couldn't bring my whole self to it." As she observed how the more senior scientists showed up in the world and behaved with each other, this career that had been her brass ring for ten years didn't look like something she wanted any longer. Kirstin wanted to see the results of the science emerge more quickly. She knew she needed to center her work in science around *kids* because kids can learn a concept, be confused, and reach a place of understanding—and at times awe—in a matter of fifteen minutes.

"We were within a few months of graduation and Frank and I were biking home at the end of another long day at the lab. We're riding along, and then I put my feet down and stand there straddling my bike. Frank notices I'm not behind him anymore and circles back. I look him in the eye and say, 'I'm going to be a high school teacher when I grow up!' (She was at this moment twenty-eight.) To his credit he just blinked and said, 'Okay?' If you had told me when I was in high school that I was going to spend my whole professional career being in a high school every day, I probably would've kicked you, and cried, and run into the woods." But having been *that kid* she knew she needed to go be with *those kids*, to see *those kids,* to believe in *those kids*, to be the adult who wanted to ask the questions and know the answers. Kirstin got her PhD in biochemistry on a Saturday and two days later began Stanford's teacher education program to learn how to teach high school science. This was not what a scientist with a PhD from an elite school and years of scientific research to her name was "supposed to do." But, other than partnering with Frank, Kirstin points to her pivot to teaching as the best decision of her life.

The teacher education program entailed coursework and student teaching.

My mom, the ever-wise Dr. Jean Lythcott, whom you've met earlier in this chapter, was Kirstin's faculty mentor, which is how I know her. Kirstin found that while she wanted her work to be about, with, and for people—this was why she'd switched from the science researcher track to the teaching track—oddly, she didn't seem to know how. "On the outside I felt like I was doing everything I was supposed to do. But on the inside I felt so young all the time. Teaching was collaborative and cooperative, and I didn't yet have an understanding of what it means to create a network of people who care about you. I had friends, but I didn't let them care for me because historically that had been unsafe and dangerous for me. I was basically feral. I would break a boundary—like by saying the hard thing too fast—and you could hear a pin drop. And I'd be like, *Oh*. I had to learn how to connect with people. I didn't know that the slow building of connection with people is a feature, not a bug." She would, over time, learn how to build connections with people. Amazing two-way connections. And this would become the foundation of her award-winning teaching style. "On the bike ride with Frank that night back when it all became clear, I suspected I would enjoy helping young people learn. But I didn't realize how much I would learn back from them."

As a student teacher Kirstin encountered Rolo (not his real name), a student who kept his baseball cap pulled down over his forehead and seemed to want to refuse to learn. "He skipped classes, failed classes, evaded even well-meaning teachers, and affected careful nonchalance about his future." She approached him and asked why he was failing school. (This was her version of the approach her drama teacher never took that day in the snow, in essence asking, *What's going on and are you okay and can I help*?) Rolo looked at her, took a chance that the bluntness of her question and earnestness in her eyes were sincere, and told her he was undocumented, which means he wouldn't be able to go to college or even get a job, so why did school even matter? Then he rattled off the names of other kids who were in the same boat. Kirstin spent the night researching scholarships and sources of support for undocumented students at local colleges. The next day she handed Rolo a packet stuffed with these printouts. The day after that, Rolo knocked on Kirstin's door and told her that he was ready to take a test he had been avoiding by skipping school, on which he got an A. He began to knock on Kirstin's door day after day. He sought help with his assignments. He began marking up texts with highlighters. He began asking deeper questions about topics he was learning about in other classes. Kirstin's behavior showed Rolo that he mattered to her, and he accepted her attention like a wilted plant takes in water.

In turn, Kirstin sought Rolo's advice. (And this offer and practice of two-way respect is what sets her apart from many other teachers.) "I began to ask Rolo for his perspective on questions I had regarding teaching practice. I may have had the pedagogical content knowledge required to coach Rolo in his coursework, but he had the firsthand knowledge of school, particularly as an English language learner, that I needed. At the end of that year, we made a somewhat unorthodox deal for a newly minted science teacher and a failing student. Once a week that summer, we met at the local library. I helped Rolo with his summer school homework; he then previewed assignments I was creating for my first full-time teaching position at another school and offered suggestions." Even though they were "puzzling over different work," they became "thinking partners" as Rolo endeavored to become a better high school student and Kirstin endeavored to become a better science teacher. "Trying to help each other pushed us each to think more deeply." Rolo invented the "What's in your head?" silhouetted faces exercise as a way to honor what was going on for students and as a source of inspiration for each student when things were tough.

After two years of classroom teaching in the Bay Area and working with Rolo on the side, Kirstin and Frank moved to Bloomington, Indiana, where Kirstin took a position as a science teacher at a very large comprehensive public high school. Her students there come from all walks of life. Some of her students are juniors and seniors gunning for elite college admissions results by excelling in AP Biology. Others are ninth through twelfth graders taking Earth and space science, which is the class for kids who have historically struggled in science and which she co-teaches with a special education teacher she calls "amazing." Kirstin wanted her classroom to be a place where kids could exhale and regroup when things are tough, so Rolo's "What's in your head?" silhouette exercise came with her. She mentored him long-distance by providing feedback on his college essays and by writing a letter of support for his citizenship application. She flew back to California for his high school graduation and tried not to cry.

Kirstin's Bloomington community feels like a crossroads of America where everyone comes and goes and not everyone likes what they see, and within that messy context Kirstin is a wizard with kids. "I teach high school science in a community that looks like the national discourse in our country. It's suburban and rural. There are students who speak with the midwestern newscaster accent and others with a southern accent. We have flat-earthers. We have undocumented kids, Black kids, first-generation immigrants. There are whole streets where the Confederate flag is flown and whole streets with Black Lives Matter signs. Our farmer's market made national news because it includes an openly racist vendor of vegetables. Many of the white thirty- to fiftysomethings in town were aghast at that. Once when I asked kids to write what inspires them about the future, a child wrote in very light print 'white power' and I learned that his father was involved in white nationalist stuff. Bloomington is also a university town, so folks come in from all over the world, stay for a few years, and leave again."

Kirstin says, "Integrity is all we've got, really," and she defines integrity as living in a way that reflects your values. She makes a careful study of her own character, and continually attends to the places where she's falling short. (She'd never put it that way, but as a third party I can tell you that's precisely what she is doing.) "Some of the most uncomfortable work of becoming an adult and being an adult is realizing when you've stepped outside your values and figuring out what to do next. I teach science and engineering and in the engineering design cycle you ask questions, then you build something based on what you find out, then you do the thing that you've planned, and then you look back at it and evaluate what happened. Then you do it all again. But the thing is: we are all engineers of ourselves. You are constantly finding a way of being about yourself. And if you can pause, and look, and say, *How's this going*, then you take these steps that in sum help you become the person that is more you. Practice and feedback. Apply it to where you are right now in your life, where you're going, and who's with you. This can make tremendous growth and peace happen for you, and develop your character."

One of Kirstin's most strongly held values is a concept she learned from Carla Shalaby, an educator at the University of Michigan, that there are no "throwaway people." The life that Kirstin, Frank, and their two young kids live in Bloomington and the way she shows up in her classroom are the embodiment of this value. "When we incarcerate people, it's like we throw them away. So, as a family we send books to prisoners and Frank teaches in a jail. When we ignore climate change, it's like we're throwing people away worldwide because there are people less privileged than us who are being impacted by climate change first. So, we made a decision when we moved here to try to decrease our greenhouse gas consumption. We try to get by on less. We decided to only have one car. We walk to work. We're vegan. We are very big consumers of secondhand goods. And as I learned and grew in my classroom practice, I realized that I think that everybody should be able to learn in school. There are no throwaway people in schools, either. So, now I'm doing a whole bunch of diversity, equity, and inclusion work in lots of different frameworks. You have to be directly involved in dismantling systemic bias and oppression. It's not enough to be friendly to the person behind you at the grocery store—although that is important! But you also have to act, to try to stand up to injustice when it happens. And, particularly for folks who hold identities that are privileged in our society, it's important that we acknowledge that not all situations are safe for all people at all times. So when your identity puts you in a privileged position in a conflict, you have even more of a responsibility to learn how to stand up. That's an essential part of adulting. We admire the people who stand up, like Congressman John Lewis and Rosa Parks, but we don't always understand that the way they lived came from whole lifetimes of thinking about how and where to push on systems to begin to dismantle them through practice and learning." So, everything from how Kirstin's classroom is set up to how she structures lessons to how she speaks with young people is designed to ensure that together, she and her students are co-building the world they want the bigger world to be.

Her students are individuals, each with a story, and Kirstin listens to them all. "Rolo taught me unequivocally that everybody holds knowledge, and that it might be knowledge you desperately need. And that the experiences that challenge us might be the most important ways to become more authentically ourselves.

"I'm still learning how to teach. But learning how to teach from Rolo that summer was just a huge level up. It had to do with me reassessing how I was in the world and who I paid attention to. Seeking varied perspectives and having to learn, that's not a bad thing. My flat-earth-espousing students remind me that people have a real hunger for the views of ordinary people to be valid. They made the point that lakes should slosh over their edges if they're on a spinning planet. So, I put water in a bucket and spin it around and around and ask them to notice what happens to water when it's pulled by other forces. My transgender students have taught me so much about what gender means, and how young people can experience gender and shifts in their own understanding of gender."

Kirstin worries about how digital culture makes students feel that they have to be perfect. "Even if you're intentionally disheveled, it's still got to look like you're someone who doesn't make mistakes." She believes every single one of her students can grow, and that the purpose of life is to practice and learn, so her classroom is a place of opportunity and encouragement, not of degrading judgment. "I set up spaces where people see mistakes as data, not as evaluation. There's no late penalty for work on nearly all assignments, and every assignment is resubmittable to one hundred percent. It means that someone will submit, I'll give them feedback, they'll submit again, I'll say, 'Oh yeah not yet,' or 'Come here and we'll talk about it.' It frees them up to know they could fail their test and still end up earning an A for the class with continued effort and questioning."

Looking back at the adults who failed her when she was young, she says, "I don't blame the drama teacher. And maybe he did start a conversation with the guidance counselor or call my father to check in. But now I wish so much that he had started that conversation with ME, that he had checked in with ME there in the snow. I'm not saying I think all my shame about my family, all the fallout I've experienced from lack of proper parenting, our family's food insecurity, my own mental health, I'm not saying that any of that would have been fixed. But it might have been a start."

Knowing that her teachers assumed she was fine, Kirstin continually reminds herself not to make assumptions. "Uncovering the assumptions we make is a vital part of becoming better teachers. I had no idea what Rolo was going through when I first asked him why he had checked out. Many of my assumptions about students continue to be inaccurate at best, including assumptions about what learning strategies will be most effective—and why some strategies flop. Questioning students directly helps. If I introduce what seems to me like an engaging lesson and students act restless or roll their eyes, I'll stop, acknowledge what I'm seeing, and ask, 'What's happening? What can we do to make this better?'"

She also drops a few crumbs about her childhood into conversations for the students who need help seeing a path forward. "It's like I'm chipping off just enough of my story to draw out their stories, and also to show an example of a time when things have been okay, that things CAN be okay, that we can actually get help, that we can grow out of the things that are difficult especially when we get help." She is therefore a trusted adult to whom teenagers turn.

"This year I've been the first person that some students have told about the hunger they're facing, the abuse in their home. I have been the person several students first tell about their desire and their plans to take their own lives. And I am so grateful every time a kid lets me help them get help."

She sums up her work this way: "I want to start conversations with kids, both within the context of the content I teach and beyond. And I want to listen, *really* listen, to what they have to say. I think, at my core, that's what I'm about as a teacher. And I want to be someone who fact-checks kids as a way to say, *I see you, I notice you, I love you.* That feels really important. I want to be a person who wants to hear the truth, who knows the power of truth in helping create inflection points in our lives. And I want my students as grown-ups to be open to exploring their own stories and to walk with others and their stories as a start."

IN SHORT: BEHAVE NICELY

Our character is what introduces us to others, and it's what they most remember about us when we leave the room, and when we leave this life. You want to be able to interact not just productively but well and joyfully with other humans. But you must balance that with your duty to do right by yourself. That's what we're addressing next.

Unpack and Reflect

- What is my definition of good character? Who in my life best exemplifies good character, and why?
- When someone gives my eulogy someday, what do I hope they will say about my character?
- If I'm being honest and unafraid to talk about it, when I look at the "'Sweet Sixteen' of Good Character," what do I need to work on?
- Is good character compatible with or at odds with my definition of success?

5

STOP PLEASING OTHERS

(THEY HAVE NO IDEA WHO YOU ARE)

> The measure of a person, of a hero, is how well they
> succeed at being who they are.
>
> —Queen Frigga, Thor's mother,
> *Avengers: Endgame*

It's Thanksgiving, a family wedding, or some other event that brings relatives together. Someone you haven't seen in a while comes over and asks one of THOSE questions:

"Where are you applying to college?"
"Where are you working?"
"What are you studying?"
"Got a girlfriend?"

Your eyes shift sideways and back to center again. Your brain is literally shuffling through all possible responses while simultaneously trying to decide whether to go with the response that gets the positive reaction, or the one that might be truer but just might lead to confusion, disappointment, or outright judgment. You shift your weight to the other foot and begin to explain . . . getting some credits at community college before going back or transferring, your major in comp sci, your demo tape, your internship with a political campaign, working construction, your entry-level job at a nonprofit, waiting tables while auditioning, a master's in teaching, the startup idea you and your friends have, a hundred-hour-a-week job on Wall Street, driving for Lyft, the fact that you have no fucking clue, the fact that your girlfriend is a boyfriend, or is pregnant, or is from a background you know this relative just cannot or will not want to relate to.

The responses are predictable.

If your answer pleases your relative, you're golden. You get a big smile, a fist bump, maybe an "Awesome," or whatever. If their face has that "Oh?" look on it, no such luck; they'll nod up and down with a tight smile, which tries but fails to mask their judgment. If they're a real jerk about it, they'll outright say that what you're doing is wrongheaded or dumb. (That actually happened to me once and it sucked; I'll tell you about it later.) But I think the most excruciating response is when they literally don't understand what you're talking about, and you try to explain it further, and instead of trying harder to get you, to see you, to know you for you, they turn their lack of understanding into a critique of your entire generation. "What is it with you Millennials? In my day we knew how to get a job and stick with it until we retired." You scan the room for someone who can rescue you from this hell as your relative drones on.

WHAT IS SUCCESS, AND WHO DECIDES?

All we ever wanted as children was for our parents to be proud of us. Truth is, we still want it. Take me, for example: I'm fifty-three and my father died when I was twenty-seven. Almost half my life ago. And to this day when I do something well and someone says, "Your father would be proud of you," I practically burst into tears. I'm still not sure why his approval matters so much, but there's no doubt it does.

If at times you've gone with the answer that pleased your relative regardless of how much it really aligned with your actual situation, plans, or dreams, I'm not here to judge you. In a lot of families and communities, "success" is pretty narrowly defined, i.e., the "right" schooling, particular kinds of work, being in a relationship with a person the family deems appropriate, a certain amount of money or status. If you're on your way down that path, you're probably getting a lot of approval from people who matter to you, and let's face it, approval feels really good. And kudos to you if you actually *want* to be doing the thing that lights other people up, or if they actually love you for who you are, dig your choices, and embrace your significant other. Do not take that for granted.

But therapists' couches are sagging under the weight of desperately unhappy forty- and fiftysomethings who did exactly what they were "supposed to do" and are exactly the person they were "supposed to be"—i.e., successful by that narrow definition discussed above—yet now ache to figure out who *they* actually want be and what *they* want to do with their life. I'm here to try to make sure that the person on the therapist's couch one day isn't you. Which is not to knock therapy—I'm a huge fan and partaker of it—but simply to say let it not be therapy for bad decisions made out of fear of disappointing your father.

What is it with fathers? Mothers, too! Parents' friends. Extended family. An entire ethnic community. Grandparents can be the worst. (True story: A college classmate of mine, from a wealthy family on the East Coast, chose Stanford over the Ivy League and her grandmother disowned her, literally.) When I was a college dean, I met with a lot of students who were in some degree of distress over "having to" study a particular subject in order to meet expectations. You can guess what those subjects were, right? Econ or finance, pre-law, STEM, or pre-med. (I have yet to meet someone who was forced to be a philosophy or theater major.) I knew a lot of Stanford pre-meds who were biding their time until they could tell their parents they didn't actually want to be a doctor. They seemed to think that time would only come when they *were* a doctor. As a fiftysomething in Silicon Valley, I know some extremely rich people who know they've won some aspect of the game of life (money; prestige; maybe reputation) but nevertheless sense that the life they really wanted to live is passing them by, now more quickly than ever. (Pro tip: Money and status and all that comes with those things cannot mask unhappiness.)

When it comes to the personal side of life, I also worked with a lot of students who performed an identity expected of them, whether that identity was based in social class, sexual orientation, gender expression, race, religion, cultural affiliation, ability, neurotypicality, or just how they socialized with peers or behaved in the classroom. And they performed that identity even though they actually wanted to BE, even knew they actually WERE, someone completely different. No matter how "successful" they were in class, or in landing internships, jobs, or coveted grad school spots, those students had a faraway look in their eyes even while they spoke with me. They were doing an amazing job at squashing their actual self somewhere way down inside of them and keeping that self at bay. It broke my heart.

Which will you be? The person who knows who you are meant to be and goes for what you want regardless of what others think? Or the person who wakes up at forty or fifty realizing that all of your choices have been made from a place of fear of disappointing others?

THE PAIN OF PERFORMING THE PART

I spent my twenties doing work I thought would validate me in the eyes of others, and was well into my thirties claiming identities I thought would bring me acceptance. Then one day I broke down under the psychological weight of it all. If I could wish anything for your journey, it would be that you get clear on who you are and what you want to do with your life sooner than I did. Although even in saying that, I know that for many of us a big component of adulting entails veering way off course, because only then can we really see where our true path lies. In other words, maybe you have to go through shit and pain in order to know what brings you joy.

It is 1995. I am twenty-seven. Dan and I have been happily married for three years, and in the year since I graduated from law school in Massachusetts we've been renting a house in a middle-class community in Menlo Park, California, just up the road from Stanford. It's our first *actual* house, a teeny two-bedroom right behind a Safeway—and it's not a fancy place. But it's sturdy and clean and it's filled with all the nice contemporary furniture we bought with the fat insurance check we received after our moving van caught on fire on the way to California. (Spending that fat settlement check instead of investing it for our future was, shall we say, a big lesson learned; I'll talk about that in chapter 8, "Money Matters.") We spend our Thursday nights on our expensive couch watching this awesome new sitcom called *Friends*. And one of our cars is an adorable red 1965 MGB named Maggie.

Professionally, I'm pretty sure *I've done everything right* and I'm, like, THE MAN. I'm a first-year associate at a prestigious Silicon Valley law firm where I work on patent, trademark, and copyright litigation matters. Every day I put on one of the five Ann Taylor suits I bought with my big salary, with either a cream or black blouse underneath. To make my biracial hair "professional" I use a curling iron and smooth it into a long ponytail that sits at the nape of my neck. I go off to work with my brand-new black leather courier-style Coach briefcase slung over my shoulder. I work extremely hard poring over legal briefs and case law about the ownership and protection of ideas. The partners and senior associates teach me, praise me, and give me more responsibility. I earn good money—actually, *great* money. I seem to be pretty good at the work. Yet on this Saturday night in the summer of 1995, nine months into this job, I'm sitting on the slab of concrete our landlord calls a back porch and I'm bawling like a baby.

I'm crying because when it comes to my work life (which, let's face it, feels like my *whole* life given the hours I'm asked to work) I get a knot in my stomach at about two in the afternoon every Sunday just anticipating having to go back the next day. To make matters worse, I feel lonely in my misery because everyone is clapping at my apparent success. On top of that, I'm ashamed for feeling miserable—my parents were loving and supportive and gave me many advantages in life. As I sit on the cold concrete behind my house that night, I give myself a talking-to. *You've been given so fucking much and here you are crying. Actual people are suffering, Julie. You are not one of them. This is not suffering. Figure it out.* (Nowadays we'd say I was acknowledging some of my privilege and feeling sheepish and frustrated in the face of it.)

I tried to work through this disconnect between an outwardly successful life and inward misery by imagining my life plotted out on a map—the choices I'd made for work and in school, the things I valued along the way, meeting Dan, getting married, and my current job as a corporate lawyer. Then I tried to zoom out to get an aerial view of my life map. Looking down on my life from such a great distance, I somehow understood that this turn toward corporate law was a big left-hand turn away from the things that had always mattered to me, which landed me on the periphery of my own life, far afield from where I thought I would be by now. I was bewildered. How did I end up *here*, I wondered through tears. How did I make such poor choices on my own behalf? *I did everything right.*

A decade hence, when I'm in my late thirties and in my dream job as a dean at Stanford, my team will have a retreat, part of which entails taking the Myers-Briggs personality inventory test. There will be twelve to fifteen of us in a large conference room with tables and big pieces of paper and markers, where we're supposed to take the test and then fashion our results into a "personal crest" that we are then to present to everyone. The exercise is intended to help us better understand where everyone is coming from, which should help us work together more effectively.

I'll learn that day that I'm a Myers-Briggs ENT/FJ (i.e., evenly split on the "Thinking or Feeling" scale, which they say measures whether "When making decisions, do you prefer to first look at logic and consistency or first look at the people and special circumstances?"). I won't know what to make of it, and as I compare my poster to the others I see around the room, I'll see that no one else has a T/F duality or any duality for that matter. Nevertheless, I've always been a fan of self-assessment and I tend to believe whatever results I get. So, I'll bend over the table drawing a stylized T/F with my red Sharpie as part of my personal crest when my colleague Sally will sidle over. Sally is a small white woman with twinkling eyes and short salt-and-pepper hair that stands straight up and out, who often rings a little Buddhist chime to get a meeting started. She'll peer at my crest for an uncomfortably long while and then look up at me wide-eyed like she's just discovered something big. "So, *that's* why law must have been so *hard* for you."

What? I'll blink rapidly. I'll have no idea what she's talking about. *I was good at it! Why does she think law was hard for me? Is she criticizing me? Do I need to defend myself?* I'll just stare at her while these thoughts course through my brain. She'll beam for a few moments, and then just walk off. Sally will go on to be a mentor to me, which some might find odd because she's a few levels below me on the org chart. No matter. She becomes someone who really sees me and will never be afraid to tell me what she's seen. I'll always remember her. We remember the people who saw us when we couldn't really see ourselves.

As I write this chapter, I'm fifty-three, and in the twenty-five years since that miserable night on the back porch in Menlo Park I managed to leave corporate law, create a new career for myself as a university administrator where I had the incredibly rewarding job of mentoring college students, and then I moved from doing that to being an author and speaker, which I also absolutely adore. Who knows, I may have a fourth and fifth career in me. And I know that whatever I do will be up to ME. I've also been on a personal journey to locate an identity for myself I truly love regardless of what others think of it, and I choose to be in community with others who will accept me for me. When I finally gave myself permission to do what I want to do and be who I want to be, my life began to feel calm and peaceful, and joyful and amazing, and good.

Between what I've learned on my own unpredictable journey, and from my thousands of interactions with humans struggling to craft a meaningful and purposeful life for themselves, here is my advice for how to stop trying to please others and instead define career success and your personal identity on your own terms:

STEP 1: Find your voice

STEP 2: Stop judging it

STEP 3: Go in the direction it tells you to go

If it sounds simple, it is. (Which is not to say it's easy.)

If it sounds hokey, bear with me. I really believe there's something to this.

STEP ONE: IN THE NOISE OF EVERYONE ELSE'S OPINIONS, FIND YOUR VOICE

When we're young, our heads are filled with a lot of noise, the noise from other people's opinions and expectations of how we should and should not lead our life. *You should do this. You should be that. Don't act that way. Act like this. Don't hang out with those people. These are the people we value. In our family, these are the people we join our lives with and this is the work that we do.*

And now that you're older, you're (unfortunately for you) the first generation to experience FOMO from all of that imagery on social media, coming at you like a constant barrage of values and expectations and judgments (even though those values and expectations really have nothing to do with the real you AT ALL). When I was growing up, we simply knew far less about what everyone was doing. And now of course people not only show you what they're doing, they curate it so you only see the good stuff. It's hard to know if you're doing okay in the world if you're measuring yourself against people who are, well, making shit up.

Many of us have at least some inkling of what *I'd really love to do and be if it was just up to me* and many of us have at least a sense of the identities we yearn to inhabit that feel truest, most authentic to us and that will allow us to live liberated and free lives. But out of deference to other people's opinions, or the practicalities, or out of respect for all the money our folks invested in us, or from a fear of disappointing those who gave us life, we convince ourselves that whatever we'd love to be and do just isn't realistic and maybe isn't even valid. Still, until the day we die there's always that little inner voice that tries to pipe up and advocate for who we are and what we want to do with our lives. It takes a lot of practice to learn what our own voice sounds like—and then to rescue it from the noise of everyone else's expectations.

Let's go back to that cold, concrete porch where I sat as a miserable twenty-seven-year-old corporate lawyer. Remember, it was 1995 (meaning the Internet's earlier days). I couldn't google "How do I get a better life?" Plus, it was a Saturday night, which meant all the bookstores and libraries were closed; I had nothing external to guide me. So, I went inside and found a piece of paper and a pencil. Then I sat down at the little round table squeezed into our kitchen and drew a line down the middle of the page. On the top left I wrote, "what I'm good at," and at the top right, "what I love." My hunch was that getting off the periphery of my life and back into the main part of it would come from knowing the answers to these questions, finding the overlap between them, and crafting my life accordingly.

Not gonna lie, the left side of the list was hard for me. I sat there jabbing the eraser end of the pencil repeatedly against the table as I waited for some brilliant insight to come. I mean I knew what people *said* I was good at. (I paid a lot of attention to what people thought of me, and why they liked or didn't seem to like me.) But the purpose of this exercise was to excavate what I knew about myself from somewhere deep inside . . . me. Finally, a few thoughts came, and they all had to do with "people." I felt a little silly writing them down. Pursuing this exercise made me feel naked and vulnerable even though I was alone in my kitchen with my beloved Dan doing his own thing somewhere nearby. If the lawyers at my firm saw this list, I thought, they'd probably laugh at me.

The right side of the list was much easier to fill out. I was able to do a true brainstorm, jotting down the first things that popped into my head.

When I was done, my list looked like this:

WHAT I'M GOOD AT	WHAT I LOVE
• HELPING PEOPLE ON THEIR PATH	• CHEESEBURGERS☺
• SOLVING PEOPLE PROBLEMS	• STANFORD
• CONNECTING PEOPLE WITH EACH OTHER	• MY FRIENDS
• BEING THERE FOR PEOPLE	• GOOD FICTION
• GALVANIZING(!) PEOPLE AROUND A CAUSE	• RED WINE
	• DAN♡

That night at my kitchen table I didn't yet know my future mentor, Sally, who in seeing my Myers-Briggs results knew clearly why I'd left the practice of law, because I value being logical but also want to take special circumstances into account (that maybe for me being logical IS to take special circumstances into account). Sally's insight about my compassion for human fallibility was not yet available to me as I stared at a rather strange list of brainstormed items. Yet my rudimentary but honest pencil-and-paper exercise was enough to reveal a bit of my inner voice, enough to give me a nudge to try to appreciate that I was indeed a people person, and that being a people person might be an okay thing to be, and that maybe, just maybe, it could even be relevant to the work I would go on to do one day.

From that first communication from my inner voice grew a life that I love. Turn off other people's voices; what is yours saying to you?

STEP TWO: STOP JUDGING YOUR VOICE

I needed the nudge from the brainstorming exercise, the nudge that made my inner voice go, "Hey, you're a people person; you should be working with people." Was it truly an epiphany? I mean, I'd always known I was a people person. But for twenty-seven years I'd thought that being a people person was just some soft right-brain trait that came along with my femaleness, in contrast to the analytical left-brain stuff I was so desperate to sharpen, demonstrate, and prove. Being a people person seemed easy, obvious, or trivial, and helping people didn't seem to be serious work, either; therefore I didn't see these things as being the important work to be done by a highly educated person such as myself.

I want to pause here to address the prevailing societal sense that goes something like this: *highly educated people shouldn't do work that's "beneath" them*. I encountered many Stanford undergrads over the years who dreamed of being on the front lines of patient care as an EMT or nurse, but felt the pressure to "use" the Stanford education to become a doctor instead. I met a similar set who wanted to teach kids but were told that K–12 education was beneath someone with a degree like theirs, and if they wanted to be in a classroom they should instead aspire to be a professor. These thoughts came from family, but also from peers, and even from a few Stanford professors. Regardless of the source, it's bullshit. There is no such thing as work that is *beneath* you. If you're good at the work and you love it and it gives you the opportunity to contribute to the world in ways that are meaningful TO YOU, and you feel like *Fuck, yeah!* when you do it, then to hell with anyone who thinks you should have done something different with your education or station in life. Sometimes this critique comes with a slightly more analytical veil, i.e., *You spent so much money to get that education; why take a job that won't allow you to recoup that cost?* Well, yes, you want to try to be making prudent financial decisions, but as long as you can pay your bills, YOU get to decide what kind of work you'll do. Even if you or others can't see the direct connection between the work you do and whatever you studied in school. Education almost always enriches the mind and the soul, and it is never ever "wasted."

So, as I started to give my inner voice a bit of leeway to speak, the insights started to come. That night at my kitchen table I got honest with myself about how the whole purpose of going to law school only four years earlier was to try to help people out of unjust situations so they could live a life of dignity in America. People like incarcerated youth, battered women, people being discriminated against as they tried to vote, buy a house, or get a job, and criminal defendants who'd had terrible childhoods, all of whose circumstances mattered to me. So, why was I helping advance corporate interests in patents, trademarks, and copyrights instead of helping humans? And how much longer would I wait before being the person I'd always known myself to be? Sitting at my kitchen table late, I was tearing up again, but this time it was tears of relief, maybe even of hope, at feeling I might be beginning to get my life back on track.

Was I brave enough to listen to this voice, quit my prestigious corporate law job, take a big pay cut, and go help people? Not exactly. It's not that simple. But I'd achieved step one (listen to my voice) and was working hard on step two (stop judging it). I started to give myself permission to be my actual self. Only then could I dream of the jobs that might allow me to put my people skills to use. I might have pivoted back to public interest law, yet somehow I couldn't; I feared that the lawyers who did that work would see me as a sellout for having gone corporate out of law school. I was afraid to face them. (And yes, I was afraid to face that truth in myself.) In addition, though, I was getting sick of the endless arguing, pettiness, and reams of paper involved in law and litigation. My dreams of helping people via my law degree were going up in smoke.

But my paper-and-pencil exercise showed me there were people I would *love* to help—right down the street, if I became an administrator at Stanford.

STEP THREE: GO IN THE DIRECTION YOUR VOICE TELLS YOU TO GO

After you've found your voice and you are no longer judging it, the final step is to go in the direction your voice tells you to go. This takes intentionality, which means making plans and working really hard to set those plans in motion. And setting those plans in motion entails daring to tell a few of the right people about those plans. Which can be really scary. But if you can get a few others to help you on this journey, by believing in you and supporting you, it will go more smoothly.

Back to me and my kitchen table. Since I was fairly certain that I wanted to shift my career to student affairs or college admissions, I might have outright asked someone in that field to hire me. But that would have been a pretty bold first move (even for me, ha!). The better first move is to approach someone in the industry, field, or career you want to enter and ask if you can take them to coffee, or get a twenty-minute conversation with them on the phone for what's known as an "informational interview." Why twenty minutes? Because even the busiest executives can say, "Oh sure, I can give you twenty minutes." In your informational interview you don't ask them for a job; you ask them about: their work, the field more broadly, how they got into the field, and what advice they have for someone like you looking to enter the field. (Pro tip: Keep track of the time, and if you're at the twenty-minute mark, say, "I just want to pause and note the time. I'm loving this conversation but we're at twenty minutes and I know how busy you are." If it's going well, they're likely to let it run to thirty minutes, because most folks structure their calendars in half-hour increments. But don't be offended if they say they need to go.) Follow up with a thank-you note. Let them know when you start applying for stuff.

The beauty about informational interviews is that you can ask for one from a complete stranger. Most people farther down the path of life than you appreciate that if you want to get ahead you have to hustle, so when such people get a thoughtful email from you asking for twenty minutes of their time to learn more about their industry, many will say yes. It is a fairly light lift for them. All you're asking them to do is talk about themselves (which most people find pretty easy to do), and since most people enjoy talking about themselves they come away feeling great about the conversation they just had with YOU, which means they are more likely to be inclined to help you, as long as you didn't misbehave during your conversation. All you need to have in hand to initiate an informational interview request is an email address for the person. Before you speak with them, go to LinkedIn and do a web search more broadly so you can ask informed questions. (The question "If I have this right, you've been in this field for ten years, at three different companies. How did you get your start?" is a far better question than, "So, what do you do?")

But now let's talk about your network, which is made up of the people you know—family, friends, classmates, acquaintances, current and former coworkers, teachers, and neighbors—and the people *they* know. These people may be able to help you get informational interviews. And they might even be able to get your résumé on the right person's desk. Now, if when I refer to networks you feel, *Lady, I don't have one*, I want you to visualize the person who comes to mind when I say, *Who cared about you?* You can begin to build your network by simply checking back in with this person. Tell them what you're up to and ask how they're doing, too. Share your thoughts about where you might be headed in life. Get their feedback and advice. And with all respect due, ask if they'd be willing to help with whatever your next step might be. Their help could be as simple as just telling you that they believe in you so that you can believe in yourself, too, or being listed as a reference, or writing you a letter of support. If your life has been such that you do not have much of a network, I want you to recognize that you may actually have different strengths, like the wherewithal to hustle and make good use of whatever resources you can find. Remember Rolo and his teacher Dr. Kirstin Milks from chapter 4, "Be Good"? I'm fairly confident that if Rolo were *ever* to ask Dr. Milks to be a reference for him, she would jump at the opportunity to do so. If you had someone like Dr. Kirstin Milks in your life when you were in high school, that person is a core part of your network.

So, in trying to make my career move, I began with some informational interviews with people in college admissions and student affairs offices at Stanford so I could learn more about the work I was feeling called to do, and how I might make some inroads as a complete outsider. Then, I wrote a killer cover letter and applied for a job in student affairs with some impressive campus references to back me up. But my résumé bore no sign of my being competent at working with students. And (I would later learn) applicant pools are full of unhappy corporate lawyers trying to start a new career. In the end, I was rejected by three different offices at Stanford over the course of three years and would get off-the-record feedback that I talked too much in the interviews and therefore they feared I was not a team player. (This is the very stuff I would get actual feedback about years later as a dean, which I shared with you back in chapter 3, "You're Not Perfect." The signs were there all along, sigh.) But I finally caught a lucky break as the fill-in for someone's maternity leave at Stanford Law School (where the fact of my having gone to law school and been a lawyer was actually an asset!).

Making the plan and acting on it was easy for me. The harder part was figuring out who to tell about it. First, since I'd pretty much constructed a life of doing what I thought was expected of me, to win the approval and applause of others, I was pretty afraid of telling the people in my life what I *really* wanted to do. (Other than Dan—my beloved, who has always seen me just as I am and loved me no matter what.) Still, I had some newfound energy from the brainstorming exercise, which was giving me fresh fuel; my voice was out and demanding to be heard. So, I started telling my dream to the universe; that is, I started telling people in my circle. Sometimes I got the thumbs up, the fist bump, the attagirl. Sometimes it went really badly.

One such experience came a few years into my job search, when Dan and I went out to dinner with a family friend of Dan's named Ken who was on business in Silicon Valley. Ken was our parents' age, and, as it happened, was a fellow corporate lawyer. I knew our dinner conversation was going to feel like a friendly sparring match as can be the case whenever you talk with a lawyer. In fact, we'd been warned that Ken's analytical skills were so fierce that he'd intimidated his own law professor into quitting his job back when he was a student at Harvard Law. I was cautiously excited. I was used to being good at these conversations. In fact, I liked keeping up, making the unexpected jab, maybe even having the sense that I was winning points.

When our food came, Ken started asking me about my work at the firm and I found myself tossing off the stories that would impress him. After he probed my responses and I felt I'd kept up the verbal repartee, I felt we'd established who we were with one another. I decided to get real and say that I was actually thinking of leaving the law.

"Oh?" he said.

I took a deep breath, glanced quickly at Dan, then looked back at Ken. I told Ken that I thought I might want to stop practicing law and instead work on a college campus in admissions or student affairs. He burst out laughing and wiped his large mouth with the cloth napkin, then threw it on the table. "You don't want to do that. Those people are mindless bureaucrats." He folded his napkin back on his lap and changed the subject.

I was humiliated. I started mumbling something about wanting to start a family and needing more manageable hours if I was going to have kids. Dan squeezed my hand under the table and looked at me lovingly. There was so much of dinner still to go. I decided to ask Ken various questions about himself, which I knew would get us from here to the end of dinner and would take the attention off me and my silly dream.

That conversation was over twenty-five years ago. When you finally have the guts to tell people what you want to do with your life, and you get ridiculed for it, you don't soon forget it. It takes tremendous courage to keep going for your dreams in the face of laughter. Particularly if those judging you are close family, or prominent in some way that matters to you. I'm here from my fiftysomething perch to say to you: Keep going. Honor your voice. Even if they laugh, do it anyway. People who judge others tend to be very unhappy with some aspect of their own life. A huge aspect of adulting is finding the courage to do what you want with your life even if those who claim to love you the most outright disown you for it. It's YOUR life. Don't you ever forget that.

GETTING PERSONAL

I just gave you a glimpse of the bumps, twists, and turns I experienced professionally en route to having a career that brings me tremendous joy. The effort it took to change careers (twice!) was pretty exhausting and there were a lot of setbacks. In short, it did not come easily for me, nor will it for you unless a lot of luck intervenes. But it is doable, and it is definitely worth it.

Right now though I want to pivot to the other side of life, the personal side. Here, you want to be completely in charge rather than let others dictate it for you—starting with your identity and where you find community, belonging, connection, relationship, and interpersonal joy. It's hard enough to walk around feeling you don't fit in your *career*; it's excruciating if what doesn't fit is your personal identity expression.

I actually wrote a whole book on the subject a few years back (*Real American: A Memoir*). I'd begun life as an innocent little kid as everyone does, but at about age three or four, I started to get the message from my community and the media that something was wrong with me and Daddy because of the color of our skin. By the time I was in high school, I'd experienced plenty of microaggressions and some outright hateful racism. When some ignorant asshole wrote the N-word on my locker on my seventeenth birthday senior year, I didn't breathe a word of it to anyone and just buried it deep inside. And that kicked off about two decades of loathing myself for being Black and trying to cope with that by being what white folks valued.

I looked "successful" during these two decades, though, right? I attended a brand-name college and law school, I became a corporate lawyer, then a university dean, both of which made me upper middle class. But through some really hard introspective work with an executive coach starting at around age thirty-nine, I came to appreciate that my driving motivation was to try to please and impress white folks so as not to incur their cruelty, anger, disdain, or disregard. Basically, I was trying to be the model Negro so I'd never be called the N-word again.

This may be tricky to understand. Am I saying I didn't want to go to law school, or be a lawyer and a university dean? No. I'm saying there are different motivations for the behaviors we exhibit and choices we make;

we can do things because WE want to do them (which is healthy) or we can do things because WE NEED OTHERS TO APPROVE OF US (which is not). I've come to learn that my primary driver in my late teens through late thirties was to "be somebody" in the eyes of other people (mostly white people) because racism had taught me to loathe myself, so I needed the approval of white folks to feel like a whole, valid human. In contrast, acting from a place of self-love means knowing you are going for those opportunities and doing those things because YOU want to do them for YOU. It's the "why" behind the what. And as Ananda said in chapter 4, "Be Good," it's knowing your why that matters.

As I alluded to earlier, the phenomenon of social media, of having a digital identity, has changed *everything*, and this is particularly true when it comes to identity development. On the one hand, social media is a godforsaken hellhole where you can be critiqued, outright bullied, or just plain ignored. On the other hand, social media allows you to easily find and connect with people who are like you and who will love and accept you for who you are, which was simply not possible in prior eras. But regardless—and this is important—social media cannot give you an identity, a sense of self, or purpose. The you who creates and animates your posts is the real you, not the posts themselves. If we begin to see our identity as who and how we are on social, we become susceptible to those likes and comments almost as if they are the measure of our worth. Research from the nonprofit Common Sense Media (where Jamie from chapter 3 works) shows that social media usage can have an outsized impact on those of us who struggle with our mental health—if we're in a good place, social media doesn't impact our sense of self but if we're struggling, research shows that positive interactions make us feel better and negative interactions make us feel worse.

When I finally became a self-loving Black and biracial person, I could say, *You know what, I don't have to be right all the time, and if some white person feels, "Oh, Julie's wrong," and if they feel that way because I'm Black, I can't control that. That's on them. You know what, I am going to wear my hair natural even if they think it's not professional because this is the hair God gave me. You know what, I am going to quit this mostly white discussion group because I'm tired of being the only one to speak up about the Black or brown or other marginalized person in the story. You know what, just because you want to make your community organization "more diverse" doesn't mean it's worth my time to be in it.* I decided I was done trying to be the model Negro or the token Black. Done feeling any obligation to explain the details of my people's history to those who have chosen never to be interested in it. Round about the same time as these epiphanies were happening I also came to accept that, *You know what, I'm also attracted to women, not just men. In fact I'm attracted to folks regardless of gender.* I left my role at Stanford in 2012 and went back to grad school to get an MFA in writing. I wrote poetry. I wrote creative nonfiction. I read my poetry about the rise of white supremacy at grungy clubs in San Francisco. I'd never felt more alive.

I was forty-five by the time I located a self I could truly love. I credit a lot of things for catalyzing this transformation, but probably most impactful was the poetry of Lucille Clifton, an African American poet whom I think of as my "literary Black mother." Her poems speak to the Black female body, to breasts and hips, to childbearing, to mothering, to fears and loneliness and joy, to men and women, to women and women, to Blackness, to food, to ritual, to the white male sneer, to sexual pleasure. Reading Clifton's collection *Good Woman* when I was thirty-eight, I began to feel that if she was possible, if these words were possible, then maybe I was possible. Clifton died in 2010. Meeting her in 2004 was a true highlight of my life.

I am: a Black biracial woman with light skin who is bisexual, butch, and queer, in a thirty-two-year (and counting) relationship with an amazing white Jewish bisexual cis-male husband with whom I have two fantastic children. Now that I've found that self, I am intentional about being in relationship and community with people who accept me as I am. The choices around where I spend my time—be it work, volunteering, mentoring, civic engagement, and just plain having fun—are all in furtherance of being in community with folks who care about the communities and concerns I do. (Pro tip: The older you get, the more secure you'll feel in making choices about who you are and where and how you can live your best life.) I'm done performing for anybody else. If folks can't accept me as I am, I no longer worry about that. That's their work to do.

And. It. Feels. Amazing.

DON'T JUST TAKE MY WORD FOR IT

Being a people person, I tend to hear from folks who want to share the various things they're navigating in life. I try to bring a compassionate ear. I try to demonstrate that I see and accept them as they are. When I hear from people who have stopped pleasing others and are on their way toward being themselves in work, in life, and in love, I am overjoyed. I hear the late poet Mary Oliver asking, "What are you going to do with your one wild and precious life?" And I hear answers. I want to give you a glimpse of what this sense of self *sounds* like. Here are three people who come to mind:

MEET ALEX—Standing Up for Who He Is and What He Wants

One day when Alex was a college student in Washington, DC, he got up early to buy himself a new set of earbuds at the Apple Store. Then he went into Starbucks for a cappuccino. On his walk home, he was stopped by a police officer who asked to see some ID. Passersby glanced as Alex put his cappuccino on the ground, dug into the pocket of his jeans, and fished out his California driver's license. The officer handed the ID back with this explanation: "The reason I stopped you is you match the description of a suspect breaking into hotel rooms and stealing Apple products." Alex, a medium-skinned, fit, twenty-year-old African American man, continued on his way back to his dorm room at Georgetown University.

It's eleven in the morning for me, but it's evening for Alex, who is now twenty-six and living in Stockholm, Sweden. I can hear the clatter of pots and pans as he moves around his kitchen. I thank him for allowing me to intrude on his dinner preparations. With the time zone difference between Sweden and California this was the only time we could both make work. He begins to sauté onions in butter and I can hear them sizzle in the pan. My stomach grumbles.

I first met Alex back in 2008 when we were knocking on doors together for then-candidate Obama. I was a forty-year-old university dean. He was a teenager. Now, Alex is in design research at the music-streaming platform Spotify. His job is to observe users and then design better ways for users to engage with the app, work he calls his dream job. "It's what I've always wanted to do with my life." I'm talking with him to understand how he knew this, how he crafted a path in this direction, and what if any obstacles he encountered along the way.

Alex traces his passion for design all the way back to early childhood when he filled sketchbooks with drawings of cars, boats, and other machines. When he was a freshman in high school, he saw a television program about the famous Silicon Valley design company IDEO founded by David Kelley and thought, *Okay, this is something I do in my free time. Something I love.* Now he knew it was an actual line of work. "That's when I said, *I want to get into this field.*" His mom encouraged him to track down David Kelley and ask for an internship. One rainy day Alex stood in Kelley's office, watching this renowned man flip through Alex's book of sketches. Kelley seemed some-what impressed. Alex summoned his bravery and asked if he could work at IDEO the following summer. Even though IDEO only hired grad students to be interns, Kelley saw something in this kid that he liked. Alex worked for IDEO every summer until he graduated from high school, and over time he proved himself to the old-timers, learned the ropes, and came to understand "user-experience," the branch of design that centers on going out in the field to talk to people, to figure out what made them tick and how to make a product or experience really good for them. All signs pointed toward Alex having a career in design. But societal pressure was about to get in the way.

Alex is a very proud graduate of Georgetown University, but he calls his decision to enroll there "my first misstep," because they had no major in design. "Everyone said Georgetown was the quote, unquote 'best school I got into.'" And what "everyone" thought mattered to Alex, so off he went. "But with no design major or even a mechanical engineering major, I felt like, *Shit, I messed up.* Then I said to myself, *Well, I'm here. I've got to figure out how to make this work.*" Because user experience design is all about figuring out what humans want and need, Alex decided that a psychology major would be the next best thing to a design major. But Alex's mom had a different opinion. Their conver-sation went something like this:

"Major in the school of foreign service. It's their best school. Be a diplomat."

"No, I want to be a psych major."

"Why."

"I want to do design."

"Psych majors don't get jobs."

Having advised thousands of college students myself, I'm used to hearing this concern from parents. I get it. She loves him. She wants what's best for him and she believes she knows what that is. But she's wrong. Psychology, one of the social sciences, is an excellent background to have in almost any workplace. Particularly in our era of automation, robots, and AI, studying psychology gives you an understanding of the most precious workplace asset of all: humans. But I don't need to say this out loud to Alex. He's way ahead of me.

"She was SO WRONG. I still give her shit for this. She thought, *This nineteen-year-old, he's fucking up, he should be in the best program at the best university in DC and that means diplomacy.* She was wrong. I ended up being a psych major. And it was because I decided, *I'm going to force this square peg into a round hole, finagle my way into design even with Georgetown having no way to study it.* My mom said, 'Fine, go into the neuropsych stuff, then. You'll get a job.' I said, 'No, I want the behavioral stuff.' She said, 'Behaviorists don't get jobs.'"

This conflict was huge. Alex loves his mom and respects her intellect, her educational background, and her years of experience. Still, his inner voice reminded him that he'd been gunning to be a designer for practically his entire life. So, he stuck to those guns.

He found a course called Reimagining the University as a Design Problem, taught by an English professor, Randy Bass. Bass was frustrated that universities like Georgetown—which originally were places to study the liberal arts—were now churning out carbon copies of students who all seem to end up in banking and consulting and he wanted to figure out how the university could be redesigned to help students make better career decisions based on their interests. This was both a design opportunity and a meta-representation of the pressures Alex was feeling, all in one. "I was all, 'This is my calling! This is the best!'" This class proved to Alex that he was on the right path, and he got a mentor out of it. "I was this psych major who supposedly wouldn't get a job, who ended up working with Randy Bass to co-create another course for my college that helps students make better decisions about what they want to be and do out in the world."

Alex pauses to tell me that it feels cathartic to talk about this. This means he's still in the process of giving himself permission to be and do what he loves. I get it. He's young. He still worries at least a bit that other people's opinions about his life may matter more than his own.

After college Alex moved back to the Bay Area and took a job in San

Francisco. He had his first long-term relationship with a guy. "My parents are very progressive but they're Boomers. They were very much in the dark about same-sex relationships. It required a lot of education on my part." A few years later, he was off to Stockholm with Spotify.

"In psychology, there's a theory that when you undertake a really big change you can actually pull off multiple changes at the same time. I wanted to take advantage of that. I wanted all that newness. Part of that was not wanting to feel like a piece of me was back in San Francisco. So, when I moved I ended my relationship, amicably. I jumped in with two feet at Spotify. I'm learning Swedish at a rapid clip. I'm out here making decisions for myself, figuring out how to pay Swedish taxes, get Swedish Internet, make new friends in Sweden. I'm learning to cook for myself so I don't eat takeout all the time. The onus is on me to live my life."

I ask Alex how it feels to be Black in Sweden? "It's better. I know there's a good amount of casual racism here; they say things that aren't 'woke.' But there isn't this 'We're gonna kill you' type of racism that I really tangibly felt in America. Here I look at the police and do not feel fear. Particularly because I'm in a cosmopolitan city in Europe, there are so many different cultures here that I don't get the 'other-ism' that I felt at home in Silicon Valley where as a Black person it's terrifying to talk to the police. My identity here is much more rooted in being the American than in being the Black guy. Of course, being the American has its own set of problems but it is far easier to walk down the street and just go about my life. My mental health is so much better here. It really is a noticeable difference. I'm loving it. Sweden is like a mental exhale. It's like, 'Whew, I can live my life.'"

He reflects on his relationship with his mom. "My mom has said, 'Mea culpa. I was wrong to say you should be in the school of foreign service. You definitely had it right.' But I also understand why, as a Black mother, she wanted me to be in the best school at the university. Her focus on prestige and job stability was borne out of the sincere desire for me to thrive with the cards our society has dealt me as a Black man, even if it meant, at the start, that it was difficult for her to see the forest through the trees." Alex is grateful for the fierce love and concern behind his mom's efforts to steer him down the right path. But he also knows that if it is to be his best life, he has to be the one designing it.

When his parents visited him in Sweden recently, it was time for another reckoning. "My mom asked, 'Are you still bisexual?' I said, 'I haven't told you otherwise. And that's a bit of a problematic question.' She said, 'Why can't I ask that? That's not problematic.' I told her, 'Yes, it is. It's bi-erasure, as if it's a status that can come and go.' She felt I'd been lying about my sexuality my whole life despite her giving me so many opportunities to come out to her. She wanted to know why I was being deceptive. I said, 'That's not what it is. It's not about you. I wasn't out to myself.'"

Alex says his relationship with his parents has never been better. "But it took some brute force. During that recent visit I said, 'Mom, look. Look around. I have a job at Spotify in Sweden. I landed the career I've wanted since I was fourteen. I am in one piece. You are here visiting me. What else do you want? You won the parent contest, whatever it is. You have a son who is employed in a field he loves in Sweden and is living his best life as a queer person. What else do you want?' She was like, 'You know what, you're right, fine. I keep pushing but there's no need. You wanted things from an early age and you went out and got them. Fine, you're right.' I said, 'Right. There's no more you can do. Let that go and enjoy your parental retirement. I will always be here for you and we are a close-knit family. I will always love you, but I am an adult now. You have to take it as a win.'"

His voice as he relays all of this is confident, not defensive, just...certain. I think it's pretty cool that Alex gets paid to care about what humans want. When humans do what they want, they thrive. It's the story of Alex's life.

MEET ELENA—Honoring Family Sacrifices with an Independent Life

Elena's entire family immigrated to the U.S. from the Ukraine when she was four, and English proved to be quite difficult for her grandparents in particular. By middle school, she'd take calls with representatives from the phone and electric companies on her grandparents' behalf and try to parse the nuances of their bills. Children of immigrants often learn adulting skills earlier than others for the simple reason that *they have to*.

Packed into a small apartment in Oakland, California, her parents took whatever work they could find, went to school at night, and struggled to learn English. Government services helped make ends meet. Relative to all of this, Elena's job was simple: excel in school. And she did. "Seeing adults you love struggle to make a life for themselves creates an internal metronome. It becomes the beat to which you must move. I was afraid of not doing right by my family, by making choices that would make it seem that their sacrifices were for nothing. It made me afraid of not being on the quote unquote right path."

College was the first hint of discord. She was at the University of California at Berkeley, and was drawn to study political economy, the intersection of social science topics with data and other quant-centric things. "But anything other than a doctor, lawyer, or engineer seemed like *not a real job* to them," she tells me. It wasn't that Elena's parents didn't love their daughter or that they wanted to control her. They just wanted to make certain that she was setting herself up for a stable life—something they'd never had. Elena's enthusiasm for juicy political science topics simply didn't seem connected to the secure future they wanted for their daughter. They feared she was making a bad decision that could harm her. So, Elena found a middle ground and majored in economics. "My sense of obligation handicapped me around my freedom of thought and freedom of decision in college. I let my family's perspective frame what I would study. I was very afraid something would go wrong. I felt like if I fail, the whole world will implode. It was like being in the skin of perpetual fear."

The fear was nothing if not motivating. She knew she had to turn her econ major into a great job out of college, and she did just that by methodically plotting her way there. She got her résumé fine-tuned at the career center, prepped for job fairs and interviews, got internships, and worked every summer. It paid off. After graduating she landed a job with the San Francisco office of Deloitte Consulting LLP, one of the world's top consulting and accounting firms, where she worked in technology and management consulting. By age twenty-three Elena was getting strong reviews, earning great money, and anticipating her first promotion. That's when she decided to leave it all behind for a nonprofit charter school organization in Oakland called Aspire, and all hell broke loose.

"My parents were *horrified* at my starting salary. My mom said, 'We worked so hard to take you *out* of Oakland. I can't believe you're thinking of going *back*.'" (Elena explains that Oakland was where her family had had their biggest financial challenges. And now Elena was going right back to where the family had started.)

For weeks, she second-guessed her decision. "I'd call home, and my parents would say, 'Why would you take such a pay cut when we spent all this money supporting you?' and I would hang up and cry. Then I'd visit them and see a lot of other adults I grew up with, and right in front of my parents they'd go at me with things like, 'Why would you go *do* that?' Like *I was their American Dream*, and I was failing to live it." It was six long weeks between getting the job offer and starting the new job. None of the elders in her life seemed happy for her, let alone proud.

I ask her how she found the guts to switch careers in the face of all that. "Deloitte was a great place to work. I just felt an uneasiness with how much privilege I saw myself having. Something felt off. I understood very clearly that this seeming meritocracy that I've done so well within—the opportunity I've been given here in the U.S.—really isn't the meritocracy I think it is. I'm white and my English sounds native. I'm just experiencing so much privilege it feels like something is off in terms of what I do with this privilege. I was reading these political economy labor economics journals that talk about the effect of each unit of education on incarceration and voter participation. The more education you have, the less likely you are to be incarcerated and the more likely you are to vote. I started volunteering with kids. I wasn't serving in a way that felt I was truly making use of my experience and my privilege to create a community I was most proud of. It all came together: I knew I had to go into education."

And what about the pay cut, I ask her? I mean, I can relate. I took a similar cut when I transitioned from corporate law to academia. Salary and cost of living are huge variables to consider when contemplating a job change, and often when we head toward greater meaning in our work, that work comes with less money. "For me it was like, 'This is a calculated risk. I'm going to a charter school organization. I'm going to make *way* less money. And if it's bad, I have only myself to blame, and I'll fix it by going back to grad school.' With all they've invested in me, for all the sacrifices they've made, I have a set of skills that are marketable. So, there is no scenario where I will call my parents and say, 'This didn't work. I'm going to move back in with you.' I have the skills not to go back, and I have pride and stubbornness so I refuse to let myself fail in this way." *It's on me and I'll handle it* was essentially what Elena was saying—a great harbinger of adulthood.

Handle it, she did. After a few years of thriving at Aspire, Elena landed her dream job at the Oakland office of the Charter School Growth Fund. Her job is to find the charter school entrepreneurs who are best at transforming education in underserved communities and support their work by giving them grants. It boils down to spreading great education practices and in so doing ensuring that more kids get to achieve the American Dream. Before long, Elena's parents saw that even if a career in education wasn't what they had initially imagined for their daughter, it could in fact lead to a stable and secure life for Elena, which is all they had ever wanted.

Along the way, Elena continued to achieve dreams of her own. She met a guy named Andrew. They moved in together. (This was another decision that her parents weren't so keen on at first, but now they all love each other!) Elena and Andrew got a Great Dane–mutt mix, Charlie, and as they trained him and focused on trying to be good parents to Charlie, they did so knowing that this was maybe a warm-up for raising actual humans of their own one day. "Everything has come full circle," Elena tells me when I check in with her a few years after we initially spoke. She is now thirty-two. She and Andrew got married. And Charlie is now the nine-year-old big brother of Emma and Levi, twins born to Elena and Andrew during the pandemic. Charlie adores them. When Elena or Andrew puts one of the twins down for a moment, Charlie comes over and rests his head on the baby's legs. Like, *Don't worry, I've got this.*

"Having children has given me a much deeper appreciation and perspective on the dynamics of being a parent. My parents are the ones supporting me through this process—both emotionally and by babysitting as often as we need them—and they share their wisdom gained from having raised me in circumstances that were difficult." Elena's parents are proud of her, both for the life she has created and for the work that she does in the world. I'm certain she doesn't take any of it for granted. "Some decisions of mine that were initially unpopular with my family ended up being great decisions. Not just for me but for all of us."

MEET OLIVER—Fully Formed, Fully Responsible, Fully Adult

Oliver is a fifty-year-old white man who was born into a wealthy British family in "Jane Austen country" in England, and as is the tradition in those circles Oliver was sent off to boarding school at age eleven. Oliver was the kid at the back of the classroom who seemed like they couldn't care less.

Oliver was assigned female at birth, and in that identity was expected to grow up and find a husband, have a bunch of children, live in a big country house, and throw lavish dinner parties. "At art school in London, I went through a brief rebellious stage characterized by motorcycles, body piercings, and a peroxide crew cut." But by his midtwenties, societal and family expectations loomed large. Oliver coped by drinking. A lot. So much so that it became a problem. "I moved away from 'being one of the boys' on my motorbike, and tried to be a girl so I could find a husband. I somewhat reluctantly returned to the fold, and married a perfectly suitable man whom my parents adored. I first got sober in 2001, six weeks before my wedding, because I was suicidal and thought that alcohol was the problem. (It was, just not the only problem)."

After a British wedding, the couple moved to Fairfield, Connecticut, where Oliver soon gave birth to a son, then another son, then twin daughters. "By 2010 my then-husband would go to work at five in the morning and come home deep into the night, leaving me alone all day with four children under the age of five. He was almost never home. One day, the twin girls were crying in one upstairs bedroom and another child was crying in another bedroom two doors down—and as soon as a child in one room stopped crying, another child would start crying in a different room of the house." Oliver stood on the carpeted landing of the stairs, holding one weepy twin while being pelted by screams from all sides, knowing it was impossible to comfort every single child at once. Even though Oliver was alone, he cast around for somebody else with more authority who should be doing the task of comforting. Then, suddenly, he realized that it didn't matter whether he felt capable of taking care of the children. He simply *had to.*

"In that moment, it was like I got up to the front of the class and became the teacher," Oliver says. "There's a pyramid of responsibility, and I thought other people would always be above me. Not so. The person at the top of the pyramid of responsibility is actually *me.*" Oliver characterizes this moment on the stairs as a breakdown, and emerged from it by getting sober again. Along the way he got the tattoo "NFBM" on his inner wrist, which stands for the title of the Led Zeppelin song "Nobody's Fault But Mine." It reminds Oliver that holding yourself accountable is the difference between being a child and being an adult.

"I was worried I was going to peel back the layers, get to the center of myself, and find nothing there. But I had a moral obligation to do the inward work on myself so I could become a complete person. I finally started facing up to everything, who I was, what I needed to do to be a good parent, and the changes I needed to make in my life so that I wouldn't continue to feel the need to run away from it. I finally came out as gay in 2011."

Now that Oliver is on a path to becoming who he is visibly and out loud, authenticity has become especially crucial. "I've known that I was trans since I came out in 2011, but I had to deal with all of this one step at a time, in bite-sized pieces, because obviously—considering where I started—it's been a lot. I came out as transgender in late 2017, and went from a tiny minority of seven percent to an even tinier minority of zero-point-one percent. I don't have a map to follow except the one I determine on my own. I have to be able to answer my own questions: Who am I? What am I? I have to fortify myself against how I will be received by most people. When I achieve this happiness from within, it'll be so worth it."

As I know from my own struggles with self-acceptance, what Oliver is aiming for takes work. When I finally loved myself as Black and biracial, my transformation was somehow obvious to others in the Black community. One woman I'd known for a few decades said, "We've been waiting for you all along," which, even now, as I type this, brings tears to my eyes. Oliver is experiencing a similar embrace in Fairfield, Connecticut, where he is both finding acceptance and playing an active role in accepting others who are searching for belonging.

Family acceptance (or lack of it) can be the hardest truth to reckon with, yet telling our truth to family is a key step toward fully accepting ourselves and living the life we want to live. "Once I'd started integrating the concept of authenticity and honesty into how I parent my kids, it became inevitable that eventually I'd have to face up to this, too." A year ago, he began the process of coming out to his eldest kids, who are entering puberty. The kids are taking the process in stride. However, his British community—those in his parents' generation and the social circle in which he grew up—are not; they see Oliver's "coming out" and involvement in the queer community as attention-seeking. Yet, for Oliver, life goes on. Perhaps he had to lose acceptance in one community to find it in another.

Oliver now makes his home in Connecticut where he co-parents his four kids with his ex-husband. He makes his living as a writer. Our conversation is interrupted when Oliver's kids yell out greetings as they come home from summer camp. "Turns out that coming out as trans is one of the best things I've ever done apart from having my kids. Regardless of how complicated it is, I feel fully formed, fully responsible, and fully adult. Like if I can do this, I can do anything." Oliver goes to join his children for lunch. It's a small act of belonging he'll never take for granted.

IN SHORT: YOU ARE THE ARCHITECT OF YOUR LIFE

As a college dean I got to sit with thousands of young adults contending with the same doubts and insecurities I grappled with in my younger days, whether it be about career or identity or all the stuff in between. My job wasn't to tell them what to do or who to be. My job was to listen well and try to open them up to their own selves by asking them good questions about the how and why of their expressed intentions. And to remind them that you must stop pleasing others because those other people literally have no idea who you *are.* Then I'd root for these young adults as they began to identify what they really and truly wanted to do, gained courage to be that person, and made choices and plans accordingly.

So, hey, go for it. Your life is different than mine. Perhaps way different. I may've made choices you don't agree with. I may be someone you'd argue with while watching the news. I may have bumper stickers that make your skin crawl. That's fine. I'm opening up about me to encourage you to open up to you.

Over time, from trial and error, and one experience after another, you start to become more familiar with yourself. You learn what excites you, and just as importantly you learn what repels you. You begin to develop that "I could see myself doing this forever" feeling, whether it's about a line of work or a relationship. You want to look for clues as to what really matters to you. And you want to get better at making decisions accordingly.

I'm asking you, Who are you? What are you good at, and what do you love and value? What kind of work would sit at the intersection of those things? Where do you find belonging? What kinds of people do you want to invite into your life? Can you give yourself permission to be that person, and then chart a path that's most right for you?

☺ = WHERE YOU WANT TO BE.

I'm rooting for you to get there. But I know that a lot of stuff can hold you back. So, let's talk about getting unstuck.

Unpack and Reflect

- Whose plans and expectations are influencing my choices in life?
- What are the things that I'm both good at doing and love doing? What kinds of paid work, volunteer work, and hobbies allow me to do those things?
- Which of my identities matter most to me, and am I living in a place and working in a space that allows me to freely be that person?
- If I was able to listen to my voice, not judge it, and honor what it tells me, what would I change about my life?

6

GET OUT OF NEUTRAL
(THE TRAGEDY OF UNUSED POTIONS)

I wanna break it in my hands
I wanna grow something wild and unruly
—The Chicks, "Cowboy Take Me Away"

This is your adulthood. It's already happening. And one day it'll be over.

Don't wait around for a sign that it's time to start. Don't try to save it for later when you might be better at it or enjoy it more. Don't expect someone else to do it for you. You get this? You're free—no longer a child who gets told what to do, and not yet dead, which sadly is a destination that awaits us all. It's go time.

You're in your "wildhood"—a period of life so labeled by authors Barbara Natterson-Horowitz and Kathryn Bowers (in *Wildhood: The Epic Journey from Adolescence to Adulthood in Humans and Other Animals*)— when you leave the care of your parents and go on important and terrifying quests during which you learn to keep yourself alive, negotiate your social status, navigate sexuality, and cultivate self-reliance. If this time in your life sounds a bit primal, it is. The book *Wildhood* documents in great detail the journey of four young adults—a hyena, a penguin, a whale, and a wolf—and demonstrates how the adulting path of these four species is astonishingly similar to that of a young *Homo sapiens* (you). As we discussed in chapter 1, the three essential components of adulting are *wanting to*, *having to*, and *learning how*. The young hyena, penguin, whale, and wolf in *Wildhood* most definitely *had to* adult and they were actively *learning how*. But *wanting to* wasn't even part of the equation for them. None of the rest of the animal kingdom gets to muse over whether they *want to* or whether they're *ready* to adult. If they don't, can't, aren't, or won't? Well, they die.

Fortunately for us, our ancestors created a human society that has some important built-in safety nets, which make life less dire for *Homo sapiens*. Yet, paradoxically, for us *Homo sapiens*, the larger the safety net we have in the form of others there to help, plan, fix, and handle stuff for us—preventing us from perhaps *having to* or even from *learning how*—the more we may grow complacent and unable to adult despite our adult-ish age. Too much of a safety net leads to learned helplessness, which leads to anxiety and depression. It's *wanting to adult* that springs open the trap and liberates us from that malaise.

So, this chapter is about some of the things that might be stopping you from *wanting to*, and about how to activate that piece of yourself.

THE THINGS THAT HOLD YOU BACK

Used to be you didn't have a choice. Children were expected to work to contribute to the household income. And once you were eighteen you were on your own and expected to make your own way. Times have changed. We've created a preciousness and protectedness around childhood (for kids who are middle class and beyond; poor and working-class families tend not to have the resources or free time that yield a precious and protected childhood), which looks like a good thing. And today, for those kids, we have a sense that you can take your time and slowly *emerge* into adulthood rather than have it thrust upon you on your eighteenth or twenty-first birthday.

But we've gone a step further. Today, if you're middle class or beyond, there's a pervasive mindset that you don't really need to hustle in your twenties because they're a time to play around and just have fun. Yes, you should have fun. (Have a lot of fun!) But at the same time, you're supposed to be figuring out who you are and what you're good at, how you're going to make a living, who you want in your life, and how you're going to make things better in the world, so you need to get going on that. Adulting is an active verb, and as you "do" it, it creates its own phenomenal momentum.

Nobody knows this better than people in their early thirties. And their therapists. Lori Gottlieb, a psychotherapist and author of the wildly popular book *Maybe You Should Talk to Someone: A Therapist, Her Therapist, and Our Lives Revealed,* is one of them. Lori and I went to college together, and we support each other in our authorly lives. When I reached out to her on Facebook to talk about the target audience for this book and to ask if she had any insights, she replied, "My practice is full of them!" I got her on the phone twice to talk about, well, you! She began by telling me, "A lot of people in their early thirties look back on their twenties and say, 'I wasn't really paying attention. I wasn't really setting up the infrastructure of my life in the way I wanted to.'" Lori will have much more to say as we continue, so much so that I think of her as the resident guru of this chapter. And I'm super grateful to her for taking the time to help me—and you! But for now, her top-level advice here is that the various things you try out and practice in your twenties prepare you for better decisions and outcomes later in life, so now's the time to get your butt in gear. Don't be that person who gets to the end of the video game with unused potions. Use them!

Adding to the list of problematic pervasive mindsets is "keep your options open" (whether about work or your love life) proffered by well-meaning but misguided relatives and peers. "Keeping your options open" sounds liberating, but it's actually a trap. Here's what I mean:

- First, it implies a vast set of options for which you can and should prepare yourself. Yes, the universe is vast and possibilities are limitless (if you are middle class and beyond), but you will go insane studying piano, premed, econ, and particle physics, so as to keep open the possibility of being a concert pianist, doctor, businessperson, and astronaut. And in your personal life, while dating apps present an endless sea of faces and bodies you can hook up with, joy comes from deep connection with others, not from forever swiping right.

- Second, "keeping your options open" implies that there's some perfect time (decidedly not now) when the right path will become clear. There is no right path and there is no time better than the present to try something out (unless you are in crisis and not able to think clearly, then, yes, focus on that first before trying out something new).

- Third, let's face it, this comment tends to come when the person with whom you're speaking doesn't like the option you're excited to pursue. In deferring to them, you give your power away to them instead of you being the decider. They love you, but they do *not* know you better than you, no matter what they say (and if they *do*, you need to change that, because you're not their pet, project, or puppet).

- Fourth, this "options open" idea literally keeps you in limbo. Well, when are you supposed to make a choice then? And what are you to do in the meantime? You can't window-shop your life forever.

- Fifth, having too many options breeds overwhelm and anxiety. Research at grocery stores shows that if you're given three jams to sample and purchase you're likely to buy one, but if you're given twenty options you're likely to just give up and go home.

- Sixth, if something arises that actually excites you, yet you say, *Naw, I don't know if I should go for that just yet*, you've basically wasted something that could have been worth trying because you were waiting for a clearer signal (from some external source) that this was a good thing to try. The tragedy of unused potions!

The fear of uncertainty and the unknown can loom like a very large monster. Particularly upon exiting childhood (which had a ton of structure, and a clear lockstep progression), the wide-open landscape of adulthood is basically one big unknown. It's completely rational and valid to have some trepidation about getting out there. But your choice is to venture out into it or stay in your comfort zone, where it's safe but nothing interesting ever happens and where you will feel stuck, I promise you. Toward this end I'm inspired by *Survivor Season 12* (Panama/Exile Island) competitor Cirie Fields, who started out saying she didn't even want to pick up leaves and rocks because of the critters hiding underneath, yet she made it to the final four. Upon her departure she said, "Fear of the unknown kept me on the couch. Now I'm aware there's so much more I can do." Confronting the unknown gave Cirie *life* (and made her one of the most popular players ever).

And, as we just discussed in chapter 5, "Stop Pleasing Others," even if you're not afraid of the unknown, well-meaning family or peers may be holding you back by lording their potential disappointment or ridicule over you. Dad really wants you to do the internship he set up for you. Mom brags about how smart you are and hints at what you might do with that. Your friends tease that the things you like to do are dumb or weird or not as practical as their own pursuits. It's hard to make that first brave choice toward a line of work, a grad school, or that person you like when you fear what everyone else is going to say about it. Hey, these folks may have their own hopes and dreams for you. But you can get stuck trying to live your life to please them. And if you manage to please *all* of them, you'll most certainly have failed to please yourself. (Remember, whose life is this anyway? YOURS.)

As I type this, I am in a LinkedIn conversation with a twenty-four-year-old stranger in France named Hugo whose parents appear to be trying their darnedest to tell him what to do for a living. Hugo watched my TED Talk and wrote me a three-page letter in response. (I love it when folks give voice to their inner self, as Hugo was doing by writing to me!) His parents had made every decision for him in childhood. After he graduated from college, they set up three internships for him in finance, which is his father's profession. But Hugo was sort of meh about the work. And now they're telling him to take a job in data science, or tech and programming more broadly, which Hugo feels no passion for. He asked for my advice. I asked him, *What kind of work would you be excited to do? What kind of work energizes you?* He replied, immediately (which tells me *he knows it deep inside*), "Physical therapy, and I know a lot about it and have years of experience—how to treat injuries, what are the issues and misconceptions with the fitness and health industry, how to fix the issues brought by sedentary lifestyle, how to make any pain in your body go away instantly, what elderly could do to maintain better health, what people are doing wrong when working out and how much time they waste in doing so, etc." Brilliant. Then the kicker. "So, maybe that'll be my backup."

Noooooooo, Hugo, no! (I didn't actually type that, but I was thinking it. I mean, this dude took the time to summarize his entire life story for a complete stranger [me] all but begging for help in getting out of his parents' orbit.) I replied, "I don't think you need me to tell you this, but GO BE A PHYSICAL THERAPIST. Go do that work. Get the schooling you need, the experience you need, and go be that person. It's a perfectly valid choice. Go be that person." But I fear Hugo is nowhere close to getting unstuck. He tells me, "I think, maybe there is a right set of words I need to hear that will change my mind, motivate me, alternate my perspective on things and set me on a track to a more fulfilling life. I'm just wondering, what those words are, and in what order." Hugo needs to hear those words not from me or his parents. They need to come up and out of him like a barbaric yawp (as Robin Williams in *Dead Poets Society* urged his students to do, quoting the poet Walt Whitman) so he can say those things to *himself* and fling himself out of his parents' orbit and out into the universe where he knows in his soul he wants to be.

CHILDHOOD CHICKENS COMING HOME TO ROOST

While we're on the subject of your parents, let's really *go there*, because how you were raised has a whole lot to do with whether you feel stuck or able and excited to move forward right now. In her private therapy practice, Lori Gottlieb finds that while many young adults express a desire for what their parents have (e.g., the family; the partner; the life filled with friends and family and holidays; a job that they like but that doesn't run their lives), they didn't necessarily have the kinds of experiences in childhood that train people to know how to achieve those things. Lori shared with me these great examples of how dynamics from childhood can contribute to young adults feeling stuck:

Regarding How to Be Present with Others: If your home environment was one in which everyone was constantly returning their eyes to a screen, including at meals and in one-on-one conversations, you may not have learned how to be present to the people who matter to you. This lack could be compounded if every time someone *was* interacting with you it seemed to be about peripheral assessments of you, like your grades or your test scores. In the aggregate, you may not have had much experience with what Lori calls "the delicious feeling of being known," the experience of someone knowing you not for your achievements but just for YOU; and because you haven't had that delicious feeling you may not know how to create it for others, which could make it hard to get a relationship off the ground.

Regarding How to Demonstrate Mutual Care in Relationships: If you grew up being taught "you do you" and "they do them," and everyone can be themselves, this modeled a way to be open and accepting of all people, which is good. However, while the openness to difference is super important and valuable, a clapback might be coming your way if you emerge from that messaging thinking, *I just need to do me; I don't have to take on responsibilities toward other humans.* There might even be a second clapback coming if the other message you got from your nuclear family was *all your needs are going to get met by us.* Did your parents behave as if their needs didn't matter? Or, put differently, did they behave as if their needs were about getting particular opportunities for *you*, like the right school, club, college, or internship? What can happen if you were raised by such parents is that your idea of a relationship is that the other person drops everything so you can do you. Then you get into relationships as an adult and you say to yourself, *Well, my experience of love is that they were going to make sure that nothing was going to get in the way of my needs and goals. So, now I'm in this relationship with someone who has their needs, and they get in the way of my needs, and this doesn't feel like love.* The contrast between what you expect from a relationship, based upon how you were raised, and what it actually takes to make a relationship work could make it hard to make a deep commitment to other people.

Regarding Disagreement, Reconciliation and Compromise: Some kids were raised with adults (such as caregivers or teachers) handling disagreements, compromise, and reconciliation for them. For example, if when you were in school one kid upset another in a serious way and the school intervened—if the adults flat out handled it, or if they initiated a conversation between the students, or if they even facilitated that conversation (giving you talking points)—the kids didn't learn how to work things out for themselves. Kids raised this way can become adults who are stuck when it comes to disagreements, reconciliation, and compromise because they don't have a whole lot of practice with *I'm going to take this risk and I'm going to be vulnerable and walk up to this kid and say, Hey, let's work this out*. If a pattern of adults managing disagreements for you was laid down in childhood, you can find yourself at a standstill when the inevitable adult-sized disagreement arises in the workplace or in your relationships.

Regarding the Hard Work of Work: If you were raised in a nuclear family where the caregivers did a lot of planning, reminding, handling, and fixing stuff that centered around you (your assignments, your projects, your tasks, chores, and obligations), you may not appreciate what it takes to get a job done from start to finish. You may not understand that almost every job has parts that aren't enjoyable. As such, out in the real world you may feel, *This is really boring, I hate doing this, I need to get another job* . . . instead of *Hey, that's part of the learning curve, and also there will be boring parts of any job*. What's extra hard is that out in the real world there is no clear path. In contrast, in childhood, you may have been told your assignment, exactly what you need to do for next steps with your homework or a school project, and by the way you may have had a college counselor or a college consultant and that person went through exactly the choices you would have (and even when there were choices, someone curated those choices for you). The end of the school years can seem dauntingly wide open for anyone, but if you're accustomed to having virtually all of your options laid out for you, it might be extra-hard for you to figure out how to create your own next steps.

Regarding Who Decides What's Best for You: If you were raised by people who always said they knew what was best for you, even as you became an adolescent and young adult, you might easily be stymied in your ability to decide things for yourself. Lori Gottlieb has clients who say, "I'm in grad school for this and I don't even know if I want to be in grad school.

I don't know myself well enough to know what I want." This applies to relationships, too, where there's a tension between *What kind of person do I really want to be with versus the kind of person my parents say I should be with*. Lori told me a story of a client who froze when her boyfriend asked her to marry him. "Everything on paper about these two people made it seem perfect, and everybody was thrilled about it, except for this woman. When he proposed, she hesitated, and he saw her hesitate. She called me for an emergency session. She said, 'I don't know if I want to marry this person. I just kept staying. I had no good reason to leave.' And I said, 'Isn't a reason that you need some time to figure out what you want?' It was like a light bulb went off. She hadn't developed this inner compass. Her inner voice was telling her, 'I don't feel connected to this person. I don't feel this person is my life partner.' But she couldn't listen to that because of the other voices saying, 'Isn't he so great' and 'He's the kind of person you should marry to have the kind of family you should have, just like extracurriculars you needed to get into college.' It's the same dynamic. She broke up with him and is now dating someone and it's 'I never felt this way before.' Now she says, 'I was always with the kind of person I thought I *should* be dating, but in this person I have the person I *want* to be dating.' By the way, the person who proposed was 'double Harvard.' Came from the 'right schools.' The new person she's infinitely more happy with didn't go to a name-brand college." If you trust that your parents have your best interests in mind regarding your work, schooling, or relationships, you might end up deferring to them at great personal cost, or feel paralyzed over the inherent conflict with these people you may love more than any others.

(Tips for getting unstuck from these and other issues start on page 144.)

WHERE ARE YOU POINTING YOUR FLASHLIGHT?

Joe Holtgreive is a professor of engineering at Northwestern University, where he also serves as a dean who supports struggling students. He knows what struggle feels like, because once upon a time he was a new student on that very campus flunking an engineering course. In this sense, his trajectory from struggling student to dean on the same campus is identical to mine. Both of us devoted ourselves to believing in students when they weren't believing in themselves. We did it because we had once been that student.

Joe has a TEDx Talk called "How a Flashlight Changed My Life," in which he explains his philosophy on how in moments of intense uncertainty—which is one of the causes of stuckness—what we focus on impacts everything. It goes something like this. You're holding a flashlight. Your *intentions* are your hand aiming the flashlight (where it chooses to point the flashlight). Your *attention* is the flashlight and the beam it creates. Your *awareness* is what the flashlight illuminates. When our intentions are unintentional (herky-jerky instead of focused and steady) we have a wandering mind. "And a wandering mind is an unhappy mind," Joe says, quoting the brain research of psychologists Matthew Killingsworth and Daniel Gilbert, which shows that whenever our minds wander, we tend to go into self-centered rumination and experience a feeling of worry. (By contrast, a focused mind is calm.)

In moments of intense uncertainty, it feels like our flashlight is jerking back and forth from options to deadlines to crises to failed expectations. It makes us feel ungrounded and exhausted. But we're the ones holding our flashlight, and with it we can be intentional, and therefore more focused, more at peace, happier, and more successful.

Picture a student who comes to Joe's office to discuss how badly they are doing in an engineering class. Joe asks, "Is your intention not to fail? Or is your intention to succeed?" The student thinks there's no difference, but Joe says there is. Joe says if your intention—where you aim your flashlight—is to not fail, then the flashlight beam (your attention) is about what failure looks like, what threatens your success, and the consequences of that failure, and what the flashlight illuminates (your awareness) is fear, rumination, threats, and a sense of I AM NOT good enough, not getting enough support, etc. However, Joe says, if your intention—where you aim your flashlight—is to succeed, then the flashlight beam (your attention) is about strategies, opportunities, and resources, and what the flashlight illuminates (your awareness) is curiosity, excitement, commitment, and a sense of I AM going to work hard and do my best to succeed.

BE CURIOUS ABOUT YOUR SELF

To be able to hold your flashlight steady and point it in the right direction, you need to know a lot about yourself. If you're kinda stuck like it seems Hugo is—if you can't give yourself permission to go for what you want, or you're stuck in someone else's script of your life, or you flat out don't know what you want, regardless of the reasons why—Joe Holtgreive would invite you to *be curious about what motivates you to stay stuck* (instead of being motivated to propel yourself forward). Is it impossible to take action because you want to keep your options open? Are you afraid to commit to this, that, or them because you're not really sure what you want? Are you not thrilled with what you are doing or who you're with, but change is scary? Are you giving up before you ever really got started because it looks like hard work? Is someone standing in your way? Do you feel you don't even know yourself well enough to know what you want? I want you to recognize the purpose in staying as you are. Because only after you're curious about why you're behaving this way and only after you recognize the purpose it serves for you can you move past it.

We can go to therapy for help in figuring this stuff out. (I highly recommend it!) But frankly, just a good conversation with another person, whether they're a therapist or not, can start to illuminate parts of ourselves we hadn't previously seen. Sometimes we know exactly what needs to happen, and getting unstuck means taking that deep breath and speaking up about it. Believe it or not, that's what Hugo did. And you're not going to believe where he is now.

Three months after Hugo first wrote me, we were in touch again. This time it was me reaching out to him to see if he was comfortable with how I'd written up our interaction in this book. His reply blew my mind. In continuing to ponder his dynamic with his parents, Hugo began to ask himself, *If my parents don't like what I want to do, why not show me something of their own?* Hugo was steadying his flashlight. It dawned on him that his father had been pushing him to do tech and programming in financial services, his own field, without ever really showing Hugo what that field was all about. "I think my father didn't want to show me what he does or deals with because he was so unsure whether I would like it at all. So finally one day, when we were sitting at dinner, I just said, 'Jesus Christ, will you please teach me something about what you do? You've been in the business for thirty years and you haven't taught me anything, I barely know what you even do! I want you to teach me.' The next day he took me to an important business meeting. I got to see how negotiations work, and it was an awesome building experience for both of us. I saw he felt easier by having me by his side. Maybe it sounds weird, but he felt more protected, like he had an ally in the room. To me, it was the first time I felt his pride exuding towards me. And wowie did that moment itself just obliterate the concerns I had about myself."

Joe Holtgreive says, "Pay attention to where you're shining your light. Tune in to the physical sensations in your body, your emotions, the stories in your own head. Choose to shine on what feeds and nourishes you rather than what haunts or distracts you. It makes all the difference." He's describing a process known as mindfulness, which I'll discuss more in chapter 12, "Unleash Your Superpowers." The point for now is, where you direct your mind determines whether you're going to remain stuck, sad, and frightened, or whether you can move forward. That power is within you. Hugo knows that now.

Hugo still cares about physical therapy. But he's greatly enjoying data science, too, not just because it's a vehicle for greater closeness with his father but because he's GOOD at it. "I finished a data science boot camp, my final project got approved, and it was extremely satisfying to finally produce something tangible that exemplifies my skills gathered during the pandemic," he says. "It's weird how one event can change a relationship. Previously, my conversations with my father felt like asthma. Right now they flow like a stream. He's excited to share with me what goes on during his day, tell me his financial plans, his approach towards things. Most importantly, he's excited to talk to me. A few days ago I joined in on his talks with wealth managers, where I saw how they approach their clients, the strategies, and products, and I saw a start-to-end creation of a portfolio. This whole process took a huge stone off my chest, just an absolute rocket thrust. I'd constantly thought that since everything was done for me I wasn't prepared for life, and suddenly that perspective is gone."

The tone of Hugo's letters to me completely flipped. The initial three-page letter sounded like a plea from a trapped person. This exchange three months later is optimistic, grounded, and unstuck. As Professor Holtgreive would say, Hugo steadied his flashlight on his intention to communicate more clearly with his parents. He felt the "deliciousness of being known" of which Lori Gottlieb speaks above. "The missing component was a sense of feeling adequate and valuable to my dad. His act of introducing me to what he does, inviting me to that world of his, is the process of creating those delicious feelings. Those moments are incredible jolts of energy that carry over to everything else you do, because the feeling of inadequacy is gone."

I'm putting Hugo's story here for you, dear reader, but Hugo has advice for parents, too, which you can flag if you need someone in your life to see this: "Maybe it's worth it for parents to take a deep breath, slow down, sit down with your kid, and finally offer something personal of your own to make your kid feel more valuable." And yes, Hugo has lessons for me, too. Like, sometimes I am too quick to say things like YOU SHOULD BE A PHYSICAL THERAPIST. (And quick was exactly my speed while scrolling my LinkedIn mail, where Hugo first found me.) As I review his initial letter to me, quoted earlier, I think I'd read it as Hugo waiting for someone to tell him what to do with his life. Now I know that what he longed for were better conversations with his father. Another reminder that I'm not always right :) Thanks, Hugo, for teaching me.

FOURTEEN THINGS TO DO DIFFERENTLY TO MOVE YOUR WORK AND RELATIONSHIPS FORWARD

Let's not mince words here. Getting unstuck takes a ton of hard work, both in terms of actual effort—to look for a better job, find a more affordable city, change your dating patterns—and emotionally. But I know you want to get out of neutral; I know you want to be engaged with work that matters and with people you vibe with and value. I know that you want to be able to count on things and people. I know you want to make a difference. I know you'd like to experience deep and abiding love with others that will buoy you no matter what comes your way. Lori Gottlieb routinely asks her clients in therapy, "What are you going to do differently to move your work and relationship forward?" Because she is so widely sought for her opinions on these things, I wanted to put her advice here on the page for you alongside mine as if we are both talking with you (thanks, Lori!):

1. *Take time to be alone with yourself.* We in the older generations had solitude imposed upon us because we didn't have access to 24/7 connection and information, and that's one element from those bygone days that is worth reclaiming. We don't want you to be lonely, but there's a huge difference between being lonely and alone. (Lori says people on their phones all the time are lonely but not alone.) As I mentioned earlier, young adults are regularly telling their therapists, "I don't know myself well enough to know what I want." So, step one here is getting to know that self a whole lot better. And you do that by being alone.

   That's because, as Lori says, "In silence is where we start to hear ourselves." (She points out that that's why we tend to come up with the best ideas in the shower where there are no interruptions!) She says you don't have to be DOING things all the time. You need a break from work, school, media, social media, commitments, and even friends and family. You need what she calls "a safe harbor" where you can just BE with yourself. Things you might do with yourself include taking a walk (by yourself), mulling your thoughts, meditating, reading a book, cooking for yourself and enjoying your meal, and writing in a journal. You'll start to get to know your inner self, and the more you do this the better you'll get at intuiting what you really want and what is in your way.

   It's crucial to practice both being alone and being okay with being alone. Not only do you learn more about yourself, but you need the capacity to be alone if you're going to be in a relationship, because the people with whom you are in relationship are not going to make sure you're engaged and taken care of every minute. This also, Lori says, is a simple truth about adulting.

2. *Turn inward. Pay attention to your feelings of discomfort.* Lori finds that young adults do not have a lot of familiarity with their own feelings (perhaps because parents and caregivers stepped in to prevent hurt or bad feelings from happening in childhood;

perhaps because they were shut down for having feelings). As a result, there's a lack of experience in dealing with feelings of discomfort, and a feeling that one's own discomfort is inherently a bad thing. It's not a bad thing. Not something to just get rid of. It's a set of things to pay attention to, think about, and honor, so you can get out of neutral and move past them.

So, be curious about your discomfort. Ask yourself, *What am I feeling? Where am I feeling it in my body? What's going on inside of me?* Lori says that when you analyze them, you can use those feelings in a positive way. If for example you are feeling anxious, a good way to manage that is to say, *What's making me anxious? Maybe I'm in the wrong job and I need to make a change. Maybe I'm realizing I'm slacking off and I need to step up my game.* There's tremendous value in asking, *What is this feeling telling me?* and *What can I do to change that?* (I'll talk about my own experiences with getting to know my own discomfort in chapter 12, "Unleash Your Superpowers.")

3. *Learn how to regulate your own emotions.* Lori says "regulate" means "make me feel calmer." And as we grow up we morph from our parents helping us regulate our emotions to being able to do it for ourselves. After looking inward and noticing what's happening for you, you might say, *You know what, I know that I'm stressed right now. I have too much on my plate. I'm going to go take a run, which helps me regulate my emotional state. I'm going to call a friend and connect with somebody. I'm going to read for a while. I'm going to create a schedule that isn't so stressful. I'm going to make sure that I get sleep.*

A great way to regulate your emotions, Lori says, is by connecting. Connect with nature by going for a walk in a beautiful area. Connect with a friend by having a voice-to-voice conversation or by writing a long letter. Connect with yourself by reading a book. Connect with your body by meditating.

Note, getting on social media, or using food, alcohol, or drugs does not count. These are things that allow you to avoid your feelings. (One of Lori's friends says, "The Internet is the most effective short-term non-prescription painkiller out there.") Social media is outward focused. It's *What is everyone else doing and how do I compare.* It's not connection, it's disconnection. It's *I'm not in that equation except to analyze and compare disfavorably.* When you scroll Instagram endlessly, you're likely trying to distract yourself from whatever feeling you're having. Then you see other people's posts and feel worse about yourself because you're looking at the highlight reels of someone else's life. Every "like" is another dose of medication instead of taking care of what you need the medication for in the first place.

4. *When with others, be present.* Nothing says, *You don't matter very much to me* like your face staring at your phone instead of at the person in front of you. If we want to demonstrate that we care about others (which can lead to deep and meaningful connection) we have to be fully present with them. This means not texting while you're talking to someone, not scrolling your feed while hanging out with someone, and instead putting your phone down and giving them your attention and your time until your time together is over. When this happens, you will discover "the delicious feeling of being known," as Lori calls it.

   Lori says you have to be intentional about being present. You have to say, *When I'm out with my friends I'm not going to put my phone on the table between us. If someone texts I'm not going to answer because for this hour I'm out with my friends.* Yes, it is really uncomfortable at first. But you have to practice starting to be present. You're likely to notice, *I feel refreshed and refueled from that hour, in the way that I don't when I'm answering texts while talking to my friend, or taking selfies while talking to my friend, or scrolling through Instagram while talking to my friend.* Lori notes that this isn't an anti-technology diatribe; we just have to be more deliberate about how we use technology, so we don't lose the ability to be present to the people who matter to us.

   Also ask yourself, are you someone that someone would want to be in a relationship with? That is, do you act in a way that you would want to be treated? If you are having trouble in a relationship, do you understand why? Because now is the time to figure that out. Maybe you're not being present.

5. *Take action, do something different, and start anywhere.* This piece of advice for getting out of neutral is a mash-up from improv, design thinking, and psychology. In improv, where you're thrown out on stage with the imperative to be interesting and entertaining without a script, the advice is "start anywhere" because that's how things get going. In design thinking, there's a "bias toward action," meaning just *go for it* and see what happens cuz that's better than doing nothing and repeating the same old patterns. And our resident guru Lori Gottlieb says that therapists will urge you to "Do something different than what you've been doing." She says if you don't know what you want in a career, or you know this job is not right for you, or you keep dating people who turn out not to be right for you, "Instead of sitting around complaining, do something different. Date differently. Focus on what you want to do professionally instead of just letting these ten years pass ruminating on why you don't like what you're doing. It's hard to say, *I'm going to be proactive and move outside of my comfort zone.*" But if you want to get out of neutral, you have to.

Lori says you can initiate a plan, and it doesn't have to be perfect but it will lead you somewhere. And that's better than doing nothing because the more you can get out in the world the better off you'll be. Whereas if you don't take action and instead just try to figure it all out in your head you don't get anywhere. Joe Holtgreive, the Northwestern dean with the flashlight analogy, says, "It's not about 'What's right?' It's about 'What's right for me?' Even better, it's about 'What's right for me *right now*?'" It's a much smaller answer to a much smaller question. Hopefully much less anxiety producing.

Lori says that since you don't have a lot of stability as a young adult (new job, new city, new people), taking action leads you on a path to more stability. She shares the story of a client who recently started volunteer work and it has opened up her community. She met all these people she would never have met otherwise. And it helped her career, which she never expected. All from getting a little outside her comfort zone on a Saturday morning.

6. *Don't bolt at the first sign of a problem.* When a client is having a problem at work or in a relationship, Lori calmly responds, "Okay, so you had your first disagreement with your boss/significant other, what are you thinking about that?" But she finds that her client has already gone to their friends, who are just as clueless, and who have already said, "Your boss is so mean, you need to quit" or "Break up with him, that's not okay, you need to be with someone who is one hundred percent supporting you." The friends' immediate reaction boils down to *This person is upsetting you and we love you and we don't want you to be upset,* and that's understandable because they're just trying to be there for you. But someone with more experience would say, "Why don't you go talk to them about it and understand what is going on between the two of you?"

Lori says that if you bolt the minute there's a disagreement it's likely because you haven't had enough practice going deep. Going deep means exploring the contradictions, making compromises, being generous, setting boundaries, asking someone to be generous on our behalf, and making hard choices. And it's the only way to make progress in anything involving humans.

Obviously this piece of advice is in tension with the prior piece. (You may be wondering, well, when do you make a change and when do you stay at it?) All I can tell you is: this is the right question. And a lot of experience at trying both tacks will help you develop better instincts over time about which is the right approach in any given circumstance. As Lori says, "You may not realize that you have good ideas and a lot of the resources and answers within you. Don't be the child who waits for the adult to tell them what to do."

7. *Evaluate those options you've been keeping open.* Remember, holding options open keeps you in limbo and may make you anxious. Ask yourself what options you're holding open right now and why, and for how much longer are you going to do that? Also, who

decides which of these options is best for you? What would happen if you closed off most of the possibilities by moving in a particular direction? If you were guaranteed that whichever option you picked, it would work, which one would you pick? Try not to let external definitions of "the right job" or "the right person" come into this. There are exceedingly happy people doing jobs you have never heard of and might never dream of doing, and there are exceedingly happy people having relationships you would never conceive of. None are inherently right or wrong. You do you. But get on it!

8. *Form your own opinions.* As my former Stanford colleagues Bill Burnett and Dave Evans, the guys behind the number one bestselling book *Designing Your Life*, would say, these are the years to develop your "Worldview" (your theory of how the world works) and your "Workview" (your theory of what work means to you). The sooner you can begin to form a sense of what you value and believe in, and what matters to you and what does not, the sooner you get clarity on which ideas and choices you want to get behind. So, get comfortable saying phrases like *What matters most to me is . . . I'd like to structure my life around . . . I'm trying to grow in these ways . . . I feel most productive doing . . . I really enjoy creating . . . I'd like to live in a world where . . .* At first, you're going to feel weird, like you're talking the way much older people talk. And that's exactly the point.

9. *Share with those with whom you feel safe.* As you make a big choice to get out of neutral—personally or in terms of work—it's incredibly helpful to have a few people in your corner because not everyone will be. When you decide on a path forward, tell the few people who will support you no matter what. Your very best friend, your loving and nonjudgmental relative, or that awesome high school teacher, coach, or mentor—that person who believed in you and wanted to support you and had no ownership over what you did and was just always there to care about you and cheer you on. I call these folks your "trusted others."

Before the larger crowd of friends and family gets wind of your plan, develop an elevator pitch to describe it—because people will have questions, and ideally your elevator pitch will shut them up or at least slow them down:

- Show up with agency, with a voice that demonstrates clarity, strength, and calmness. (*I've decided . . .*)

- Inject your sense of self and/or your values. (*Because I've always known X about myself . . . Because I've always loved . . . Because I believe so much in . . . Because I want to try . . .*)

- Define your next step clearly. (*For the next eighteen months I'm going to get my certificate in X/I've decided to move to X and do Y/I want to let you know I am in a relationship with X . . .*)

- And because defense is often the best offense (*I know this may not be what you had in mind for me . . .*)

- Then end with a request for support. (*But I hope I can count on you to support my decision/believe in me/love me regardless.*)

Prime your trusted others to be there for you to respond to whatever fallout comes. Maybe they can pick up the phone proactively and talk your parents off the ledge. It might even give them pleasure to do so.

10. *Change your relationship with your parents.* Lori and I agree that a true signal of adulthood is whether you can be an adult instead of a child with your parents, because changing your relationship with your parents moves you along in life in a really significant way. So, yeah, it's time. (It's hard, I know! But it's time. And I'm here with this entire book to support you in this. Don't forget that.)

The hard question is of course *how to change your relationship with your parents.* And although you may hope they simply start treating you like an adult, the hard answer is *it's actually all on you*, because you can't change someone else, so your relationship with your parents won't change until YOU bring something different to it. The good and even miraculous thing is that once you *do* show up as an adult with them, they will most likely start treating you as an adult (or have a tantrum about your trying to be an adult, which is them acting like a child, so . . .). So, Lori would ask, "What are *YOU* gonna do differently to change the way they interact with you?" Lori recommends you start by talking to them like one adult talks to another. (They're not going to instantly become completely different people. But they'll hear you in a different way.)

It may be that you're still childlike in the sense that you're just continuing to let them handle everything, and they show no signs of stopping, but you're starting to realize it's problematic. If this is the dynamic, I recommend you ask for a time to talk with them (that'll signal to them it's something important) then say, *Okay, folks, thank you for all you've done to get me to this point. Now it's time for me to do more for myself, and I have some thoughts on where we could start. . . .*

Or you may be showing up as a child in that you blame your parents for things that happened in the past, such as expressing to them that the reason you're having trouble launching is that they didn't do XYZ or did too *much* of XYZ, instead of taking ownership for your life. If you're thinking, *My parents won't let me do this* or *My parents made me go to law school*, that's the child still protesting against their parent. Lori says you need a different relationship with them where you aren't wanting something from them that they can't give you (like going back and changing the way they raised you, which is impossible for them to do). She says your parents can still give you a lot though, especially when they're not the target of rage. She encourages you to figure out *your* life, and talk about what *you* want to do *now*. Being in a fight with your parents about the past is the very definition of stuck.

Adulting means doing your own thing, and inherent in that is the strong likelihood that you will disappoint people you love to a small or even large extent. You should flat out accept that you may disappoint your parents. This may sound glib or flippant of me, but I do not mean it that way. We are nearing the middle part of this book, and this message is the hinge on which the whole argument of the book turns. Your task is to examine your fear around that and let it go, because it's *your life*. Yes, a piece of you wants to live up to whatever vision they have always had of what your life would be. But what you want out of this life is always more important/significant than what someone else wants it to be about. I'll go so far as to say that doing what's right for you—even if they threaten to never speak to you again—is the number one sign of adulting. I encourage you to ask yourself these questions: *Whose judgment do I most fear? What would the fallout look like were I to disappoint them? What would I do? How would I cope? How would it feel to be doing that thing I know I really want to be doing, even if it meant I lost their support?*

11. *Be ready to fail, and try again.* Life is not an all or nothing test. There is no cutoff after which the powers that be say, *Nope, too bad so sad, you failed.* Every day offers a new chance. Making and owning your own decisions is an ever-ongoing process. You're discovering then becoming who you are, allowing yourself to evolve and try different things and not get stuck in labels. You balance that with figuring out what remains consistent—how you want to move through the world. As I've mentioned before, there is no failure, because there is no one right path. There are experiences and what you learn from them, and more experiences and more lessons, and you keep trying to be the person you want to be—and you keep going.

   Stefania, whom you'll meet more fully later in this chapter, launched an extremely successful company when she was forty, despite not having any money or a business degree, and here's how she says she did it: "It's because I had failed at so many things. I failed at pursuing a career in my major. I failed at finances thanks to college credit cards. Failed at negotiating my salaries. Failed at being truthful about my wants and needs in relationships. Failed at my marriage. Failed at trusting my instincts. Failed at sticking to diets. You name it, I failed it. And yet, at the age of forty, I was still standing. And I knew that failing with a new company would be the least scary or life-impacting thing out of all these other failures. But then the company took off like a rocket. My cofounders and I were *right* about a problem that needed solving. That gave me the confidence to look at life in a new way. I thought I had to have it all figured out at twenty. Definitely by thirty. Nuh-uh. Failure not only taught me resilience, but it taught me to never stop thinking about what's next." Dear reader, Stefania didn't leave many potions unused! She drank them up. And now she says this, "Every time I have stepped even just a toe toward any discomfort, good things have happened. I hope that my kids get how important failure is sooner than I did. Yes, I tackled the finances, ditched the marriage, figured out what I wanted in a relationship, learned to trust myself, lost eighty pounds, and almost a decade later I have an award-winning business. When I was twenty, I wish someone had told me to try everything and not be afraid of failing. It's the only way to figure out what you're supposed to do."

12. *Accept your lack of control.* If you were in charge of most things, then you could decide precisely what to do for your job, where to live, with whom to share your life, whether and when to have kids, and so on. But, you're not in charge of most things. The way your life unfolds will be heavily influenced by chance, luck, and other people's decisions and choices. Your task is to walk the path of your life knowing that you will get hit from the left and right by stuff out of your control. Some of those hits will knock you down and you'll decide, *Well, that was a disaster,* and you'll take a different path as a result. Some of those hits you'll bounce back from stronger and more determined on that very path. Some of those hits will turn out not to be hits but nudges that open you to something completely new and wonderful. Accept your lack of control and trust that you have what it takes to keep going no matter what. Adults exert their agency knowing that they live and work within complex systems that have lives and cultures and functions of their own.

13. *Hustle.* By hustle I mean get out there and make it happen. My former student Lexi Butler, now thirty-two years old, has devoted

her career to the PR, compliance, and privacy side of tech at NetApp, Airbnb, Facebook, and Twitter, where she counseled managers on how to behave more equitably and coached young professionals on how to squeeze the juice out of their experience. Her advice on hustling? "My career has gone through multiple remixes but the foundation is still the same. I work extremely hard to either get better at what I am doing or to get out as smoothly as possible. You have to have the grit and the tenacity to take ownership of your life and your possibilities. Have the informational interviews, go to a therapist, talk to friends, think about your strengths, but if you don't put things into action, nothing will ever come of it. Do the work. This freedom isn't free."

14. *Begin to cultivate that deep, abiding sense of who you are, no matter what.* I call my son Sawyer's high school friends "The Elephants" because of the sound of their voices and bodies booming against the ceiling and walls of our home. One of them told me, "What I do to enjoy myself is based on my body and athleticism, so as I get older what am I going to do? I won't be a cool skater anymore and I'll just be some old dude. I'm going to sit there and rot." Another "elephant" then replied, "You have to find sources of happiness that aren't just based in some external thing that could go away at any time, like your body, or some ultimately self-destructive habit—the degenerative shit—but an internal happiness." And to both I'd say, it's making plans that are stable no matter what, because you know who you are no matter what. I've always been a people person who wants my work to be about helping people. I've tried to help people by being a lawyer, a university administrator, an activist, a writer. But I also wanted to be a singer who moved people with my words and voice, and a broadcast journalist who moved people with my words and voice, and an elected policymaker who moved people with my words and voice. I never did those things for a living. But I kept the spirit of those ideals inside of me—use your words and voice to help people—and I've brought that to every single thing that I did choose to do. When you take you with you, wherever you go and regardless of what happens, you'll be all right.

DON'T JUST TAKE MY WORD FOR IT

It sucks to be stuck—stuck in the second tier when the jobs go to first-tier people, stuck trying to start a family when it just isn't happening, stuck in the wrong grad school program, stuck in a bad relationship, or stuck in a complicated family dynamic. These are the stories you'll read next. But it feels absolutely amazing to drink your potions and get out of neutral, which is what happens in all but one of these stories. (I included the outlier because hearing what "still largely stuck but working on it" sounds like may inspire you in its own way, too.)

MEET MICHAEL—Hustling His Way out of Neutral

It is early morning when Michael calls me. He is in his midthirties, a vice president at a company in corporate America. His wife, Michelle, is in the senior leadership at my gym, and when Michelle heard me talking about writing this book she suggested that Michael would be a good person to talk to because his trajectory toward adulting entailed a lot of hustling.

As Michael and I talk, he is getting ready to go into the office before taking off on an international flight later that day. His wife is at work. His fourteen-month-old son is with the caretaker nearby. Around him, I can hear the soundscape of his family home: dogs woofing, the clatter of tumbling Tupperware and baby gear. The place he is in now must feel tranquil compared to the homes he grew up in, where his three siblings and numerous stepsiblings chased their interests under the watch of his divorced parents and their partners, who were lower-middle class and struggled at times to make ends meet. We're chatting today so that I can understand how he got from that childhood to this adulthood.

Michael's parents grew up in the Brooklyn projects but established their family lives in Milford, Connecticut, a coastal town between Bridgeport and New Haven. Education had been their ticket out of the projects, yet education took them only so far. His mother was accepted to Yale, but couldn't afford to attend. His father didn't have money for college either, but fought tooth and nail to get an education by starting in community college and eventually earning a degree in civil engineering.

"For my dad, it didn't matter where we went to college as long as we went.

He would always say, 'School is an important opportunity. Take full advantage of it.'" Michael did work hard and was a high achiever in elementary and middle school, earning straight As and making big plays on sports teams. He was naturally competitive and driven. "I kind of had a chip on my shoulder," he tells me. Then came high school. Freshman year, nothing seemed to come easily anymore. Balancing homework and sports was challenging in a way it hadn't been before. Michael's transition from childhood to adolescence proved a tough one.

"Getting a job at sixteen was the best thing that ever happened to me," Michael says. "It allowed me to balance my priorities." Tackling work and school simultaneously turned out to be a happy tandem for Michael, so he chose to go to Northeastern University in Boston because of its unique work integration program known as "co-op." Starting sophomore year, Northeastern undergraduates are required to alternate six months of academic study and six months of professional work for the duration of their time in college. Michael started out as a premed major, then switched to finance and accounting with a minor in biology. Northeastern has a global network of employers, spanning almost every industry, that are eager to hire well-trained college grads. By senior year Michael had lined up a post-graduation position with the accounting firm PricewaterhouseCoopers (PwC). He was bartending in Boston to build up his savings when life decided to put a wrinkle in his *best-laid plans.*

Spring semester of his senior year while at work, Michael got wind that the Swiss investment banking company UBS had booked an exclusive recruiting event at the bar. Only students from the Ivy League school up the road (Harvard) were invited. He rearranged his schedule to be able to work the party, and he hid copies of his résumé in one of the cubbies on his side of the bar. After the cocktails and glad-handing were over and all the Harvard seniors had gone back to their side of the Charles River, one of the guys in a suit who'd run the event approached the bar to hand Michael a big fat tip. "I don't want your tip," Michael told him. "I want to meet your HR recruiter and hand her my résumé."

The HR recruiter would one day become a major mentor to Michael, but that night she promised only to put his résumé in the slush pile. Still, she'd liked his moxie and passed the résumé along to colleagues when she got back to the office. Someone decided to give him a chance. "After a grueling, rapid-fire round of interviews called 'Super Day,' I was one of eighteen students who were hired to work at UBS straight out of undergrad, and the only one who wasn't graduating from a so-called Tier One school. My nickname on the trading floor was 'Tier Two.'" Tier Two would go on to be hired by a hedge fund customer of UBS in California, and get an MBA at UCLA before he'd make a shift to Google, where his career would span ten years, three promotions, and the release of a Virtual Reality/Augmented Reality (VR/AR) system. We're on the phone together two weeks after the consumer electronics company HTC recruited him to be their newest vice president. He is about to be flown out to Taiwan to present his strategy to CEO Cher Wang. He will sit alongside twenty-four other HTC leaders whom the CEO has selected for being crucial to the company's success. Next week is his thirty-fifth birthday.

Michael has agency in spades. He knows what he wants, and he will fashion an opportunity for himself out of whatever ingredients he can find around him. It was agency that made him switch from premed to finance and accounting for his undergraduate major. Agency made him rearrange his work schedule so he could work the bar when the Harvard students and UBS came calling. And agency led him to make choices in furtherance of what he wanted for himself as he rose up the corporate ladder. But more than agency has led to Michael's success. He has done a lot of thinking about that.

"Being able to talk to anyone on their level has been crucial," he tells me. "Being authentic, empathetic, and inclusive has been key. I actually care about the well-being of my team members, and that turns out to be an asset in the workplace, because success only emerges from a healthy team environment. Nobody on my team ever feels that their voice isn't being heard. Everybody in the room is accountable."

Michael sees accountability as the outcome of a linear process that starts with empathy. When you empathize with someone, truly care about who they are and where they're coming from, and demonstrate that with active listening, Michael says, it allows the other person to be authentic. This leads to the "trust/non-trust stage," and ends with accountability, which in its simplest form is reliability: *Do you do what you say you're going to do?* The most valuable skill in this process is active listening, Michael says. "To create a shared vision, you have to actively listen," and this principle applies whether you're working on a team to drive the success of a company or whether you're cultivating a social community that will help you live your best life. And active listening is a key skill for building relationships you can rely on in any context.

"I'm successful because I can talk with my wife about the amount of travel I have to do for work." I relate to what Michael is saying, because for the entirety of our kids' lives Dan has been the primary parent (with a lot of help from my mom) while I held down a busy full-time job. I feel both lucky and grateful. "I'm successful because I get to give my kid a bath when I come home from work, and it's the best fifteen minutes of my day. It's never going to be competitiveness that will be the thing that makes you successful, because success often has nothing to do with winning. Relationships are everything to success."

I ask him about the role of failure. As we'd talked through the details of Michael's upward career trajectory, he'd first said that he ended up moving to California to work at Google because he "wasn't in love" with his work as a trader and decided to finally act upon his desire to be in tech. But once we began discussing the importance of failure, he revealed more of that story to me. He tells me that when he left UBS he didn't make the move for tech, and he didn't make the move solo; he was actually headed for a different investment bank and his girlfriend was going to move out to California with him. This was the first step toward them getting married, getting the house, and having kids, he tells me. "My career goals consumed my focus. I was sure my goals would carry us into the future we desired." But that future never came to be.

"I failed in that relationship because I projected myself onto her. I wasn't really listening to what her career goals were. I was a passive listener, always thinking about the next thing I wanted to say," Michael tells me. "She wanted to be an actress, and when she came to me to discuss her taking the risk of a career shift, my response was, 'Why are you talking about acting? You graduated with a degree in veterinary services.'" She left him. As he told me that story I got a much clearer idea of where Michael's empathy and active listening came from. And how humbling it must have been for someone accustomed to making things happen to come up short on the home front.

We finished our conversation and hung up. Hours later, I was making lunch plans and my phone rang. I recognized Michael's area code and answered the call. This time, Michael's voice came to me strong against the background of traffic noise. Turns out Michael had kept thinking about failure as he finished his pre-business-trip tasks at home. He was thinking about it as he packed his briefcase. And he was thinking about the relationship between failure and success as he got into his car, mounted his cell phone to the dashboard, and called me as he headed for the airport.

"There's a failure I didn't mention that should be included," Michael said. "So, I left investment banking to work at Google in their mobile division and then switched to virtual reality, but I need to tell you why. A few years after moving to California I met Michelle, the woman who would become my wife. A few years later we decided to start a family, but we went through three years of fertility issues and procedures. These issues led to multiple miscarriages and one pregnancy ended in a termination. My motivation for transitioning from mobile products at Google into VR/AR was the idea of creating my own family in an escapist environment. I wanted to enter a virtual reality space where I could have a child and the family I always wanted, even if it wasn't real."

He told me about how dark things had gotten for him and his wife in real life. They both were repeatedly undergoing treatments with outcomes that left them feeling powerless, which made them rigid and controlling in other areas of their lives. This meant their friends no longer wanted to be around them, so with every miscarriage, their grief and loss were compounded by the loss of friends. There are a lot of pauses in our conversation, and I thank Michael for opening up to me.

Michael's work in virtual reality didn't sate his craving to be a father. Their IVF doctor urged them to consider adoption as a way of just letting go. "We did a few adoption seminars, learned about the process, and signed up with an adoption lawyer out of LA who told us it could be a few years to find a baby that had no drugs in its history, which was our stipulation. We said to ourselves, *Cool, no problem, we don't think we'll end up going with adoption anyway.*" Two months later, Michael and Michelle got a call late one night. "It was like, *There's a woman going into labor in LA. You've been chosen to be the adoptive parents of her baby. You have seven hours to get here now if you want this baby. If you want to do it, it's time.*" They knew nothing about the birth mother or the baby. They dropped their Jack Russell dogs off at Michelle's parents' house and drove through the night from the Bay Area to LA. When they arrived at the hospital the baby was three hours old and in the NICU (neonatal intensive care unit, which is for struggling newborns but also for those without parents). They met the birth mother, signed the papers, and took their son Jackson home.

There's more. My first conversation with Michael was a few years ago, and so I wanted to circle back for an update. Michael is now thirty-seven years old and vice president of ecosystems at a global bank, where he's working hard to make point-of-sale lending easier for regular consumers like you and me. (Picture a way of purchasing goods that is as easy as using a credit card, but that comes with a much lower interest rate.) Jackson is now a happy, healthy three-and-a-half-year-old, and the big brother to baby Chase, who is just over a year old. "Once we had Jackson we assumed that we weren't going to have our own baby. The weight was lifted off our shoulders." Michael and Michelle stopped thinking about conceiving a baby and focused on the baby in their arms, on each other, and on rebuilding a happier life, given the toll the IVF years had taken on them. "When Michelle got pregnant we were so excited yet not excited because we thought something would go wrong as had happened too many times before. The fourteen-week genetic testing went fine, but we were still not excited. We finally got excited at about twenty weeks when we could really say, *Okay, this baby is going to be born healthy.* When you've been beaten up so many times, you expect the worst. And when the worst doesn't happen you don't get excitement; you get four and a half months of thinking the world is going to collapse and fall apart on you."

I wanted to share Michael's story with you because I was drawn to how he hustled to create the opportunities he wanted for himself, how he chose to derive lessons from the wrinkles in his best-laid plans, and how he deploys what he's learned in order to help others whether in the workplace or on the home front. "It took a while for Michelle and me to figure out how to be open with our adoption story with people we barely know. What we learned was, *Whatever, it doesn't matter.* We now see that our story inspires hope and optimism in folks that might be on a similar journey. Once you learn to let go of the stress and control and start allowing the environment around you to feed your soul, amazing things can happen."

MEET JIM—Stepping Off a Fast Track That Was Going Nowhere

Jim's parents emigrated from Korea before he was born and raised him near St. Louis. His life from there was on a fast track. He graduated from high school a year early, majored in public health at Johns Hopkins University, and landed a spot at Harvard School of Dental Medicine. All according to plan. But in 2000, toward the end of his second of four years in the dental program, he began to feel deeply unsure about what he was doing and where he was headed. "Dental school felt like a gravitational pull taking me in a direction that I didn't like. And if I did nothing, it would keep pulling me there."

Looking back, he realizes he first began to feel uncomfortable when it was time to figure out what to do after college. "I hadn't been exposed to a lot of different paths and hadn't sought out all the different options. I knew about professional schools. Knew I liked science. Figured I'd get a graduate degree." Medical school held no interest but "something about health care was interesting." So, the choices, it seemed, were: dentistry, chiropractic, or podiatry. "If I'm being honest, it was about a good lifestyle and a stable career, and between teeth, back problems, and feet, teeth seemed the most appealing."

Once made, the decision brought relief. "I was like, *Great, I'm just going to do it. I don't have to think about it. It's a laid out, regimented process.* Then I got into Harvard. And that validated my direction, because you don't say no to Harvard. So, I went." He enjoyed the first year, which was science on steroids. "You just learn about the body. Very theoretical. Super interesting." In the winter of the second year he got his first glimpse of actual dentistry. Standing there with his hand inside someone's mouth, he felt…nothing. "I started realizing that if I'm not excited about this now, how am I going to feel one year from now, or in five or ten years?" Then the guilt set in. All the money his parents had spent, all the time he'd invested, not to mention that "everyone" knew what he was studying and where. All of that strengthened the gravitational pull compelling him to keep with the program. Plus, he didn't have a different plan. But as he got to the end of his second year, the pull felt not only inevitable but unbearable.

Jim left dental school. (Please note, there's nothing wrong with dental school. It just wasn't the right place *for Jim.* As with me and corporate law.) He went on a bit of a whirlwind exploration into the unknown to figure out what he really wanted to be doing with his life. He's now a forty-three-year-old vice president at BetterLesson, a New England–based company that helps K–12 teachers level up their game. He has a wife and a son, and he is deeply happy.

More than twenty years after sidestepping a fast-tracked life that wasn't right for him, Jim is on the phone with me. "I can still feel the pit in my stomach when I summon the memory of that gravitational pull and what my path was going to be if I stayed in dental school. I couldn't imagine feeling that every day for the rest of my life. The hard (and right) question to have been asking myself was, *Is dentistry the right thing for me?* But I couldn't bring myself to ask myself that. So, I asked easier questions—questions I could handle thinking about and that I thought would make sense to family and close friends—questions like,

Am I burned out? And, *Do I just need to take a break?* But I'd been on a pretty predictable path all the way through life, so people were thrown even by my saying I might need to take some time off. A close friend from college said, 'What are you *talking* about?' Mom was like, 'What do you mean take a break? Go finish, then start working.' There just wasn't understanding. They chalked it up to me being a bit frivolous and wanting to play, versus the reality, which is that I was really unsure about what was going on. I'll own a lot of that, because I didn't open up to them. I was worried about their reaction. I didn't even have an answer to the logical question, 'What else would you do?' I just wanted to not do it, give myself space, and see what would happen."

The hardest person to convince was the one to whom he owed so much: his mom. Jim's father had passed away while Jim was in college. He and his mother were—and are—extremely close. "All my life and still to this day I'm a momma's boy. I love my mom dearly, and I respect what she says a lot. If she wants me to do something I'm generally taking care of it for her. This was the first and maybe only deviation in my life from that."

His feelings boiled down to guilt, betrayal, and fear. "I felt guilt, because I was and am still today appreciative of everything she and my late father did for us. I felt a bit of betrayal because I'd agreed to a plan and I was trying to go off of it. And I felt scared because when we're doing a plan that we both agreed to, there's a shared risk, and if it doesn't work out, it's oh well, we tried. But this was all me going out on my own limb. If it didn't work out, what a fool I would be. It felt really scary to own this decision. What is the reaction going to be? How does this change how my mom views who I am and how people are going to view who I am? I felt that stepping away from dental school was going to be really, really high stakes for something I was both sure about yet not sure about, if that makes sense."

Somewhere along the way Jim went from trying to convince his mom that she should let him take time off, to giving himself permission to do what he needed even if his mom didn't quite understand it. It took a series of conversations over a few months as his second year in dental school was drawing to a close. "What I call Phase One was where I lightly introduced the idea of taking time off, and she quickly shut it down. 'No. Can't do that.' But my need for a break didn't go away and I knew I had to bring it up again. Phase Two was: 'I think it'd be good to take some time off.' She came back at me with the guilt—the *I invested in you* angle. And when the need still didn't go away, I raised it again. We were now at Phase Three. She said, 'Why do you want to do this? Just finish.' Which led me to say that I was having bigger doubts. 'Then what else do you want to do?' To which I didn't have an answer, and *that* didn't really go over that well." He laughs. Jim was pretty good at powering through tough things, but the gnawing feeling of discomfort associated with being stuck on a path he did not want to be on was not going away. It was growing. With the wisdom that comes from experience, Jim now says, "If I'd had the skills to have the direct conversation with my mom, I would have. If I'd had those skills, I also probably wouldn't have been this far down the wrong path before saying something."

With the green light, or at least not the red light, from his mom, Jim took a leave from dental school, and "finally had the fun of asking myself, *What are the things I've always wanted to do but couldn't do because I was on a pretty rigid path?*" He calls it "The Year of Randomness." He competed in a Tae Kwon Do tournament in Kentucky (and won a gold medal), backpacked in New Zealand, taught test prep, and became a paid 'background actor,' aka extra, in Hollywood, ending up in *The Princess Diaries*, starring Mandy Moore and Anne Hathaway.

At the end of the year "off," he'd experienced a good amount of unwinding but hadn't done much reflecting on what he wanted out of his career. He extended his leave one more year (keeping his options open) and reached out to his dean of students from college, who suggested he come back and work in admissions for a while. "I instantly loved being back on a college campus. There's an energy there. Intellectual growth. An exciting time of life. A spark. Something about that setting inspired me more than I ever felt with dentistry. I didn't know what exact role I would want on a campus. But that feeling of inspiration was the feeling I needed to feel."

The terrifying day we call 9/11 happened while Jim was working in admissions at his alma mater, Johns Hopkins. Although different from the COVID-19 pandemic in many ways, 9/11 was similar in that, for many, it led to a reckoning about what really matters to them. For Jim, "9/11 hammered home the importance of people coming together, and that helping to build community is an important part of what I want to do." He was twenty-four when 9/11 happened. He felt super clear that he wanted to stay on a campus forever and work with students. By then he knew family and friends would think it was a ridiculous decision, but he went for it anyway. He pursued a one-year master's in education (back at Harvard), then became assistant dean of first-year students at Bowdoin College in Brunswick, Maine.

Then a woman a few years into her role as dean of freshmen at Stanford—me—put out a job description for an assistant dean and Jim jumped at the opportunity. That's how I know him. And I hope you can see why I thought his life trajectory would make him the perfect person to inspire freshmen to think about what they really wanted out of life. After three wonderful years he left us and went to get his MBA, which led to work in a number of different companies, and ultimately his present position at BetterLesson in Rhode Island. The random jumps from being stuck to unstuck, from avoiding the gravitational pull toward the wrong thing to feeling the flow of the right thing, all of those steps make sense when you look back on your decisions in life. But if you'd told a twenty-year-old Jim that he would go to dental school but quit, get a medal in martial arts, act in a few movies, become a university dean, get an MBA, and help lead a company devoted to supporting teachers, he would have just laughed at you.

Now forty-four years old, Jim knows that in the fight over dental school, his mom just wanted to make sure he would be in a good, successful, stable space in life and was worried because she saw her son turning away from a good opportunity without a well-formed plan. "I see how that was tough for her. But still, her initial reaction of trying to shut it down versus explore it was not what I needed at the time." He knew deep down she would accept and support the change eventually, but in the moment he also knew he needed more than his mom was able to give him, even while holding tremendous love for her. Being able to hold both of those truths in your head and heart is an important part of how you get out of neutral.

MEET STEFANIA—Exiting a Relationship and Entering a Better Phase of Life

Stefania Pomponi is a fifty-one-year-old straight biracial woman. Her mom is Korean American, born in Hawaii, and her father is Italian, from Italy. She got her undergraduate degree in art history at Loyola Marymount University in 1991, and after a career in the sales and marketing side of tech and then another career as a public school teacher in an under-resourced district, she and her best friend co-created the field now known as social media influencer marketing. So, on the one hand, she found meaningful work for herself and made her mark in that part of her life with apparent ease—but she also stayed in a bad relationship throughout her twenties and thirties, and it's that aspect of stuck-ness that I wanted to know about.

Stefania and Matt met at a club in Northern California when they were twenty-two. It was 1992. She was a recent college grad temping in Silicon Valley. He was an entry-level tech engineer. They both loved the underground music scene and kept spotting each other at raves. When they finally worked up the nerve to introduce themselves to each other, the first thing Matt needed to know was whom Stefania was voting for. It was a presidential election year. When she replied "Bill Clinton," he hugged her. They loved the same music. They loved to dance. They began to love each other. Eighteen months later they got married. Eighteen *years* later, with three kids in tow, she ended it. It was many years later than she feels she should have.

I think it's safe to say that Stefania was looking for stability and reliability and did not want to repeat the pattern of divorce that she'd seen growing up. Her mother's first husband (Stefania's father) had cheated. Her mother's second husband had serious mental health issues that would one day be diagnosed as bipolar disorder. Her mother's third husband, whose name is Tom, was and is a keeper. Her mom met Tom when Stefania was sixteen and married him when Stefania was nineteen. Stefania calls him her stepfather. "He's one of those free spirit types and completely on the level. Treats everyone with respect and courtesy. I appreciated that as a teen—he was a great role model and sounding board. I could go to him with problems or questions. There was no judgment. Ever." And he would turn out to be there for Stefania when it counted most.

Stefania learned young that she did not necessarily measure up in the eyes of others. When she attended preschool in her father's home country, kids threw sand in her face. Her biracial features were off-putting to some of the other children, and she was being raised bilingually, which meant her Italian wasn't as fluent as the other preschoolers'. "By preschool I knew I was different than the other kids." Later, a lifelong involvement in ballet was abruptly ended in the sixth grade when a new teacher told her she had the wrong build. "She told me I wasn't the right shape to be partnered. What she meant was, I was too fat." Stefania nursed this wound for two years until the movie *Breakin'* turned her on to hip-hop. The same studio that had rejected her now offered a "Street Dance" class taught by a different teacher. When she walked up to class on the first day and "Billie Jean" was blaring from the speakers, she knew she was in the right place.

So, it was a big deal to be feeling really at home in the NorCal rave scene, and meet a guy she could bond with over Chicago House DJs, Eric B. & Rakim, and the Beastie Boys. "Matt was—is—a really sweet guy," she tells me. "He's the son of Berkeley hippies who raised him Buddhist. He has a kind and loving heart and good intentions. Believes that karma is a real thing. He created electronic music and had musical aspirations. I liked that he was creative." No signs that anything was going to go wrong.

When they conjoined their lives, Matt had a good job as a systems administrator and an excited outlook on life. Stefania had a degree in art history and was working in sales and marketing for a Silicon Valley company. But Matt didn't seem to know how to (or want to) be an adult partner. He avoided the harder bits like bill paying and figuring out how to plan for the future. He sidestepped daily chores like shopping, cooking, cleaning, and laundry. "We fell into traditionally gendered roles even though we both worked. I think we never really had a conversation about it."

Matt also came and went autonomously, as if his actions only impacted himself. "And he'd just blow things off. He'd say, 'I'm coming home from work at six.' And six p.m. would come and go. Eight p.m. would come and go. Ten p.m. would come and go. There was never a reason. I told myself he must be incapacitated, lying dead in a ditch, that's why he hasn't called and isn't returning my calls. We missed so many plans—a concert, the ballet, dinner with friends—because he didn't come home."

Over the years they attempted counseling three times, the first after about six years of marriage. "In counseling we talked about upkeep of the house and came up with strategies to make the work of the marriage more equitable. I was raised with chores, and Saturday was cleaning day. I like things tidy. He was raised in a much freer way, with not as much importance placed on the functional running of a household."

In therapy, Matt said he didn't like to be told what to do, and didn't want to be held accountable to any schedule. "He had a rebel nature that superseded any manners or propriety. My point was, 'You can be a rebel, but still show up for things when you know you have to.' I'd say, 'Take responsibility. I mean, be playful, retain that spirit, but we also have adult responsibilities.' It became clear that he didn't want to grow up. That's all great when you're twenty-two. Not always awesome when you're forty-two."

Matt wanted children. But Stefania wanted to know that she could count on him first. "I told him, 'We'll talk about kids when we're thirty,'" and that bought her a bunch more years. She used that time to get a teaching credential and taught children who lived in the inner city, were often bilingual like she was, and lacked things as basic as pencils, paper, and books in their poorly funded public school. When Stefania turned thirty, little had improved on the home front, so she was in no hurry to start a family. Thirty came and went. Thirty-one came and went. But the clock was ticking. In 2002, at the end of her third year of teaching, Stefania was thirty-two and gave birth to their first child, a daughter. She quit her teaching job and became a full-time stay-at-home parent. Two years later, their second daughter was born.

She and Matt had their second round of counseling in 2002 shortly after their first daughter was born. "Kids don't make it better—just different. We had a distraction from our situation. We could focus on them. This time in counseling I was holding a four-month-old baby in my lap. We were both not happy, and we were too co-dependent to get out of it. Even when you're unhappy there's some comfort in knowing you're not alone in your misery."

I ask her what changed her mind about having kids with Matt. "You revisit things so many times. Part of the reason I waited so long to have kids was I just felt I wasn't sure about this guy. The writing was already on the wall that he wasn't ready to be a responsible adult, and kids don't make things easier if your relationship is not already strong and you don't have tools to work things out. But I wanted them. And I was running out of time. It wasn't like a turning point where things were suddenly better."

Stefania was now doing all the parenting on top of doing all the household chores. She needed help and advice, and mommy blogs were becoming a thing. "I didn't want the books that were like, 'Just wear your baby, and do these three things, and the crying will stop immediately,' because that's an idealized view of parenting that I knew wasn't going to work for me. Sometimes you need to put the baby down. I'd begun to read the Craigslist parenting forums. They had real stories, which I wanted, because parenting was hard as shit. The forums said things like, 'I had a shitty day and I can't listen to my kid cry anymore and I'm home alone,' and I was like, 'Wow, this is real. I can relate.' Turned out many of those parents were writing on those forums to get traffic on their blogs, which were a super new thing then and they just seemed like online diaries. From a marketing perspective, I thought it was fascinating. From a storytelling point of view, too."

Stefania and Matt and their children were living in San Francisco by then, and living in a big city with babies was a whole new ball game. She figured other new parents were struggling, too, so she started a lifestyle blog from an urban standpoint called *CityMama*. "I wrote the parenting stories I wasn't hearing elsewhere. Like, 'How do you deal with groceries and a baby on the bus?' That gained some attention, which then launched the next phase of my career, being hired by AOL to write for their parenting site and eventually hiring bloggers for them, including my best friend, Cat. That was my first paid blogging job. In 2004, I had my second daughter and transitioned to working for Viacom/Nickelodeon. I had this series of amazing jobs. You were hired for the way you wrote, the connections you had, and how many connections you could drive to the content. I knew how to drive traffic. By 2005 and 2006, these major media companies started to figure out that parents are a huge money-spending demographic, and if you had compelling parenting content that attracted a lot of eyeballs, you could throw ads up against that content and sell a lot of shit. They hired bloggers at five dollars for a three-hundred-word post and at the time bloggers were happy to do that. If you could do five three-hundred-word stories a day, that's twenty-five dollars. If you're a stay-at-home parent, or you have a job but just wanted some running-around money, that was a good way to do it. And it helped you get your name out."

Thanks to blogging, Stefania's life became more public. But she remained extremely private about what she was going through with Matt. Her mom was nevertheless paying attention. "There was a pattern of my ex not being home because of work, or staying late at work. My mom saw me doing all the parenting work, being the one that was at home and doing all the things. That didn't sit well with her. She never overtly said, 'You should leave.' But she did say, 'When you start thinking *my marriage might not be the right thing* it's about three years before you actually do something about it.' She told me that when my first child was a newborn, then my three years turned into ten years."

I ask her how it felt *inside* her to be in a marriage that wasn't what she wanted. "I was unhappy and felt a lot of fear. The judgment of family, friends, and coworkers. The unknowns, like, what happens if I'm alone, will I be able to make it, where do I go, where will I live, who would support me?" She kept the details of her marriage private from even her closest friends. "I didn't want to disrespect him by airing dirty laundry. I just felt, 'Okay, every marriage has issues. Mine are maybe worse? More insurmountable?'"

She coped by bargaining with herself. She says, "I knew I was unhappy, but it was always, 'Well, if I can get through this, then I'll get to the next day.'" With my mom living in Hawaii, I would hold out for vacation time, thinking, *If I can get to Hawaii I won't have to think about being unhappy for two whole weeks.* I lived to escape."

In therapy her desire was to be thought of more often. "Any sort of a birthday present that wasn't an afterthought, or a Christmas present that wasn't purchased on Christmas Eve at nine p.m." Why didn't she think she deserved better than that? That's something she says she hasn't worked out fully, even today. "Coming from a divorced household, there was the pressure of *I have to make it work. At all costs. This has to work. We have to figure it out.* I've always felt glad and relieved that my mom made the choice to leave the bad situations of her first two marriages. I don't know why I couldn't apply that to my own. I wanted it to be different. I was going to break the pattern."

From 2006 to 2008, Stefania was a consultant to PR companies or brands who wanted to be connected to bloggers. "My goal was never to start a company. It was just to improve the connections between the brands and the bloggers because those connections weren't always good. The branding value of bloggers was a new frontier for marketing, but the bloggers were very savvy about their influence, and that situation made for some unsavoriness that was gross to me. It was my industry, and there was plenty of room to add a layer of professionalism and ethics. We began calling our bloggers 'influencers' and we began holding them accountable in exchange for much better payment, like one hundred dollars a post."

Advocating for the needs and rights of others may have contributed to a strengthening resolve within Stefania. She began to feel resistant in marriage counseling. "There was too much hurt, a lot of words spoken and not enough action shown. I was told to be patient. Let him make mistakes and not jump all over him for trying. He would hear my need for help as 'Oh, she needs help *when I'm available*.' Take laundry. If I asked for help it was because the laundry had already been sitting for days and I now needed to do more, but there was already laundry in the machine, so let's get it folded and put away. His thing was 'it would get done in its time.'"

By the third round of counseling Stefania was done. "I was there to go through the motions, quite honestly. I had already said all the things, and tried all the things. I knew that anything he was going to do to 'show appreciation' wasn't going to land. I was there to save face or performatively show I was trying to work on things." They separated for a few weeks in 2010, and in their reconciliation conceived their third child, a son. "But one day he just didn't come home at all and stayed away for days, and I didn't care." It was the summer of 2012. She had a rising third and fifth grader, and a sixteen-month-old baby.

This is where her stepdad Tom comes back into the picture. "I keep my cards close to the vest. I'd never told Tom how frustrated I was in my marriage." But he had always been a source of encouragement and support. Once in high school, when she had been saving to buy a used car (a 1982 two-door white Honda Civic hatchback), Tom had loaned her the last bit of money. She had set up a payment plan and she would come to him with coins in her hand to pay him on time. She knew if she came to him to say, "Hey, can I borrow $400," he would say yes with enthusiasm, and that was a comfort to her. But she didn't ever want to take advantage of Tom's generosity. So, she would come with handfuls of nickels, and slowly she paid off the loan.

One day in 2012 Tom asked her the question that would change everything. "I'd been more open than ever with my mom about my marriage, Matt's behavior, and my unhappiness. And that was enough for my mom. She must have talked to Tom. And Tom said, 'Are you staying because it's financial, because if so I'll take that worry away from you. If that worry is away from you, what are going to do?' And I was gone the next week. He truly gave me my life back in so many ways. I hope whatever my kids need, I'm in a position to be able to do that, too, cuz god damn I don't want them to spend ten years longer in a relationship than they have to."

This is why we need friends and family who have our back. They don't have to have all the money in the world. When their will and advocacy for us is strong, it can be the force we need to do what we've known for so long is right. "By then I was in a trance. I don't know how it happened actually. That was my mental state at that time. Unconscious. But conscious. My parents stepped in and did everything. My mom found a house a few towns away, they called the movers, the movers came and packed everything, moved us, unpacked everything. Years later I was finding things in random places."

I asked her how she actually made the decision to leave. "I think I had run out of ways to bargain my way out of staying. I finally had a hammer to the head. I realized if someone is not coming home that means they are so unhappy they don't want to be there. And I also felt rage that as a mother I could never do that and never *would* make that choice not to come home. He could do that because he knew I was reliable. But at the end of the day he was not a reliable person. That was the moment I was like, *Oh, okay. I'm not about this life anymore.*"

I ask how it *felt* in her body when she was rid of Matt. "Light. Like my feet were not touching the floor. So light. A relief that I can't even put into words. All of the things I had worried about and been fearful about and were holding me back were immediately gone. I felt fearless in that moment. Granted, I had the support of my parents, but all the other things I had worried about—external judgment and all the 'what ifs' were gone from my mind. I didn't care what people thought. I was out. It was like a jailbreak. It was a whole shift in my thinking. I had done the biggest 'what if,' the scariest thing, and nothing else mattered anymore."

It makes perfect sense to me that while Stefania had felt like she didn't matter in her marriage, simultaneously, in her professional life, she had been giving voice to others and ensuring *they* were rewarded for their efforts. After being a major presence in the mommy blogger space with her *CityMama* blog, and after being a consultant for major brands, in 2009 Stefania and her best friend, Cat, founded Clever Girls, a company that would ensure bloggers were paid fairly for the stories they wrote about products. This transformed both the blogging and marketing spaces, and the new field of social media influencer marketing was born. Their first client was Heather Thomson, who designed for Diddy's Sean Jean brand and for Beyoncé's and JLo's brands and would go on to be on the *Real Housewives of New York*. Back then Heather had launched her own shapewear brand called Yummie Tummie. She hired Clever Girls to get her brand connected to influencers. Stefania and Cat recommended to Heather that the marketing for her brand needed to be real women bloggers who were tired of having to suck their gut in all the time. "This included many body-positive and fat-positive influencers who weren't waiting for the mainstream to catch up with their desire to look fashionable and cute. Realizing what an untapped market this is, brands like Yummie Tummie had to change or they were leaving billions of dollars on the table. My company's role has always been to lift up influencers." The Clever Girls support for Yummie Tummie was a major success. From then on Heather Thomson embraced inclusive sizing.

Then, one night in early November 2013, fifteen months after she split from Matt, Stefania was up late reading Reddit after her kids had gone to bed, and she came upon a spate of intriguing yet vague posts about an event happening in San Francisco the week following. The posts reminded her of a Make-A-Wish event in Seattle she'd seen unfold, where a bunch of people came together in secret to make a dying child's dream come true. By now it was midnight, and she was trying to track down an email address for the Make-A-Wish Foundation. "If you're pulling an event together in SF, I'd love to help out any way I can," she wrote. Then she went to bed. At 8 a.m. she had a response. "Yes, this is us, we need help. A child named Miles wants to be Batman for the day but we're having trouble promoting it."

Stefania came to the rescue.

"At Clever Girls we'd been plugging along being the little agency that could, doing our good work behind the scenes, but we never had that one case study that lets you easily explain at a cocktail party what you do. I said to Make-A-Wish, 'Okay, you want to gain awareness and support for Miles's wish to be a superhero. You need help with promotion. The event is in eight days. We can definitely help you there. Let's create a unique hashtag.' So, we came up with #SFBatKid and we started with our own network of influencers. We said to them, 'Hey, you might be interested in helping kids, or you might be into superheroes, or into helping wishes come true. Can you share this tweet saying something amazing is going to happen in SF next week?' And that just exploded. In my initial conversation with the leader of Make-A-Wish she'd said, 'We're giving this child an experience doing different things in SF, and we're going to be making these stops and we'd like 30 people at each stop.' I said, 'Would you like to add some zeros to that?' The promo started happening purely on social media. They were seeing a thousand hits per second on their website on the second and third day. We did the social media. Apple stepped in to manage the PR. That was the week that Twitter went public, so they had other things going on, but we wanted the characters involved to be able to tweet during the day *as the characters* involved, you know, like as the Penguin. People already had those handles, but Twitter said, 'They haven't used those handles in years; you can have the handle now.' We told the story, and people felt something, and that's the key to making something go viral." Stefania had gotten unstuck from Matt, and now she was unsticking both the Make-A-Wish Foundation *and* Twitter. This girl was using her potions. This girl was on fire!

Stefania was forty-two by the time her marriage to Matt was all over. I ask what advice she would offer others in a similar situation. "The signs were there from the start that this was not who you needed to walk shoulder to shoulder with in this life. I was not paying attention. He had not lived on his own before we moved in together. That's definitely something that is a life experience everyone needs to have. Two, it was helpful to think about my mom saying when she thought about could her marriage survive, that it took her three years to make the decision. I hung on to that as a kind of permission to even think those thoughts. If I was thinking these things there was no need to rush to judgment, I could take my time. I'm grateful for that; it was like a crack in a door and all I had to do was step through it. Three, but at the same time I didn't listen to my gut and I did not trust myself. People say you have gut feelings for a reason. Yet so often we ignore them. Ever since then I've tried to pay attention to what my gut is telling me, cuz it's usually right. If we don't feel good about a situation or a person there's a reason; I mean, that's your body talking to you. I wish I had listened sooner. I spent ten years not listening to my gut and not trusting myself. That's a lot of time.

"Now I try to live like I don't have time to waste on things that don't serve me, including relationships. I've learned to trust myself and relearn what it's like to live on my own, and be okay with being alone. I'm not lonely in any sense. I don't feel a pressure to need a constant companion. Companionship is lovely, but I feel no external pressure to rush into it."

MEET BEN—In the Process of Getting Out from Under

Ben (not his real name) is a thirty-year-old straight biracial man (Asian/White) who lives in Tampa, Florida, with his parents. When my research assistant, Leigh, first spoke with him a few years back, he told her, "My sister and I are essentially prisoners in our mother's house." This felt incongruous to me and Leigh, because at the time Ben was in his late twenties and had already earned two graduate degrees. From outward appearances, it would seem that he was capable of achieving a good degree of independence.

As I was finalizing this book I checked back in with Ben, hoping that he'd been able to untangle himself at home and thinking I might put those lessons on the page for you. I learned that while in some ways he does have greater control over his life, in other ways he is as entrenched as ever in a restricting relationship with his parents. Ben's story is a reminder that when people in our lives are unwell, becoming unstuck ourselves can be especially painful and difficult to achieve.

In our initial conversation, Ben had characterized his situation as follows. "I have two graduate degrees. Two retirement accounts. I own my own condo here in Tampa that I rent out for extra income. I know how to invest money, address mail, write a check, file my taxes, drive a car, operate a computer, create a résumé, interview for jobs, and cook enough to survive. These areas of my life do not bother me as an adult. However, I do not feel like an adult at the moment because I still live with my parents. I lost my job, which set me back from my goal of moving out, but that's not the real reason why I can't leave. My mother is the biggest oppressive force in my life that keeps me from reaching for what I want to do. Exercising any agency over my life is like going through an emotional war, because she cannot be left alone." Why Ben's mother seeks to control Ben was unclear, but her impact on his agency has been extreme. He describes his life as being "on a leash." His father, who is seventy and on permanent disability, is "hands-off," neither involving himself nor intervening. Ben's mom is fifty-two. Whenever Ben has attempted to make a break for adulthood, his parents insisted that his idea was financially unsound. For example, after he did well at community college and wanted to attend the University of Florida, a two-hour drive away, they argued, "Why would you go there when the University of South Florida is right here? Why would you spend money on moving and on renting an apartment when you don't have to?" They seemed to have no understanding that a young adult might naturally yearn for greater opportunity and more independence even if that opportunity and independence cost some money. Years later, Ben bought a condo with his own savings, but they refused to let him live in it! "I was told it made no sense for me to live in my own place when the family could get income out of renting it. My parents are not that well-off. And they asked me, 'How do you expect us to pay for everything?' So, I didn't go to college two hours away. And I didn't move into the apartment I own. The 'financial efficiency' argument is their move when it comes to approving whether or not my sister and I can do something." In my early conversation with Ben, I noticed the language he used, noticed that he spoke of his parents "approving" whether or not he could do something, and I found this language odd for someone close to thirty years old. I realized that any psychologist reading what Ben said would deduce that however awful Ben felt about being on "a leash," the leash must have felt better to him than the alternative.

In our first conversation, Ben acknowledged that in some ways his mom's behavior is consistent with her upbringing in a multigenerational Taiwanese family. "She had four generations of her family in her house growing up. Coming here, she still has that mentality. And even though my childhood had many problems, I did enjoy being physically close to my grandparents and cousins. Familial support is a nice thing to have. I don't want my family to be gone. But, in my life, if I want the support of my parents, it comes with the cost of having a leash put on me. I have been turned into my family's secretary, tracking the payment of bills and completing any tasks that require communication with third parties like scheduling deliveries and appointments. The upside is, I know how to operate our family's household without them. But there is this layer of oppressive obligation that changes these tasks from 'everyday business that every adult has to do' to 'a list of demands from parent to child.'"

I want to pause here and be respectful of the cultural differences between how Ben's Taiwanese mother behaves versus the stereotypical American idea of independence. I am not critiquing cultures that rely on intergenerational interdependence in terms of living arrangements and financial support. What I *am* here to say, however, is that any person regardless of ethnicity or culture will wither psychologically if we do not have ownership over the basic choices a human makes in life—what to do for work, where to live, and with whom to share our lives. There is nothing wrong with the expectation that offspring will help support parents financially. But there *is* something wrong if that child, now an adult, has no life of their own because their life is servile to the life and choices of their parents. Adult children are not pets to be led on a leash or even servants. We can be respectful of generational hierarchy and cultural mores yet expect to be treated on a human level as adult equals.

As Ben and I talked more, I came to learn the painful price he paid for going "off leash": abandonment. When in his midtwenties he had approached his mom about wanting to move in with a friend, the retaliation was swift. "She went to my room, began to throw my stuff around, and talked about how she has all this space now that she can use. I don't need that in my life. If I went ahead and went to school away from home, oh boy, I wouldn't be able to focus on doing well in school because my mom has a complete meltdown every time she gets a whiff of me leaving." Here Ben is referring to what happened when he studied abroad in Germany and the UK while in college, and again when he took a seminar in the Czech Republic while in grad school. "Going to Germany was the first time I took decisive action on doing something I wanted to do toward my objectives. The day I was leaving, she woke up and treated me like I didn't even exist. She didn't even say hi." While abroad, he was hardly in touch with his mother; at most, they spoke once on Skype for a few minutes. "She generally doesn't acknowledge that I exist when I'm gone. She says talking to me would be 'too painful.'"

Those trips abroad furthered Ben's academic and professional interests, but he longed for his parents to respect the path he was on. "If my duties to my professional career and academic interests were put above my parents' knee-jerk reactions, I would feel the respect an adult deserves," he told me. But Ben's mother seemed to lack respect for every little thing he did. He said, "At Walgreens last Saturday, I picked up an item that I was thinking about buying, and right there in the aisle my mom screamed at me that I couldn't buy that because it was too expensive. I'm almost thirty. Do you know how degrading it is to have your mother yell at you in a Walgreens to put back a bottle of mouthwash because it's four dollars? A lot of my shopping tends to be online now. I just have to make sure I intercept the bill before my mom gets to it. She'll go through my mail, open my birthday cards, even discard something without knowing what it is. I go on Amazon and I pay eight dollars and thirty cents for the same mouthwash that was four dollars in the store because I can't go shopping without my mom tugging on my leash."

The one freedom Ben's parents gave him—and it was a big one—was the freedom to choose what he studied. He started off in business at community college, gravitated toward English in undergrad, and then received a master's degree in library science and a second master's in English/rhetoric writing and digital media studies, focusing on student empowerment. "Making my academic plan was the one thing that made me feel like my own person. That's why I like to connect other people to their academic path. If I could find freedom in my plan of study, then I can help other people find freedom in it, too." I relate to this idea big time, because after making a choice to be a corporate lawyer, where I was miserable, I pivoted to working in academia because I wanted to help the next generation make better choices than I had made. And yet, I found it ironic that Ben's research focused on agency and was centered on how to *give students agency* just as he was hoping his parents would give him agency. Having agency given to you is not how agency works. A person can take it away by keeping you on a leash, but they cannot give it to you. They can avoid standing in your way, but regardless of whether someone is in your way or whether there's absolutely nothing at all in your way, you have to seize your agency (your ability to make your own choices and take your own actions) for yourself.

When I circle back two years later to catch up with Ben as I'm finishing this book, I hear some great news. He received a full scholarship to law school and a second scholarship from the American Association of Law Libraries, owing to his master's degree in that field. He is halfway through his law degree, and is doing so well there that the faculty have approached him about teaching a class in legal research and writing. He's setting his sights on a judicial clerkship after law school—a very prestigious opportunity—and a possible career in bankruptcy law.

I ask about things with his mom. "Things are still tough at times, but I can say things have never been better, honestly." I ask him what changed. "After my interview with Leigh [my research assistant], one thing that kinda stuck with me was that if you have control over at least one aspect of your life—like when I separated my finances and got my own bank account, something I've guarded [and] which gives me a little bit of separation—it seems to help. After talking with Leigh, it got me thinking about other areas of my life where I could exert more control."

He decided to tackle his weight. (Weight hadn't come up in the first call, so I'd had no idea it was of concern to him.) "I've been overweight since kinder-garten, and since our last call I've lost one hundred and forty-three pounds." Wow. He did this by deciding to be in charge of what he ate, which provoked his mom, who "shows love by shoving an ungodly amount of food at you." But he kept his goal front of mind, and after shedding seventy pounds, he decided he felt comfortable starting to exercise, and that, too, became something he could control. "I am now in the best shape of my life. That's not the stereotype of thirty. But my better days are right now."

He started teaching English composition, at the same community college he had attended years back, while going to law school at night. "I'm guiding my career. I have faculty status. Taking control of my eating, and exercise, and how I want to be has really opened up a lot of avenues for me." I ask him how he *feels*. "Losing the weight helped me feel better about myself, for one, and makes me feel more independent. In a roundabout way I think that interview with Leigh has actually helped me." Leigh turned out to be that one caring person who can be respectful and still ask the right questions that help nudge a person out of neutral. She opened Ben up further to what Ben wanted for himself. I'm so happy for him, and of course I pass the news on to Leigh.

But a lot remains the same. Ben's mother nags him about his food choices at almost every meal. She fights about the clothes he wants to buy. She interferes with his relationships. His most recent relationship lasted about six months and ended four years ago. "And that's part of the reason I don't date, although I'm trying to get out there more now. I just feel like it's really difficult dealing with her and dating. She sees me dating as a threat and it's ammunition to start fights. I learned a long time ago, if I'm dating I'm not telling her."

Ben's mom even needles him when he goes out with friends, as if he is a teenager with a track record for misbehaving. "I am normally able to come and go without too much trouble, but she gets nosy and asks, 'Where are you going? Who are you going to go see?' If I stay out past dark she does have a tendency to give a tantrum over that. She will call me repeatedly until I answer, and bark at me to come home because it's late. It happened during finals when I was studying at the law school library." I ask him how he copes with this. "I'm very upfront and honest. I'll usually just tell her where I'm going and who I'm going to be with. Other times, let's say I'm going to meet a bunch of friends for a birthday party and she doesn't know these people, so I'll just go. I've learned to stay calm on the phone and make it appear like I'm having a normal conversation even though I have my mom melting down on the other end because she wants to know where I am and what I'm doing. A whole other realm of awkward. But barring her getting nosy, or it getting late and I didn't clear it with her ahead of time, it's fine."

Not gonna lie, hearing what happens if he *didn't clear it ahead of time* makes me want to scream, "He's a GROWN-UP." And maybe I want to scream on Ben's behalf because I have a memory of feeling this in my own body, albeit under much easier circumstances. As I mentioned in chapter 4, "Be Good," when Dan and I were in our early thirties we bought a house with my mom that we could not otherwise afford so that our kids could attend the so-called best public schools. Mom was continually curious about our comings and goings. She'd say things like, "So you were out early this morning?" And when I came home late, she'd ask where I'd been. These rather innocent questions drove me nuts. I felt watched. Like I was seventeen again. Still, although I found my mom's curiosity intrusive, she wasn't oppressive or controlling like Ben's mom is. I can't begin to imagine what this degree of surveillance feels like for Ben.

So, I am truly heartened when Ben tells me he's in therapy. I ask him who convinced him to go. "I got health insurance and signed myself up." This is good. It means he knows he needs help dealing with his situation. "Part of counseling has been learning tools to help negotiate tension and conflict with my mom. Even though my therapist can't diagnose her, she gave me the book *Stop Walking on Eggshells: Taking Your Life Back When Someone You Care About Has Borderline Personality Disorder.* I've been working quite a bit on how I approach my relationship with my mom." I ask him for an example. "If I were to sum it up it would be awareness and empathy. Awareness is just my mom is the way she is and might not change ever. Like when we're eating out: she expects me to order beef because 'Beef is getting your money's worth.' If I'm aware of those situations when she's going to try to exert control over particular things, I can usually avoid an argument. Empathy is because my mom has genuine experiences of painful emotions and hurt reactions to certain things. Whether she has been actually slighted or not doesn't matter, because she feels as if she has been harmed. Being able to approach my experiences with her from an empathy perspective changes our interactions and lets us get over our experiences more quickly instead of me being reactionary when she's being reactionary. Instead of being two screaming morons, someone has to be the grown-up."

Ben is still living with his parents. What's more, he tells me, "I kind of have to at this point. Adjuncting at a community college is great professional experience but it doesn't exactly pay the rent." Just to be clear, I don't think there's anything inherently wrong with living in the same house as your parent when you're grown. It's all about, *Do you have agency in the house? Can you come and go as you please? Are you contributing to community but also allowed your own space?* Hearing this thirty-year-old relay the small degree of control he has in his life, I express a lot of empathy. I also decide to ask a tougher question: "When are you going to move out?" He sighs and replies, "When I can. Goal is full-time job with benefits. Then I can move out."

I ask him what's going to happen to his relationship with his mom when he does move out. He replies, "I honestly don't know. She'll probably end up wanting to follow somehow. I don't know what her world would look like with both her kids moving out. She works full-time and has her own stuff going on. It'll be a new frontier to negotiate. One thing me and my therapist are working on—although it's very slow and difficult now during COVID because telehealth is not the same thing as going to the office—is learning how to create and hold boundaries. It's my next phase of development I need to work on.

"While I am well aware that my life would be a lot different if I left, it's just the home we live in now—I couldn't afford similar accommodations elsewhere. Here I have my own office space with diplomas on the wall, a bedroom and bathroom, and a nice dining table, which is a good place to have conference calls because of COVID. And I'm in a suburb so I have miles of sidewalks I can walk. I'm trying to make the best of where I am."

Ben's situation with his parents is extreme. His father is disabled and it's quite possible that his mother suffers from borderline personality disorder that only her therapist could, for sure, diagnose, so it's on Ben and his sister (who has moved out) to figure out how to carve out an adult life for themselves. Ben is taking steps to disentangle himself and set himself up squarely in the future, even if his unusual situation makes this a slower and more profoundly emotional process than it might be for others. "I've seen other people with their parents. When things go wrong they can count on them. But if I moved out on my own I could not count on these two to bail me out on rent or car payment, any of that. As things have been going, since they're getting older and I'm getting older, I've basically been the one balancing the checkbook, making sure things are getting paid, knowing where the money is going. Dynamics have changed in the last couple of years. Living here, I feel like things are more stable with us together in terms of finances and such. If I moved out, if they decided they didn't want me to watch over their stuff, things would go to hell very quickly. It's more stable; it's safer being here until I have my own income that could support me."

And perhaps even more important than solidifying his own income, Ben is fortifying himself emotionally and psychologically. He says it's a "daily grind of getting to where I want to go, on my own, self-sufficient, while interacting with and helping with my family on my terms. But I recognize I still need to congratulate myself a little bit more. I have anger issues. Trying to work on bettering myself and being in a more positive healthy spot. People have met my mom and they think she's a sweetheart."

If I could shine a light on an example of when Ben first snatched his life from the jaws of control it would be this: When he was eighteen, his parents added him to a joint checking account and expected him to deposit his income into it. "My paycheck would come, get deposited into the joint account, and my mom would spend my check out from under me to pay their bills." So, what did Ben do? He figured out how banking worked, and set up his own secret account. Seven years later, when he was twenty-five, he opened an IRA to save for his retirement. "My mom could not stomach the idea of me funneling money into an account and locking it away for the next forty-plus years. She had a massive meltdown over it instead of thinking she'd raised a responsible adult." Ben has continued to fund that account for five years now, and as you will read in chapter 8, "Money Matters," funding a retirement account is one of the smartest things you can do with your money. Go Ben, go! "One of the best things I ever did was opening my own checking account and having my own finances separated from those of my parents. I believe the freedom to have your own money should be basic to any human being. I cannot tell you how valuable this inch of freedom has been for me." I hear it, and I applaud it.

Even though the challenges I've dealt with in life are very different from Ben's, at the end of our call, I tell him that over the course of my fifty-plus years, I've learned that even those of us who aren't involved with people as tenacious as his mother can't control others, and that the only thing we can be in control of—if we work hard at it—is ourselves. He told me these ideas resonate with him. "I'm trying to work on myself, to be better. I'm trying to keep that growth mindset and grow into the person I want to be."

I'm rooting for him. You know I am.

IN SHORT: MOMENTUM IS THE NAME OF THE GAME

When you're transitioning from childhood into adulthood it's natural to be stuck in neutral sometimes. It's scary to try things and scary to leave behind the thing you're currently doing. Even if that thing is holding you back—as they say, the devil you know is better than the devil you don't know. But this life of yours is meant to be lived: actively, intentionally, and, more often than not, with some measure of joy. You deserve that. So, get in that driver's seat and start to power your life. We're headed toward relationships next, and that's going to take a whole lot of action and intention on your part!

Unpack and Reflect

- Where am I stuck, and what do I think is keeping me stuck? What options am I keeping open, and why? What would I gain and lose by opting for each thing? What am I waiting for in order to decide?
- Which, if any, of the "Childhood Chickens Coming Home to Roost" show up in my life?
- Which of the "Fourteen Things to Do Differently to Move Your Work and Relationships Forward" do I most want to work on?
- Where and with whom do I feel at ease, comfortable, and free? Where and with whom do I feel less able to be myself?

7

START TALKING TO STRANGERS

(HUMANS ARE KEY TO YOUR SURVIVAL)

Don't talk to strangers.

—Everyone

Back in 1981, a young Florida boy named Adam Walsh was abducted from a mall by a stranger and murdered. His horrific story was turned into a 1983 made-for-TV movie, which became the second-most watched television show of all time (during an era when there was no Internet or streaming, and even recording shows on VHS tape to watch later was a new technology). In other words, on that particular October night, at the exact same time, everyone and their mother paused what they were doing and sat in their living rooms and watched this show, and it happened to be a show that scared the bejeezus out of everyone. For families across the country, the concept of "stranger danger" became more frightening and more real. It may be the one concept that all Americans, regardless of gender, race, religion, or political affiliation, have rallied around for close to forty years.

Accordingly, most Millennial and Gen Z children were raised with the mantra "Don't talk to strangers." This meant have no verbal interaction with strangers and of course don't go off with them anywhere, either. But it morphed into making no eye contact with strangers, and having no little chitchats with strangers on sidewalks or in stores. Then it became ignoring strangers entirely. A lot of kids grew up not just afraid of the very idea of strangers, but literally not knowing how to interact with them. As a result, kids didn't learn to navigate the social cues given off by someone they didn't already know. And then they graduated from high school and went out into the world, where their life was full of . . . strangers.

Here comes what may be the most obvious point I'll make in this book: we're all strangers to each other at first. Then, somehow, we become acquaintances with some of those (former) strangers, and some of those acquaintances turn into neighbors, friends, colleagues, mentors, lovers, partners, and fam. Research from the fields of evolutionary biology, anthropology, and social psychology shows that we are a highly social species who *must* interact cooperatively and kindly with one another not just to get stuff done but to be emotionally well. Research even shows that interactions with people who will forever remain strangers to us (i.e., the person on the street who passes by) also have positive mental health effects on us.

In short, not only is it *okay to talk to strangers*, you want to. You gotta. Let's go.

WE'RE ALL HUNGRY FOR REAL CONNECTION

I'm in airports a lot, and sometimes I pause to watch people interacting with their loved ones at the departures curb, right before the TSA line, or where people come out from Arrivals. They put a hand on a shoulder. They put forehead to forehead. They hug. They jump up into each other's arms. They kiss. They cling to one another. They refuse to be parted. As they pour their feelings onto each other, I press tears from my own eyes and have to look away. Human touch is an old, animalistic instinct that ensured our survival. These moments I witness at airports are the plainest evidence that human connection matters profoundly to us, and makes what can at times be a bleak, monotonous, and mortal existence feel divine.

Yet there's a crisis of disconnection—of loneliness—in our modern age that was identified quite notably by Robert Putnam in his book *Bowling Alone*, published in 2000, and has been taken to a whole new level with the technological advancements of the twenty-first century. It feels like a strange paradox, right? We're desperate for connection with each other yet we live in a time where technology brings us closer together than ever. (You want to see what your friends are up to? No problem, social media brings their words and imagery straight to a device you constantly have with you. You need some advice from someone? No problem, various websites, blogs, and apps give you access to data, opinions, and perspectives from around the world. You want to hear great stories? No problem, innumerable podcasts feature people telling their tales and books now come in audio.) Yet with a few exceptions all of this technologized connection doesn't nourish our souls the way in-person connection does, and the fact that we let technology do for us what direct contact with humans used to do for us exacerbates the problem.

There's something else awry in our highly technologized social culture—real life gives way to performance. We leap to social media to report whatever achievement we've unlocked—to demonstrate our worth and to feel good about ourselves (and/or our kids). It's like a highly curated scream into the wind: "See me! Tell me I matter!" (I'm not criticizing you for using social media; I'm constantly on there, too.) All of those likes and comments give us a delicious hit, a temporary high, a bit of soothing. But that hit doesn't last. It actually makes us hungrier for more. Meanwhile, we *think* we know so much more about each other these days thanks to social media, and by some measures we do, but seeing a high school friend's wedding pictures, or seeing a former colleague's vacation photos doesn't connect us the way a phone call with either of them would.

Even modern parenting—which *appears* to offer greater connection between parents and children than ever before—is a big part of the disconnect. Yes, we parents are *always there. Always* aware. *Always* on top of everything. Not a single piece of homework, or quiz, test, project, playdate, practice, game, rehearsal, recital, performance, application, date, or deadline need escape our watch or, often, our involvement. But being aware of everything about someone is not necessarily the kind of connection that makes that person feel seen and supported. It can come to feel like constant surveillance, distrust, or judgment.

Lori Gottlieb, the Los Angeles–based psychotherapist and bestselling author who offered us so much good advice in chapter 6, "Get Out of Neutral," sees a ton of people in their twenties and young thirties in her practice and told me that whatever the problems presented are, "I always come back to relationships. If you don't understand the way people perceive you or the impact you have on other people, you're kind of walking around blindly. And it matters in work and it matters in relationships and it matters in how you relate to yourself. Understanding how you relate in the world is the most important thing you can have as an adult because if you don't understand how you relate in the world, you're going to keep running into the same problems and obstacles, and like *Groundhog Day* you're going to end up in the same place. You're going to say, 'I don't understand this, or why my boss said that, or why this person broke up with me, or why I'm so depressed.'" In *Friendship: The Evolution, Biology, and Extraordinary Power of Life's Fundamental Bond*, science journalist Lydia Denworth shows how kids' brains are wired to learn about cooperation, reciprocity, loyalty, and trustworthiness from interacting with other kids. But what is unique to your generation, Lori Gottlieb says, is that you often did not learn those lessons and get that feedback from other kids because your childhood relationships were so micromanaged by adults.

So, I'm here to say that we, your elders, may have failed in not allowing you to experience enough how-to-relate-to-others feedback earlier on, and by our not allowing you to get that feedback from your peers, you might have missed the message that relating mattered and you might not have gotten a lot of practice in improving relationships. Lori also notes that people your age are not "hanging out and doing nothing" as much as prior generations did at your same age. (When we were your age, we would hang out a lot and talk about everything and nothing, and just goof around.) So, you get out in the world and may not know yourself really well or how to just be regular and chill with other humans.

I try to tackle this loneliness and disconnection in my work, broadly. When I'm not writing books, my professional life mostly entails showing up in various cities and towns to discuss those books. In my keynote on the harm of overparenting I tell parents that when we question our kids about deadlines and accomplishments we aren't fostering the kind of connection that matters psychologically. I say, *Our kids want to know they matter to us because they exist, not because of their grades and scores and accolades and awards.* Then I say, *And guess what, they're no different from us in that regard. WE want to know we matter, too, not because of our job or house or the amazing thing we posted on Instagram or whatever, but because we exist. We are all hungry to feel seen, to know we matter. To someone.* No matter what part of the country I'm in when giving this talk, people in the audience stare back at me with wide eyes that shimmer with tears. My eyes are usually teary by that point, too, because I, too, often feel disconnected. These moments to be vulnerable with an audience and feel their vulnerability in return are moments of connection. I would rather not be disconnected. But it's a relief to know I'm not alone in feeling this way.

It's getting really bad. The former prime minister of the United Kingdom, Theresa May, called loneliness "the sad reality of modern life for too many people." To combat it she established the world's first ever "minister for loneliness" position. (It sounds like it's ripped from the pages of *Harry Potter*, but it's real. Google it!) Japan reports that elderly people (particularly women) feel so lonely that they commit small crimes that land them in prison because of the connection and care they'll get there. In 2017, U.S. surgeon general Vivek Murthy wrote that loneliness is "a growing health epidemic." The organization that studies the wellness of college students in the U.S. (American College Health Association) has been tracking loneliness in college students for years, and in the most recent study (Spring 2019), 59.4 percent of male-identified students and 70.1 percent of female-identified students reported feeling lonely at some point in the last year. Both of those stats are up close to 20 percent from 2009. A 2018 study about loneliness in U.S. adults conducted by the health insurance company CIGNA found that:

- **Nearly half** of Americans report sometimes or always feeling alone (46 percent) or left out (47 percent).

- **One in four** Americans (27 percent) rarely or never feels as though there are people who really understand them.

- **Two in five** Americans sometimes or always feel that their relationships are not meaningful (43 percent) and that they are isolated from others (43 percent).

- **One in five** people report they rarely or never feel close to people (20 percent) or feel like there are people they can talk to (18 percent).

- **Only around half of Americans** (53 percent) have meaningful in-person social interactions, such as having an extended conversation with a friend or spending quality time with family, on a daily basis.

- **Generation Z (adults ages 18–22) is the loneliest generation** and claims to be in worse health than older generations.

- **Social media use alone is not a predictor of loneliness**; respondents defined as very heavy users of social media have a loneliness score (43.5) that is not markedly different from the score of those who never use social media (41.7).

There's a wound, a strange detachment, felt by us all. But this important national survey shows that it can be particularly acute for people your age.

I imagine you know this. Sense it. Even feel it within you. (Or is it *so* normal that while you can express that you're lonely, you don't necessarily feel that it's problematic?) It doesn't just hurt us in the now. It's killing us, slowly. Lydia Denworth's *Friendship*, which takes a scientific approach to studying the value of this thing we often take for granted, says loneliness is "friendship's opposite" and "as deadly as cigarette smoking." Okay, so it's dire. Literally.

So, this chapter is devoted to human connection whether it be with the stranger on the street or the lover in your bed. We have the capacity to save ourselves. The antidote to all of this loneliness is simply: each other.

STRANGER THINGS

Let's start with the simplest type of connection. You leave your house. You go places. Who do you see? Strangers. Research shows that even the briefest eye contact with them is good for you. Adding a little smile is better. And talking with them makes you happier still. Counteract all your impulses from childhood and go for it. Research proves it'll be GOOD for you. Note how I keep citing science and research in this chapter? It's because I'm feeling the need to *prove* to you that this human connection stuff matters. You may have been told that your twenties are all about work and career and that you can focus on your human relationships later, but if you've been told that, you were *duped*. Picture yourself as a train on a railroad track. Work is one of the two rails supporting the train and allowing it to move forward. Your human relationships are the other track. If you fail to build that track, your train goes careening off into the bewildering darkness.

Back to strangers. The Germans have a phrase, "wie Luft behandeln," which means "to be looked at as though air." We English speakers might say, "They looked right through me." Picture it. You're in a store, at a party, a restaurant, in the center of your campus, waiting for a train. Someone scans around looking for something, someone, and you meet their eyes, but they just pass over your eyeballs as if you're part of the wallpaper. While many New Yorkers famously pride themselves on not just their ability to ignore each other but on their *desire* to do so, research shows it's actually kind of a shitty thing to do. Sorry New Yorkers, I love you, but.

Professor Kipling Williams at Purdue University in Indiana set up a study where a young woman walked by the participants and either made eye contact, made eye contact with a smile, or completely ignored them. Then five or six steps later someone stopped them and said they were conducting a study and asked questions about how they were feeling. Even those who received just brief eye contact from the young woman felt a greater sense of inclusion and belonging. "Just that brief acknowledgment, that brief glance—with or without a smile—made them at least temporarily feel more socially connected," says Williams. Those who were completely ignored felt even more socially disconnected than the control group who hadn't seen the woman at all. Being ignored by her harmed them.

The U.K.'s minister for loneliness is doing a nice job of promoting interaction with strangers. If that sounds like something you want to try, check out their website (bemoreus.org.uk) for some very cute videos they've put together, including one with little children chatting up strangers in a coffee shop and one with comedian Andy Parsons chatting up strangers at a mall. The advice emerging from them is things like "you have to be aware of people," "it requires a little effort," and "make small connections every day."

And a side note here: I completely respect that eye contact and connecting with strangers may be a big deal for you. I'm not here to say it's a simple thing we can all just *do*. If you are on the autism spectrum, for example, it is likely hard, perhaps very hard, to do it. Or you may have social anxiety, which makes it difficult. Or you may have had some rough life experiences that make you instinctively keep your head down for self-protection—particularly things like abuse or people acting with prejudice toward you on the basis of your skin color or religion. Or culturally it may be the case that your gender is not supposed to look people in the eye. But if it is *remotely* possible for you to make eye contact with a closed smile I encourage you to try in places where you feel safe. You will likely get better at it the more you do it, and you'll get the feedback from others with their eyes and their small smiles that will encourage you to do it more often. It really is *so* good for you.

Now shift your thoughts from true strangers to the familiar folks you don't really *know*, yet you see regularly—the barista who makes your beverage of choice; the janitor at work who dumps your bin as you burn the midnight oil; the subway conductor; the postal carrier or UPS driver; the office security guard; the grocery clerk; the server at your favorite restaurant; the owner of your favorite bookstore; the receptionist where you work out. In their book *Consequential Strangers: Turning Everyday Encounters into Life-Changing Moments*, authors Melinda Blau and Karen Fingerman call these folks (as you can guess!) "consequential strangers" (another term is "weak ties"). Blau and Fingerman say, "Our intimates anchor us at home, but our consequential strangers make us feel grounded in the world."

So, these folks' faces have become familiar to you, but are you going the next step and talking to them? Do you know their name? Knowing their name opens the door. It will change their day for the better if you can say, "Hey, so and so, how's your day going?" They'll quite likely beam at you, and thank you for asking, and so your day will be changed for the better, too. You'll feel better about yourself both because you've done a good deed and because you'll have gotten some juicy human connection. Maybe they'll ask you how you are, and wow, if that happens it will up the interaction value even more. Weak ties and consequential strangers are like protein boosts in your smoothie. Pow. Give it a try sometime. If their name isn't on their badge, gather up your bravery and *ask them*. Work hard to remember it.

And then there are the cocktail parties, the open houses, the work gatherings. These have always been opportunities for awkwardness, and now that we have our phones for company, it can be that much harder to go up and meet someone because you have to prove you're more interesting than whatever they're scrolling. Remember those phones aren't offering the juice that we humans need to really connect. If you're the host of the gathering, whatever it might be, you can help everyone practice starting to be present by making it a no cell phone situation. Everyone will have to deal with those awkward moments of *I don't know what to say right now*, or *I don't know what to do right now*, or *I'm just going to have this awkward silence with these people on the couch*. But at the end, everyone will tell you they had the best time. Because odds are quite good that after ten or fifteen minutes of awkwardness, they'll have discovered that a real human beats a phone.

HOW'S THAT WORKING FOR YA? (COLLEAGUES)

Next up: colleagues in the workplace. You know them. You bitch and moan with them. You might go to lunch with them. You do projects with them. You sit in meetings with them. Some work environments are fantastic at facilitating human connection, but plenty are not. (In chapter 11, "Make Things Better," I mention the *Forbes* "Best Employers" list, which is a tool you can use to investigate workplace norms in this area.)

How often does something like this happen to you? (Picture two colleagues who know and like each other walking past each other.)

> 1: Hey, how are ya!
> 2: Good, you!
> 1: Good!
> 2: Good! (shouted over the shoulder) We should get coffeeeeeeeee.

I didn't even use question marks after the questions, because this is a formalistic exchange rooted in manners and offered with good intentions, yet the person asking is not really asking, and the person responding is not really responding, and neither is really listening to the other. We might as well be going, "Quack Moo Cock-A-Doodle-Do."

I'm serious!

The ability to change this meh dynamic is within your power. But do you? You're busy. You're late. Got stuff on your mind. Somewhere you gotta be. The coffee part I think you mean. Because you know you *do NEED to connect*, and that person and coffee are as good a set of variables as any. But you don't. Because you can't. Who has the time? Meanwhile you're checking your phone. I challenge you to pause and say to that person, *You know what? Let's schedule that coffee RIGHT NOW or it'll never happen.* Then schedule it. Then DON'T CANCEL. Sit down with that person and that coffee and lean in with some of the really good opening lines you'll see later in this chapter. And while getting together in person is clutch, virtual is better than nothing. I combatted loneliness during the pandemic by meeting with fellow authors (my "colleagues") on Zoom. It became a lifeline.

Just to put a pin in why you really need to connect with the people you work with—like it or not you probably spend more time working than doing any other thing (except sleeping). So, your chances of having meaningful human connection are actually greatest *there*. Plus, on a very practical level, the people you work with form a huge part of your network. (Remember the networking tips in chapter 3, "You're Not Perfect"?) You need these people you work with to show up for you when you're thinking about getting a new job. They're more likely to do so if they feel you actually give a damn about them. Research shared in the book *Friendship: The Evolution, Biology, and Extraordinary Power of Life's Fundamental Bond* shows that "it takes between 40 and 60 hours to move from an acquaintance to a casual friendship, from 80 to 100 hours to call someone a friend, and over 200 hours of togetherness before someone rated as a best friend." Coffee dates are a great way to get your hours in!

COMMUNITY CONNECTIONS

Researchers say that one of the reasons we're so lonely is that many of the mechanisms that used to be in place to foster human connection have simply fallen away. Religious worship among adults was at an all-time low in 2018, according to a Gallup poll, which found that only one in two Americans reported belonging to a church, synagogue, or mosque, which was a twenty-point drop since 1999. And involvement in community organizations, clubs, and leagues is also waning. A lot of these types of entities were organized not only around religious beliefs, but were for a certain gender, or class of people, or race/ethnicity. I'm guessing that as we've taken sledgehammers to those norms, we may inadvertently have thrown the baby out with the bathwater. In any case, a weekly or monthly function with a set of people with whom we share a common interest isn't a common thing in the ways that it once was, and those who don't find new ways to engage regularly with community risk real detriment to their wellness. *Who has the time?* you may be thinking. Yet isn't it clear that you need to make the time?

Our neighborhood connections have also thinned considerably. When women weren't in the workplace they were the unelected yet unequivocal leaders in the community, fostering daily interaction and making meaningful connections. I'm not trying to throw us back to those times—I am acknowledging that when we women finally gained opportunity in the workplace, and as dual-income earners became the norm in families for economic and personal enrichment reasons, our neighborhoods lost the leaders who had created and tended those important ties. To take gender out of it, nobody is at home during the day anymore. This makes our sidewalks, streets, parks, playgrounds, and corner stores feel more lonely.

So, we each gotta find our people some other way. Maybe you love to sing? Find a choir. Maybe you love to read? Join or form a book club. Maybe you want to work on your writing? Enroll in a writing workshop. Got a dog? Frequent the dog park. Enjoy rock climbing? There's a rock wall club near you. Go to your school reunions. You're not starting from scratch with any of the people there—this interest you have in common with the folks there *is* the ice breaker allowing you to connect deeper more quickly. In the "Don't Just Take My Word for It" section of this chapter, you'll see just what a visit to the dog park or rock wall can lead to!

You—we—also need more actual connections *of* the flesh. Hugs. Pats. Non-sexual cuddling. (Sex matters, too; I'm just saying it doesn't have to be sexual activity to be a meaningful in-the-flesh connection.)

Humans need touch. Not having someone to hug regularly can actually be devastating. Some say that we all need four hugs a day for wellness. My friend Marcia Baczynski co-founded the concept of "Cuddle Parties" to offer people access to non-sexual human connection. It was a huge hit. Seventeen years later, they are going strong in nineteen countries (North America, Europe, Africa, Asia, and Australia) with over one hundred trained facilitators. Their website (cuddleparty.com) describes the experience as "a structured, safe workshop on boundaries, communication, and affection." Three cheers to them for what they're doing to combat loneliness.

I want to acknowledge that you may have had experiences in life that made you wary of humans, made you feel that the last thing you want to do is have to rely on people, let alone cuddle with them. I appreciate that and am not trying to push you farther or faster than you want to go. I'm just here with information that human connection *with the right people* IS good for you, and with a faith that those right people are out there for you even if it may take some time to find them. I also want to acknowledge that you may have been raised with a set of values that suggested that relying on others made you weak. I'm not interrogating those values so much as offering something different—the evidence that connecting with people strengthens you in ways that feel really good without asking you to give up your individualism, sense of self-reliance, or autonomy.

NEIGHBORS

As strange as it may sound to you, given that I'm a big extrovert, for at least ten years I didn't know anyone on our street. Back in 2002, Dan, my mom, the kids, and I moved into the house we now live in—one we'd bought and spent a year rebuilding because it was truly damaged (it had a six-inch slope from the front door to the back door because of how the land had settled over the years). Some of the neighbors hated the new construction so much that they made a petition to get us to change it. One tried to take us to mediation to change the design of our new house. (I told the mediator, "The house project has been approved by the city, so there is nothing to mediate. But if my neighbor wants to have a mediation designed to improve our relationship I'm all for it." I never heard back.) One set of neighbors just stopped talking to us altogether. Most of the rest didn't seem to hate us—they waved back at me if I waved at them first—but we'd never exchanged even a cup of sugar, let alone had a decent conversation. We live on the end of a cul-de-sac and for years when I drove home, turned onto the cul-de-sac, and pulled into my driveway, which was at the top of the circle, I felt that I was entering a bullseye of scrutiny, a kind of unwanted connection. This deeply bothered me.

Many of my neighbors were elderly. Many were the original owners from when the neighborhood was built back in the late 1960s, and all of them were white with the exception of a Chinese family that had moved in shortly before us. One of my next-door neighbors, a woman named Nancy, would occasionally call me about a concern over something we were doing in our yard or to our house. When an ambulance came for her and we learned a few days later that she'd died, I was both sad and mad at myself for not having made the effort to know my neighbors better.

I think I'd been waiting all along for them to welcome me with an apple pie or something. But it finally dawned on me that I could make an effort, too. One of the elderly white women, named Eva, had actually been quite kind during the house-design phase. When we held a meeting in our driveway to discuss their concerns, she stood up in front of her neighbors and said, "This doesn't feel like a very Christian thing to do." So, I set out to try to connect with Eva. She and her husband, Gordon, would go on walks down the sidewalk, arm in arm, and one day when I was driving by I pulled over to say hi. Then I told them how much it had meant when they'd stood up for us at the community meeting. I told them that some neighbors still don't even wave at us, which made me feel kind of bad. Eva patted my arm and said that was just nonsense and Gordon agreed. Every few weeks I'd see Eva and Gordon out on their walk when I was driving and I'd always stop and we'd chitchat for a few moments, then continue on.

Meanwhile another set of neighbors, Rob and Rita Varney (he in his late nineties, she in her late eighties) had started doing walks around the cul-de-sac together, him in his wheelchair, which she pushed from behind. When I pulled over and said hi one October day, Rita said, "We always try to stay up long enough to see your kids on

Halloween—what time will they be coming by?" Man, that brought tears to my eyes. Who knew! Sawyer and Avery were probably five and seven at the time, and the neighbors two doors down who refused to say hi to us wouldn't even smile at us when we brought the kids by on Halloween. Yet here were some other neighbors three doors in the other direction who actually looked forward to seeing our children! I went home and told the kids that we'd be changing up the order in which we visited houses on Halloween that year—that Mr. and Mrs. Varney were *waiting up* for them.

Soon things began changing for Eva and Gordon. They weren't out on their walks very often. Gordon looked to be slowing down physically, maybe having health issues. I checked in. Kept a closer watch. Turns out Gordon's mental cognition was in decline and his kids from his first marriage had decided he needed to live in a memory care facility. I was able to say goodbye before he moved out. Eva was wrecked.

I began going over to her place every now and then to check in on her. One day she invited me inside. She sat on a chair in her living room and I sat criss-cross on the rug to pay deference, respect, as if she was a grandmother and I was her grandchild. I asked her about her life with Gordon and a beautiful love story unfolded. She'd divorced her first husband in her forties. Went out a lot with girlfriends. Decided on a whim to get a tattoo, and did I want to see it? *A what?* I'm thinking. And there it was. This beautiful yet simple little butterfly about an inch in diameter on her left shoulder. Her second marriage was to Gordon, who turned out to be the love of her life. (I was in my forties at the time of this conversation, and all of a sudden Eva was no longer an elderly woman to me but someone who had once been my age and had dealt with the shit life throws you at that stage.)

With her "Gordie" gone, Eva saw no reason to leave the house. She became a recluse. I was talking with Rita Varney and Rita's grown daughter Natalie in the cul-de-sac one day. We were all concerned about Eva. I was forty-four, had just left Stanford, and was a graduate student once again, this time in an MFA in writing program up in San Francisco. I had this sense that a monthly writing group might get Eva out of the house, and foster community among all of us. But by now, as you know, I'd become much more collaborative, so instead of just imposing this idea on my neighborhood, I wanted to approach Rita with it, because she was in her early nineties by this point and I really saw her as the "Grande Dame" of the cul-de-sac. So, I brought it up. While Natalie clearly liked the idea, Rita seemed really skeptical. But when I pressed the point about Eva, Rita said she'd participate.

I started the Maybell Way Writers Collective seven years ago, and until COVID we'd met once a month almost without fail. We're all women, and we range in age from forties to nineties. Eva never came, but to my surprise, given her initial reaction, Rita never missed a single meeting. As she'd grown more frail, Natalie, and then my mother, became her typist and scribe. Her tales of a childhood in the navy, of a life married to her beloved Rob, who was a noted physicist during the Cold War and had long since passed, and her feelings toward her Black housekeeper all kept us rapt. When Rita died a few years ago, Natalie stood up at the memorial service and read a statement Rita had written about how much the Maybell Way Writers Collective had meant to her. "Even though when Julie raised it, I thought it was a *really stupid* idea. . . ." Everyone at the service busted out laughing. We could all picture Rita's face when she thought something was silly, and hear the scorn in her voice. I laughed the loudest. I hadn't been sure she originally thought my idea was silly— now I knew! It made her unflagging participation month after month that much more sweet.

WHO SHINES THE LIGHT ON YOUR PATH?

Mentors are another category of people who emerge from our community connections and with whom you want to have a strong relationship. A mentor is someone usually older, definitely more experienced, who is squarely in your corner. They're the elders in your childhood whom you want to go see when you come home after time away, that one awesome high school teacher who believed in you, the boss you no longer work for but who makes you smile when you think about them, the people you asked to provide a reference for you or a letter of recommendation. They've always seemed to really dig you. They take an interest in you, not your achievements or next steps in life, but in *you*.

The best mentors don't give you answers. They ask you good questions that open you further to your wants, needs, and dreams. Having been a mentor to many students over the years I thought of my role as shining a light on their path, to illuminate it, to show them things they wouldn't otherwise have been able to see. (Look back to chapter 3, "You're Not Perfect," for tips about how to cultivate a relationship with a mentor at work.)

I can picture the faces of my strongest mentors. A white professor named Jim Steyer, who was the first professor to really *see* me in the college classroom, who urged me to speak up when he could see my brow furrowing with questions but I was afraid to raise my hand, and who nodded his head vigorously as I offered answers to complicated questions, demonstrating not just to me but to the entire class that my thoughts were good ones. A Black professor named Kennell Jackson, who was the resident fellow in the dorm where I lived for three years and who mentored me for twenty years, though I was too afraid to get close to him and it wasn't until he was dying that I realized how much he cared for me; still, his wisdom (which I initially took as judgment) was always with me and is with me to this day. When I was desperately seeking to leave corporate law and work at the university, Jim Montoya, a Latino man serving as Stanford's dean of admissions, turned me down for an entry-level job and said, "I'm not giving you this job, Julie, because you could have my job one day and this is not the right place to start." Jim would go on to be the person who whispered "Dean of freshmen?" in my ear, a position that thanks to him seeing something in me became a job I would indeed go on to do for ten years, which would become the reason I wrote a book on parenting that I would be asked to write a sequel to. That's this book you're reading right now, which I can trace all the way back to Jim. Then there's Maryellen Myers, a white Buddhist Aikido master who was my executive coach in my final years at Stanford and who knows my shit so inside and out I'm sure that if there's any truth to the concept that we picture five people when we die she will be one of them.

Now fiftysomething myself, I seek to mentor others whenever possible, which is not to say I don't still need mentors of my own. I do. I mentor young writers, particularly emerging Black writers (but I am open to all). I've mentored a young white man in prison for drug possession who asked for my help with an essay he wanted to share with his fellow inmates (you'll meet him in chapter 10, "How to Cope"). I've mentored a kid kicked out of high school for bad conduct. I've mentored lots of people who were miserable in their careers or personal lives and needed help finding the way to what was next.

I think of all the roles I've played the role of mentor pleases me the most. A mentor believes in a person when they sometimes can't believe in themselves. It's the care of a parent with none of the responsibility. I hope as you emerge into your adulthood you will be able to name and connect with a few mentors. And I hope you'll soon find yourself in the role of mentoring and enjoy helping other people out if you aren't already. The research shows that even for kids who grow up in the most trying of circumstances, if they have just one caring adult, their life is going to be okay. This is the silver bullet of human connection. Knowing you matter to just *one person* can make all the difference in the world. As we saw with high school teacher Dr. Kirstin Milks in chapter 4, "Be Good," even if no one was there for you, you can settle the score with the universe by being that one person for someone else.

FRIENDS

My neighbor Rita had moved from stranger to neighborly acquaintance to familiar face to community connection to friend to revered elder. My life is all the richer for it. Actual friends, not just people you've friended or followed on social media, are people with whom you have some kind of mutual connection, care, and concern. It isn't a friendship if you know a ton more about them than they know about you. Just like sex, if it isn't mutual it isn't good.

Although you may find yourself with little motivation to do anything at the end of a long day of work other than scroll and binge various forms of media, human connection is so important to your wellness that you've got to make time for friends, too. It's likely you're at least texting these people pretty regularly. Better than texting are synchronous platforms such as FaceTime or Skype, battle royale games such as *Fortnite* or *PUBG*, MMORPGs (massive multiplayer online role-playing games) like *World of Warcraft* or the *Elder Scrolls Online*, or online party games such as those made by Jackbox. Synchronicity means what you communicate and what the other person communicates is happening at the same time, in tandem, in response to each other, so these interactions are better at fostering human connection. Texting, in contrast, is asynchronous, which means you can send it and they don't have to be there in order to receive it. They receive it whenever they do and you may not be there when they respond. For this reason, texting and other asynchronous technologies offer a connection that is far less juicy.

But you need more connection in the actual flesh—the truest type of synchronous connection—with these people. Poker. Book club. Coffee. Hiking. Shopping. Dinner. Game night. Hoops. Bible study. Comedy club. Dancing. Theater. Other forms of play. Shit, what you need is more *laughter*. And when you're with people, in a group or particularly one-on-one, don't be that person who constantly looks at their device. Yes, there are times you *have to* check your phone because your dog is sick, your boss is on a rampage, you're on call with your kid, or your parent is having a procedure. Fine. *Say* that, then, and adhere to that as the *only* reason you will break from the person you're with. But don't start scrolling when someone is literally across from you having a conversation with you. That is body language for "What's happening with these people online is more interesting than what's coming from you, the actual live human in front of me." It's incredibly rude and makes the person across from you feel like shit. I have a friend who does it A.L.L.T.H.E.T.I.M.E. and one of these days I'm going to find the courage to say to them, *Um, could you not do that? It makes me feel like you're more interested in that than in what you and I are talking about. In me.*

If you're flaky in person like this, or generally flaky in terms of not getting back to people, you're teaching people that they can't count on you. You may at some point be wondering why you don't have good friends or close friends you can confide in. If that is happening, it's worth a moment of introspection. (Hey, I get it. I'll cop to not being great at nurturing my friendships a little bit later in this chapter.) Being a reliable friend is key. Doing what you've said you're going to do and doing it consistently matters. Being trustworthy. Just plain showing up and checking in. Learning how to be a good friend is the right thing to do—your friend benefits, of course—but it also staves off depression and anxiety in *you*.

THE CONNECTORS

Some people have that *group of friends they see all the time*. Often, it's a same-sex group of people who go out together. Divorced moms. Bros from college. Grad school friends who travel someplace annually together. Church group. I've never had that. Frankly, I'm more comfortable in a group of guys than I am in a group of women. (Can't really explain why that is, except to say *I know how to be around men*, whereas with women I often don't know what to say or how to join in. Meanwhile Dan is the exact opposite. And that's probably a reason we vibe so well!) Gender issues aside, I love being around humans, so I've felt envious whenever I heard of people going off for their regular you-can-count-on-it friendship fun. Seriously, at my age, I know people who have been gathering annually with a group for thirty years, and I'm glad for them that they have that and sad for me that I don't!

But something special happened on Election Day in 2016 while I was at the local Safeway stocking up on champagne and hors d'oeuvres with which to celebrate the election of our first female president. I'm standing next to the chilled beverages when this woman eyes my very full cart and says, "Having a party tonight?" I say yes, and we chitchat about how exciting it's going to be, and about how we're both trying to do 'champagne math' to be sure we have enough to go around. Then she leans in and whispers, "Do you live around here?" And I tell her yes, I live in Palo Alto and she tells me she lives in Los Altos, which is right next door. And she says, "Cool, I like to reach out because there are so few of us here." Kanesha is Black, too. And she's right. While Silicon Valley is diverse in many ways, there aren't a lot of Black folk here. So, she decided to create a group of professional Black moms who could just be ourselves with each other. We meet when we feel like it. Sometimes at someone's house, sometimes at an art exhibit, or a restaurant (and, during COVID, on WhatsApp). The conversation is just about life, work, kids. Once, a brunch went four and a half hours because we just *didn't want to leave*. When Toni piped up that her eldest son had been pulled over by the Los Altos police seventeen times in eighteen months nobody said, "Well, what was he doing?" or "The police are just there to protect us." We all knew what was going on and what a relief it was to be in a room where everyone just *understood*. I've only known these women for a few years, but the connection with them pulls deep into my heart. Thank you, Kanesha!

So, I've come to appreciate that there are opportunities for connection all around me, and I'm getting better at noticing and strengthening them. My work takes me all over the country, and in the early years of being on the road my mantra was "Get in/Get out/Get home." This meant when people I didn't know well would write and say, "You're going to be in my town, want to get coffee or drinks?" I'd decline. (Seeing people I didn't know super well felt like *more work* somehow; if they were close friends, though, I said YES!) Then I'd go on with the actual work—giving talks, answering questions, signing books, which meant I was surrounded with people, a few hundred at many stops—and yet feel *incredibly* lonely. I came to appreciate that although I get eye contact and beautiful smiles from these strangers, in the aggregate they're not filling my relationship bucket because ours are one-way connections. These folks have read or heard about my work and they value it and me; they have a degree of knowledge about me that I can't possibly have about them, so it's a non-reciprocated way of knowing. I greatly appreciate their interest in my work and the fact that they've come out to see me with everything else that's going on in their life, but I don't know a thing about *them*. And if I sat down for a meal with them, it would be hard in one hour to get to know them in any way that resembles the way they already know me.

But these acquaintances who reach out, these folks I went to school with or worked with long ago? I now understand just how valuable that connection with them will be and I jump at the chance to meet up with them. My old mantra "Get in/Get out/Get home" has morphed into "Oh yes! I'd love to have coffee/dinner/drinks with you." And when we're together, I'm not the author who showed up to give a talk, I'm a person who asks questions that deepen my understanding of who they are, what matters to them, what's good in their life. I work hard to ensure I'm not taking up more than my share of the conversation. I do this for my own self-care. It's a practice on top of a practice on top of a practice. One I cherish.

GETTING TO KNOW YOU

"Where do you work?/What kind of work do you do?"
"Where did you go to school?"
"Where are you from?"

These are the questions we seem to need to ask a person upon first meeting them. But they're the dullest questions known to man. You might disagree, if, say, you have the kind of job that makes people's eyes pop with delight, or if you went to a school whose name makes people drool. (Pro tip: The eye-popping and drooling makes you feel good about yourself for a few moments. But don't mistake this for people actually *liking* you or *having any sense of who you ARE*.) What's wrong with these questions is that they yield facts in response. They're not conversation starters.

Want to go deeper? Want to really connect? Maybe you're thinking, *No, not really*. If so, Ha. Here's a reason to be motivated: When you have a truly great conversation, not only do you learn more about the person but they emerge from the interaction feeling they really like YOU. "How's your day going?" is a good opening line with anyone, and a downright act of kindness with strangers from the grocery clerk to your Lyft driver. If you want to try to get a person to open up a bit so you can start to get to know them, try one of these three *great opening lines* you can ask anyone: 1) So, what's *good* in your life these days? 2) So, what are you working on that really *matters* to you? 3) So, what do I need to know if I'm to really know you?

Or, ask one of these additional *great opening lines* for fam or friends you haven't seen in a while: 1) Is there someone important in your life you want me to know about? (Pro tip: It's phrased without gendered language, which means you're open to hearing about anyone they might want to share about.) 2) I really want to get caught up on what's going on in your life. Can we make some time?

When you're on the receiving end of these questions, size them up and ask yourself if you feel safe being open. If not, go with a generic response. If yes, you feel safe: Let delight fill your eyes. Tell them something really good. And/or look them in the eye more seriously and tell them the thing you're really struggling with and what you're doing to work on it. And then, and this is key, be sure to reciprocate. Remember the best human connection is two-way, synchronous. Don't be that person who talks all about themselves, then walks away. The easy transition is, "Okay, enough about me. How about *you*?"

PRACTICE SHOWING UP AS YOURSELF WITH OTHERS

Dr. Carrie Kholi-Murchison (who goes by Kholi) is a queer Black woman in her midthirties and the director of people and culture at the health and wellness company Whole30. Her cool job is "to facilitate helping people heal, grow, and own their health on their own terms." Kholi understands well the value of going deep in our interactions with others—yes, even at work!—and uses "radical transparency" to help teams of colleagues work through recurring personal conflicts. Radical transparency is something you can learn, too. It requires, first, something I mentioned in chapter 5, "Stop Pleasing Others": the important skill my coach Maryellen taught me, which is learning how to notice what you are feeling in your body and why, as a way to help uncover what was triggering an emotion. I'll teach you how to do this in chapter 12, "Unleash Your Superpowers," but we're here in our relationships chapter right now, where emotional triggers are very relevant, so I want to be sure to note the idea of radical transparency right here.

Kholi says radical transparency requires being vulnerable. "We're taught bravado. To posture, so that we don't appear to be hurt. Nobody teaches us to say, 'I'm scared.' 'I don't know.' 'I need help.' But these are things we need to communicate." Kholi's queerness gives her tremendous empathy and insight into who feels able to be themselves in the world and who does not. "As queer people, we learn when we're young that who we are is wrong. Not just our desire, but literally our very being. And we're rejected not by people who don't know us but by people that we love, want to rely on, and want to be in community with."

She helps teams examine the nature of their feelings through journaling. She has them write down, "My three favorite things today were . . ." and "The things that really drained me were . . . ," and she has them write down where they felt those things in their body. Then she helps them analyze their patterns over time. Kholi says if having a formal journal isn't your thing, just literally write or record these things somewhere; get them out of your body. Being able to jot down for yourself what that thing made you feel, where you felt it in your body, and noting that to yourself over and over shows you, *Oh, here's something I need to work on or I need to communicate to someone else.*

When Kholi talks a team through the results of their journaling exercises, she presses people to say how they felt, not how someone else "made them feel." "If you start explaining what happened to you, instead of sharing where the feeling is located within you, your colleagues [or roommates or friends or lovers] won't understand the impact they had," and the real impact on you is what people need to know in order to better understand you and to be motivated to change the way they're expressing themselves to you.

Radical transparency takes practice. Showing up as our authentic self with others takes practice. Being ourselves in relation to other people, all the people in our lives, takes practice. So go ahead and start practicing. Too many young adults have been told they don't need to work on relationships until their careers are settled. But relationships are an essential component of building a career—and relationships form the marrow of life! You don't just arrive in life as a thirty-five-year-old knowing how to be good at human relationships. They take practice. Particularly if we have to undo patterns from childhood that make it more of a challenge for us to feel safe and seen with others and to communicate effectively with them.

THE LIFE-SUSTAINING POWER OF A CLOSE FRIEND

The gold standard when it comes to human connections are the close friends and family we actually *enjoy* being around. (My definition of "close" is: I know *much* of their shit, they know *much* of mine, and we love and accept each other anyway. This means we've been deeply vulnerable with one another, and have shown up for each other when times were grim. We've probably also had a tremendous amount of fun together.) You might think of these people as "amigos," "bros," "buddies," "buds," "compadres," "fam," "homies," "mates," "pals," "peeps," "posse," "tribe," etc. (Pro tip: Some of these terms are culture-specific and if your culture doesn't inherently use a term, as is the case for non-indigenous people with "tribe," I recommend that you not use it. You have plenty of other great terms!) Regardless of the terminology, you know who I mean. And I know how much they matter to you.

My phone buzzes at 1:45 p.m. on a Monday in early November when I am determined to devote every available moment to writing this very book. I'm behind on my deadline, and with my speaking schedule and the upcoming holidays I have very little time to get an entire book written. The last thing I need is an interruption. But it's Andy.

I've already told you I'm an extrovert. I genuinely enjoy being around people and I make friends easily. When I was eighteen months old we'd just moved from a house in Lagos, Nigeria, to a high-rise apartment in Manhattan, New York. I was missing my Nigerian friends so badly that I toddled over to my mother at the kitchen sink, tugged on her apron string, and said, "Friends, Mommy, friends!" Certain there must be other small children living in this building, she took me down to the huge lobby where we sat on a couch across from the bank of elevators. After about twenty minutes, an elevator opened to reveal a mother and a small child about my size. I ran toward them, arms outstretched, shouting, "Frrrrrrrrrrrrriend!" I guess you could say I'm kind of a risk taker, too. My mother sat there clutching her heart hoping this little stranger would reciprocate my good intentions. That little stranger, whose name was Gabrielle, became my friend, and introduced me to other small humans, named Faye and Tina. My risky little effort was oh so worth it.

More than five decades and many more moves later, I'm blessed to have had a number of good friends intersect my path. And I tend to still be an outstretched-arms kind of person. I come in for big hugs, I scan your eyes for your unspoken feelings, I hold you in your pain and struggle, and if I really trust you I'll open up and share some of what I'm going through. But over the years, life got busy. I put my work, my marriage, and raising kids first. So, while I have a great career that brings me excitement and wonder, a partner I am still madly in love with after thirty-two years, and two amazing children I feel lucky to call my own, I can count my close friends on maybe two hands. I feel sad as I type this, particularly as I wonder what the less-than-close friends are feeling now, whether they get it, because they prioritized other things, too, or whether they're out there somewhere feeling rejected by me (I hope not). I never want to be a person who hurts others. Yet friendships need tending to or they'll shrivel up and wither. The truth is, I've underattended many of mine.

Andy and I hardly ever see each other because he lives in DC and I live in California. And we only talk a couple times a year because . . . life. And we don't even belong to the same political party. But we met as twenty-one-year-olds with passion and impatience about America and a clear conviction that we could do something to make our society more just. Ever the optimist, he walked around as if he had springs in the balls of his feet. His eyes flickered with intellect, his smile was a yard wide, and his jokes made us cackle, double over with laughter, and wipe our eyes. This white male Jewish young Republican was totally unlike me, and yet totally my kind of guy.

When I published a memoir about my experiences with racism back in 2017, Andy called me up to congratulate me. There was warmth in his voice like when a parent tells you they're really proud of you. He said he remembered the op-ed I wrote in college about experiencing racism when I was four years old, and he was thrilled that I'd continued to write about all that, and that it had turned into an actual *book*. I sat there going *What* as he said all of this. I literally had zero recollection of having written that op-ed, or of having had the guts to describe my experiences with racism in such a public forum at that relatively young age. I'd basically forgotten the bravery of younger me—and as Andy praised me I sat there thinking, *Where did that brave self go and why did it take her close to thirty more years to publish on the subject again, and my God how had Andy remembered?* And then he tells me how sad it made him then and now to read about some of the tough stuff I'd experienced. Being seen and thought of so deeply is I think a good definition of "Love." And I've gotten it from Andy countless times. So, when Andy calls, no matter what, I answer.

Andy is brilliant and has an important job in DC, but he is always unassuming. He asks if I have time to talk. I hesitate because my unfinished book is literally staring at me from my enormous monitor, but it's

Andy. Forty-five minutes later, we've gotten caught up on the trajectories of our kids' lives. The things that bring us pride—his son's brilliance in math, my daughter's transition to a college she loves—and the things that worry us about those same kids. The scary things that are happening with older loved ones. The shitty things that are happening with work or at home. And we also talk about the one-off moments of abject joy, like our primary relationships—his with Amy, mine with Dan—that make the hell tolerable and make the good days divine.

When I can hear in both of our voices that we're feeling tugged by whatever tasks await, instead of segueing to *Goodbye* I decide instead to go deep and ask, gently, if he's taking care of himself. He laughs and says no, not really. Says he knows he needs to, but life is so fucking busy. And I smile and think about the doctor appointment I've been putting off because for all kinds of fucked up reasons I feel like I have to lose weight before I can go see a doctor. I tell this to myself, but even this is too vulnerable to share with Andy. Instead, I tell him I'm in the same boat, and that I'm not going to be that friend who nags him to go to that doctor's appointment. "But I do want you to know that I get it, and how hard it is, and that we also need to take care of ourselves as we're taking care of everyone else," I tell him, as I'm telling it to myself as well. "People are counting on us to be there for them," I tell him. "I'm counting on you to be there," I say. He says, "I know. I need you, too. My parents are in their eighties and are getting sick. And one day they'll be gone and we're in our fifties and we're up next." I hate hearing this, because I do not want to die. But I also love being frank and clear about the years moving on, because facing it head-on feels better than cowering in the corner and hoping the truth will pass. I tell him, "You matter to me, And (my nickname for him). You really matter. I want you to know that I don't have that many close friends and I know we hardly ever talk but you really matter to me." He goes, "I love you more than I can possibly show." We both have tears in our voices now, these two fifty-one-year-olds who met in college, who hold each other over the phone line as we face the howling darkness.

I don't need research to tell me that having Andy in my life means we'll both live longer and more joyfully.

WHAT LOVE LOOKS LIKE

And of course, there's Dan.

Dan and I have been together a whopping thirty-three years and married for twenty-eight. I'm proud of that. Because three decades of togetherness didn't come easy, and hasn't always been fun. There were the doldrums where we coexisted like roommates. There were a couple painful years when we were very disconnected and had to try to find our way back to each other (therapy FTW).

We enjoyed eleven amazing years before Sawyer and Avery arrived (seven as a married couple). But like most couples we found that babies changed things between us. We wanted them badly—went to some lengths to conceive them, in fact—and we were lucky to have both healthy and "easy" babies, who became delightful toddlers and children. And my mom was with us, helping us raise them, so we had more couple time than the average pair of new parents, by far. So, it wasn't the kids themselves. It was that once they arrived the rhythm of our life—which frankly I think we'd totally taken for granted—was completely disrupted. Whereas life used to be about him, me, and us (and work, and family, and friends), and felt long and languid and silly and sensual and hopeful and fun, now our daily schedule had a shorter radius. Everything revolved around our kids' sleep, meals, poops, and play schedules. We were tired, which meant we were impatient with ourselves and with each other.

As adorable and amazing as the kids were, I really missed this *other* adorable and amazing person my mom calls "Sir Dan." We couldn't even seem to connect when we *did* connect—as on our semiannual "love trips," the two-night getaways every six months, which were the ingenious advice of Dan's grandmother, "Nana." We'd started going on them when Sawyer was six months old and have done so without fail every six months since. They'd been amazing for the first few years but in 2002, three years into parenthood, the trip was rather meh. The obligatory photo to capture the moment via tripod (it was the era before selfies) shows us looking like we're trying desperately hard to look genuinely happy. And failing.

That was the year of our tenth wedding anniversary and we threw a party in our backyard. We invited four couples who were more or less at our age and stage, as well as my older brother George and my mom. Saw-yer (three) and Avery (one) were tucked away upstairs with a babysitter. We splurged on a caterer who brought delicious food and drink, fine linens, and sparkly lights. Our guests sat along the long edges of the table that stretched across the grass and Dan and I sat at either end. Me being bold and never at a loss for words, I stood to toast Dan. With my cham-pagne aloft I smiled and said, "You know, there were times over this past year when I wondered if when we got to this point we'd even have anything to celebrate." Our guests looked down at their plates or off into the distance. This was a reveal, yes, but I could see in some of their eyes that they got it. They were in the throes of parenting young children, too. Sir Dan stood at the other end of the table, raised his glass, put his other hand on his heart, and smiled. "I'll wait for you if you'll wait for me."

This is what love looks like.

Almost two decades later that scene still takes my breath away. My brilliant introverted partner made it all okay. He was telling me, us, and our gathered friends and family that there was nothing wrong with us, that this was circumstance, and that it would pass. I can't swear what I looked like or sounded like in response but it was some combination of a cocked head and tears and an *Awwwwwwwww*. Even so, I'm not sure I believed him—just saying it doesn't make it so. But I desperately wanted him to be right. This was the person who, upon celebrating finally getting pregnant with Sawyer, gave me a diamond necklace and said, "This is for us to remember what we had *before* we had kids." Like he'd had a premo-nition. I clutched at this necklace as I sat and ate the fancy anniversary meal. The necklace was a talisman, a portal to a memory of an earlier time, a promise that he and I would feel that way about each other again.

Right he was, although the easier time of it came slowly and it would be years before the deep connection returned and I didn't need to clutch the diamond necklace as a reminder. Kids outgrew feedings, diapers, and naps, and started to become a little more self-sufficient. When the kids were eight and six, he found this idea online:

1. Print the statement "I love you because _____" and frame it behind glass.
2. Get a dry-erase marker.

3. Take turns writing on the glass with a dry-erase marker however often it feels right to you.

Dan created a little framed statement for us, and we must have exchanged that thing a thousand times by now and worn out two dozen dry-erase pens. We've written things like, *I love you because* . . .

Of Saturday morning.
Of how you look in that t-shirt and those jeans.
You like the soft cushiony spaces of life.
You're not grossed out by weird body stuff.
You talk to me about what's bothering you.
You help my mother out.
You help your mother out.
You wore that cowboy hat.
You have a lot of faith in us.
You make me feel like the moon and the astronaut.
You like to watch me grow.
You cried out for me in your sleep.
You're the one I want to come home to.
You said yes.
You say you'll handle everything and you mean it.
You came home early yesterday to spell me.
You make people laugh and cry.
You sang me a poo song when my tummy hurt.
I can feel you loving me as I sleep.
You know the right thing to do and you do it.
You knew right away that you were sorry.
No one else loves the way you do.
Even when things are blah you're still the most beautiful thing in my
    life.
You come get me when I'm hiding from myself.
You ran out of words for love.
You know how to snake the shower drain.
You meet me at the edges and in the middle.
You look longingly at me in public.

You came home as soon as you could.

You came home.

*The racy things—though not included here—are also important to note. And to that point, I can't write a book on adulting and not mention sexual intimacy, yet what am I going to say? Sex is how we got here *and* it's good for you. It's a most ingenious creation of the universe, hormones, nerve endings, and God. Go get some. What you do, with whom, and with how many, is none of my business. As we told our kids when they were teenagers, as long as it's: 1) safe, 2) consensual, and 3) mutually pleasurable, go for it. And let me underscore the mutually pleasurable part. Don't be that person who only cares about getting their own needs met.

FOR THE LONG TERM

The longest study of humans ever conducted (called The Harvard Grant Study, which followed a group of men from their early twenties until the end of their lives) has kicked off a zillion findings over the decades. Perhaps the greatest, most universal, and most critical is this one: "Happiness equals love, full stop." ("Full stop" is old-fashioned language. It comes from the time of the telegram, which was a way to communicate a written message instantly over the phone and was routinely used to communicate overseas during the first three-quarters of the twentieth century. At the end of a message the transcriber would type: "Full stop." As in "That's it, that's all there is.") Today we might say, "Happiness equals love, period."

In his "What Makes a Good Life?" TED Talk, Robert Waldinger, the researcher currently responsible for this seventy-five-year-old study, says, "Just like the millennials in [a] recent survey, many of our men when they were starting out as young adults really believed that fame and wealth and high achievement were what they needed to go after to have a good life. But over and over, over these seventy-five years, our study has shown that the people who fared the best were the people that leaned into relationships with family, with friends, with community." He continues, "So, this message, that good, close relationships are good for our health and well-being, this is wisdom that's as old as the hills. Why is this so hard to get and so easy to ignore? Well, we're human. What we'd really like is a quick fix. Something we can get that'll make our lives good and keep 'em that way. Relationships are messy and they're complicated and the hard work of tending to family and friends, it's not sexy or glamorous, and it's also lifelong, it never ends."

But you gotta.

When they looked at who was healthy at eighty years of age, it had nothing to do with the person's cholesterol levels. It was who had been happiest in their relationships at fifty.

Having hit that milestone fairly recently myself, I think this is an opportunity for me to go and kiss Dan.

DON'T JUST TAKE MY WORD FOR IT

MEET AKSHAY—Strengthening Ties While Staying True to Himself

Akshay is a thirty-six-year-old gay South Asian/Indian male physician who grew up in Michigan and now lives in Chicago. He was estranged from his parents for ten years because they refused to accept the fact that he was gay, but he refused to let them go. This is his story.

In 2007, when he was twenty-two and about to graduate college, Akshay came out to himself, his friends, and his parents all at once. I was his dean. All the time I'd known him he'd had a distant look of fear in his eyes, like an animal backed into a corner. While he was warm, funny, brilliant, and earnest, something was clearly *wrong*. So, when he came out, it all made sense to me, and I thought it was wonderful to see him beginning to give himself permission to be himself. His parents had the opposite reaction.

"With anything said to my parents over the phone there's a risk of them overreacting or not reacting in the way they intended. So, I'd told them by email." His dad immediately flew out and took Akshay to a Hindu temple, where he paid a priest to pray to try to "fix" Akshay. "There were all these monuments to gods and goddesses in front of me, and the familiar scent of the incense. It felt like me versus all Indian people, all Hindu people. I remember feeling, *Not only is my dad not accepting me right now, but my whole culture is rejecting me.*

I felt like I had done something truly horrible. After that we went back to Dad's hotel and I was sitting on the bed talking to Mom on the phone and she was telling me, 'This can't be possible. Don't do this.' After my dad returned home, I would occasionally talk to my mom on the phone, but it was business-like and not addressing things head on. When I would ask to talk to my dad, Mom would tell me he couldn't talk to me even though I could hear him in the background." It went on like this for a couple months but then his parents swept it under the rug.

Akshay's parents grew up in India and met just weeks before their arranged marriage in the early 1980s. She was highly educated, and a singer of some repute. He was an engineer. They followed his career prospects to Dow Chemical, headquartered in Midland, Michigan. A few years later, Akshay and his fraternal twin brother were born. "My brother and I always had a business-like relationship with my parents. We were defined by our achievements rather than our identity. Gotta look good on paper. Be valedictorian. Do this and this and this. I was number one in our class of four hundred and my brother was number two. When the garage door opened and Dad was home, we'd better have done what he expected. There was never a true connection of getting to know who we were and what we wanted from life."

Instead, his parents valued status and outward appearances. "It really mattered what other people were saying about us. Whenever I did a performance or recital—I played violin and piano—all we'd talk about was what other people had said about the performance. Never 'We're so proud of you, you worked so hard for this.'" His parents also lacked an emotional connection to each other and seemed to have little in common. "My brother and I had this theory that because of the pain of their marriage they were living vicariously through their children. Maybe if they were really strict and had such high standards for us growing up we'd be super high achievers and somehow make this all worth it."

Akshay was headed to med school after college but spent a gap year doing research. He supported himself on his stipend of $20 an hour—his first tantalizing taste of being in charge of himself. "The transition from living in a dorm where my parents paid for room, food, and tuition, to my research job where I supported myself even if it was paycheck to paycheck was the first moment I felt that I didn't need to rely on anyone." A year later he enrolled in the medical school at the University of Michigan, which he chose for its excellence, the in-state tuition, and the opportunity to be physically closer to his parents, which he hoped would increase the chances of repairing things with them. (It did not.) He took out loans to pay for tuition and living expenses, furthering his sense of independence from his parents. And he began to frequent the gay bars and clubs in Ann Arbor and for the first time explore what it meant to be a gay man. "It was to some degree a nice distraction from the issues with my parents. But it wasn't enough to offset it."

A year and a half after he came out, in the midst of his first year of medical school, Akshay tried once again to connect with his parents, this time with a detailed ten-page letter. Again he was met with rejection and the sense that it should not be discussed further. "I had a lot of support from my friends, and my brother. But with my parents I felt I'd tried enough times to get them to try to accept me. I was just giving up at that point. Now our relationship was very strained, even worse than it had been before I came out. We would talk about superficial things, and we could all sense that if we ever got into something more personal it would cause trouble and more conflict. My twin brother and I continued to lead parallel lives. He was also becoming a doctor. They'd ask him if he'd 'found a girl,' and he did meet someone in his residency whom they accepted into the family. Yet they were not asking me the same thing because they didn't want to know the answer. For lack of a better word it was a 'Don't ask, don't tell' situation."

Akshay began to struggle with anxiety and depression. He graduated med school in 2012, did a three-year pediatric residency in New York, then moved to Chicago for a fellowship in pediatric hematology and oncology, which would become his specialty. Along the way he'd dated a number of men, but "when feelings would come about I would shut them off and move on to the next person." He credits a great therapist in the Chicago area for seeing him through some very tough times.

In 2017, he was on the phone with his dad talking about his brother's recent engagement. "After maybe eight years of not talking about my sexuality, he hinted to me about 'finding a nice girl to marry.' That hit me really hard. It seemed like such a small comment to make, but I responded with anger. I told him, 'We've talked about this before. I'll just tell you that nothing has changed.' That was the end of the conversation. There was no acceptance or interest in trying to learn more." Akshay was thirty-two, and it had been ten years since he'd come out.

In the summer of 2018, he was in his first serious relationship. He invited his boyfriend to his brother's wedding but brought him "just as a friend." "We never held hands or did anything to publicly show that we were a couple. My sister-in-law's family could tell though, and they were very accepting. My parents, on the other hand, were polite to him but kept their distance. I saw my mom and dad looking over at us and I could just tell that they knew."

Later that summer Akshay wrote the letter that would change everything. "Back in 2007 I was very defensive and angry, like, *This is normal. This is this. This is that. It's not going to hurt me. I'll be fine.* Whereas I wrote this new letter from a place of love. From wanting to repair my relationship with them. I said, 'I'm writing this not to make you feel bad or guilty or because I want to vent or am confused, but because I want to repair what is clearly a very damaged relationship.' One of the most important things I said is that 'I would not be reaching out if I didn't love you and value you as my parents. I wish badly that we could move forward in a relationship based on honesty and authenticity in the time we have left together.' I don't go into too much detail but I make very clear that I'm standing my ground in terms of who I am, that this is something that hasn't changed, if anything I have become even more secure in my identity. And I was finally able to make clear what I have gone through as a result of their rejection, which is not something I had been able to do up to that point. I told them about the anxiety and depression. Told them it's been crippling at times, and has interfered with my ability to have meaningful relationships with friends and people I date, and interfered with my ability to focus at work. So, I made it very clear to them, no holding back, what this shame, rejection, discrimination has done to me. Because one of their biggest attacks on me ten years ago was *Look what you're putting us through.* I wanted to make it clear that as much hurt as I was putting them through, I went through something even worse as a result of their rejection."

As Akshay reads this letter to me I can hear the strain in his voice. "I felt like I had to be the adult in the situation. For my whole life, I was the child who had to check boxes to be worthy of their love and acceptance. But in this situation, I had to be the adult and teach them something about what I had learned, and take some responsibility for my relationship with them rather than wait and wait for them to try to repair things on their own. I really held my ground. And re-reading it gets me emotional. But I'm also really proud that I am mature enough to focus on my intentions—repairing the relationship with my parents—rather than the potential negative consequences or worst-case scenario. I had faith that if I told the truth, and it came from a place of love and wanting to heal and help my parents and me move forward, I couldn't go wrong in sending this."

Akshay's dad wrote back within a few hours. 'Dear Akshay, I love you more than I love myself. I simply like you to lead a healthy and very happy life. Understanding your feelings from your email I fully accept the path you've been forced to pursue. Stay in touch, love Dad.' Even though this was only "halfway there," Akshay says, "this was a better response than anything I've ever gotten from him by far." His mom responded, "I ditto dad's letter to you. I love you dearly and want your happiness. Hope you will not be distant."

He continues, "It was a win to just not have a rejection. Clearly something had changed in them. Clearly they had learned something. But most telling was when my mom and dad called me that evening. They said, 'We love you no matter what.' And that just brought tears to my eyes. I can't remember ever hearing that before from them in my entire life. I finally had some hope that we could work through this. My dad then said, 'You were too small to remember how I used to hold you both in my two hands for hours and hours. I do remember! God bless you both. Take care!' Akshay knew that this was a big step for someone who is otherwise emotionally removed. "So, it felt very touching. Showed me how much love he really does have to give."

In 2019 Akshay reconnected with Nick, a white guy from Indiana. "He's someone I had seen a few times many years earlier with whom there had been an emotional spark. So, I texted him one day, and we hung out for a couple of months, and started dating officially that March. After quarantining separately during the pandemic, I moved into his space, and more of a permanent move is coming in the next month. It feels wonderful. I feel like I've met my soul mate. He's not just my partner, he's my best friend. We're really close and really kind to each other. Having that deep friendship as a foundation is really critical." Nick is also a doctor—a psychiatrist, to be exact. "I think that's part of the connection. It's wonderful to be with someone who gets that I work with sick kids and their families, who understands what it's like to spend your day giving so much to others."

As you might expect, Akshay told his parents about Nick by email. "It wasn't long after I started dating Nick that I informed my parents about it. They've been so supportive. They've met him twice. In the fall of 2019 they came into Chicago for dinner and drinks with us, and told me how nice he was and how much they liked him. Then for Thanksgiving, we all went down to New Orleans, where my brother and sister-in-law live. Her family is there, too. My parents spent a lot of time really getting to know Nick. Due to the pandemic I've only been able to FaceTime them since. They go out of their way to ask, 'How's Nick doing?' instead of me forcing the subject. And then when the pandemic happened, they said, 'How is that affecting his practice?' This would be their chance to not talk about it, yet they ARE. That's by far and away the most convincing sign that they are inclusive and accepting. They know that he matters to me and they accept that it's real."

I used to tell my students that adulting is doing what you know is right for you, and even if the people who ostensibly love you most threaten to turn against you, you do it anyway. Akshay was there. "I had reached that point that they may disown me for life. But it didn't matter. It's so much more important to be authentic and be who you are than worry about the consequences of what showing your true self would lead to. It's about the intention and being whole and having integrity." And as he grew whole, he became able to try to pull his parents back into his life. From a place of strength. "Now I'm in a position where I wake up each day and it's hard for me to believe they accept me. There was so much momentum from feeling rejected by them. For me to turn around and see that what I thought was going to be impossible for the rest of my life—my parents accepting me—has now come true is still something I'm trying to wrap my head around. It's been that shocking." And that wonderful.

My final question is about the emotionally gut-wrenching nature of his job. After all, every day he works with kids who have a blood disease or cancer. His job is to diagnose, treat, and heal these kids, but it doesn't always work out that way. I ask him if because of his upbringing it's hard to be emotionally available to his patients and their families. Turns out it may be the opposite. "Nick recently said, 'Given how you were raised, it's kind of a miracle you turned out how you turned out.' With my patients and their families I think of them as my own. It's possible that one thing that drew me into pediatrics was being able to immerse myself in the families of my patients and really feel like I'm part of those families. I wonder if subconsciously I enjoy working in this field in part because I didn't have that closeness and that feeling of family growing up. I always wonder if this is my way of pouring out all the love and the connection that I would have liked to have with my own family. I feel a pull to be connected to them. It's not the learning about their diseases and treating them that matters most—as rewarding as that is, the most rewarding is being able to foster really close connections to patients and families."

I told you that when I worked with Akshay as a student, his eyes revealed something was really wrong. Now when I see pictures of him simply being his whole self, his eyes are gleaming and bright. Having loving and secure relationships with people who love you for who you are makes you feel *alive.*

MEET JOE—Forging Relationships to Follow His Dreams

To look at Joe you might miss some of the more salient aspects of his identity. He and his partner, Emily, are pandemic-era transplants to the Republican stronghold of Auburn, Alabama. But Joe supported a progressive candidate in the 2020 Democratic primary. "I think I blend in rather well. I'd probably look very normal in a MAGA hat. I'm used to being presumed to be on their side but it becomes clear when I open my mouth that I'm probably not. I know that I come across as friendly and open. And I look friendly, too. I'm like a Labrador: I'll say hi to anyone, but I have no problem growling or barking or biting." Joe's life is a study in relationships—with his father, his best friend, his partner, himself, and now with his new, conservative community. He takes things as they come and does not flinch. He has come a long way to become this person.

Joe is a thirty-two-year-old straight white man from Dallas, Texas. His parents had six marriages between them. They divorced when Joe was two, and he was raised by his mom in a middle-class community. His father is wealthy, having been born well-off and having made a fortune in executive recruiting. Growing up, Joe stayed with his dad every other weekend and for summer vacations. "My dad called me every day, did the soccer games, the family vacations. But getting him to show up for and support what I was passionate about is where tensions began." Joe lacked for nothing except perhaps the certainty that he was loved no matter what.

Joe met his partner, Emily, when they were undergraduates in the theater department at Southern Methodist University (SMU) in Dallas. He was a senior, directing a scene from *The Tempest.* She was a first-year sharing her audition monologue and song for the freshman showcase. "Emily crushed it, and I was looking for strong actors for my *Tempest* scene, so I went up to her and asked her to be in it. She loves to remind people that I didn't ultimately cast her (I picked a different scene altogether), but we both agree that this was our first use of our love language: we are attracted to good people and good work." Love was indeed floating around in the air. They dated briefly. But Joe didn't know what he wanted in a relationship or even how to be *in* a relationship. And the relationship he most wanted to work on was with his very-hard-to-please father.

Joe hoped his dad would show up to see the plays he was acting in or directing, but no. His dad didn't seem to understand the whole theater thing— neither its validity in the world nor its importance to Joe. When Joe dropped seventy pounds of excess weight in college, his dad acknowledged the change, but then pinched the fat on Joe's belly and said, "Well, what about this?" Then, there was the family money. The kind of wealth Joe's family possesses is held in various financial accounts that must be managed, including a trust fund that was left to Joe by a grandmother who died before he was born, which she'd stipulated was "to be used to follow your dreams." Joe's father oversaw all of this money, decided where to invest it, and kept a close watch on how Joe spent it, which caused Joe anxiety. "For years, if I was going to do even the simplest banking transaction, my hands would be shaking." Joe also didn't seem to have a good head for business, which frustrated his father. One summer during college, when Joe was part of a directing workshop in New Mexico, through the SMU-in-Taos program, his dad called to yell at him about a snafu with a business matter Joe had been handling. "I'm in tears in Taos because my dad is yelling at me for not knowing how to do business well. All I can think is I need to be a good capitalist. I need to figure out how to make the MOST money.

"I had no interest in my dad's field, but I wanted to achieve in my field what my dad had done in his." So, when Joe graduated from college, he took off for Los Angeles with his childhood best friend, Tommy, also a theater kid, who had just graduated from Syracuse University. They found an apartment. Tommy quickly got work as an actor. Joe got cast as an extra in commercials and on *Glee*, which felt cool and allowed him to support himself for quite a while. Yet television work simply made clear to Joe that his passion was the stage, where everything happens in real time, in one take, and you have to own whatever you say. Plus, the loudest voice in his head—that of his father—told him he had to get a "real job," and to his father, being an actor was not that. But maybe helping other artists get their careers going could be.

Joe landed a coveted job at one of LA's top talent agencies, where he scouted talent for commercials and helped clients navigate deals. "I was that annoying person watching TV who always said, 'Hey, I know that person! I know that person!'" Meanwhile, Emily was becoming a revered member of the SMU theater community. She visited Joe once in LA, "but it was totally platonic." They "kinda stayed in touch but not really." Years later Emily would say that she'd known right away that Joe was "the one." But it would take Joe about five years and a lot of on-again, off-again with Emily before he figured it out for himself. Getting ahead at work was his priority.

Joe was now on the fast track to becoming an agent, and he began thinking, *Maybe this is what I'm supposed to be doing*. "I was getting what my dad would call 'no-bullshit experience,' building up that callus you get by working in the industry and becoming more shrewd, cold, and capitalist." It was hard work but also glamorous. One of the aspects of the job he loved most was going to comedy venues and theaters to scout talent. "The most badass I ever felt in LA was having a business card with the name of a reputable talent agency on it. It became *This is who I am*." When he visited his father at his home in Palm Springs he'd take a stack of papers from the agency with him. It was the first time Joe was doing work his father could relate to. He remembers feeling like, *Look! See! I have real big-boy work that follows me home! It's a real job! See?* Sometimes when Joe visited, his dad would bring out some weed, and they'd smoke together. Then his dad would turn around and criticize Joe for smoking too much. On the phone with me, a decade later, Joe sees his father's criticism of his work, his weight, his use of weed and alcohol, and how he handled money this way: "There was always something to control."

Being an agent-in-the-making was fabulous, until it wasn't. "Actors would turn down a two-day commercial in Santa Monica that paid seventy-five thousand dollars because they didn't want to deal with the traffic. Or they'd say, 'It's cheesy. I don't want people to see me in that light.' I get it. They're artists. No actor wants to be a commercial actor. You can feel like you're whoring yourself out. But it's a year's salary for two days of work! The theater person in me said, 'You can't *do* that. You have an *opportunity*. You have to *take it*.'"

In general, the theater person inside Joe was starting to yell louder. In early

2014 Joe turned twenty-five, which in his mind was the age by which you're supposed to be doing what you want to be doing with your life. Tommy was making it as an actor and was helping to develop a show that would become a Broadway musical. (How cool is that?!) But Joe, while successful by many measures, was fucking miserable. One night while Tommy was out of town, Joe was hanging out at his friend Nolan's apartment and had what he calls a breakdown. Pacing around Nolan's kitchen, Joe started shouting, "I've checked off all the boxes. I wear a tie. I work nine to five. I'm doing what I'm *supposed* to be doing. I'm becoming more successful. I'm not *afraid* of working really hard. I just want to work at a place I *really* like!" He tells me that it felt terrifying to think about abandoning all this success "just for my own happiness." (As if his own happiness is a trifle.) He told Nolan, "There are realities of being an adult: You have to have a job to pay your bills. But the other reality is insisting on happiness." Nolan watched Joe spew all these feelings, then said, "If you had to pick either acting or directing, which one would you choose?" Suddenly, everything became clear for Joe. He wanted to be a director. This meant going to grad school, which meant moving to a place where he could build his theater résumé, which meant leaving LA, which meant abandoning his and Tommy's plan to take LA by storm. Joe remembers, "This meant I would have to risk disappointing my best friend, someone whose approval I greatly valued, in order to do what I *knew* I had to do for myself."

He slept on it. The next morning, he called Tommy and relayed what had happened the night before. "Tommy just heard me out. No criticism. Didn't make me justify it. He just said warmly, 'Well, go then. Do it.'" Reflecting on this a decade later, Joe realizes that his best friend, Tommy, had just given him his "first real whiff of baseline respect and trust." Or what psychotherapist Lori Gottlieb calls "the delicious feeling of being known." Thanks to Joe's growing sense of self and the support of his best friend, a happier life was beckoning. Joe didn't want to waste any more time.

With a newfound sense of purpose and urgency, Joe quit his job, moved back to Dallas, started directing local theater to build up a portfolio of work he'd be able to use to apply to graduate school, and reconnected with Emily, who had just graduated frm SMU and was directing a local show. He may not have known then *why* Emily mattered to him, but he knew she *did*. Their respect for each other as theater artists was immense. He calls her "an amazing diplomat with so much goddamn grace." He thinks she admires his uncompromising stance on things he believes in. They dated off and on. Sometimes they'd go two-stepping in Fort Worth. "We kept coming back to each other. We were obviously attracted to each other, but what drew us back was the work. The love and joy of directing theater and doing it at a high level and knowing it was good."

Together they built a new way of putting on performances in their community that they billed as "House Party Theatre," which is exactly what it sounds like—a live theater performance in a location where a party is also underway, such as a living room or an art gallery. Under this umbrella, Joe and Emily produced everything from classical to experimental works. They turned the concept into a theater company. It became a thing. Other nontraditional theater organizations began to proliferate in Dallas. The crowds grew so large that they had to worry about the fire marshal. Joe and Emily grew more confident that their work was at a high enough level to be worthy of it being their profession.

Professionally they were a team of equals. Personally, they didn't know what they were to each other. He was into her, and she was into him, that was clear. His reasons for breaking things off were always perfectly rational, at least in his own mind, and he was always kind about it. "After I had broken it off yet again, Emily said she didn't think we could even be friends, let alone be romantically involved again. But I was always very insistent that, 'Yes, we *can* be friends. It doesn't have to *be* a relationship. I just knew I loved her as a *person*.'" The push and pull left Emily bewildered. Her parents had been together for thirty-five years. She knew what being in a long-term, committed relationship looked like and required. And she knew that what she had with Joe was not it.

One night in January 2016, they were just hanging out as friends in Joe's kitchen, sharing songs with one another, like "Oh, have you heard this? Let me show you this."

As Joe remembers it, "Eventually, a song we'd danced to before came on, and I said to her, 'Not being cliché, but do you want to dance?' So, we started two-stepping, not making it a thing, not being romantic. Songs keep shuffling out of this crappy speaker in my kitchen. Then we get a slow song. And I say to myself, *Dude, what are you doing? What are you waiting for?*" And then it got cosmic for Joe. He got the strong sense from the universe that the whole purpose of going to LA in the first place, and being miserable in the work he felt he was "supposed to do," and having the epiphany about happiness being what matters, and moving back to Dallas, "was so I could be in the right frame of mind, and have this discovery right here in my kitchen about who Emily is to me." That night, he realizes, "She's this person you can look dead fucking through and let them also see through you and you're not afraid. There's an invitation to be honest, a shared respect," and he told himself, *This is the partner you've been waiting for.* Unlike Emily, who had her folks as role models, Joe had had no road map for love. But he did have a road map for hurt, and he was desperately afraid of going there. "She had every reason to tell me to fuck off. But she didn't." Emily seemed, in her own strong and gracious way, to nudge him out of that terror and into her arms.

"Emily deeply cares about those in her circle and is very protective of her time. The amount of time she was investing in me? It's like she sees something in me that I'll never grasp." Joe's voice trails off, then he yells at me teasingly for making him go there. I get it. This kid grew up with a father's love intertwined with judgment, leaving him with a fragile sense of self. He tells me that Emily is "strong enough that she doesn't need anyone, so the people in her life are one hundred percent at her discretion." It's almost like Joe is saying, *I can't believe she chose me.*

Once he and Emily were officially a thing, it was time to meet each other's parents. First, they drove to visit Emily's parents, a pair of artists and educators who live in South Carolina. At the time, Emily was putting on a new play, and her parents wanted to hear all about it. They asked things like, "Hey, how are rehearsals going? Is that actor still giving you trouble? Have they mastered their lines? Is the staging still a headache?" When they all got up to get more to drink, Joe pulled Emily aside. "They know everything about what you're doing. You just share it? You don't have to justify anything to them?" And she said, "Yeah, why would I?" Another epiphany for Joe: In a loving relationship, *why would you have to justify yourself?* The relationship between Emily and her parents had that "delicious feeling of being known" quality, like Joe's friendship with Tommy. "That's when I knew that how I was raised and what I've accepted as normal is unhealthy. Not that Emily's family is perfect. But having a baseline respect for people and their choices, just being able to say, 'I love you,' instead of 'We're a family, so you have to do as I say' is everything." Then Emily's parents wanted to know more about Joe. "We'd driven all the way from Texas to visit, so they knew that this round of dating must be serious. They took an interest in me. Listened to what I said. Even in this serious moment, I didn't have to justify one goddamn choice I was making to them." Meeting Emily's parents showed Joe that Emily was a safe path forward. And maybe even showed him what a relationship based on unconditional love looks like.

Joe then took Emily to visit his dad in Palm Springs. "We went for a walk in his neighborhood. My dad thoughtfully inquired about Emily's passion, which she explained is directing. Then she described the work she and I are doing with House Party Theatre and how well it's going. My dad sounded intrigued and downright supportive. Then, in the next beat, he looked over to me and said, 'Since *your* theater company is a failure, what are *you* going to do?'" Now, it was Emily's turn to pull Joe to the side. She whispered, "He knows we do the same thing, right?" Joe explained to his dad that it was the same theater company and that they'd never taken a loss financially, which was a badge of honor for Joe and Emily, and something Joe knew his dad should respect. "But he shrugged it off," Joe remembers, "reinforcing his opinion that I was wasting my time." As awkward as it was for Joe to be needled by his dad in front of Emily, he was glad that Emily witnessed how he stood up to his dad. "She saw that I wasn't willing to bend or break."

Back at home, House Party Theatre continued to thrive and launched them both on their MFA journeys. Emily went to the University of Iowa and Joe headed to Brooklyn College in New York, where he joined back up with Tommy, who was now starring in a Broadway musical. For Joe's final project (known as his "thesis show"), he directed *Lear*, a play written and originally directed by the highly touted experimental playwright Young Jean Lee, the first Asian American woman playwright to be produced on Broadway. *Lear* is about children becoming adults in a way that their father didn't envision. It takes the shape of a young adult's mind breaking apart as the nuclear family deals with the impending death of the father figure. The family members each tell their own story to themselves, each dealing with the reality of their story of what's behind the mask they wear for themselves and for each other. "The show was very hard to do, and it was the first time in my artistic career when the cast, crew, and I were like, *We* know *this is good.*"

It's not hard to see why Joe chose this play for his thesis show. "This play was me saying, 'Dad, this is who I am. This is what I do. I love you, Dad. Do you love me back?'" I don't know why we need our father's approval so much, but so many of us...do. I wrote about feeling this myself in chapter 5, "Stop

Pleasing Others." It's an ethereal yearning for connection that seems to defy logic. "He hadn't seen any of my stuff in ten years. I had hopes that he would fucking see it." I picture Joe's father as continually refusing to hold Joe's outstretched hand.

But Joe's dad did come to see the show. He flew out to New York the day before the show, and hung out with Joe and Tommy. Joe steeled himself for a difficult conversation, because his dad had been critical of Tommy's choice to pursue theater, too. Yet, when Joe's dad asked Tommy about his career, he listened, nodded, smiled, and praised Tommy. "Then my dad turned to me and said, 'When are *you* going to get a real job?'" Joe took a deep breath. He knew that the following night might be his last chance to prove to his dad that his work *was* real. That his work mattered. That *he* mattered.

Closing night went great. The cast and crew gave Joe a bottle of Jack Daniels, and invited Joe's dad to join them at their cast party, which was being held at a fancy bar. But as a recovering alcoholic, Joe's dad avoids bars, so he said he'd just head back to Joe's place. Joe waved the cast away with a smile, and said he'd catch up with them later. As he and his dad walked back home, Joe's father said, "Shit, you can do it!" The tone was congratulatory, maybe even a tad proud. This was something Joe, now twenty-nine, had been waiting to hear for most of his life. But then his father started talking about how the MFA meant Joe could become a professor. It became clear that he thought Joe was getting an MFA for the *purpose* of teaching. "I realized, *Oh man. I like teaching. And yes, I may need to teach on the side. But like, directing, that's where I should be.*" Joe tried to explain, again, that directing itself was his passion. His dad pressed, again, the importance and legitimacy of a different path.

Back at Joe's place the two of them sat down and started smoking a bowl together. Joe wanted to pregame a little before meeting up with his cast, and cracked the Jack Daniels. His father called him an alcoholic. "I'm like, *Dude, I'm getting ready to go out and celebrate.*" His father said, "It's sad. You've changed so much since LA." Joe replied, "You mean since I decided to insist on my own happiness? I HOPE I've changed.

"It killed me that he comes and sees the show, then seizes on my drinking. Like it's not okay that I want to go out with my cast and celebrate this huge accomplishment. It was always something. It could have been, 'You smoke too much pot, or you weigh too much, or you don't make enough money.' That was always the pattern. I would be this Labrador retriever and come back with this duck in my mouth and he would be like, 'Great. Where are the other ducks?'"

Joe had had enough with this person who barely knew him and always rendered judgment. "I was like, 'You get to make declarations about who I am and about my character because you're my *father*?'" In the months to come, his father started hounding Joe about money again. He told Joe to relinquish control over the trust account from his grandmother. Joe refused; an official at his bank made clear to Joe that this money was *his*. "I was threatening autonomy to a controller." His father became increasingly threatening by text, and even contacted Emily and Tommy to say that Joe was an alcoholic and needed an intervention. Joe wondered if he and his father would even *have* a relationship if money was out of the picture. "I think he couldn't believe that I could love him or be interested in him for anything other than his money, which breaks my heart, because my dad is not a bad person."

Joe sent his dad an email asking for a relationship without conditions. "I said, 'I don't want to fight with you. I love you. You're my dad. I don't want there to be all these fucking conditions about what I have to do to merit success and afford you entry into my life. I just want you to be a human being that I love, and just coexist.'" His father replied, "Well, if we are going to have a relationship without conditions you need to get one thing straight." And that was it. Joe was done.

"We had a relationship founded on money. He's paid for my schooling, and carried me for thirty years. I think about it as *I've never had to learn to walk because you carried me this whole way. And now that I'm learning to walk on my own, you're mad at me for not knowing how to walk? BUT YOU CARRIED ME! Of course I don't know how to walk. Anytime I tried and fell down, you'd yell at me for not knowing how to walk and insist that this is why I need to be carried.*"

Joe gained autonomy by opening his own checking account and by asking his bank to take his father's name off the account that legally belongs to Joe. They seemed to do so happily, as if Joe was not the first thirtysomething to rightfully wrest control of money out of a parent's hands. This made Joe happy, too. But the psychological freedom was even greater. "My breakup with my dad was a terrifying prospect. I'd had no experiences to suggest I could really stand on my own without being carried, except for the fact that I trusted that Emily and Tommy—the two most important people in the world to me—wouldn't waste their time on me if I was who my dad seems to think I am. Their faith in me showed me that maybe I bring something to the table, too. Then, I did my thesis show, which proved how much I'd grown professionally. Emily and Tommy plus *Lear* intersected and solidified my confidence that I could end this toxic relationship with my dad." He decided to break up with his dad. He ceased communication with him and they no longer have any contact. Sometimes that's how life goes.

Life went on. Joe got happier. He moved to Iowa for Emily's final year of her MFA. (Her program lasted three years while his lasted two.) The money from his grandmother helped make ends meet in Iowa. Joe and Emily deepened their commitment to each other and got engaged. During the pandemic a friend offered them jobs at his theater company, in Auburn. Emily is director of development, a paid job with benefits, and Joe is associate artistic director, which is part-time; he supplements that income with odd jobs. Emily also has another job on the side. "We don't compromise when it comes to the importance or value of our work. We recognize we're artists. It's not, 'Oh, he *also* does theater; she *also* does theater.' No. We're theater artists."

Their family includes two cats, Masha and Pip, and two dogs, Charlie and Abner. At their dog park in Auburn they meet people whose politics differ from their own. "We all love our dogs. I'm hypersensitive to any possible common ground. At the dog park, or walking down the street with our dogs, I have positive experiences with people who are going to vote for someone I abhor." These interactions spur Joe to ask himself, *What is that person's story?* He explains to me that a dog is a reflection of its owner's humanity. "Your dog tells on you: If a dog is good, it has a good owner, but if your dog's an asshole, you're an asshole. I can't hate these people and like their dog at the same time, and maybe that's a privilege I have. But there is something there. We are both in this dog park. There are rules in this fenced area. We don't hold the same values outside of this area, but we understand that our dog's behavior is a reflection of us. Maybe we're not as entrenched in our polarized views as we think we are, because each of us is here with a dog that we care about, and the recognition of us as people who all care about dogs, at least, is abundantly clear. In those moments, we love our dogs and don't care about politics. Maybe we're telling a bit more about the truth of ourselves when we open up to each other in the dog park." Joe describes this potential bond between conservative and liberal dog owners as "standing in a weird doorway." I find his musings surprising—because I am not a dog owner, so maybe I just don't get it. But his musings also show me a path forward and give me hope.

"If two years ago you'd said, 'You'll be in Auburn,' I would have said, 'What went wrong?' But to be white artists in the South trying to do anti-racist work feels meaningful to me. We're more needed here. There are fewer barriers to reaching policymakers. It's small, and we get to be honest and have these conversations. If we were with a bigger company we probably couldn't be bold and say, 'Hey, we have to talk about some shit.' I'm really questioning. I'm understanding that we are in the presence of real evil. The bell has been rung for this higher calling, and I have no grasp of the scale of what's at stake or of how much hope has been lost, but Emily and I are here for this moment. Ten years ago my thought was, *Make this into a career. Get the awards. Have the money first, and THEN I can serve with my art.* Now I just want to serve. I realize the moment is calling us. If I'm going to do anything meaningful in the face of it, I've got to do it now. I need to see if I can put this pile of money that's in my name to some constructive use."

Joe and Emily are in the work fully, and they're in it with each other. The wedding will happen when crowds of people can once again revel safely in person. But Joe doesn't need a piece of paper from the state of Texas or Alabama to tell him that Emily is his forever. "We both wanted a companion to share this work with. The theater world is so small, so when you see it in other people, you're like, 'She is *it.* She's the rich material I recognize like stardust.' I am certain we collided when we were supposed to, and we stuck when we were supposed to, and now that we're in Auburn we know, *Oh dude, we're on a BIGGER ride than we ever thought and we have very specific roles to play.* We let each other worry about what we should be worried about. And we're each other's stable place. There's a prevailing notion always that *I've got you.* When the shit hits the fan, we will be shoulder to shoulder facing it. We want someone we can fully face the world with."

MEET ASHLEY—Doing the Work to Be in Relationship

Ashley is a thirty-four-year-old newly out queer Black woman who lives in Boston, Massachusetts. She has a master's degree, and her career has centered around social justice in the higher education and nonprofit sectors. She loves hiking and rock climbing, which she self-describes as not the Blackest set of interests! From her responses to an adulting questionnaire I posted online a few years back, it was clear that Ashley has put a tremendous amount of intentionality into being in community, friendship, and relationship with other humans, and squaring the seeming contradictions in her identities, passions, and pursuits. I have her on the phone to get her insights. But first a bit more background on Ashley.

Ashley was raised Southern Baptist Evangelical in Hampton, Virginia, and outside Fort Lauderdale, Florida. Her mom was a single parent who, despite the challenges of raising a child alone and on a working-class income, managed to be there in all respects for Ashley. For example, when Mom sensed that Ashley was being bullied in the third grade, she put Ashley in the car and drove around the neighborhood until they found the girl and then Mom proceeded to chew the girl out. And when as a cheerleader in high school Ashley got injured by a kick to the mouth, Mom had some really choice words for Ashley's coach. Ashley went away to college up in Gainesville at the University of Florida, where she majored in English. In her senior year, her mom was diagnosed with a type of soft-tissue cancer called leiomyosarcoma, but it seemed to be stabilizing so Ashley went off to Philadelphia to serve as an AmeriCorps fellow in an organization that was addressing poverty. As Ashley's two years with AmeriCorps were drawing to a close, her mother fell and broke her hip, which revealed that the cancer was spreading. She came home to care for her mom while supporting herself with a job working with students at the university. Her mother died a few months after Ashley moved home. And although Ashley was part of a large extended family, she now felt like she was on her own.

Ashley was twenty-four and entering her "wildhood"—that concept we covered in chapter 6, "Get Out of Neutral," when you leave the care of your parents and go on important and terrifying quests during which you learn to keep yourself alive, negotiate your social status, navigate sexuality, and cultivate self-reliance. Ashley was about to do that, and because cancer had taken her mom, she was basically alone in the world. Like a wild young-adult animal fending for itself, she was about to experience the bewilderment of having no home and hearth to fall back upon, and no one to reassure her as she sought to bond with others. She would reckon with having to do much more for herself while also doing for others. She would struggle with how to stick with roommates when it felt easier to walk away. She would grapple with how to make real friends in a society that lives increasingly online. But before any of that would happen, and because we're not wild animals but humans, Ashley was offered a lifeline from the community that understands grief. I lost my dad when I was twenty-seven, so I know that we who lose a parent young are unwillingly initiated into a community most of our peers simply do not know exists. (I'll share more about my personal experiences with grief in chapter 10, "How to Cope.") That community was there for me, and it would be there for Ashley, too.

It began with a very special dinner party. The Dinner Party is an organization for people in their twenties and thirties who have lost a loved one. It has chapters all over the U.S. (thedinnerparty.org) and after Ashley's mom died, an AmeriCorps friend who had also lost a parent recently reached out to encourage Ashley to join. The Dinner Party is a simple concept. You just sign up for monthly gatherings with a small group of people in your town with whom you'll gather over supper and talk about your loss. These connections were instantly meaningful to Ashley, and it wasn't long before she passed The Dinner Party invitation along to another friend who'd joined the community of young people who'd lost a parent. These ten years later, with all of that well in her rearview mirror, Ashley still describes herself as someone who "tends to friend people whose parents die."

Most of Ashley's mentors had come from the field of higher education, so in grappling with her next steps she decided to pursue that path, too, with a focus on anti-poverty and anti-racist work within the context of student advising. She uprooted herself and headed far north to Burlington, Vermont, where she enrolled in the University of Vermont (UVM) master's program in higher education and student development, whose social justice mission suited her well.

One of her first tasks in Vermont was to locate the local chapter of The Dinner Party. Finding none, she created a chapter and led a "table" of her own. In the years since, her friend group expanded to include a number of people who have lost loved ones, which becomes a unique point of connection and mutual understanding. "They're my support system. We do holidays together. We all have really dark senses of humor, which is great. One of us will be freaking out about something normal, and someone will be like, 'What's wrong with you?' and they'll be like, 'My mom is dead!' And we get it."

She can see how her mother's death has changed her perspective. "I remember what it felt like to encounter someone who'd suffered the death of a parent, and I wouldn't understand, and I wouldn't want to hear about it. I'd just be like, *Ugh, I hope that never happens to me*. In some ways, it's the ultimate nightmare." Now she's that person who notices when friends appear to be taking their parents for granted. "I'm at the age where people are fighting with their parents about a lot of stuff. One friend is in an argument with her parents about her significant other, and has taken the side of her partner against her parents. I would never say, 'Stop it, my mom is dead.' But in conversation about these kinds of things, I do try to ask, 'Where do you see the love in what your parents are doing?'"

With her master's degree in higher ed from UVM in hand, Ashley got a position in the UVM admissions department, where her job was to recruit talented low-income first-generation students to come to the university. This had been her trajectory in life and now she would be responsible for ensuring others had that same opportunity. She loved meeting with students and their families and loved being a representative of a school she respected so much. But after three years, the constant travel was wearing her out. It was time to figure out next steps. In 2016 she got a job with the Bridgespan Group, a Boston-based global consulting company that helps nonprofits and philanthropists become more impactful in their work. She moved to Boston, where once again she was alone.

"I remember when I was just getting out of college and had overdrafted my credit card account, and I called my mother to help me figure out what I needed to do. Now, I don't even think about calling a parent for help, because I can't. I feel the lack of support when big things are happening. When I moved from Vermont to Massachusetts I was like, *Everything has to go right because I have no fallbacks*. Those situations set a fire under my belly to really support myself and be strong."

She had to meet people. Somehow. This time around when she moved it wasn't to a college campus, which tends to be a place where you can easily meet new people. "When I moved to Boston, I didn't know anyone and totally lacked the skill of how to meet people." Now she was one of thousands of twentysomethings taking the T (the name for Boston's subway system) between home and work, walking the cobblestone streets of this historic city, and braving the tough winter. A feeling of aloneness was settling down around her. Her first idea was to find a local chapter of The Dinner Party. This would prove to be easy as there were many "tables" in the Boston area. Unfortunately, there was a long waitlist, but Ashley had scaled that mountain before. She just created and led a new table of her own. Her grief-counseling community was in place. Check!

Next up was finding roommates she could stick with, which was, at times, rather complicated. She was gaining some insight into her childhood dynamic with her mother, about how it had served her then and how it might be underserving her now. "My mom had this incredible warmth, and she was also very much a force. I was very shy and didn't have any of that force. My mom just wanted her kid to be okay." Here Ashley reflects on the bully situation in third grade, and the cheerleading injury in high school, where in both instances her mom swooped in and handled it. As a result, Ashley thinks, "I never really developed the skills to handle conflict on my own." But if you're going to live with people, you're going to have some conflict. It's just natural. And normal. Yet… "Whenever I had roommate drama, I would just move. I didn't even know how to handle it any other way." After a few years and a few uncomfortable roommate situations in Boston, it was clear that moving in response to conflict was not going to be a successful long-term strategy.

Ashley relocated to a house with five roommates, one of whom had been there for many years and was clearly the guy in charge. Each roommate was assigned one part of the house to clean, and if that chore didn't get done on time, the offending party had to pay everyone else in the house twenty bucks, for a total of one hundred dollars. Ashley's chore was to clean the kitchen and she was supposed to do it every Wednesday night. In her second week of living in the house, she forgot to do it. When she woke Thursday morning she immediately remembered and she raced to the kitchen and cleaned it. But it was too late. As far as the roommate in charge was concerned it didn't matter if you forgot your chore, or just blew it off, or were just new, or whatever. "He was like, 'You broke the rule.' And he was stubborn about it." Past roommates had willingly not done their chores before and had to pony up their hundred-dollar debt to the community. Yet Ashley felt she was just paying rent in exchange for space in the house and "didn't see myself as really 'living *with*' these people." As with prior roommate conflicts, Ashley's instinct was to leave. "This person was really mad at me. I didn't feel like I had the skills to navigate that. It just felt overwhelming at the time. I've always been pretty conflict-averse. I thought to myself, *Okay, gotta move—but I can't! I've been living here less than a month!"*

Something about moving out of a place after living there for so short a time all because she couldn't have a conversation spurred Ashley to get some advice. "I talked to another roommate and was like, 'What do I do?' This room-mate helped me get a better understanding of where the guy in charge was coming from. Once I saw it from his perspective, that his friends had moved on, all of these new people including me were coming into the house and wanting to change the rules, and all of those feelings were coming out on me, it made more sense. They told me to talk to him, so I sat down with him and had a conversation about the problem. We figured it out. I got that we needed an accountability system and he got that we needed to have a punishment that people feel okay about. We ended up changing the rule. The new rule is that if you don't do your chore you have to do everyone's chore the next week. It benefits everybody." (Frankly this sounds WORSE to me because what if the flake doesn't come through and no one else cares because now it's someone else's job, so the house never gets cleaned! But it worked for Ashley and her roommates, and that's what matters.)

"My mind is still blown that a simple conversation resolved the whole sit-uation. We're good now and I can't believe it. Sometimes, I think my mom would see that I couldn't do something, and she would go ahead and do it for me. What could've helped me more is if my mom had sat me down and had a conversation around conflicts—*How do you feel about this situation? What can you think of doing?*—then I might have developed some of those resolution skills earlier on."

While Ashley was working hard to address her tendency toward conflict avoidance on the home front, there was also the matter of friendship to deal with. Ashley wanted friends, as all humans do. Not just people she could see once a month in a support group for grieving twentysomethings, but *friend* friends. "I had been in school where it's so easy to meet people. I hadn't had to make friends without context. I was just so lonely. I didn't know anyone and didn't know how to meet people. And I hadn't really developed any hobbies." She tried the friend-meeting app Bumble BFF (the friendship portion of the dating app Bumble). "I got on this app not for long-lasting friendships but as a way to meet people, and as a way to have folks to do things with, and to get out of my shell a little bit." Being twenty years older than Ashley, I have never used an app to make a friend, so I need a short explanation about how an app can help you do this. "You have a dating profile basically, but you talk more about your interests, what you like to do, and what you're looking for in a friendship. If you swipe right on people, a chat opens up and you start conversing. You're like, 'Okay, I like going to spinning classes, why don't we check out a class and have brunch afterwards?' If you really hit it off you keep hanging out. Ideally, it's organic and based on shared experiences."

So, finding friends via an app was fine, except when it wasn't. "You can come to a conclusion about someone pretty quickly. When you're dating at least you're like, *Okay, we don't want to date anymore.* But with the premise of friendship, if you don't even want to be someone's friend, it's both really awkward to stick it out and also awkward to never talk again. When I was first getting into rock climbing, I did a hangout with someone who shared that interest. You normally build off of that shared interest, but we literally didn't have anything else to talk about. When it's mutual, it's easy. It's just, *Okay, nice meeting you, have a great life.* You just walk away and you don't ever talk again. If it's not mutual, it's awkward. Ideally you say, 'I had a great time but I don't really see this going anywhere and I don't think it makes sense to get together again.' Sometimes you just ghost people."

In the months when she was trying to meet people online, social media was a disappointing enticement. "I noticed that when I was lonely and went on social media, it made me even lonelier. I felt as if I was connected because of 'likes.' As if liking someone's post was actually a meaningful way of interacting with them—but it was a false level of connection that didn't satisfy my deeper need for connection. Social media allows you to passively consume information—and of course everyone's trying to show only their best self, regardless of what's happening in real life—it's only background noise. So, I deleted Facebook. At first, I didn't know if it would be possible to stay connected with anyone being off Facebook, if I'd be left out of things. Then, I went through a really bad friend breakup. I deleted all my friend-making apps, too. I was getting serious FOMO."

The online terrain was proving to be somewhat treacherous, so Ashley did a throwback and decided to try to meet humans in person. "I went to the rock-climbing gym for the first time in my life. I met people. And through those people I met other people. I didn't grow up doing any of those outdoor things. Those spaces are new to me and I found I love engaging in them. Soon, I had a real community. Meanwhile I'd been off Facebook for a month, and I felt really good. I tried staying off for another month. I ended up meeting a really great group of girls that like outdoors stuff. We go hiking together. I developed a large group of friends. I developed a community, in person. By being off Facebook, I got a deeper look into my friends' lives, going past the façade of 'having it together.' People had things to tell me in person. We could have deeper conversations. Real intimacy. There's such a surplus of people to interact with online that getting rid of one little account can act as a natural filter." During the pandemic Ashley found these friendships to be a lifeline. "Now that we're all trapped in our homes it's so important to have a sense of community. Because I built those friendships through things that I loved doing, those friendships have a great foundation and have really sustained me." She's gone back on Facebook during the pandemic, but mostly just to stay up with members of her extended family.

I ask Ashley if she can think of an example of a friendship she has that wouldn't have started online but *did* work by starting in person. "I think of my friend Sierra. We both love to rock climb. If I'd seen her on the app I don't think I would have swiped on her as a friend. First, I would have thought she was too cool. She just had that look. Or just given the trite things people put in their profiles I might have thought she was a little basic. But on a climbing trip we started taking about growing up in extremely religious environments, and that unearthed a lot of stuff for us both. This is not something you would casually bring up on a profile or that would come up just hanging out. We really bonded over that stuff."

Real people with whom Ashley could share real interests and have actual in-person experiences proved to be more fun and meaningful than whatever friendship she was trying to get generated online. I am so happy for her, and I want that for you, too. But I feel like your parent telling you to take your vitamins. Like, *Here, reader, go have some in-person interaction. It's GOOD FOR YOU.* By which I mean I either sound just old or obvious. But, like, yeah. It's how humans have always done things. We are a social species. The research proves that we need other humans in our lives in order to feel good and safe, and to survive. And yet the Internet with its magical front door of social media, and the ability to use our phones to text, chat, and share photos and imagery has become the way we do business with each other. Still, it doesn't give us the juice we need to squeeze from human interaction. While some folks do enjoy online connection more (because IRL just doesn't work for them, and that's valid, and I'm happy for them that online connection is a thing available to them), for many, if not most of us, online is just not sufficient. If we didn't intuit this before the pandemic, I think we do now. I guess you could say that Ashley was an early adopter!

As I go back over Ashley's story, there's something here about Ashley being flung out in the world only to ultimately come back to what she knows to be true about herself. As I reread her words, I see that being intentional about relationships has mattered to Ashley all along. "I have distinct memories of being in kindergarten and being at a playground birthday party and thinking to myself, 'I can't wait until I have control of my life and I don't have to be here.' I've always really valued the freedom to choose the people I get to have in my life, and my independence. Now that I'm an adult and I'm living that independence, I have to be responsible for myself and responsible to other people.

"I've been focusing on my own security lately. Even as a kid, I thought adulthood would feel secure—I still have a false sense that there will be a certain point in adulthood where I will have achieved everything I need to achieve, I'll be locked in and I can just stay there. It's hard not to observe other adults and think, *Oh, so that's what it's like to have made it. I bet they don't have to worry about stability.* But that's not accurate. Everything can change at any moment. Like my friends who've been dating people for five, six, seven years, many of them are breaking up and not getting married. So, the future that they assumed they'd have together isn't happening. I've been thinking about Beyoncé recently in this regard. There's so much stuff Beyoncé has gone through—her husband cheated, she had a miscarriage—and she's *Beyoncé*. She's not safe just because she's Queen Bey. Nobody is exempt from the difficulties of adulthood because of who they are, or how far into success they are."

Life is looking pretty adult-ish for Ashley, and in really good ways. She likes Boston. She is passionate about her work at the nonprofit organization Bottom Line, where she manages a team that mentors over two hundred first-generation college students in the Boston area. And in the fall of 2019 she went back onto an app (Tinder) where she met Martha. They started to dig each other. Right before the pandemic began it became "*official* official," but they both wanted to limit their exposure so they couldn't touch or even be within six feet of one another for many months. Then it became time to take the next step in their relationship and spend time with each other without it being so complicated, so they moved in together. With her uncomfortable experience with roommates and household rules in mind, I ask Ashley if she and Martha are setting up boundaries and expectations. "We need to. Definitely learning. It's a challenge to live with anyone. We're figuring out how to do that. I've never lived with a significant other before and neither has she." Ashley calls this her "biggest adulting move yet."

"When I think about the future of my adult life, it really comes down to how to relate to other people. I know so many people who are lonely right now. How to relate to each other is really what we all have to figure out." I agree with Ashley. How we relate to each other is everything.

IN SHORT: RELATIONSHIPS ARE THE MARROW OF LIFE

Human connection is fundamental to your survival. And being able to be in functional, mutually enriching relationships with others in the workplace and at home makes life so much more enjoyable.

Take a deep breath. We're going to turn to some stone-cold realities. Money doesn't make the world go round but it sure can help you get where you want to go. That's what's up next.

Unpack and Reflect

- With whom do I feel "the delicious feeling of being known"?
- What is hardest for me about connecting with other humans?
- My most valuable relationships (including weak ties, workplace relationships, neighbors, mentors, friends, and family) are with whom? What can I do to strengthen those ties?
- If I am in a partnership, what am I doing or can I start doing to deepen that relationship?

8

MONEY MATTERS

(HOW TO MAKE IT, KEEP IT, AND

MAKE IT WORK FOR YOU)

I would rather give you twenty-five thousand dollars than spend it on a party that lasts for five hours.

—My father, on the occasion of our wedding

This was the last thing I wanted to hear from Daddy. The words NOT HAVE A WEDDING ARE YOU KIDDING ME coursed through my veins like a log flume on an amusement park ride. It wasn't so much anger I felt as confusion. What the hell was he even talking about?

Twenty-eight years of blissful marriage later, I know exactly what he was talking about. He was talking about the magic of compound interest, which, generally speaking, holds that if you invest your money in the stock market it doubles approximately every eight years, which would have brought his $25,000 investment to over $200,000 today had I not spent it on . . . cake.

Okay, there were other expenses besides cake, but you get the point. That's a lot of money. And, yes, weddings are a once-in-a-lifetime event where you most definitely want your friends and family to see you declare your eternal promises to each other. And you want it all to go as you dreamed and you want all the photos to be perfect. (We went for black-and-white photography, which in a pre-Instagram world was really rather sophisticated for a couple of twentysomethings.) And you will savor those memories and retell those stories for a lifetime. But: a lifetime of spending on what you think you really want *now* means you will always have only one marshmallow instead of two. You want two marshmallows. Even if you don't like marshmallows, you'll want two of them. Two is better than one. Trust me.

THE MARSHMALLOW EXPERIMENT

Okay, so what am I talking about? I'm talking about this awesome little study conducted at Bing Nursery School on the Stanford campus back in 1972 in which a psychology professor named Walter Mischel gave a bunch of tiny children one marshmallow each and then told them that if they waited fifteen minutes to eat it they would get a second marshmallow. Some kids gobbled the first one down. Others waited the fifteen minutes and got two, which presumably they then gobbled down. The professor tracked the children for years—these are my peers, so they're now in their early fifties—and found that, as they grew up, the kids who waited the fifteen minutes for the second marshmallow were more "successful" across many measures including on standardized tests, in school, and at work. Whoa.

Turns out, if you are the kind of person who has the self-control to delay gratification by sacrificing a bit in the here and now, there will be a bigger payoff down the line for you. It also turns out that even though some of the little kids in the original experiment seemed to come by their self-control naturally, self-control can be taught. We can learn how to delay gratification. There's hope for two marshmallows for us all. (There's an important caveat here with the marshmallow experiment that we cannot overlook, which is that when researchers tried to replicate this experiment much more recently, they found that *why* kids were able to delay gratification had less to do with willpower and more to do with affluence. When poor kids were offered that first marshmallow, they ate it, which was smart for them to do given their life circumstances. The affluent kids probably figured they'd get THREE marshmallows once the test was over. How hard was it really for them to wait, comparatively speaking? But I digress.)

There is a simple analogy between the marshmallow experiment and spending money. If, rather than consuming all of your money now, you invest some of it, you'll have more money in the end. Not to say life is all about money. But you want to have enough to live the life you want to live, and to help the people and causes you care about. Earning money can't be only about saving for the future because what's happening in your life in the present matters, too. (You don't want to be an indentured servant to your sixty-five-year-old self, as my friend Mary likes to put it.) But to be responsible for your twenty- or thirtysomething self while also being responsible for your sixty-five-year-old or even eighty-year-old self? That's part of the challenge of being an adult. Yes, it's a pretty complex set of issues to balance. That balance is what we're going to talk about in this chapter.

IT'S ONLY MONEY, SO WHY AM I CRYING?

It doesn't seem like it necessarily should, but money brings out our emotions, sometimes to a surprising degree.

What we first knew about money came straight from our parents' or guardians' behaviors and attitudes—how they took care of the basics like food, rent, utilities, and medical care (or didn't); their attitude toward material possessions; whether they gave way to the impulse of the moment or refused to buy anything they deemed unnecessary; whether they could be transparent about purchases or felt the need to hide them; whether one parent needed permission from the other to spend; whether money led to fights—these memories form the soundtrack that plays in our mind whenever we start thinking about money.

Then we overlay our own attitudes and choices about money on top of all of that stuff from childhood:

Am I spending my money on the "right" things (and who decides?)

Do I have credit card debt, and how do I feel about all of those purchases?

Did I fund school with student loans, and do I feel good about that investment or do I regret it?

Am I opening my bills (not to mention paying them) or does it scare me to do so?

Is my career choice "worth it" whatever that means (and who decides)?

Doesn't my education mean I should understand money better than I do?

Do I trust my significant other with financial decisions?

Am I using money as a way to demonstrate my worth?

Am I being taken advantage of by this seller? By this friend?

Am I okay with this person sharing expenses with me?

Am I still on my parents' payroll and does that feel okay?

Why do I feel guilty about buying something nice for myself?

I'll admit that money has flat-out made me cry. Mostly when I've realized I've done something extremely irresponsible or uninformed. I got my first credit cards when I was in college. The banks pretty much lined the hallway of the student union eager to sign up naïve young spenders like me. Not to blame them. Okay, partly to blame them. But I was the one forking over the card at expensive restaurants and in expensive stores for really unhealthy psychological reasons as it would turn out—like I wanted store clerks and waiters to know that I was not the stereotypical Black person who could not afford whatever they were selling. Very fucked up, I know. Still, regardless of the complex psychological trauma that made me pull out the plastic, I know the responsibility for what went on those cards ultimately lay with me.

I didn't really understand how a credit card worked—that I should only use it to buy things I could cover with the money in my bank account. *I mean, of course, I knew this.* But I didn't have a method for tracking my expenses; I relied on just remembering, which proved to be a fallible method. So, when the credit card bill came each month, I was often a little surprised by how high it was, and over the months and years surprise turned into being completely taken aback. On top of my purchases, there was the interest they charged—an enormous amount of money in and of itself, the sum of which kept adding up. Soon I was just paying the minimum balance, which I would one day learn is almost every bank's strategy for keeping customers forever indebted. (Pro tip: If you only ever pay the minimum required, you will never pay down the debt and you'll end up paying far more in interest fees than you ever paid for the items you purchased. Do not be fooled. This is how they GET YOU.) By the end of college, I owed at least $3,000 on my two credit cards combined ($6,219 in today's dollars), my first job paid an annual salary of $20,000 (before taxes), and my rent was $500 a month (a lot of money back in the day; yes, I'd opted for the high-end apartment complex as part of my efforts to live large). So, how was I going to pay off my credit card debt? I put my head in the sand and just hoped the problem would go away. It didn't.

Two summers later, I was twenty-three years old and had moved back east to live with my parents before starting law school. Dan and I had gotten engaged and were in the throes of planning a wedding, to take place the following summer. I'd forwarded my mail to my folks' address, so everything including my credit card statements piled up on their kitchen counter. One night they approached me and I could see from their faces that it was serious. My mom said, "We want you to start your new life with Dan debt-free." Daddy handed me a check for $3,985, the amount of my debt in full. I felt my heart pounding in my head. Tears fell down my face. I accepted the check. (Having family who can rescue me is an enormous privilege, I realize, and I treat it as an obligation to pay it forward to the next generation.)

Fast-forward fifteen years and I'm a college dean in my late thirties counseling students. My students were the recipients of a very expensive college education, and as they mulled over what to major in and what to do for a career, they were also worrying about how to invest the money spent on their college education wisely, so as to make the most of it. But my response to them was that while yes, you want to make good financial decisions, remember that this is *your one life*, in which you have to figure out who you are, and what you are good at, and what matters to you, and then go do those things. My feedback was about glimpsing joy and then having the guts to pursue it. About meeting obligations, yes, but also about funding dreams. And even though it may seem odd to talk about things like joy and balance in a chapter on money, I do believe that value system works here, too.

My former student Denae emerged from college and grad school with roughly fifty thousand dollars of student loan and credit card debt. She came from a working-class family. Not only was Denae's debt much bigger than mine was, but unlike me her family could not bail her out.

Denae went very public on Facebook about her debt and her desire to pay it off, sharing how she was curtailing all expenses, from food and rent to social life, while still living a reasonably fun twentysomething life in New York. Her posts got a ton of likes but virtually no comments, which perplexed her. Then the private messages started pouring in. "I need to learn this!" "Tell me how you did that!" "Could you give me some advice?" Denae had hit a nerve. Her college-educated friends were ashamed that they did not know more about personal finances and were afraid of letting anyone but Denae know. As she worked on her own situation, she counseled her friends privately. We'll hear more about her journey at the end of this chapter.

I'm hoping that here you'll find some encouragement about how to make money work for you instead of it being a thing you're ashamed about or confused by or that causes perpetual anxiety. I'm hoping you'll come to realize that money isn't simply a left-brain (analytical) thing, but a deeply right-brain (creative) concept. Your relationship with money gets at the most fundamental questions you will ask yourself in this lifetime. There is no one *right way* to earn or spend your money. As for the crying, we cry less about things, money included, when we know *why* we've made certain choices. We shed fewer tears when we're spending money on the things we've decided matter most to us. We might even shed happy tears when we've made a choice that paid off well, and we're proud of ourselves for whatever we sacrificed to get there. Waiting for those two marshmallows, then savoring them, can sometimes bring us joy.

BIG-PICTURE ECONOMICS

Before we get to the specifics of you—the earner, spender, and saver—you need to understand the larger economic context you're operating within. It boils down to this: The mathematical equation comprised of "income" on one side and "rent/mortgage, food, utilities" on the other is way out of balance for many people in many communities today. When your grandpa launches into a critique of how your generation is lazy and doesn't know how to work as hard as he and his friends did when they were your age, he's flat-out wrong. Some of these examples will help you (and him) understand why.

It used to be that a person in this country could count on the concept of what society calls "upward mobility," which went something like this: A child would get a better K–12 education than their parents got, would go to college if their parents didn't (or attend a better college than their parents did), would get a better job, make more money, get a better house, etc. (Obviously this concept privileged some more than others, particularly when it came to getting a home loan and buying a house, which were opportunities systemically denied to Black Americans in a conspiracy of bankers and realtors nationwide that lasted for much of the twentieth century.) But in the main, regardless of your racial, ethnic, or socioeconomic background, over the many decades of the twentieth century, Americans of all backgrounds tended to see their offspring's situation improve over what they had. This is also known as achieving the American Dream.

Unfortunately, the America your grandparents and parents may have lived in is very different from the America we live in today. In the year of my birth (1967) the chance of a child growing up to earn more than their parents did was 90 percent. By 2017, that rate had plummeted to 50 percent. In that same span of years, student loan debt skyrocketed. So, young people are not only not outearning their parents, but their monthly bills have a huge new component most of their parents' did not have. Taking just these two things into account, the American Dream appears to be a fade-to-black Instagram filter, just in time for you to inhabit your adulthood. Great. Oh, and a pandemic.

"Minimum wage" used to mean something you could really count on, but today not so much. When President Roosevelt created the concept back in 1938, in the aftermath of the Great Depression, it was meant to provide more than subsistence-level money, and would ensure that people could earn enough to live on. A worker (almost always a man, back in those days) earning the minimum wage made at least enough money to support a family of three above the poverty line. Eighty years later, in many communities around the nation the idea that a minimum wage could sustain one person, let alone a family, is laughable. Today, there are very few counties in the United States where a person working full time and earning the minimum wage can manage to rent a one-bedroom apartment.

What's a reasonable wage, then? A good rule of thumb adhered to by financial planners is that a person should spend no more than a third of their gross monthly income (*gross* meaning your pay before taxes) on housing, which makes it possible to afford other essential expenses such as food and utilities. I live in the San Francisco Bay Area, where a number of towns and counties have raised their minimum wage to the so-called living wage of $15 an hour. I know that sounds like a ton of money to those of you for whom the minimum wage is more like $8 an hour. And yes, at forty hours a week, a $15-per-hour wage computes to a monthly salary of $2,400 and an annual salary of about $30,000. (To compute an annual salary, assume 50 weeks worked x 40 hours worked per week = two thousand hours worked per year.) But what's a monthly gross salary of $2,400 going to do for you in a town where the median rent for a one-bedroom apartment is $2,700 ($32,400 a year), which is the case in many Bay Area towns? Obviously, in communities like mine and plenty of others, we desperately need our local elected leaders to pay attention to this gaping hole in the fabric of the American Dream; we've either got to be paid more or we've got to prevent housing costs from rising, or both. But in the meantime, each of us has to focus on keeping going. It's on us to do what we can to create a better situation for ourselves. Sometimes that may mean uprooting ourselves and finding a community where we can afford to live, work, and thrive. I'm not trying to tell you where to live. I'm just encouraging you to think about *whether* where you live is financially sustainable. (Pro tip: You can easily search for surveys and lists about cities that are attractive for young adults in terms of job opportunities, cost of living, and lifestyle.)

Wages that don't keep up with a rising cost of living and substantial student loan debt feels like the biggest financial problem facing young adults today. But some subtle yet no less serious changes are also at play. Once, when unions were more prevalent, employment felt like a hand-shake of mutual obligation (whether commanded by law or unions or, occasionally, out of the goodness of the employer's heart), and you would get a job, keep a job, and have that job for the rest of your life. That "one job for life" concept hardly seems to exist anymore, and in some ways that's good; it's exciting to have the freedom and flexibility to change jobs and even careers. (I'm on my third career as I write this and have enjoyed the mobility and the opportunity to regroup, refresh, and start anew each time.) But in other ways this loosening of the bonds between employer and employee has led to an erosion in confidence about individuals' financial futures. Can you count on being at company X in five years? Will company X be *around* in five years? What *can* you count on?

As labor laws protecting workers' rights eroded during the past couple of decades, the concept of "unpaid internships" arose, which is where companies get free labor from you, and you get experience for your résumé but zero actual dollars to put toward your bills. (Of course, you have to be well-off enough even to contemplate taking an unpaid internship [for example, your parents are heavily subsidizing your bills if not outright supporting you], meaning those who are already advantaged get the résumé boost from the awesome, yet unpaid, job, while those who can't afford to work for free lose out on the career-enhancing job opportunity.) This disproportionally disadvantages the poor and working class, as well as people of color (who are less likely to have family wealth), and queer and trans people (who are less likely to receive family support even if their families have the means to help).

On top of the cruelty of unpaid internships, after the financial crisis of 2008 (which hit those just starting out in the workplace quite hard) we saw the rise of the gig economy—the idea that a human could and should cobble together a sustainable income by being a permanent freelancer or consultant doing this and that for an hourly wage or a one-time fee. While there's a ton of flexibility and freedom in that arrangement—you can set your own hours and choose what work you will and won't do—such jobs come with no traditional benefits (for example, health, dental, vision, life insurance, a retirement plan with matching employer funds). This can seem fine when you're young, fit, healthy, and have no dependents, but it's really dicey if your tooth cracks and requires a crown, if you need a good mental health practitioner, if you get a scary diagnosis, or if a baby is on the way.

Then there's the side hustle, that additional job you take on to augment a regular full-time job. For example, public school teachers who hustle as Lyft drivers are big in my neck of the woods, because the salary a teacher makes isn't enough to cover the basics in a high-cost-of-living environment. The manager of my local food pantry told me that retired teachers form a disproportionately large segment of their clients. A side hustle (or two) is how many are getting by. There's something wrong with a society in which teachers, some of the most important members of our community, don't make enough to support themselves throughout their lives. Maybe you and your generation will join together to right this and other wrongs, as we'll discuss in chapter 11, "Make Things Better."

For now, we're talking about something more basic: your income. And do not despair. You have a lot of control over your choices. Where to live, what to do for work, and how to spend your dollars, that's all up to you. So, the remainder of this chapter is about how you can be in charge of the challenging but ultimately rewarding choice-making that will allow you to balance your financial priorities and structure a life of joy.

I DON'T WANT TO DIE

First, let's talk about death. (You're thinking, WHAT?! But bear with me here.) Because deciding to plan for our financial future requires accepting the uncomfortable truth that our lives will one day end. Believe me, I know that this is the last thing you want to talk about. Yet we have to, at least for a moment.

My younger self was so afraid to think about dying that when the thought accidentally wandered into my brain I would shudder to try to shake off whatever had prompted it. But recently I lost not one but two dear college friends in their early fifties, Magnus and Eric, and their sudden deaths almost exactly a year apart made me start to wonder if I was going to make it to fifty-five, let alone seventy or eighty. There comes a point when the immortality we felt as teens and young adults gives way to the certainty that our life is finite.

Contemplating death also means facing the real possibility that there may come a time when we can no longer take care of ourselves. None of us wants to be impoverished, feeble, or alone in our final years, yet we can't take for granted that family or friends will inevitably be there for us. But let's assume that you have good relationships with your family. Even if all goes as well as possible, there is still going to be immense sadness. Secretly, I've hoped that Dan and I will die at the exact same moment because I can't bear the thought of living for even one day without this person who is such a mensch that literally as I'm typing this, he walks into my office and gives me a vase of yellow Gerbera daisies that he picked out just for me. (Mwah!) Yet if I'm so afraid of feeling sad when I think about the big picture that I can't think about it, then I'm avoiding a really important truth, which is that I will (I hope) get old. And if I avoid that truth I may fail to plan for the later years of my life, and for the costs of the end of my life, financially. The actual costs of avoidance, not to mention the emotional stress of it, can be enormous. So, let's *not* avoid that topic.

THE "R" WORD

Long before your eventual demise will come the stage of life called *retirement*, a time of greater relaxation after your years of being an active working person, usually marked by fewer obligations and for many people, more travel. I've only just started thinking about retirement. (I've been all about *What am I going to do next?* not *When do I get to stop doing all of this?*) So, I get it if you want to skip this portion of the chapter. But you really shouldn't. And hey, you made it through the death bit, so why quit now? Whether it's taking care of your body or your bank account, adulting requires thinking about your present and future self because your older self benefits when your younger self has thought ahead.

Aside from the few among us who can count on large bequests from wealthy relatives in the form of money or real estate (congratulations if that is you), the remaining 99 percent will not inherit a sum of money that sets us up for life. So, we need to talk funds for your retirement years, which will come out of three buckets: what the government will do for you, what your employer will do for you, and what you will do for you. Let's begin with the government, where the short answer is: probably not much.

What I mean is, you may have heard about Social Security, another great idea conceived by FDR in the wake of the Great Depression that was meant to ensure that senior citizens (as they were then called) were not destitute in their old age (which was considered to begin at age sixty-five in those years). The deal was that workers would pay a small amount from every paycheck toward the Social Security "trust funds," as they are called, which would grow faster than inflation and yield money that would be there to support those workers once they were out of the work-force at age sixty-five. The thing is, it didn't actually work that way—it wasn't like the money from a person's paycheck was put away in their very own savings account, for *their* use decades later at age sixty-five. Instead, the money a person put away was going to pay for *someone else's retirement* right then. The ultimate intergenerational compact; the ultimate pay it forward.

But then the Baby Boomers became the largest generation in American history and they lived longer than their elders, and Gen X (my generation), which followed them, has far fewer people. So, it's a math problem: there just aren't enough Gen X workers to cover Boomer retirees who are plentiful in number and are living forever. This is why you hear about the Social Security trust funds running out. (There will always be some money in them as long as current workers continue to contribute to them; folks are just likely to get a smaller payout than they used to get.) Congress could conceivably come together to figure out how to fix Social Security, to be sure that the younger workers of today receive benefits commensurate with what older workers have and will continue to receive. (Frankly this is an issue begging for Millennial and Gen Z activism, if I may say so as a humble Gen Xer who will one day count on y'all to pay for my Social Security.) But the bottom line is, the estimated average payout in 2020 is $1,503 per month. And while that will rise between now and when you retire, unless you plan to retire in a very low cost-of-living area, and/or you plan to live extremely fru-gally, your monthly Social Security payout will almost definitely not be enough to meet your monthly bills as a retiree.

In addition to the government Social Security program providing less retirement support than our parents or grandparents could count on back in the day, very few employers provide retirement pensions any longer, which was a guaranteed amount of money your employer would provide you after you retired (or to your widow/widower upon your death). Unionized workers tend to fight for and receive pensions, and a few industries continue to provide pensions today as a rule (including the military, local and state governments, nursing, public schools, fire-fighters, police). But when it comes to private employers, the percentage that provide employees with a pension today stands at about 17 percent, meaning most of us cannot count on having an employer-funded pension upon retirement. At the end of the chapter, we will meet Wesley, who has an employer-funded pension, and you will see how the loyalty between employer and employee completely changed the trajectory of Wesley's life. Bottom line: it's on us as individuals to make wise choices now so that when it comes time for us to retire, we're good. This is where you come in as the savior of your future older self. It's on you to put the right amount of money away for your retirement. You can even live a bit more simply in the now, acquiring and holding on to only the things that truly "spark joy," à la Marie Kondo, so you can save more and have more to spend in your retirement! Hey, maybe you'll even be able to pass on some kind of sweet inheritance to your own kids or grandkids. #Goals.

Speaking of goals, book titles scream about retiring early and traveling more, as if retiring early were the whole purpose of life. But, remember, if you're figuring out who you are and what you want out of life as we've been discussing, and you give yourself permission to do those things, you might be thrilled to get to do those things for as long as possible. In fact, research indicates that humans tend to wither when we retreat from working life completely. So, to my thinking, we don't want to have to stop working until our bodies and/or minds have really petered out, at which point it's like, *Okay, I guess my time here in this body on this earth is coming to a close, I've set aside funds for these final years of what has been a great life.* (Of course you may decide to take a job that doesn't bring you joy now, hoping that after thirty-plus years of doing it, you can put your feet up on a dock somewhere with a fishing rod in one hand and your favorite beverage in the other. I'm not telling you *what* to think about your retirement; I'm just telling you to *think* about retirement. See the difference?)

THE BALANCING ACT: EARN, SPEND, BORROW, SAVE

Picture a spending spectrum with your most important needs on one
end (such as food, shelter, and medication) and your "maybe one day"
dreams all the way at the other end. Once we are able to meet our most
basic, urgent financial needs, we have a tremendous number of choices
about how we earn, spend, borrow, and save. And the concept of how
you "should" make such choices (often in the form of other people's
expectations and opinions) is not a terribly useful gauge.

How we allocate our resources is personal. And our priorities vary
considerably over the years and decades of our lives. One day Netflix
and Two-Buck Chuck are our primary sources of entertainment, then
maybe it's live concerts, then maybe it's airfare and a hotel to see that
band you love so much play live one last time before they retire. (This is
me and the Eagles!) One day, it's a used car to replace the used car that
just got totaled and that the insurance company won't completely pay
for. Another day, it's that vintage car we can't afford to buy our partner
but that we can rent for a day on the occasion of his fiftieth birthday.
One day, it's a birthday gift for a friend and then that same friend has
a GoFundMe to help with something serious. One day, it's our student
loan payments, and the next, it's starting to fund a 529 plan for our own
child's college education. One day, we start saving for a down payment
on a house. One day, our own medical issues take center stage. One day,
we go back to grad school to pursue that passion that can no longer be
denied, even when everyone says it's a silly idea. Regardless of when or
whether any of this happens to you, my point is that your financial decisions are just that: yours. They may be wildly different from the choices
your friends or family would make. That's okay. Don't ever forget that.
It's *your* one wild and precious life, *your* money, and *your* choices.

For example, don't let anyone tell you that it's stupid to take out
student loans to pay for art school or to become a social worker. Sure,
those degrees are not likely to lead to high-paying jobs (such as what
you could earn in medicine or law, which are other degrees people
will take out big loans to pay for). But if your heart and mind are telling you that you want to be a painter, or work with kids in the foster
care system, then you should go do that. Just know that you are most

likely making a trade-off of finances for job satisfaction, and maybe that means you need a second job, or you need to move to a more affordable town, *and be okay with that.* And hey, remember, I've been there. I went from being a corporate lawyer to being a university administrator to being a grad student in my forties who hoped to make it as a writer. Each time I pivoted toward a new career, I initially made less money than I had made previously. (It helped hugely that Dan was there to back me up.) Yet each change in the work itself made me that much happier. Don't make the mistake of going into a career that other people think constitutes "success" just to have a big salary. Inside the fancy buildings that house law firms, hospitals, and investment banks lurk more than a few miserable employees, and no amount of income compensates for outright hating your job. When I was in law school, I borrowed $79,500 to pay for tuition, room, and board—that's $137,841 in today's dollars—and my salary as a first-year lawyer was $77,000, which, according to financial planners, was a student loan debt that "made sense."

Whatever your job may be, you're going to earn some money from it (that's the point!), and whatever your after-tax take-home pay turns out to be, you don't want to be spending all of it. You want to spend less than you earn so you can put a bit of money away for emergencies, for bigger purchases, and of course for your retirement. When Dan and I were just starting out, we didn't save any money because we felt like we needed literally every dollar we earned. (In hindsight, I see that fewer take-out pizzas would have yielded the savings that seemed out of reach!) As we grew up and became more expert in our fields, we made more money. Dan was at the startup that became Pandora. I was a dean at a prestigious university. One day, twenty years into our marriage, we were like, *Wait, we're making so much more money but where's the savings?* The problem was that we'd never been savers. Other than putting money away for our retirement, we'd been spend-what-you-makers. We were truly idiots on this front. Don't make that mistake.

The best way I can explain what was going on for us is that each of us basically had a secret number in our heads that we knew represented too big of a splurge. We never discussed a specific amount with each other, but somewhere in our minds we knew that there was an amount that crossed the line. From the start of our relationship Dan and I chose to put all of our income in one pot and pay our bills jointly, rather than have his income and his bills on the one hand and my income and my bills on the other, and maybe some third pot of shared money and expenses. Not everyone does it the way we've done it. When we were first dating, our splurge limit was maybe $100. By the time I graduated law school and we were married that amount was maybe $250.

My guilty pleasure has always been clothes, but not in the way you might expect. Having been a plus-sized butch woman for most of my adult life, I have a really hard time finding affordable items in my size and in a style I love. This makes the necessary task of clothes shopping emotional for me. As Dan and I started to earn more income, our splurge limit went from $250 to $500 and beyond. And when it came to clothes shopping I always hit the splurge limit and I'd actually get a little teary as I pictured myself walking in the front door with my bags and letting Dan see what I'd bought for myself. To his credit, he was super supportive of my shopping challenges and never made me feel badly for those expenses. But the tears were the clue from my own body that I knew I was uncomfortable crossing that particular financial line.

From clothes to dinners out to home furnishings to nonprofit donations to travel to things for the kids to the miscellaneous things you can find on Amazon, over the years, Dan and I kept raising our splurge limit, and we got to a point where we were hemorrhaging money. It just kept going . . . somewhere. The bulk of my income comes from being a public speaker, which means I often don't bring in much money in the summertime. Despite making enough money by all objective measures, two summers in a row we found ourselves going, *Wait. How are we going to pay the bills?* Which was ridiculous, because overall our income was higher than it had ever been.

Dan and I sat down for a serious conversation with each other about saving 5 percent or maybe 10 percent of our income in order to see us through the slow income months, and maybe even to achieve our life-long dream of having a second home on the Northern California coast one day. Then we realized that the only way we were going to achieve either of these goals would be to cut our splurge limit by 90 percent. For example, whereas we'd gone all out to the tune of a thousand dollars on a designer recliner (both artsy and cozy) for our living room, now that we needed to buy a second recliner, we would allow ourselves only one hundred dollars for that second chair. This was a radical concept for us. (You should have seen us moping around the much cheaper furniture store.) But, it worked. We found a recliner for a hundred bucks. Bonus: This is the recliner our family and friends always gravitate to. They love it!

The other thing that radically changed our financial picture was a lesson I learned from a family of modest means who were working hard to put away money for their kids' college and their retirement. When their biweekly paycheck came, they immediately cashed it and put 10 percent of it in an envelope marked "college" and 10 percent in an envelope marked "retirement." Whatever was left over went to rent, food, and all the other expenses for that part of the month. Once a month, they deposited the savings from those envelopes in the bank so they could earn interest.

This practice reflects a philosophy called "Pay yourself first," which means that instead of hoping to have some savings left over *after* you pay your bills, your savings become your most important expense and you take care of that first. Taking a page from this book, Dan and I set up a new bank account to be the holding pen for summer expenses and another account to hold funds for our coastal dream home. When income comes in, we pay those accounts first. This ends up forcing us to reduce all of our other expenses, whereas in the past our immediate expenses were out of control and we shortchanged our longer-term needs and wildest dreams.

As I've already admitted to you, in my early twenties I was turning to credit cards as the way to purchase things I truly could not afford. If you do that too often or for too long, you will find yourself in a financial hole that will feel impossible to climb out of. I mention this again to raise a separate point, which is that you will not only owe a terrifying sum, but you may have ruined your ability to get loans for big things such as a car or a house. What I'm talking about here is your credit score, which is something you want to keep track of. Your credit score is a rating of your reliability as a bill payer and it will impact your ability to purchase one of these bigger-ticket items. A good credit score (which you get from being good at paying your bills on time) can also entitle you to a lower interest rate, or, if your score is not good, it can subject you to higher interest rates. There are many different credit score companies out there, and each can use slightly different metrics, but all are going to be looking at whether you pay your bills in a timely fashion and how much of your allowable credit you are using at any given time. For example, just because your credit card company is allowing you a $10,000 credit limit (which, if you're wired like me, will make you go, "Woo-hoo, I'm rich!") that doesn't mean you should borrow the maximum! That upper limit is there for you to draw upon in a *true* emergency only. A good rule of thumb is that for purposes of maintaining a good credit score you should not borrow more than 20 percent of your credit limit (across *all* credit cards *and* all installment loans you may have, including mortgages, student loans, etc).

Essentially, Dan and I had to adopt a different mindset about ourselves as spenders. Live like a grad student even when you can afford to live far better, then watch how your dollars grow.

GROW THOSE FUNDS: THE MAGIC OF COMPOUNDING INTEREST

I turned to my friend Chris Andrews for the nitty-gritty on how to grow your money for later years. Chris is a Millennial, and a kick-ass financial adviser with Northwestern Mutual (a company that offers various insurance products as well as financial planning advice). He wants you to know first and foremost that "one of the biggest advantages of saving for retirement early in your career is time. Time is the driver that allows compounding interest to fully work its magic." The magic he's talking about is what happens to compound interest.

Compare the following:

The twenty-two-year-old who starts putting $1,000 per year ($83.33/ month) into a tax-deferred investment account, and continues contributing $1,000 per year until they retire at age sixty-five. Assuming a 7 percent *net* (after taxes) average annual investment return, this person would have over $283,000 available to them upon retirement.

The thirty-two-year-old who starts saving that same $1,000 per year. By waiting ten years to get started saving for retirement (assuming the same

7 percent *net* average annual investment return we allotted to the twenty-two-year-old), this person will have only $136,000 available upon retirement.

So. Even though on the surface it may have seemed that a difference of ten years at $1,000 per year would yield a difference of only $10,000 plus some interest, because of the magic of compound interest (which means the interest *plus* the principal together get reinvested every year) the difference is much greater. By being able to put $10K away between the ages of twenty-two and thirty-two, our wise twenty-two-year-old has over $147,000 in extra money available to them by age sixty-five! WHAT!!!!!

Look, I know some of you right now are like, *Fuck, I'm already thirty-four so I'm basically screwed.* Hold tight. That is not the takeaway here. The takeaway is START PUTTING *SOMETHING* AWAY NOW. Start. JUST START! Your older self will always be grateful that you started. Because guess what? That thirty-two-year-old who is really pissed at what they didn't do at twenty-two is still better off than the forty-two-year-old who is only starting to invest. Let's look at those numbers:

The forty-two-year-old who starts investing $1,000 a year (with the same 7 percent net average annual investment return) will have only $62,000 available upon retirement at age sixty-five.

Okay? And look, we're talking about saving $1,000 a year, which is $83.33 a month, which is $2.77 a day. You read that right. For the cost of a cup of coffee, tea, or juice, with no additional work or sacrifice required on your part, you are accruing big bucks for your retirement. So, why stop there? Imagine if you could save not just $2.77 a day but $10 a day. TEN BUCKS. Here's how that would break down if you started doing that at forty-two versus thirty-two versus twenty-two years of age:

The forty-two-year-old who starts saving $10 a day has saved $3,650 by the end of the year. If they put that money into an investment account, and they continue contributing $3,650 per year until they retire at age sixty-five, assuming a 7 percent net average annual investment return, that person will have over $225,000 available to them upon retirement—a far greater return than if the person had only saved the equivalent of a cup of coffee daily ($62,000 at retirement).

The thirty-two-year-old who does the same thing will have over $498,000 available to them upon retirement. Again, a pretty awesome increase over the $136,000 they would've had had they saved only the $2.77 daily.

But let's look at the twenty-two-year-old who starts saving $10 a day. Watch out. Cuz that person would have over $1,034,000 available to them upon retirement. BOOM.

Ten bucks a day. Seventy bucks a week. Easier said than done, I realize. But when you look at the magic of compound interest, it kinda makes you want to try, doesn't it? And, remember, don't beat yourself up if you don't manage the ten dollars a day. There are lots of reasons why that might not happen. The message is: Just put away something. Do the best you can. If you fall, get back up and start again. You can do this.

FINANCIAL VEHICLES THAT DRIVE A BETTER FUTURE

Chris Andrews also wants us to know that while saving money is the first and most important step, the next step is optimizing that saved money for tax efficiency. "The government uses the tax code to incentivize certain behaviors in the U.S. population. In order to get more Americans to save for retirement, the government is essentially willing to subsidize certain accounts so that more money stays with you and less money goes to taxes over time." This means that *where* we save those dollars matters.

First off, you need to know that a retirement account is sometimes called an IRA (which stands for individual retirement account) and sometimes called a 401(k) (because of the portion of the tax code that references them). I will use these terms interchangeably. Now, since many people your age are in the gig economy, I want to start there. The upside to gigging is the freedom to decide what you want to do when, and where. The downside is no employer providing "benefits," such as the various insurance packages that help protect you from this and that, and the opportunity to have your employer contribute to your retirement savings. In short, if you're in the gig economy, looking after your future needs is all on you. Chris recommends that you start with a Roth IRA. "It is probably the most flexible and impactful way to save money for retirement and should be at the top of their savings priority list. Investing your money in a Roth IRA doesn't require any kind of employer plan or benefits, and it's easy and very low-cost to set up." Basically you go to one of those online investment platforms, like Fidelity, Schwab, or Vanguard, open a Roth IRA, and start socking money away, which allows taxpayers under the age of fifty to set aside a maximum of $6,000 per year in after-tax dollars for their retirement. The growth on the money you put in is tax-deferred every year and can be withdrawn entirely tax-free after age fifty-nine and a half. (There are penalties if you withdraw it earlier.) Note, as of 2019, the rule is that this vehicle is available to single taxpayers earning less than $137,000 and married couples earning less than $203,000 annually. So, it's not an option available to all income levels, but it is available to most. And let me also acknowledge that many folks would really struggle to put away $6,000 a year (that's $500 a month or $17 a day). But to see why it's worth trying, let's do some quick math:

> The forty-two-year-old who sets aside $6,000 every year will have over $371,000 at age sixty-five . . .
>
> The thirty-two-year-old doing the same will have over $819,000 . . .
>
> And the twenty-two-year-old doing the same will have over $1.7 million. (And remember, because this is a Roth IRA, if you've waited until you're at least fifty-nine-and-a-half to withdraw it, these funds are tax-free!)

I'm fifty-three and, yes, Dan and I at some point started being more responsible with our money (not before we squandered the fat settlement check for $25,000 we received for the items damaged and destroyed by the fire in our moving van, which was the second time the universe tried to give me twenty-five grand to invest for my future, the first being my wedding). This is where I go, *Why didn't I start acting on this stuff sooner?!?!?!* Basically, because I didn't listen to my father. Ha.

Now, if instead of gigging you are working for an employer that provides benefits, that employer may, as part of the benefits package, offer you a 401(k) retirement account (or a 403[b] account if they are a nonprofit organization). You can save either pre-tax dollars to the traditional 401(k)/403(b) (this means the money gets taken out of your paycheck before it ever gets to you, as with your federal and state tax withholdings) or after-tax dollars to the Roth 401(k)/403(b). (As of 2019, the annual maximum people under fifty can put away is $19,500.) The traditional 401(k) can be better than the Roth because you're investing *pre-tax* dollars, which means the money that will one day go toward taxes (upon your retirement) will be what you made from the compound interest magic. But a Roth IRA is also a good choice because, should you have to withdraw the money early, there's no penalty on the amount you contributed (there's a penalty only on the interest), and once you're over fifty-nine-and-a-half you get to withdraw everything that's in there tax-free.

Chris offers this example of the difference between how you can spend money from a traditional IRA vs. a Roth IRA: "Let's say that you're sixty-five and you need ten dollars for a coffee—because that's what a cup will cost then! If you have money in a traditional 401(k), you'll need to pull out twelve or thirteen or fifteen dollars (depending upon your tax rate in retirement) in order to net the ten dollars to give to the barista. But if you have your money in a Roth 401(k), you'll simply need to pull out ten dollars because all of the money in your Roth account is tax-free."

The key, says Chris, is that "two options are available, and both are good. If you're early on in your career and not earning much, the Roth is great because you are taxed on your earnings at a low rate and you can withdraw it all later tax-free. However, for those with a well-paying full-time job, the traditional 401(k) can be good because you get to delay paying taxes on the money until retirement, when you might be in a lower tax bracket." Chris often recommends to clients that they do some of both, if they have that option available to them.

Here's an added bonus about some employer-based retirement accounts that is VERY wonderful. Sometimes employers offer to match a portion of what you contribute to your retirement account. This is FREE MONEY, so if your employer makes this available don't leave it on the table. To be clear, they don't just hand you the money; you need to contribute a certain amount of your paycheck to your retirement account yourself first in order for them to match that money, and each employer sets the percentage they require employees to contribute before they will match your funds. Find out the percentage they require you to contribute in order for them to match and DO IT. Your creaky older self will be so damn grateful. (Pro tip: If you're weighing a couple of different job offers, ask the person doing the hiring, "Do you match employees' 401[k] contributions, and if so, to what extent?" This is a key but often not well understood benefit and may factor into your analysis of which job is ultimately best for you.)

And, of course, you don't have to limit your contribution to the amount matched by your employer. Depending on your other bills, you may be able to afford to contribute more, perhaps even the maximum allowed by law ($19,500 annually, as of 2019). While having money taken out of your paycheck is a sacrifice, many of us find that we don't notice it's gone because it was never in our hands in the first place. It ends up coming off the top like the various taxes that are withheld from our paychecks. And then slowly, over time, your retirement savings sit there growing and growing until you need them.

You should also look into the various kinds of insurance that protect you from large expenses and from true catastrophe (including medical, dental, vision, renters/home, car, and life).

DON'T JUST TAKE MY WORD FOR IT

My two experts in this chapter are Wesley, a fifty-nine-year-old man who has been able to provide a much higher quality of life for his wife and child than he had growing up. And Denae, my former student, now thirty-six, who managed to get out from under fifty thousand dollars in student loan and credit card debt while living in the greatest city (and one of the most expensive) in the world. And the bonus with Denae is that after getting out of debt, she became a certified financial adviser so that she could help other people through the tears, and grow their money for their retirement years!

MEET WESLEY—A Commitment to Be Responsible

Wesley and I met during the friendly chaos of a wedding rehearsal and family dinner when my sister married his mother back in 2005. This was the first wedding my kids would be old enough to remember, and at four and six years of age they were excited to get to be a flower girl and a ring bearer in the ceremony. I remember thinking how cool it was that my kids would grow up knowing that two women (or two men) could get married just like any heterosexual couple could. It wasn't that way when I was young (just as interracial marriage was illegal in many states when I was born), and I would never want my own children to take these hard-won rights for granted.

For almost his entire career Wesley, an African American man, has worn the brown shirt and shorts of a UPS driver, which enabled him to move from being a member of the working poor to the working class to being a solidly middle-class family man who is comfortable and content these many years later. I wanted to understand the mechanisms Wesley employed to become upwardly mobile, to get his piece of the American Dream despite a fairly challenging financial start, so I called him up to talk about that. We happened to speak on the very day he'd received his thirty-year pin from UPS, which meant some special benefits were about to kick in.

Wesley's father was about to graduate with a doctorate in computer science when he died of a heart attack. Wesley was nine. Suddenly a single parent with two young kids and in desperate need of work, Wesley's mom made clear that he needed to step up. "When I was really young, my mom was like, 'You're responsible for getting yourself to school.' I had to get here and there and do these things myself. I mean she cooked for me, and got me clothes. But quite frankly she didn't have time to take me places like school, work, baseball practice, or football practice." So, Wesley has been largely responsible for himself since he started high school, and most of the guys he hung out with were in a similar situation. He worked part-time at Wendy's, and made $2.35 an hour. About a third of his high school classmates went to college. "The rest were just like me," he tells me. "They might have gone to community college or they went into the service." Wesley graduated from high school feeling he didn't have the tools he'd need to succeed on a four-year college track.

He moved out of his mom's house and enrolled at a community college in Gainesville, Florida, called Santa Fe College, while working part-time stocking shelves on the graveyard shift at a Winn-Dixie supermarket. He bounced around between apartment complexes in Gainesville and had three different roommates in that first year. "I was trying to balance work life and school life while paying the light bill or the gas bill on time. Stuff like that was an issue for me. It took me awhile to get my arms around it. There were things I did that put that first semester in a tizzy. It was like *Animal House*. Drinking beer, partying, going to school sometimes, and working. We were basically big kids. I had to grow up."

Wesley's manager at Winn-Dixie had seemed supportive of him going to community college but would assign him shifts that interfered with his class schedule. When Wesley balked, his manager said, "Oh, no. We need you here working." The manager would say things like, "There's nothing out there for someone like you." Wesley switched to the graveyard shift to accommodate work and school, but that kind of schedule proved to be exhausting. "I wasn't yet an adult who would have been able to make all the right choices and hang in there with school. I wasn't in control of everything at that point, but I worked, and paid my bills, and stayed independent." He dropped out of school and worked full-time at Winn-Dixie.

At twenty-three he met his future wife, Angela, a white woman who was a few years younger than him. It was 1984. They would marry thirteen years later. "But from the start we made a commitment to each other to be responsible for each other. That's when I feel like everything stabilized. I felt fully *adult* adult. I don't want to say everything completely came together then, because there were always pitfalls and stumbles in the road. We were living on the fringes. We weren't broke, but we still had the power turned off every once in a while and there was no money for vacations. I made four dollars and ten cents an hour. I'd look at people's houses and ask myself, 'How the heck do you get a house like that?' I remember when a brand-new car cost three thousand dollars, and then it seemed like all of a sudden they were twenty thousand, and I'm asking, 'How in the hell do you pay for that?'"

Wesley had been stocking shelves full-time at Winn-Dixie for about three years, and "had pretty much thrown in the towel on school," when at Christmas dinner his uncle Quitman pulled him aside and delivered an unexpected message from his deceased father. "Something your dad always said was, 'No matter what job you get, stay in school.'" Winn-Dixie was a dead-end job, and Wesley knew it. So, the advice was right on time.

He went back to Santa Fe College, and in 1988 he took a part-time job with UPS loading the famous brown trucks internally known as "package cars" that you see in cities and towns across America and in lands as far away as Nepal. He worked a split shift: 3 to 9 a.m. and 4 to 8 p.m. "I went to school between shifts and would study with the books in my car." He made more as a part-time worker for UPS than he had working full-time for Winn-Dixie. Before long, Wesley got the coveted offer to be a UPS driver full-time, his dream job. But he declined it. He wanted to complete his associate's degree. His father's advice, delivered through his uncle Quitman, had stuck.

During his last semester Wesley was chitchatting with his professor after class one day and mentioned that he'd turned down a full-time job with UPS earlier that year. The professor stared at him and asked what the salary was. "I told him they start you at thirty-eight thousand, and you probably make in the fifties with overtime. He looked at me like, *What are you thinking?* I was like, 'I can do it next year.' He said, 'Um yeah, that would be a *good* idea.'" Wesley's professor was making the point that this was a great career opportunity and that in taking it, Wesley would be making more money than a lot of people with graduate degrees were able to make.

He was now more eager than ever. Angela wanted to get married soon. Wesley was ready to get started on his full-time career with UPS. He earned his associate's degree from Santa Fe College in 1994 and became a UPS driver. "It was a big step for us. And it was great. My first full-time week there I thought to myself, 'This is something I could retire at.'" More than thirty years later, that dream will soon come true for Wesley.

He and Angela married in 1997. "I made a commitment to Angela that these next ten years were when we have to make our money and put money away for retirement." As I listen to him outline their strategy I'm struck that somehow Wesley heeded retirement advice that I'd never heard, even though I was the one raised middle class. Or maybe I'd just ignored the advice because I'd already started life with a bit of a silver spoon in my mouth and didn't feel the need to worry? "We'd had some help," he explains, "and some good fortune," as he puts it (in the form of his mother, her wife, and Angela's mother helping them put a down payment on a condo before they were married). "It had taken three months for them people to put the loan through," Wesley tells me. "I'm Black, with no credit history, and I didn't know to go to a bank, so I was going to a broker. They kept calling my job over and over again asking, 'Is he still working there?'"

Eventually the condo deal went through and their financial life began to slowly take a more reliable shape. "It seems small and trivial," he tells me, "but when I could take a vacation with Angela and pay our bills *before* we went away so we didn't get hammered when we got back, that was a big deal. It took me years to do that, probably after working for UPS for three years." They bought a house. Some years later they sold the condo for a $90,000 profit, which they used to pay off the mortgage on the house. This meant they could sock much of Wesley's salary away for retirement. In the meantime, Wesley worked incredibly hard with no letup.

Studies show that UPS drivers get in and out of their truck five hundred times a day, which drivers feel mostly in their knees. All of that bending, hoisting, and shock absorbing can add up over time. "I worked twenty years before I ever had a Saturday off. The package cars are not air-conditioned. And of course you have to drive the truck without killing someone." But going all the way back to his days stocking shelves at Winn-Dixie Wesley has known how to do an exemplary job.

The higher-ups liked him from the start and kept trying to recruit him for management positions. But a mentor convinced him that it was more beneficial financially to stay right where he was. "Management isn't what it's cracked up to be. They work you seventy-two hours a week. I decided to just *work*." He loves it. It's the type of work he wants to do. As a kid he sensed he wasn't going to spend his life behind a desk, and he hated being inside a building all day. "I knew I needed to be outside, moving stuff, sweating. Seems to be something that clicked with me. If I ever sat down in one place, I'd fall asleep." And the benefits are great—medical and dental are entirely paid for with the exception of a $250 deductible per year.

Wesley's first real opportunity to retire comes when he hits twenty-five years of driving at the tender age of fifty-nine. He'll get a pension of around $3,000 a month, and he'll pay just $500 a month out of pocket for benefits for himself and his family. "It'll be killer." As someone who has never had an employee pension program, I hear that loud and clear, and I'm even a little jealous. Plus he maxed out his 401(k) contributions and bought a little bit of UPS stock with every paycheck. All of that money he set aside has been sitting and growing and just waiting for him, Angela, and their son, Wesley III.

Wesley says he's proudest of what he's been able to provide for his son, who was born in 2001. "Our next big investment is for Little Wesley's college education. He's a pretty intelligent kid, and he earned the Florida Bright Futures scholarship, which covers seventy-five percent of his undergraduate tuition and fees."

Recently Wesley and Angela sold stock and bought some land on a lake he's been going to since he was a boy. "A buddy of mine lives out there now. Finally, we realized we want a place out there, too. When we use some of that 401(k) money and build our second home, it'll be worth quite a bit. After my UPS retirement, I plan to charter my twenty-three-foot Grady-White saltwater fishing boat to tourists interested in the grouper and Spanish mackerel you can catch off the Florida coast. Then I'll go find something to do maybe thirty hours a week or so. I'm not going to be able to just sit on the front porch and do nothing." I can practically see Wesley and his family living the American Dream, and it looks really good from here.

MEET DENAE—She Set the Intention

Denae grew up in Fort Worth, Texas, in a family of "working-class Black folk," and was the first in her family to attend college. She was thirty-three and newly debt-free when I first interviewed her for this book. She'd graduated from Stanford with a BA in drama in 2006, received an MFA in performance and choreography from Florida State University in 2010, then moved to New York City to pursue her dream of being a professional dancer. She worked with world-renowned choreographers, toured internationally, and produced original work.

However, she owed $32,000 in student loan and credit card debt from her undergraduate and graduate school years, and the average professional dancer salary in NYC was $22,000 a year. She felt her debt was "deciding what I should do with my life because I couldn't afford to take on low-paid projects or unpaid internships that were often stepping stones for new artists." But then she took charge. She paid down all that debt *on an artist's salary in three years*. And she told me how she did it, so I could share it with you.

"In New York City, you can spend a ton of money on food. I committed to a plan to save money, which often meant I only went grocery shopping once a week. There were times when my plan to get debt-free was so hard, all I could do was laugh at myself. I'd walk blocks out of my way to avoid restaurants I like and make Snapchat videos saying, 'Not today, Shake Shack!'"

Let's start with where Denae's debt came from. While a Federal Pell Grant and scholarships covered much of her undergraduate tuition, room, and board, she still had to take out student loans. To cover other living expenses, her father had her apply for a credit card. She used this for expenses such as plane tickets home to Texas, clothing, and textbooks. Her dad paid the minimum amount due each month while she was in school, Denae told me, "and after graduation, the balance was gifted as my responsibility to pay off."

Her MFA program at Florida State offered a graduate teaching fellowship that covered only a portion of her tuition, room, and board. So, again, she needed student loans and another credit card for grad school expenses. With her two degrees in hand she owed over $32,000, which, with the planned interest payments, would total about $50,000.

Credit card debt is a huge problem for many of us. As I've already mentioned, looking back on my college years, I realize I didn't really get how plastic worked. I loved the cachet of the shiny rectangle with its raised numbers. It made me feel I belonged in the group of wealthy people who ambled through the manicured atrium at the fancy shopping center in my town. When I ate out with friends and the bill came, I'd pull out that card and plunk it down, sometimes paying my share, sometimes paying for all. It made me feel successful to pay for my friends' meals. I didn't treat the card like a checkbook, though, where you record what you've spent and add it all up so you know when you're nearing zero. With credit cards, there seemed to be no zero. It seemed I could just keep spending. Until, by the time I graduated from college, I couldn't fathom how I'd get enough money to pay what I owed. I was also ashamed of the debt and afraid to talk about it with anyone, including Dan, who was my boyfriend at the time, and my parents. I worried that my debt said awful things about me and my worthiness. I was a graduate of a top school headed off to a top law school, but my debt felt like a huge F.

Unlike Denae, though, I was economically privileged. So, when I was in bad shape financially, I had a safety net in the form of my parents, like a trampoline beneath me that could help me bounce back. As I've already told you, my parents paid off my credit card debt while I stood there with tears running down my cheeks. It's still hard to admit that I don't have good money instincts. Denae, however, is a different story!

Like many in her generation, Denae had student loans that were outsized compared to the salary she could command after graduating from college. And that's not just because Denae is an artist. For many who started adult lives during the Great Recession, full-time work was hard to find, and salaries stagnated in ways that, according to economists, will, over time, continue to affect economic prospects for this group of people. Still, regardless of what factors caused any of us to get in over our heads, we have two choices when our bills outpace our income. We can throw up our hands in anger and despair and avoid the topic altogether (that is, do the things that will just drive us further and further into debt)—or we can try to commit to a plan that can get us out of debt. Denae chose the latter. I'm here for it!

"On top of a low income and my large debt, I lived in an expensive city," Denae told me. "But I'm a contemporary dancer and the heart of the industry is in New York City. About three years in, I was at a cattle-call audition. This is the kind of thing where you sit on the floor with five hundred people waiting for hours until your number is called to audition for two spots. I was really worried about money. I told another dancer, 'If I don't get this job, I'm going to have to get another day job, because Sallie Mae wants her money.' I did not get that job, but I did start making a plan to get rid of my student loans.

"I read *Predictably Irrational* by Dan Ariely, which is about habit changing in spending, and was inspired to set a date to be debt-free and to make my journey public. *Okay*, I thought, *I want to get out of debt and I'm going to do it in three years by my thirty-second birthday!* Then I posted that on Facebook. When I set the intention I was like, *I don't know how I'm going to do this*. But I had told Facebook, so the goal was set.

"If I only paid the minimum payments, I'd pay nearly fifty thousand dollars over ten years on my approximately thirty-two thousand dollars of student loan and credit card debt. I got aggressive about finding additional gigs, cut my expenses down to the essentials, and made additional payments above the minimum whenever possible. I would literally walk extra cash to the ATM and make credit card payments. I would wear one or two outfits all season with different accessories. Nobody really cares."

As Denae recounted what it was like paying down her debt, I did the numbers in my head. Her discipline astounded me. I hadn't even heard how she was eating or affording a place to live—I was kind of afraid to pry further—but I needed to know how her plan worked. So I asked.

"My grocery budget was forty dollars a week plus ten dollars for picking up a meal when I needed to do that. There's a Trader Joe's and a gourmet grocery near me; I chose the Trader Joe's. I'm a small person, but a professional dancer has to eat enough to dance eight hours a day. I had to buy the right food *and* set aside time for meal prep. I prepared meals with fiber, fat, and protein to get that feeling of fullness. I ate a lot of greens, rice, beans, sweet potatoes, chickpeas, basmati rice, black beans, and avocado. I made sure I was always carrying snacks so I didn't buy food between rehearsals. When a coworker at a temp job ate my fruit in the fridge without asking, I made a sign that said: 'Please do not eat my food. I am paying off my student loans.'

"Finding stable, affordable housing also played a big part in paying down my debt. I live in artist housing now, which is like winning the housing lottery in New York. You have to prove you're working in the arts and meet the income requirements. Then, there's a long waiting list. I called every month to check my number. After ten months on the waiting list, I was offered an apartment. Here, a 200-square-foot studio rents for between $630 and $950 a month, including utilities, cable, and access to free rehearsal space. This helped me save money while making art because NYC rehearsal space averages twenty dollars an hour. My place is tiny. It feels like an adult dorm room. But it's fine.

"I get around by subway and set aside money for cabs in case of emergencies. Sometimes I purchase Uber or Lyft gift cards to limit my monthly spending. When I finish the gift card, I tell myself, 'That's it. It's gone. Figure something else out.' I've found it's easier to budget when you have finite funds available, rather than just trying to remember not to spend so much.

"Socializing and going out in the city also stressed my budget. My fancy New York friends would invite me to pricey bars and events. It was always hard to say no. I told some of my friends outright that I was on a tight budget, and they were cool with that. If they invited me to an event beyond my budget, I'd say, 'I'll swing by.' I'd literally show up for a few minutes, connect with my friends, and when they were seated or started to make their way inside the concert venue, I'd leave.

"Typically, my artist friends were much more cost conscious. We'd do things like get comp tickets for each other's shows and have everybody bring five dollars' worth of snacks to gatherings to make sure everyone ate well, affordably. There's also so much you can do for free in New York. A friend created a public 'Calendar of Free Events.' We would pre-party before going out, and I'd have an amazing time for less than ten dollars."

After listening to Denae relay her financial habits, I was squirming a bit. I'm a lot older than her, and don't have anywhere near her discipline or ability to sacrifice. I was actually taking notes for myself! Denae's friends were doing the same—an unexpected windfall that came from setting her intentions to be debt-free out loud and on Facebook.

"I have also learned how to budget for the erratic income that is the reality for many artists. I would get cast for a two-year project paid quarterly, then land one day as an extra on *Orange Is the New Black*, then spend three weeks at a residency in Trinidad and Tobago, then a half day dancing as Serena Williams in a parody of Beyoncé's *Lemonade* on *Late Night with Seth Meyers*. The checks would all come at different times. I had to develop a system to make sure my regular bills were paid on time while also setting aside money to pay down my debt."

And the goal itself—to be debt-free in three years? "I finished on time—a little bit before my thirty-second birthday, in fact.

"To celebrate, I threw a party for myself in Brooklyn called 'Denae's Debt-Free Fiesta!' Sooooo many people came out. People were like, 'Tell me how to be debt-free!' It was interesting, because when I first started posting my process on Facebook, I wouldn't get a lot of comments. But privately in my direct messages, I would hear from EVERYONE. Folks were dealing with debt across professions and across economic class. Some folks lamented about not learning about personal finance in school, others had questions about their student loans, and others wanted to share about a credit card they just paid off. In a way, it was one of my most impactful art projects that I didn't plan for."

Denae massively inspires me. She learned about paying down debt by studying the problem, then deploying what she learned with discipline. And three years after I first interviewed her for this book, I caught up with Denae again. She's still debt-free. She wants to be of service to countless others who are struggling with debt, so she's pursuing her Accredited Financial Counselor® and Certified Financial Planner™ certifications, working as a financial coach at a nonprofit, and developing her own financial wellness platform.

The year 2020 tested her methods. She lost friends, colleagues, neighbors, and a close family relation to COVID-19. Her financial counselor position at a city-funded organization was classified as "essential" at the beginning of the pandemic, but she was terrified of taking the NYC subway every day and getting sick. She quickly switched companies. The economic shock of the pandemic on New York City resulted in many of her friends moving to the suburbs. Theaters closed, and there were few places left to perform. Meanwhile, Denae's apartment building is sandwiched between a hospital, jail, courthouse and police station. "Black Lives Matter is my life," she says, and she spent the summer walking out her front door to hundreds, "probably thousands," of people marching for Black Lives Matter in Brooklyn.

"Some days I don't know if my exhaustion is mental, emotional, spiritual or physical," she says. "But you know what type of problems I don't have right now? Money problems. I did the work of getting my finances in order, paying off all of my debt, building an emergency savings fund, and intentionally building wealth seven years ago. When the chaos of 2020 arrived, I was prepared. I was injured in the fall of 2019 and had to suddenly cancel dance performances, but my emergency fund was there. I did lose income, but I had no debt and a low cost of living. I could recover. I knew how to get back on track. I had been developing a second income-earning skill set in finance in the event I couldn't dance, so I was able to quickly pivot and find a job in financial services."

According to Denae, "Your future self will thank you for getting your finances together now. I could not have predicted a global pandemic, but I had a plan in place in case of a financial emergency. What can you start doing now to help your future self?

> Save 10% of any money that comes into your life. Saving is a habit you can get really good at. This habit will protect you on your financial journey.
>
> Pay as little interest as possible on any money you choose to borrow. Try to keep interest rates on your debt under 7% if possible. If you don't qualify for this interest rate and you must borrow money, try to stay under 10%.
>
> If you owe debt with an interest rate over 10%, address it ASAP. The money that companies make from charging you interest helps them to pay their shareholders, who probably own yachts. Unless it's your yacht, don't make yacht payments.
>
> Shift into a wealth-building mindset. Financial wealth is only one type of wealth. Build the life that fits your vision of a fulfilled life utilizing all the types of wealth.

"When I was paying off my debt, I was gentle with myself in the months I couldn't afford to make extra payments, but the debt eventually disappeared, and it feels amazing not to owe anyone anything. It also brings me joy to envision how I want to build wealth rather than stressing over how to pay down debt.

"As a financial services professional now, would I recommend everyone pay off their debt aggressively like I did? Not necessarily, because everyone's situation is different. I didn't have kids or any financial responsibility to other people. It's best to do your research, seek out trustworthy sources, and build a strategy that works for you." Denae herself is of course one of those trustworthy resources. She's listed in the resources found in Appendix II.

Looking back at her story, Denae realizes how much she learned in the few years after she and I first spoke about her debt. For example: "That credit card debt I complained about my father 'gifting me' after college *was* actually a gift. Since he had paid the payments on time for four years, I had a strong credit history when I graduated. Now I see that what he did was beneficial."

And when she says that, I can't help but notice that a theme in this chapter is about listening to our fathers.

IN SHORT: CONTROL YOUR MONEY INSTEAD OF LETTING MONEY CONTROL YOU

Getting a handle on how money works and how you can make it work for you will help you feel like more of an adult and will help you make your dreams come true. But even more important than having the money you need is understanding who you are and what you need in order to be balanced and well. You looking after you is probably the most important thing you need to do. Let's go there next. Let's get personal. Let's go from cold, hard cash to warm, soft you.

Unpack and Reflect

- How do I feel about my relationship with money? To what extent is it hard for me to think about and talk about money, and if it is hard, why is that?
- What do I wish I understood better about money?
- Is anyone keeping tabs on my money with me? Do I want their involvement or not?
- What are my financial concerns and goals? How much more money could I be saving per month right now? What steps can I take to make my money work better for me?

9

TAKE GOOD CARE

(OF YOURSELF)

Everyone is dealing with something. We just have to love other people for who they are. Hope they love us, too.

—Dr. Claire Brown, *The Good Doctor*

You're young, which may make you feel immune and immortal. If so, you're in danger of not listening to me right now.

Or maybe you're not feeling immortal at all. Maybe you're feeling sad, scared, overwhelmed, sick, or like a disappointment. Or unseen.

I'm very much here for you, regardless of where you are in this.

Stay with me.

I'm fifty-three. And according to the medical profession's body mass index, I'm obese. There, I said it. I don't feel obese. But this is out there as societal judgment of me. I love myself anyway (also, thank you, Lizzo). In addition, I was diagnosed with mild asthma a few years ago, and I am pre-diabetic and hoping I don't get the real deal. And I think I might have anxiety but it's never been bad enough for me to go see anybody about it. And I'm a stressed-out Type A micromanaging control freak. Is that a thing? Hahaha. No cavities though!

This book is about you, not me. But I'm sharing about myself, because I want you to understand how much I am not judging you based on what you weigh or what you may or may not be diagnosed with. And I want you to also understand that I am well aware that I can't possibly know what you may suffer from or struggle with. But even given all of that, I feel I have to point out that if life is a nice long bicycle ride, *your body and your mind are the two wheels that propel you forward*. So, you want to take care of your body and your mind. I'm not here to advocate for one type of self-care approach over another. I'm just here farther down the path of life shining a light back at you, and in the blinding light that is in your face right now I want you to realize that one day you'll be fifty-three, possibly less healthy and less strong than you are right now, in various ways, and less able to make meaningful pivots. So, at the same time as you're figuring out what you're good at and what you love, and going off and doing those things, keep in mind that your adulthood will be a longer and more enjoyable ride if you also seek to know yourself as fully and accurately as possible, and take care of that self. Bottom line: since the future you wants to live an awesome life, future you is saying, *You gotta take care of us.*

A WORD ABOUT LANGUAGE

I see you. You're an amazingly unique individual. It's a challenge here on these pages to try to speak directly with you and also with everyone else reading this. This chapter will be extra hard to get right because it is about the innermost-what-comprises-you stuff. I'll share examples you may not necessarily really relate to. But just know that I'm trying, and I hope you'll give this chapter a try, too.

I'm going to use the term "situation" to encompass everything from mental health challenges to issues with your physical health (ailments, illnesses, and diseases) to differences in the way you learn and process information. Struggles in any of these situations can greatly if not pro-foundly impact your quality of life. My overarching message here is to do your best to understand *who you are*, and *what you are contending with*, and *what you need* in order to thrive. And I want you to be kind to yourself about who you are even if the world seems to be sending different messages about your worth (if not outright trying to "fix" you).

I'm also going to get specific with my examples, at times. And while I always do my best to refer to groups of people in the way they want to be referred to, those self-given labels can and do change over time, and people outside of any particular group can lag in understanding the preferred terms. I know about this when it comes to ethnic and racial identity, for example, where, before "Black" and "African American" were in vogue, we were "Negro," and yet some folks still call us "Colored" (which we do NOT prefer). Queer people have claimed the term "queer" back for ourselves, though it was once used as a slur against us. (Similarly, the words "mad" and "crazy" were used as slurs against people with schizophrenia, and many people avoid using those terms for that reason.) I claim queer for myself, which I prefer to use over what is more literal (for me)—bisexual—because queer has come to be an umbrella for all non-straight and non-cis identities and I feel it best captures who I am. I remember when people routinely said "Oriental" and folks started saying, "No, call us Asian." And when people routinely said "handicapped" or "special needs" and folks started saying, "No, call us disabled." I remember when genderqueer people began to ask that assumptions not be made about pronouns, and began to create gender-neutral ones that affirm their identities. I remember when most did not know what "cis" meant, which of course we now use to refer to those whose gender identity matches how they were labeled at birth, in contrast to "trans," which means the opposite. In the emotions realm, I am told that for some people "mental health challenges" and "the mental health community" are preferred over anything that equates mental health with "illness," while others in this community do prefer the term "mental illness." And in the cognitive realm, I'm told that autistic people created and tend to prefer the term "neurodiverse." I'm told that "neurodivergent" is a preferred umbrella term both for people who are on the autism spectrum and for those who are differently wired in other ways, including around learning, attention, mood, social interaction, and self-control. I'm told that some people prefer to be called "differently wired" if they have "learning differences" or if their mind gets at things differently than is considered the "norm." But I also know that there are people who feel saying "learning differences" instead of "learning disabilities" is problematic, because whatever they struggle with feels very much like a disability in a society that has failed to notice, care about, or accommodate their needs. I'm told that to be gifted and at the same time have learning differences is to be "twice exceptional." And I'm aware that as I go to some length here to try to be inclusive of all folx in my mentions, I'm almost certainly leaving out other designations due to my own ignorance.

I also know that each individual has the right to use the terms that are most meaningful to them. (I prefer "Black" over "African American" to describe myself, for example.) And that everyone, regardless of identities, differences, and diagnoses of one kind or another, is a unique individual. No two neurodivergent people are alike, in the same way that no two Black people are alike. I respect and honor differences even as I try to write one book that addresses and appeals to everybody. This is sensitive terrain and I'm doing my best not to inflict damage as I go.

In short, this chapter attempts to honor our myriad differences while speaking to what we have in common in caring for ourselves. There are things that we should take into account no matter who we are when trying to deconstruct, construct, and maintain a healthy adult self.

A BRIEF HISTORY OF SOCIETY'S APPROACH TO MENTAL HEALTH AND LEARNING DIFFERENCES

As I write this, one in two eighteen-year-olds has a diagnosis. This is a huge shift from prior generations. So, where mental health challenges and learning differences may once have been relegated to an asterisk in a book, now they deserve to be at the center of the page. There's a reason the animated series *BoJack Horseman* is so popular. Through a story about a washed-up Hollywood star who is a horse, the show somehow meaningfully brings up addiction, depression, racism, self-destructive behaviors, sexism, sexuality, trauma, and a whole host of other challenges we humans deal with every day. I'm here for it.

To hear my twenty-one-year-old son Sawyer tell it, there are more memes on mental health than on any other subject. I've learned from Sawyer that the conventional attitude toward those dealing with mental health challenges or neurodivergence goes like this: *Can't you just . . . (push through/make a list/be happy)?* And that if you can't "just" perform well-being and neurotypicality (i.e., fit at least somewhat into the system and be so-called normal) then you don't belong in this so-called society. He shows me memes in subreddits (his favorite social media space) and I do my best to understand them. Even though I don't necessarily get the imagery in the memes and am hopelessly lost about all that goes unsaid in such formats, I've learned enough to know that these memes are about recognition of the struggle, compassion, and support, and I find all of that highly encouraging.

In the first two decades of the twenty-first century, the U.S. saw an enormous upswing in the anxiety, depression, loneliness, and suicidal ideation experienced by children, adolescents, and young adults. When I was an administrator at Stanford, from 1998 to 2012, students were going to the counseling center in such numbers that we had to hire more therapists and doctors. (And Stanford's campus was no different than any other in this respect.) We also saw a huge increase in diagnosed learning differences. Things are not as they used to be. I'm deliberately saying this out loud here because too many people my age and older think, *What is it with these kids?*, instead of *Wow, things really have changed.* I know things have changed. The jury is still very much out on "why" but prevailing theories include: 1) more kids are likely to be diagnosed for things that went ignored or untreated in prior generations due to a reduction in stigma; 2) environmental factors may contribute to the increase; and 3) a lack of autonomy in childhood is correlated with increased anxiety and depression in children and young adults. I can't opine on the "why"; I just want you to know that I know things may be harder for you than the other older folks in your life seem to appreciate.

When my fellow Gen Xers and I were growing up, mental health challenges and learning differences were something people whispered about, as they did about cancer. You felt bad for the person. If the person suffering from such difficulties was in your family, you might have even felt embarrassed or ashamed. The pervasive societal mindset went something like, *They are deviant.* Or *It's their own fault.* Yes, even those attitudes were an improvement over earlier days when people were routinely subjected to barbaric treatments or simply locked away (and unfortunately even today, a psych ward can be a very traumatic place for people). But however much progress had been made by the time Gen X came along, in our childhood the prevailing attitudes that we heard about mental health challenges and learning differences were unfeeling and harmful.

Still, I know the older generations had no basis for understanding what we now know about the brain and body chemistry, stress and trauma, genetic predispositions, and the way the environment and experiences impact our genetic makeup, which is a relatively new field called epigenetics. You're fortunate to have been raised in an era of robust scientific research, an explosion in pharmacological support, and a greater societal awareness of, acceptance of, and resources for mental health challenges and learning differences. Chances are, if you've got a situation, someone in your family, community, or school noticed it, spoke up, and tried to help you out. Or maybe you took it upon yourself to get that help. You may have a diagnosis. (You may also NOT have a diagnosis, but the pain and suffering you experience are valid, too.) If you have access to professional care and resources, you may have a doctor, therapist, psychiatrist, or coach. You may have had or currently be undergoing treatment. You may have meds, strategies, services, support, and other ways of dealing. You've grown up in a time that's so much more awake and alert to these things. That's a good thing. But learning differences and mental health challenges are so common that they should be called normal. And we still have so far to go toward understanding and full acceptance of all people into all realms of life.

DISCOVERING HOW YOU FUNCTION

When it comes to adulting, there is perhaps nothing more core and personal than figuring out who and what you are and how *you* best function, so that you can keep on functioning. Owning your own situation requires first figuring out what your situation is, to the extent that figuring it out is possible (which might entail a diagnosis or a recommendation from a clinician or expert of some kind), then accepting and embracing that this is a part of you. This can be a back and forth as we learn different things about ourselves and have different experiences as that self. There can be progress and setbacks. That's all normal.

You may be newly discovering the facets of yourself that need particular care and attention. And if you're discovering that you're objectively different from the prevailing norm in your family or peer group, it can be a shock. You may go through a bit of mourning that your differences were not supported, recognized, or named when you were younger. You may have internalized in childhood that you were a disappointment, problematic, stupid, or that something was just plain wrong with you. My friend Debbie Reber, who wrote the book *Differently Wired*, tells me, "There's a tidal wave of young adults who are just discovering, *Oh, THIS is what was going on with me all along*. Some people are relieved. Others are pissed. Everyone is kind of owning it in different ways."

Hearing about these different kinds of reckonings cuts close to the bone for me.

Sawyer was diagnosed with ADHD (Inattentive Type), dysgraphia (trouble with the physical act of getting ideas out through writing), and a wee bit of anxiety when he was in the fourth grade. We got him a handwriting helper, and he saw a therapist regularly for a while. But in hindsight, I think Dan and I saw him as so smart and accomplished that we felt these things weren't that big of a deal or that he would grow out of them. This was a mistake. I have his permission to share all of this with you.

In elementary school, because the act of writing things down was so hard for him, he was allowed to take a small recording device out to the playground and dictate his stories, which we would type up for him. I used to get teary listening to those tapes, because here was my distractable kid with all kinds of playground noise and shouting kids in the background trying to pull his complex ideas out of his brain. Somehow, he did it. In middle school we were allowed to "sign off" that he had worked for a very long time on something and should not be penalized for not finishing, an accommodation I believe he used all of three times. At the end of middle school we were told he did too well in school to be included on the list of kids who would get accommodations in high school. We were angry. (At the meeting I said, *You mean if he was getting Cs he could get accommodations but since he gets As he cannot?* Like accommodations were to improve grades instead of to give kids with learning differences some relief. I remember Sawyer looking over at me, as awareness of that unfairness sat deeply in his eyes. And their answer was "yes." And Dan and I—with all of our goddamn education and privilege in life—nevertheless felt too overwhelmed by this complicated world of IEPs and 504s, and by the unstated implication from the authorities that we were wrong to ask for these things for our son, so we didn't do anything about it. Besides, Sawyer was getting As.)

Fast-forward through high school, where he did very well, although homework every single day was a complete slog for him and by sophomore year it was taking him five hours a night. In junior year, after years of resisting medication, he began taking it for homework, which reduced the load from five hours to three. I remember his pediatrician's astonishment when we asked for his sign-off that Sawyer could run track, because it was the clearest evidence that Sawyer now had two hours a day "back" to do with as he wished. And he did very well on standardized tests, refusing to take extra time for reasons I'm not sure of, and we didn't push him to do it, either. And then he went off to a rigorous small liberal arts college, did not seek accommodations, and began a slow crash and burn where workload and responsibilities outpaced whatever the meds and family support used to do for him, and he began to do poorly, and not believe in himself, and then do very poorly, and he was also struggling and then suffering emotionally. (And need I remind you that I, his mother, am a former college dean who used to help other people's kids for a living?)

Somehow, I'd managed to help other people, yet failed to help my own son. Mine wasn't just a failure to help him. It was a failure to *see* him.

When Dan and I finally got how hard things were for Sawyer, and Sawyer had come to this conclusion himself, he decided to take a break from college. We set him up with a good psychiatrist who could help with both meds and talk therapy. And we decided we really needed to better understand ADHD and anxiety ourselves. So, we bought a bunch of books on the subject and read them round robin, filling them with Post-it notes as we went. When Sawyer came home for the summer he went to use the printer in Dan's office, where the books were stacked on Dan's desk. "Mom, I saw the books in Dad's office," he told me. My heart sank. I was afraid he'd be angry and feel we were pathologizing him. He looked me dead in the eye and said, "Thank you for trying to understand who I am." He was smiling.

Any parent reading this is in tears right now. Because the last thing we want is to harm our kids. But here Dan and I were, loving Sawyer oh so much, yet ignoring, not learning, not understanding, thinking we understood when we did not. I cannot go back in time and change my responses to my son's needs, but I go forward fully committed to being the parent my child deserves, and I want that understanding, that experience of being seen, for you, too. So, if you relate to this story, just put a Post-it note on this page and give it to the person who needs to read it.

OWNING YOUR SITUATION

Once you begin to know how you function, accepting and embracing yourself is the next step, and that can lead to a level of self-acceptance I call self-love. Owning your situation is a complex, iterative, lifelong process of continual self-exploration and acceptance of that shifting self. My former student Amanda Gelender, an organizational strategist, writer, mental health advocate, and social impact expert in Amsterdam, puts it this way: "For a lot of folks it's not as simple as, *I got my diagnosis and now I understand how I work and I need to move on to self-acceptance.* Self-love and healing are nonlinear and shift over time as you grow and encounter new experiences and challenges. You may get a diagnosis that resonates with how you've felt your whole life and it makes you feel understood, relieved, and connected to a community of people who get you. You may have a doctor who dismisses or misdiagnoses you, causing additional pain and delayed treatment. You may have periods of stability and wellness followed by periods of deep pain and relapse. Your struggles may stem from ongoing abuse or trauma that requires systemic change to fully shift. It may take trying many different healing modalities before you find what best feels good to you. It's a lifelong process to build an honest and loving relationship with yourself: honoring your changing needs, desires, and struggles with as much patience and compassion as possible."

I know from personal experience that understanding and accepting the self can be an elusive goal. Self-love means you feel good about yourself intrinsically (i.e., inside of you), as opposed to feeling good about yourself only when you get extrinsic evidence of your worth, in the form of feedback that others value you or your accomplishments. (Note:

self-love is *not* narcissism. Narcissism is an obsession with the self and a refusal to see one's own shortcomings, while blaming others and having a lack of empathy for them.) The beautiful thing about self-love is that when you have it, no one can harm you emotionally, no matter what they say or how much they exclude or ignore you. This is because you know intrinsically that you are worthy of dignity and love, and if someone cannot offer it to you, you realize it's a problem within *them*, rather than it being about you. You may be having an *Oh please, it's not that simple* reaction right now, and I get that. Try to stay with me.

A lot of factors can undermine our ability to feel self-love. Living in a capitalistic economy means we've been taught that a person's worth is a function of their ability to produce output that can be commodified and sold to others. That is, capitalism teaches us that our value is equal to the amount of money we earn (or, worse, the amount we have, even if we didn't earn it). So, if our bodies or minds can't or won't do what capitalism values, it can make us feel judged not only as less valuable but as less *human*. Disability activists continue to be at the forefront of the effort to question and redefine societal worth. At a societal level, messages like Eurocentrism and thinness as beauty standards can also impact how we feel about our worth. Says Amanda, "Mainstream society and media upholds a very narrow, Eurocentric standard of beauty, so if you're not white, thin, cis, and/or able-bodied, it can be challenging to feel represented and affirmed for who you are. Self-love exists in the context of entrenched power systems and industries that profit from people feeling unattractive and unworthy."

And, at a micro-level, our family upbringing can impact how we feel about our worth. Some of us were raised to feel we're worthy of dignity and love no matter what (if that's you, cherish that aspect of your upbringing and be grateful); others of us were harmed in childhood to varying degrees, and have to do the work to counteract the message that we're not good enough as we are, or that we flat out aren't wanted. When I say "do the work," I mean the growth we can achieve through therapy or other forms of conversation, mindfulness meditation, journaling, and other practices that allow us to acknowledge, name, process, and let go of the negative messages we've received about ourselves. Learning to appreciate our own worth can be extremely challenging work, but my journey has shown me it's worth it. Self-love is an Avenger-level emotional invisibility cloak; *when you possess it, it allows you to interact with* all *other humans and be completely emotionally unscathed.* Betcha want it now, right?

But we're not Avengers, and other humans are a huge part of our journey—and they are who they are and they do what they do. So, we have to do the work not only of trying to love ourselves no matter what but also of owning our situation when in community with others and asking for what we need. If you have a "visible" situation, it's possible you get some support for it or at least recognition about it. People may be more likely to take you at your word when you express your needs as compared to someone with an "invisible" situation who may not be "believed" when they try to share about their struggles and needs. That said, plenty of people with visible situations are not listened to and don't get their accommodation needs met, either. And, if you have a visible situation, it may also lead other people to make assumptions about your needs and what you can or can't do. They may try to over-help you, particularly if you are blind, deaf, have a physical disfigurement, are in a wheelchair, or have a prosthesis. And of course many people have both visible and invisible things going on, and may be seen and validated around some aspects of what they're dealing with but not with all of it. Then there's the stigma to which you may be subjected that comes from other people's ignorance or prejudice about your situation. Their ignorance is a problem within them, but it doesn't mean it doesn't sting when it hits you. It's a lot.

"Invisible" situations—such as being neurodivergent, depressed, or anxious, having chronic migraine, or having autoimmune diseases such as chronic fatigue syndrome or multiple sclerosis (MS)—present a different set of challenges because people don't "get it" or "believe" us when we express our needs. I learned this firsthand from my friend Kris, who has MS, which is one of those diseases you can't necessarily "see," yet I've known it to take over Kris's body completely.

In the summer of 2019, Kris, Dan, and I had traveled to the border town of Clint, Texas, next to El Paso, to protest our government's treatment of migrant children. For two straight days, Kris went all out. She made and held signs, shouted at cars, organized and supported volunteers, and talked with the media. Then on the third day she was curled up in her hotel bed unable to move because the pain and fatigue were absolutely debilitating. The next day, after she had recovered a lot of her energy and was in far less pain, she taught me about the concept of "spoons," a metaphor created close to twenty years ago by Christine Miserandino, who has lupus. Miserandino used spoons on a dining table to quantify the amount of mental and physical energy she possesses on any given day, which can be measured and must be rationed if it is to last. Healthy people have an unlimited number of spoons every day, but chronically ill people have a limited number, and everything they do— get dressed, get breakfast, make phone calls, make a sign for a protest— takes away spoons until they're gone. A chronically ill person might run out of spoons well before a day is over and will need rest to replenish the spoon supply. As Kris taught me, "If I borrow spoons from tomorrow to get through today, I have fewer spoons the next day, so it's worse."

For those of us with seemingly limitless or easily rechargeable energy, the spoons metaphor can help us appreciate that energy is a finite resource for those with autoimmune or other chronic and often "invisible" illnesses and serious mental health challenges. My point here is that if you're dealing with something chronic and invisible, I encourage you to think about whom you trust and can feel safe with, tell them about your situation, and ask for their understanding, as Kris did with me. And if you're not already aware of the metaphor of the spoons but it relates to your situation, check it out (#spoonie is a very popular hashtag on Instagram and Twitter).

Another important way to own your situation is to continue on with your supports, whether they be services or meds even when you're leveling up to start college or grad school, start a new job, or move to a new community. To some, these kinds of major transitions can feel like a place of arrival, as in *I've achieved it, I don't need my services, supports, or meds anymore*, or a place of greater consequence, as in *I can't ask for services and supports here because of the stigma*. All of your supports are serving your needs and are not something to be ashamed of. However tempting it is to stop your services, generally speaking, stopping your services is not a very adult thing to do, and it can actually be dangerous, especially at a transition point in your life (which inherently involves extra stress), to abandon the very things that have been an important source of support for you up to this point. (Unless, of course, your body is telling you that something you're currently doing is harming you—this can happen in particular with medication.) I'll go so far as to say that "owning your situation" includes choosing schools, jobs, and communities that offer clear evidence that people like you are welcome and can thrive there. (In the same way that if you're queer, for example, you want evidence in advance that the new workplace, grad school, or community you're about to enter is a safe and welcoming space for you.)

And no matter where you are, to really own your situation you gotta find your people. You may be able to find them in your school, workplace, or community. But one of the brilliant things about the Internet is that it allows you to find others in the same situation all over the globe, and enables you to connect, support, and just BE, without your situation having to be a THING—swapping tips and strategies, and commiserating and consoling one another when days are challenging. Online communities combat isolation and are quite literally a life-saving connection for people every single day. We saw this a lot during the pandemic.

HOW TO TELL IF YOU'RE SUFFERING

An acute health problem is hard to miss: You have severe chest pain. Your bone is broken. You can't do the basics of feeding yourself and keeping clean. But it's harder to notice the slow creep of depression, a tumor, the inability to engage in society, or pains that grow from mild to worse over time. At some point you've gone from *I don't feel so good* to *I may be in trouble* to *I need help right now*. How do you know when it's time to seek help? And how can you intervene on your own behalf in time?

Whatever your situation may be, as my dear friend Donnovan Somera Yisrael says, "suffering is the best indicator" that you need to get help. Not that Donnovan believes that you should wait until you're suffering. To the contrary—he's all about prevention. I love this guy so much. I've known him since college and over the years he's had this way of simply walking up to me, seeing me in my suffering, and helping me feel less alone in it. I'm so glad he agreed to give you advice, too.

Donnovan is a senior health educator for mental health and well-being at Vaden Health Center at Stanford, where he helps students to live better and suffer less. Physical pain and the suffering that can stem from it is pretty easy to detect unless you're in a heap of denial. But mental suffering comes, at first, with less discernible pain. Donnovan says we need to be attentive to even the smallest manifestations of suffering. Things like "fatigue, feelings of overwhelm, rumination, worry, self-criticism, analysis paralysis, and unhealthy self-doubt." These seemingly small things can actually lead to a stage that Donnovan calls "stuckness," which can then lead to procrastination or worse. He says, "A body that stops moving gets stiff or constipated. Water that stops moving is going to stagnate. Money that stops moving causes a recession or depression. When emotions stop moving, there's a depression also. So, one good indicator of healthiness is movement. Whereas if you're stuck, that stuckness is a good sign to go get help." As with your car stuck at the side of the road, Donnovan says, you don't want to just sit there. "Ideally you go find a mechanic to get it moving again." Or a therapist, physician, or other type of healer, as the case may be.

Having good mental health is not just about getting partially out of the deep hole you may be in. "The opposite of languishing is actually *flourishing*," Donnovan tells me, quoting the research of sociologist Corey Keyes, who promotes the idea that health is not merely the absence of disease. Donnovan says we need to get good at detecting whether we are flourishing or languishing by asking ourselves, "Do I have an enriching life? Do I have a life that has growth? Do I feel curiosity? Do I have juicy issues to wrestle with? Do I experience occasional states of flow (a sign of experiencing engaging work/activities)? Do I engage in work that gives me a sense of purpose? Do I know my 'why'? Do I feel a sense of connection with others? Do I feel that I am part of a community? Or is it no, I am feeling stuck or blah, I am stuck in vicious cycles like procrastination, or in problematic relationships." (Pro tip: You can teach yourself to discern whether you're feeling these things by developing a mindfulness practice, which I'll tell you about in chapter 12, "Unleash Your Superpowers.") Donnovan says if we're having trouble getting ourselves out of a repeating pattern, we need to consult with someone. "You've got to get your car moving." By this he means go find someone you can talk to. But what if you can't ask for help?

THE HURDLE OF ADVOCATING FOR YOUR NEEDS

If your ankle appears to be sprained or you're coughing up half a lung, your friends are likely to tell you to go get it taken care of. But if your suffering is hidden from others, you have to develop the courage to become an advocate for your own right to get help. The more you're suffering, the harder it can become to self-advocate, of course; it's a very slippery slope. And many of us have a hard time showing vulnerability to others.

Donnovan acknowledges that asking for help *is* a sign of vulnerability. But he is an adherent of the researcher Brené Brown, who teaches that "vulnerability is *the* gateway to *all* the good stuff in life," as Donnovan puts it. "We need to make a mindset shift from believing asking for help is a form of weakness to believing asking for help is what smart and successful people do."

Donnovan uses "mini spiels" to try to convince his students that it's smart to ask for help. As I shared with you in chapter 3, "You're Not Perfect," Donnovan asks, *Do you know that Michael Phelps had a swim coach, Simone Biles a gym coach, and Serena Williams a swing coach? What are YOU so good at that you don't need help?*

And he then asks: *How many of you are happy to help someone else out but won't ask for the same thing from others?*

Well, after asking those questions, Donnovan tells students to *practice* asking for help: *Identify items on your to-do list with which you could ask others for help. Even the simplest thing (have a friend pick up your favorite snack when they were going to Trader Joe's anyway) will get the ball rolling, and the other person may even be happy to do it and it may strengthen your bond.* Dr. James R. Doty, director and founder of the Center for Compassion and Altruism Research and Education at Stanford, adds, "Fear of judgment stops us from asking for help. What we don't realize is that so many people want to help us."

THE STRONG THING LURKING WITHIN YOU

There's an emotional muscle within you that serves as a huge source of protection if you know how to exercise it. It's called resilience, and here's how it gets built up: Picture yourself learning to walk. You sucked at it. Up you went and down you fell any number of times. Definitely did not get it right on your first try. But then at some point you were able to make sense of how it worked, and your strength and balance improved as part of the process, and you began to get a sense of the environment around you, and off you went, ready to tackle the next thing . . . stairs!

My friend Adina Glickman likes to use this visual metaphor when talking with clients about developing resilience. For years she provided academic support and coaching for Stanford students who struggled with time management and procrastination, and the underlying situations for which those things might be symptoms. Now Adina is in private practice as an academic, life, and career coach. She teaches that "what's happening in that learning-to-walk process is not that we're just having a purposeful goal (*I want to walk*) or just persevering (*I'm going to stay at this*), it's that we are learning from the experience. Resilience is our ability to look at what our setbacks have been and make sense of them and learn from them."

When a client is facing a big setback, Adina walks them through a prior setback and the process they went through to move on from it, which she knows will help them weather the current situation. "Finding resilience inevitably follows an arc of expectation, disappointment, feeling crappy, connecting with people about it, getting other perspectives, and then the feelings change, and the life circumstances change, and the wind blows the other way. I'll say, 'You've had someone not want to go to the prom with you. You got rejected from a school you wanted to go to. You've had some kind of experience you can integrate into what is happening now.' Actively reflecting on that helps you process it." Here's an example:

> Client: When he turned me down for the prom, I wouldn't leave my room for three days.
> Adina: So, when it was the first day, do you remember feeling *I'm never fucking leaving my room again*?
> Client: Yeah.
> Adina: Then what happened?
> Client: And after three days I was sick of being in my room.
> Adina: Right. Feelings change.

Clients will tell Adina, "If I start crying I'll never stop." To which she says, "No, you won't keep crying forever. Maybe you'll cry for a few hours, but you'll get thirsty. You'll go get a drink of water. While you're drinking you won't be crying and there'll be a brief interruption. Maybe you'll start crying again, but then you'll have to pee. Time evolves, life evolves, then the phone rings." The lesson here is that you've been through something rough before, but your feelings changed then, and here you are now in another rough situation and in time your feelings about this will change, too.

Sometimes we get dismayed by our own inability to cope with something. Adina says, "A lot of people say, 'I'm a strong person, why am I so upset?' Or, 'I've done a lot, why is this bothering me so much?' But being resilient is not just about *you*—it's about *you within your context* of what you can reasonably be expected to handle right now. It's about starting to understand what one's place and capacity is in the world, and how that needs to be modulated according to what that world looks like. We're not going to tell Black men, 'Relax when you get in the car,' because that's just fucking insane. And we're not going to tell women, 'Work harder and you'll make as much as men,' because there's more going on than that. There's a context in the world. And each of us has to understand how much we influence context and how much context influences us."

She also advises clients to seek out the experiences of others to make more sense of what they're going through. "Being young means you don't yet have a large accumulation of your own experiences, which is why it's essential to connect with others to learn about how other people have handled things. Simply collecting stories of a variety of perspectives helps create forward motion in how your own feelings can evolve. When you can take on an experience that's bigger than the one inside of you, that's perspective. Your pain becomes 'not me in the world alone'. The ability to breathe some room into what you're feeling is what helps the feelings change."

The better you get at "experiencing your experiences" the more resilient you become, according to Adina. "By the time you're thirty, you'll have a bigger collection of experiences and more reference points. And you can say, 'Oh, yeah, I remember that happened and it felt really crappy and I didn't see beyond the hurting at the time, but I got through it.'"

Adina likes to help the people she works with think about the "event horizon," which is the amount of space and time you're able to envision beyond what you're dealing with now. Having a longer event horizon helps you to "be able to make sense of it all." As an example, Adina says, "The older you get, the farther around the corner you can see. So, when we're five years old, our brains haven't developed much yet and we don't have a sense of time, so our event horizon is very immediate. It's *What's for snack?* or *Do we get to go to the movies?* When you got to high school, if people asked you to make a five-year plan you were like, *I don't know what the fuck I want to do in five years. I can do a year maybe.* But the older you get, and the more years you have lived, the more you can say, *I can envision a longer future because I have a longer past.*"

This resilience thing is pretty awesome. And much as we might like to snap our fingers to make us resilient, or enroll in a class to get certified in it, or have someone create resilience for us, we can't. Life is our teacher. If you've had some tough times, it might encourage you to know that the rougher life is, the more resilient we have the potential to be, if we do the work to "experience our experiences," as Adina puts it (which is to do the work of feeling the feelings and processing them, with help of a professional if possible). Meanwhile, some commonly available life experiences naturally teach resilience, too, such as playing a team sport. According to my private equity friend (whom I quoted in chapter 3, "You're Not Perfect," who seeks to hire the best people possible to do the often high-stress work of deftly investing rich people's money), "To be resilient, people need to practice failure, particularly collaborative failure, so that they don't get that hormone rush that incapacitates them the minute something isn't perfect. The people who've played team sports seem to have it. It's what many of our best employees have in common. These employees harken back on the lessons and experiences from team sports in terms of navigating the workplace. They've lost a lot of games and still got recruited as an athlete. That's an irony, right? The athletic recruits weren't necessarily on winning teams, and it's not that they didn't make tons of mistakes, and often they made those mistakes in public. Yet they're still valued. Imagine if the academic side of things could create a learning environment that naturally builds resilience, too."

Indeed. I'd like to see someone imagine that. But that's a different book.

THE SECRET POWER OF GAMES

The most common mental health challenge facing the human population today is anxiety. If you're dealing with it, I've put a list of support resources in Appendix II, in case that's helpful.

But I want to tell you about something that may be new to you when it comes to managing anxiety. There's research out of Oxford University in England that shows how anxiety (and PTSD, too) can be treated in the moment by playing certain games. (For real!) I read about this in the book *SuperBetter*, by Jane McGonigal, whom I'll tell you more about in a second. But for now, the point is that researchers have found that video games that require massive, constant visual processing (such as *Tetris* or *Candy Crush*) as well as card games that do the same (such as *SET*) "help us stop imagining what might go wrong," and as such can block anxiety. This is because "anxiety—just like pain, traumatic memory, and cravings, requires conscious attention in order to develop and unfold." While anxiety can be a useful response to real threats and stressors, Dr. McGonigal says, "If the anxiety is *not* helping you identify concrete positive steps you can take, but rather is simply creating distress, play a game. Likewise, if the anxiety is trying to talk you out of doing something you truly want or need to do (like getting on a plane, giving a presentation, or going to a social event), go ahead and block it with a few minutes of play."

Jane McGonigal was the first person on the planet to get a PhD studying the psychological strengths of gamers and how those strengths can help gamers to be good at real-word problem solving. How cool is that? She's like a wizard from the future whose mission is to advance us to a better time. She says her number one goal in life is to see a game designer nominated for a Nobel Peace Prize. I had the pleasure of meeting Jane when a colleague brought her to campus to talk with sophomores about how to think about choosing a major.

Jane's knowledge of how playing games online can create real-life strengths is not from her research alone. She's had personal experience with this truth. In 2009, she suffered a mild traumatic brain injury and had to begin a monthslong process of resting her brain to try to get it back to normal. The pain in her head was constant, which meant she couldn't read, write, talk, or even just think for very long. Over time she began to feel despair, and eventually those feelings turned into thoughts of suicide. One day she realized, *I'm gonna have to turn this into a game or else I'm going to kill myself.*

So, she created a character and a game for herself called *Jane the Concussion Slayer* (after Buffy the Vampire Slayer); she later renamed the game *SuperBetter*. By naming her bad guys, developing some power-ups, recruiting a few allies, going on quests, and tracking these things each day, Jane made it through the extended post-concussion recovery period, achieved her epic win, and came out healed. As she puts it, "I didn't just get better. I got superbetter." Jane shared her game online, and after it had helped close to half a million people and had been studied by a number of independent researchers, she wrote a book about it called *SuperBetter: The Power of Living Gamefully.*

The *SuperBetter* game is alive and well today, as is Jane. *SuperBetter* has been used by people battling depression, cancer, addiction, weight issues, and plenty of other obstacles. The game is also used by people who don't necessarily have an especially difficult situation to improve but who just want to level up some aspect of their life. I encourage you to think about what gaming techniques can do for your real life and the real you. Please know that I'm not trying to minimize your struggle at all. I just want to mention this cool technique, validated by many scientific studies, in case it can be of use to you. Download *SuperBetter* to your phone, name your epic win, and get going.

SELF-CARE CHECKLIST

My friend Joe Holtgreive, the professor and dean of engineering at Northwestern University (the guy with the flashlight analogy in chapter 6, "Get Out of Neutral"), sees a lot of students who are brilliant but stressed out. And because Joe believes in the human spirit as much as he believes in the principles of engineering, he convinced "the powers that be" at Northwestern to let him establish an Engineering Office of Personal Development, which teaches engineering students things like improv, swing dancing, and emotional intelligence "as ways of inviting my students' spirit into their work." But just because he built that opportunity didn't mean the engineering students would automatically sign up. And in fact, they didn't. So, he came up with a rationale that would appeal to their left brain: "Self-care is a pragmatic approach to peak performance." That did the trick!

Based on what I've learned from Joe and from my own life, here's a guide to self-care. (Pro tip: You don't have to buy a bunch of products to do self-care. It doesn't have to be a replica of some perfect image of whatever you saw on Instagram. Self-care can come in many ways and forms and doesn't need to require money or consumerism or appropriation of a culture that isn't yours.) My self-care checklist is just about old-school *care of the self*: i.e., *you*.

1. *Breathe deeply*. Duh. But are you aware that this romantic dance between your heart and lungs is a potent regulator of your feelings, as well as the foundation of your physical health? Get to know that breath of yours: what works it up and how it calms down. That awareness will lead to greater heart and lung health. It's also a way to return to a state of greater relaxation when anxiety hits.

2. *Get good sleep*. When you were little, your parents probably made you go to bed by a certain time, and one day you'll be an older person who may have a hard time staying asleep no matter how hard you try. So, these years in between have the potential to be your wonder years of sleep when YOU get to decide when and where and how to get those ZZZs. Oh, and if you're the type who brags about how little sleep you're getting, you need to stop. You may have come by it honestly, like if your parents thought you should get all As no matter how much sleep went by the wayside. And maybe you're in a workplace with the same mentality (startup culture, for example). But still, stop. Bragging about not sleeping creates a culture of "who had less sleep than whom," which is harmful. (It's like bragging about being constantly intoxicated,

which, hey, if that's you, that's something else you're going to want to stop if you're ever going to be a functioning adult.) Your body and mind literally (and I do mean literally) recharge and renew themselves as you sleep. A good and long healthful life flows from it. So, how about you start doing whatever you need to do to be bragging that you got your full eight hours?

3. *Drink water*. Scientists say humans can go roughly three weeks without food but only three to four days without water, because without water your organs start to shut down. (Puts *Survivor* into a whole new context, doesn't it?) Many drinks contain water (like juices, sodas, coffee, and tea). But you should also down a plentiful amount of actual water every day in order to keep your engine humming smoothly.

4. *Move your body*. Your body needs you to pick your activity of choice and do it. If your capacity for movement is limited, get assistance from a caregiver or a physical therapist. Yoga, Pilates, calisthenic exercises, tai chi, and lifting weights are slow but steady ways to sweat and get really strong. Get your cardio on by walking, swimming, running, doing martial arts or group classes, playing some kind of game with a ball, dancing, gardening, or biking. Regardless of which kind of moving you do, the goal is to get your heart and lungs as strong as they can be, and develop agile muscles, joints, and limbs. You also want that sweet mood rush your body produces when you work out, from endorphins. Some days during the pandemic these endorphins I got from working out on my treadmill saved me from pretty hard-core frustration and even, at times, I'll admit, despair.

5. *Eat nourishingly*. Food is fuel. And just the act of slowing yourself down to make it and savor it is good for the soul. I'm old enough to have seen a lot of food fads come and go. I would never tell you what diet is best for your body and your lifestyle. Your task is to figure out how *you* need to eat in order to feel satiated and have

good digestive health. And if possible you should enjoy eating. (Which I do not say lightly. If you feel like you have an issue with food, I encourage you to seek help for that. Also, the "Don't Just Take My Word for It" portion of this chapter will feature someone with an eating disorder, which you may find helpful.)

6. *Claim your agency.* If you were raised by very protective parents who always had to know where you were and what you were up to, by micromanagers who told you what to do, needed updates on every detail, gave constant reminders, and/or were very critical, or by overhelpers who cheerily handled and fixed every little thing for you, your parents or guardians may have undermined your agency, which is the bedrock of both wellness and executive function. Taking good care of yourself means telling these well-meaning folks, "I love you, but I've got this. Or at least I'm going to try." This will be a huge step forward in creating healthy boundaries with them, which is essential if you are to function as an adult. This is another one of those paragraphs in this book you can mark with a Post-it note and hand over to the person, if need be. (Pro tip: New research shows that parents who assuaged your fears by preventing you from experiencing them may have helped turn those fears into full-blown anxiety; e.g., you're afraid of the dark/your parent makes sure you're never in the dark; you can't be alone/your parent makes sure you're never alone; you only eat certain things/your parent only prepares those things.) Something else to discuss with parents and therapists if this resonates with you.

7. *Process your feelings.* My British mother and her people shudder at the thought of having any feelings, let alone talking about them to others. Many of my Asian friends and colleagues say the same thing about their parents. Then there are the authoritarian parents, regardless of nationality or ethnicity, who took the "it's my way or the highway/because I said so" approach to childrearing and simply did not seem to take your feelings, opinions, or

needs into account. Also, there are the neglectful or abusive parents who were absent or harmed you. (Give a nod of gratitude to the universe or God if you were NOT raised by such people!)

Regardless of what your family is like or how you are raised, it's normal to feel sadness, disappointment, fear, frustration, and anger. Bottling up those feelings may (seem to) work in the moment, but over the long haul those emotions then stay with you, weighing you down like stones in your pockets, hampering your ability to interact with others in a kind and calm manner. So, you need to have an outlet for your feelings, such as writing in a journal, meditating, creating art, and talking with other humans.

Stretching the horizon out a bit from your interior self to the world beyond, let me acknowledge that regardless of whatever's going on in your life at any given moment there are the larger forces at play over which you have little or no control. Loneliness has been brought on by the modern era's busyness and by reliance on technology to handle what humans used to do with and for each other. Existential threats like climate change, income inequality, deep political divides, structural racism, and rampant gun violence take their toll. And that was stuff we had to deal with before COVID-19.

Dwelling on all of this external stuff can bring you down, but pretending it's not happening isn't good for you, either. The key is to acknowledge it, process it, and keep going. Talk about the things that concern you with friends and family. Then take time to speak of some positives for which you are grateful. And always focus on the things you *can* control, which are your breath, your values, your actions, and your reactions. You are stronger than you may realize.

8. *Find balance with social media.* I'm not going to tell you to get off Instagram, but I am going to remind you (as previously mentioned in chapter 5, "Stop Pleasing Others") that research shows that if you're struggling emotionally, or with your sense of

self broadly, then social media greatly impacts your mood (good interactions make you feel better about yourself, and bad things make you feel worse). However, if you're more emotionally strong, then your social media feed has little effect on how you see yourself. So. You know best where you are with all of this. Are you endlessly scrolling as a way to self-soothe? If so, try an in-person conversation with a good friend instead, or read a book. Other people's curated lives and potentially explosive opinions should be taken in small measure. (For social media's impact on keeping you stuck or the ways it might impede [or help!] your relationships, revisit chapter 6, "Get Out of Neutral," and chapter 7, "Start Talking to Strangers.")

9. *Ask for what you need.* I for one have had a very hard time with this. I learned at a young age that I was not likely to get the emotional support I needed, which felt like rejection. So, I became an adolescent and young adult who tried to get people to intuit what I was feeling without me having to outright ask. (This was a way to avoid being rejected, but rarely led to the outcome I was looking for.) Only in my forties and now fifties am I starting to be better at asking for what I need. I encourage you to try it. It may be the quickest path to the relief or solution you're looking for.

10. *Get regular checkups.* A lot of young adults don't do this, so let's drill into why. Maybe you can't afford health care (or dental, or vision), or you feel that you've been judged by the healthcare profession and you refuse to go back (I get it; believe me). These are valid barriers to accessing care. If it's about finances, find out whether your community has a health clinic for low-income people. Also, look into how the Affordable Care Act is administered in your state. If you're fortunate enough to have health/dental/vision insurance, USE IT, even if you feel and maybe are 100 percent healthy. Ideally, you're having a physical annually, where you get the various tests and vaccines recommended given

your age, gender, health risks, and lifestyle. You should be able to open up to your doctor/nurse without fear of judgment or ridicule, so if they seem biased against you for whatever reason, find a new provider.

If you're sexually active and not monogamous, find out your STD status every six months so you can be informed and inform your partners. Your teeth should be cleaned and examined ideally twice a year. Your vision should be checked as needed given your issues. Bottom line, your wellness matters regardless of how many dollars are in your bank account and how obnoxious that one doctor was to you. And things like elevated blood pressure, a growing bump or mole somewhere, or high "sugar" numbers (i.e., blood glucose) could lead to much more serious things down the road. So, take that big leap and go deal with the body you have now. Your older self will be glad you did.

11. *Get therapy*. Wouldn't it be nice to have a person sit and listen just to you for an hour each week? Maybe your feelings are big enough to warrant some time with a therapist. As someone who has benefited from therapy I'm here to put in a big plug for it. (Pro tip: There are plenty of affordable therapists out there [and yes, plenty who charge an arm and a leg]. Many offer a sliding scale based upon your ability to pay. Also, if you have options for health insurance, choose a plan that offers "behavioral health," which is the term insurance companies use for the stuff the rest of us call mental health.) A good therapist will help you unpack all the shit you've dealt with and are dealing with. You may just come to feel so connected to your therapist that you'll be sad to leave them when you're feeling better. But feeling empowered to head back into the world is the best feeling of all. And they're always there if you need to go back. And hey, if you were raised by the type of folks who didn't want you to have feelings (see above) bucking that trend is having hella agency. You're saying, *My family may not believe in feelings, but that's their thing. I am in charge of my life and I get to decide what resources and supports I need.* Boom.

Remember psychotherapist Lori Gottlieb from chapter 6, "Get Out of Neutral"? She thinks people wait too long to go and talk to somebody. "What people don't realize is that part of being an adult is taking care of your emotional health. It's not optional. It's not gravy to feel good—you have to feel good to be a functioning adult. I think people are waiting for the depression where they can't get out of bed or for the anxiety that really interferes, but what I suggest is that when you feel *I don't really know what it is but it's something*, that's enough. You need to *prioritize your emotional health*. It affects your relationships, friendships, family life, professional success, and people need to prioritize it and not put it on the back burner where there are all these other things from their to-do list."

One final thought. Just like with meds, you need to be sure your therapist is working *for you*. Dan and I were in couples therapy in 2014 and we happened to have an appointment on the day the unarmed Black teenager Mike Brown was murdered in Ferguson, Missouri, which would go on to be a foundational moment in the Black Lives Matter movement. Consumed by the news and feeling pretty distraught, I burst into our session about ten minutes late, and apologized by announcing what had just happened. Dan looked at me with tremendous sorrow on his face, but the look on the white male therapist's face was *What is WRONG with you?* We kept seeing this guy for many months, but looking back, I lost trust in him that very day and should have found someone new without delay. If you find that your therapist doesn't seem to get you, or doesn't share your worldview, it's okay to break up with that therapist and find a new one.

12. *Be smart about your meds.* Often people emerge into adulthood feeling like *Okay, I made it, I don't need my meds anymore.* I caution you against just abandoning meds when you get to the next stage of life because if you're on meds they may have helped you get to this point. (In the "Don't Just Take My Word for It" part of this chapter, you'll read about a guy with bipolar disorder whose

most frequent struggle is with himself over taking the very meds that stave off his mania.) That said, says Amanda Gelender, "Medications can be very complicated for neurodivergent folks. You of course want to take medicine if it supports your wellness, and for some it's a privilege to even be able to consistently access medication. You also need to listen to your body and intuition about whether your meds support you and respond as safely and healthily as possible (going off cold turkey is not a safe move). I have been on dozens of psychiatric medications—I've gone through periods where they have supported me, periods when I was overmedicated and extremely unwell from the myriad of damaging effects, and periods when I took time to slowly taper off of my meds to test the waters of an unmedicated brain. There is no one-size-fits-all approach to mental health treatment, and meds are just one of many options—we should center access and autonomy and never shame people for being on or off meds. We do the best we can with what we have, recognizing that it's very hard to access wellness within a health system that profits from our illness." And remember always that whether or not to be on meds is very personal to you and your situation even though others may have a similar diagnosis and prescription. Sometimes we posture with friends about being on meds or off meds or feeling worse or better about ourselves vis-à-vis our peers when we stop them or go back on them. Everyone is walking their own path. Try not to let someone else's decision or judgment make you feel bad about what you need to do for you.

13. *Hang around your people.* In chapter 7, "Start Talking to Strangers," I shared about how human connection is key to your longevity. So, taking good care of yourself includes developing a strong connection to a handful of people you really dig and who dig you. (Pro tip: Note, this absolutely does not have to be in person. Some people find that MMORPGs are a comfortable and meaningful way to connect with people. Others find Twitter and Reddit to be places to meet up with people who share deep interests and

concerns. And the pandemic showed us that online may be the only way we can safely connect in certain circumstances.) What we're going for here, whether in person or online, is the concept of chosen family, which is a set of people (whether individuals or a group) with whom you feel a sense of belonging, to whom you feel loyal, and with whom you derive a sense of meaning about your life. These people are key factors in your ability to take good care of yourself. Some of us have that with our family of origin, some of us don't. You get to decide who your people are.

14. *Laugh and play.* As with exercise, laughing releases endorphins, the neurochemicals that temporarily mute your sense of pain, stress, and anxiety. Tell jokes. Watch comedy specials on Netflix. Go to a comedy club. (Pro tip: Do not try to tell jokes at work or in a group of acquaintances. Humor works because it presses on topics of discomfort. Since people care about and tolerate different things, one person's hilarious is another person's horror. The last thing you want to do is tell a vegan your favorite joke about eating a pet pig. Trust me.) And play means just that. PLAY. Do enjoyable things. Silly things. Lighten up. Relax. Unwind. Play.

15. *Give and get hugs.* My father was a public health doctor and very much a practitioner of Western medicine, yet being raised by a stepmom who was a Native American/Black woman, he learned to respect wisdom that predates Western science. In 1980, as assistant surgeon general and head of the U.S. Public Health Service, he organized a conference on alternative medicine and brought home a T-shirt for me from it that read, "Four Hugs A Day." I was twelve or thirteen. Back then we thought that ideas like hugs being medicinal were kind of woo-woo so this shirt was like, wow. Now, we know from research that hugs release the "feel-good hormones" serotonin and oxytocin, which rise when we touch, hug, or sit close, and lower stress hormone levels, reduce blood pressure and heart rate, and might even lessen our

sensation of pain. There's evidence that even hugging a pet or a stuffed animal provides you the same benefits, so if you're not around people (or people you feel good about hugging) you can still get some of those benefits.

16. *Have orgasms.* Ha! I'm guessing you weren't expecting this one. But this is a book on being an adult, and sexual pleasure is a part of a healthy, functioning adult life. You can do this with others or just with yourself. (If you grew up with taboos against masturbation, or female orgasm, it's time to toss those harmful mindsets to the curb.) When you have an orgasm, it releases the powerful neurochemicals dopamine and oxytocin. Dopamine is pleasure. Oxytocin creates a sense of trust and intimacy. Orgasmic pleasure is available to people of all genders, sexual orientations, and relationship statuses. You don't need anyone's permission to go for it.

17. *Have a gratitude and guidance practice, somewhere . . .* Far be it from me to tell you what exactly to do on this one—you may be very religious; you may be spiritual but not religious; your values and beliefs may be 100 percent secular. The point here is to have some kind of belief system and engage it regularly for support and motivation. Have some place you go, even if just inside your head to your inner thoughts, where you think about what and to whom you're grateful, and where you ask for guidance and support in growing in the ways you most need to. Remember, you're not expected to be perfect. You're growing. You're going to continue to learn and grow until you take your last breath. A practice of giving gratitude and seeking guidance can be your compass here.

18. *Forgive.* Nor is it my place to tell you how you should react to or feel about all you've been through. I'm speaking only to what can happen physiologically *to you* when you hold anger and trauma inside of you: it can end up being a compounding hurt. I'm here to try to help you prevent that from happening or undo it if it has happened.

I used to be really good at being angry. My emotion plus my words were a potent weapon, both sword and shield. My whole family is good at it, frankly. But somewhere in my early forties, I began to appreciate that any anger bottled up inside of me is like a wild horse running around frantically in a pen. It isn't good for my heart or blood pressure. (It isn't terribly pleasant for the people around me, either.) So, even if you're not ready to forgive a person, it may be worthwhile to do the forgiveness work for your own sake. It doesn't mean you're condoning the hurtful thing someone did, it just means you've decided to release that hurt from you. Forgiving returns your power back to *you*. Inherent in this bit of advice is forgiving yourself, too. My friend Adina Glickman puts it well: "Your anger is making your blood boil, not theirs. Your anger is locking you up, not them. Holding on to your anger is like drinking poison and expecting the other person to die. It would seem like forgiveness is about letting someone else off the hook but really, it's about letting yourself grow."

Adina adds that when the person you're angry at is yourself—for inflicting hurt or failing at something—"forgiving yourself requires a willingness to be generous with yourself." Evaluate what happened. Figure out what you might have done differently and could do differently next time. Forgive yourself for it. Your mind can then stop bringing it up in flashbacks and move on. Here's where your gratitude and guidance practice can be of tremendous help in processing what you need to forgive yourself or others for. And for really tough wounds, you may benefit from therapy.

19. *And finally, never underestimate the power of a 15-minute nap.* While I'll confess I've never been a napper (I can neither fall asleep easily in the daytime nor am I happy waking on command), Joe Holtgreive from Northwestern swears that short naps of about 15 minutes can change your life. Duration is key, because if you go for too long and enter REM sleep you'll wake up groggy. (This may sound paradoxical because REM sleep is

said to be the "good" sleep. The point is that napping isn't about getting "good" sleep, it's about giving your batteries a quick boost. Think of short naps as a quick power-up rather than a full recharge.)

<hr>

DON'T JUST TAKE MY WORD FOR IT

MEET TONE—Taking Care of Himself by Getting to Know Himself

Just so you know where we're headed here, Tone's story is about the importance of processing feelings, and will touch upon youth suicide. I've known him since he was a sixteen-year-old sophomore in high school with my own two kids. That year, three of Tone's friends took their lives, which no person should ever have to go through. As Tone remembers it, "When the passings happened, what really hit me was that these were not freak accidents. It was their own choice. Even though we're very, very privileged here in Palo Alto, my friends were so mentally depressed that they felt the need to do that. I immediately bottled it up and tried to keep on going about my daily routine."

Tone was working hard and excelling, but the grind was taking its toll. It was all about taking the "good" classes, getting into the "good" colleges, and having a "good" job in life. I got to know Tone a bit in the aftermath of the student suicides. I was one of many adults in our community who were trying to help our kids process what they'd been through and bring reform to a community whose definition of success was making life really stressful for kids. Every time I interacted with Tone in those days, the look in his eyes said he was a million miles away. Now twenty-two, Tone has been to hell and back himself, and is well into his recovery. He was willing to share what he's been through, in the hope that it could help you. I'm very grateful to him.

"My parents are from China," he began. "I was born in Singapore and moved to the U.S. as a baby. In China, if you have a mental health problem, it's not discussed. As an Asian man, even here, no matter how you're feeling, it's like, *Don't talk about your emotions, keep your head up, keep going about your normal life.* That only works if you're dealing with stuff that isn't that serious. But for something as traumatic as what happened in high school, that wasn't the best advice." Yet Tone did somehow manage to keep his head up. And in those rare moments when he was outwardly struggling emotionally, his parents said, "Oh, you're going through puberty. It's part of growing up."

He chose to attend the University of Michigan, where he could immerse himself in world-class academics and indulge his love of sports. He arrived in the fall of 2017. But just four weeks into his freshman year, "something felt off" when he walked into a lecture hall. "I remember looking around, and I started freaking out because it seemed like everyone was staring at me. My head was all over the place. My chest was heaving. I was short of breath." He ran out of the building. He would later describe this as his first panic attack.

His mother just happened to be visiting him at school that week. He told her what had happened and said, "I need you to check me into a hospital so I don't do something stupid." He had dealt with mental health issues in high school, "but never like this" where he felt he wasn't in control of anything. He realized, "I can't keep putting this off anymore." As he put it to me, he needed "actual help."

Unlike in high school, Tone's mother now got it. "In asking her to take me to the hospital, I was one hundred percent vulnerable. Clearly it wasn't just me being sad, or a single moment I could just 'get over.' All of my cards were on the table. Seeing my raw emotions made it very real for her. It was, 'Oh, what he's going through is serious.'" At the hospital, Tone was diagnosed with depression and anxiety, and hospitalized for more than a week. When he was discharged, his parents brought him home to the Bay Area, where he entered an Intensive Outpatient Program (IOP), which typically entails group and individual therapy for six hours a day, five days a week. Early on in this process, he went to the grocery store near home and saw someone from high school. "Just seeing them, not even talking to them, made me have another mini panic attack. I ran into the store's bathroom hyperventilating and just tried to calm myself down."

The IOP was the first time in Tone's life where he was allowed (and encouraged) to uncork all the emotions that were bottled up inside of him. The few times he had tried therapy in high school had been awkward because he felt pressured to speak even when he had nothing to say. But the IOP offered a ton of group therapy, which was a format that really clicked for Tone. "It meant I could interact with others who were getting their mental health checked on. Hearing and providing input on their stories helped me process my own emotions." The low-stakes, zero-pressure environment was a relief to him, yet it had the structure he needed to keep from spiraling.

After six weeks in the IOP, Tone segued back to more conventional one-on-one therapy, which he was now more open to. He didn't vibe with the first few therapists he met with, but kept trying to find the right one. "It's like trying on a pair of shoes," he tells me. "The right fit for you is essential in order to get the right treatment."

In the fall of 2018, Tone started his freshman year all over again, this time at Santa Clara University in Silicon Valley, near his home. While trying to fulfill credits for the art requirement, he stumbled upon a class called Life Writing, which an online reviewer called "life-changing." It made him go, *Hmm, I could probably use a life-changing experience*. Unfortunately the course got off to a slow start when the professor, a former monk, opened class with a five-minute meditation, which Tone saw as an opportunity to just close his eyes and do nothing. But by the second week of the course, Tone realized he'd "felt really calm during the meditation and even for a little afterwards, and I didn't feel so much social anxiety that day." He stayed in the class, and paid attention, and along the way learned the value of journaling, how to practice mindfulness, and the sheer value of opening up to other people.

"That's why I'm so open to talking about my mental health now. The only way you overcome these humps is through conversation. Everyone gets therapy in some form, be it talking to friends or parents, posting blogs, doing art, creating music. Opening up and talking can be extremely difficult. And when you have a traumatic experience, it's difficult to even rationalize what happened. But talking about it is the best way to process it and make your way toward recovery."

The Life Writing class inspired Tone to start tracking his mental health every day. "Every day, first thing in the morning, I meditate to find out if I feel any discomfort anywhere, and if there is anything stressing me. Every night, before bed, I journal by actually putting pen to paper and thinking through why the thing is stressing me and how I can stop stressing about it." He found these tools particularly helpful in the time of the pandemic and in the face of the traumatic stimuli on social media about Black lives.

When I ask Tone about his future, I'm somewhat surprised to learn that he's majoring in finance, because finance *can be* one of those default majors for people who aren't sure what else do to. I poke and prod a bit about the *why*. He laughs. "I'm not sure yet if it appeals to me, to be honest. But I needed to declare a major, and I know that finance is pretty flexible and will open up a few possibilities. What I really want to do is be a therapist. It's definitely something I am considering for later on in life. But I know I don't yet have the mental strength to focus on other people. I'm just in no position to help others right now." I ask him how his parents feel about the idea that he might go into psychology, and am surprised when he says that they support it. "After seeing how good therapy was for me, they've been encouraging me to go that route. They feel I would have something to offer other kids."

It seems to me that Tone knows himself better than he did before, and he agrees. "That's how I'm seeing it," he says. "Along the path through sorting out your mental health you also get a better idea of who you are as a person." What would he tell his younger self if he could go back in time? "Really evaluate why you do the things you do. It's easy to get lost in what you think you're *supposed* to do. You have to know your why. If you just want a top school and a nice-looking job because *that'll look good*, that's not the right thing to be chasing and there will always be something more to chase and you'll never be okay with yourself as a person. It's more important to find out who you are as a person and what you're passionate about. Do something because you *like* it not because it'll improve your chances of getting into a college. Join a club not because it looks good on your résumé but because you're passionate about the cause.

"No matter how bleak it gets," he goes on, "there is always tomorrow. And whereas sucking it up is the easy way out, at least in the short term, if you don't confront your emotions, they will catch up to you. Realize that it is always okay to stop and take a break. You have every right to feel the way you do. It's important that you do right by you and get the necessary treatment. Take a gap year, time off from college, whatever. You need to treat your mental health really preciously. It sticks with you for the rest of your life. And if you don't take care of it, it'll eat you up alive. Looking back at it, the first couple months after I'd dropped out of college and felt cut off from society, I thought, *I can't believe this happened to me*. But these years later I can see that it was single-handedly the best thing to have happened." He says, "It made me see that I need to *do right by me*."

MEET SARA—Taking Good Care by Embracing Better Values

Heads up, this is a story about having an eating disorder and OCD.

Sara was one of my students at Stanford. She's now thirty and lives in Tempe, Arizona, where she is doing a PhD at Arizona State University in education policy, and she's thriving. But ten years ago, Sara developed an obsessive-compulsive disorder called trichotillomania, which means you constantly pick and pull at your hair or split ends; she also developed a severe eating disorder. In the late fall of her junior year of college, though excelling academically, she hit rock bottom psychologically. "I was like a little dog out in the street that has minimal interaction with humans or any other creature and just does its thing and finds a safe space to sleep at night and that's it. You don't take enjoyment in things. You're just, *Let me go through the motions and let me not die.*"

Sara grew up in San Juan, Puerto Rico, with a twin brother and two sisters who were two and three years older. Both parents were native to Puerto Rico. Her father spent most of his childhood in Chicago, and her mother grew up in relative poverty on the island. Her father had talents and promise but endured a set of extremely traumatic experiences, including serving in the Vietnam War, for which he earned two Purple Heart medals. By the time Sara was young, her father had fallen into alcoholism and was sometimes abusive. Her mother, whom Sara describes as brilliant, kind, and hardworking, became a pediatrician and did whatever it took to hold the family together. She was known in the community for going above and beyond to serve anyone in need. She set a high standard for effort and achievement, a standard that Sara was eager to follow.

Sara and her siblings attended the same Catholic school from pre-K through high school, and Sara's academic talents were apparent early on. "I was good in every subject. Give me a textbook and I can read and learn from it. Stand up in front of me and I can listen and remember. I have always had the privilege of being able to learn the way Western education wants people to learn, and I was able to squeeze the juice out of that. I won spelling bee championships. I took the PSAT in ninth grade and scored better than everyone else in my school. But math was where I really stood out. I represented Puerto Rico nationally or internationally every year of my life from seventh grade until I graduated. I was literally the best math student of my year in Puerto Rico."

But Sara began to feel she was either perfect or she was inadequate. There was no middle ground. "In eighth grade, I came home and said to my mom, 'Hey, I got a 92 on this Honors Spanish test,' and she said, 'What happened to the other 8 points?' I know now that what she was really asking was if I understood the mistakes I had made and had learned from them. She wanted excellence *for* me, but I took that as meaning she wanted excellence *from* me."

Sara remembers the first time the pressure began to feel unrelenting. "I was sixteen and I'd just gotten back from the Mathematical Olympiad of Central America and the Caribbean in Venezuela, where I'd won a silver medal. I was running some errands with my mom when she got a page saying one of her patients had been admitted to the hospital, so we rushed over there. There we were in this very somber environment when one of her doctor colleagues came up and said, 'Oh, this is one of your daughters, which one?' My mom said, 'The mathematician!' The colleague said, 'Oh you, I've heard so much about you!' My mom said, 'Yeah, she was just at the Math Olympiad in Venezuela. She won a silver medal. It would've been better if she got the gold medal, but we're proud of her.'" Fourteen years later, this memory is still painful. I can hear it in Sara's voice. "I was staring down at my shirt trying not to cry. It was my absolute favorite shirt. The band Green Day was on the front, and it had a hood and kangaroo pockets. Staring down I noticed a hole in the fabric right where the pocket is sewn onto the shirt. I wanted to burst into tears because of what my mom had said, and also because my favorite shirt was ruined."

There was no way to raise these concerns at home. Sara even kept her struggles from her siblings, with whom she was otherwise quite close. "To her credit, my mom realized she had hurt me that day at the hospital, because she immediately put her hand on my back and brushed her fingers through my hair in a comforting way, like when you regret something as soon as it leaves your mouth. And the rest of the day she was ridiculously sweet and nice to me. But I've never heard my mother apologize to anyone. For anything. Ever. Because she was just trying to keep things from falling apart all the time. My feeling was, *Damn, even though I'm the best academically on the entire island I'm still not good enough for my parents.* You kind of feel like shit. And you kind of aren't excited about living on a fairly regular basis but you just deal with it. I thought, *I'll go to Stanford and everything will be peachy keen.*"

But Sara was about to go from the frying pan into the fire. At Stanford, "the guy across the hall had been in the junior fucking Olympics in crew or some shit. Someone else had started a gaming software company at sixteen. I didn't really see that there was anything special about me. I was just this kid from Puerto Rico who was good at math." Her dorm mates, whom she describes as "cliquey and mainstream, meaning white or white-adjacent," constantly complimented Sara for her appearance—not her intelligence or kindness. "All I kept hearing was, *You're so pretty. You're really skinny. You're so exotic.* I felt that my Puerto Rican-ness made me weird to them, and the power dynamics of being among white and wealthy folks was reeeaaaally evident, even though I wasn't aware of these concepts at the time. My eating disorder began pretty much as soon as I got there."

When Sara came home for summer break her mother could tell that something was up. (She was a pediatrician after all.) "We started to talk about it in the car one day but got interrupted. I wanted to continue the conversation, but she completely changed the subject. I'm sure she thought, *It's just a phase.*" Sara returned to Stanford, continued to do well academically, and continued her disordered eating. "I know the body needs nutrition and without it, it starts to eat itself. But I was doing well. It wasn't disrupting my schoolwork or my research."

But junior year things got worse. "I would compulsively pick and pull at my split ends to relieve my anxiety. (This is the trichotillomania.) One night at around midnight I ate a bowl of Special K cereal, which felt like a binge. Then I stayed up for four more hours just picking at my split ends because I was so anxious about having eaten the cereal. I would often spend hours and hours almost completely still, not doing anything, just trying to stop myself from having a breakdown. There was no enjoyment, no communicating with anybody, it was just straight-up misery. One day I was having a granola bar, which was the only thing I was going to eat that day. My roommate said, 'Oh, can I have a piece?' I was able to keep it together in front of other people, and I did with her that day. But internally, I completely lost my shit. I went outside and walked around and around for two hours. *This cannot be fucking happening, this is my food, this is my only food.* Another day I worked off seven hundred calories on an elliptical because I had eaten an apple."

In late fall of her junior year, Sara sought help from the adult living in her dorm known as a resident fellow. "I said, 'Yo, I'm not in crisis mode, like not being able to study, or like my body is shutting down right now. But mentally I am in crisis. I can't make decisions. Who the fuck has the energy to study when I'm starving. I feel like I'm in hell. Every day is a struggle.'" A resident fellow is a trained counselor, and what Sara had just said to him were non-negotiable red flags. "My RF said, 'Okay, I hear what you're saying. And I don't like hearing this from people. And you need to agree to therapy or I'll have to involuntarily commit you.'" She says her RF wasn't trying to back her into a corner. He was trying to wake her up to the reality that her life was in jeopardy and the time to change that was right then and there. "I agreed to go to therapy. I called my mom to tell her. I told her, 'I don't know how to *eat* anymore.' She said, 'But you're smart! What do you mean you don't know how to *eat*? Three meals a day like we've done forever?'" Sara told her mom that she hadn't eaten normal meals in six months. Her mom pointed out that Sara had been home for the summer, implying that Sara had eaten then. Sara asked her mom if she'd ever seen her eat. Her mom said, "You told me you had." Sara said, "I lied." There was a long silence. Knowing that Sara has low blood sugar, which can cause her to faint, her mother asked how she was managing to keep that at bay. Sara told her about her so-called snacks: eight orange Tic Tacs and a stick of gum. Sara told her mom, "I am five foot five and I weigh one hundred and five pounds."

In therapy Sara unearthed the sources of the pressure. She felt a tremendous responsibility to her teachers, math coaches, parents, and even her ancestors who had all sacrificed so much to see her get this far. "It was, *Just don't waste your fucking time, or anyone else's time*. Like I had to stay alive while doing as much as possible to honor the sacrifices of the people who came before me." She then needed to learn to like herself as she was, not as a function of her grades, what she looked like, or how much she weighed.

She began opening up to her friends about her challenges. I ask her how she knew whom she could feel safe with and count on. "The friends I'm closest to have been vulnerable with me and vice versa. If my pain shows up and they don't back down, I know I can trust them." One friend introduced a whole new philosophy of caring to Sara. Sara had apologized to this friend for taking up so much of her time one day, and the friend replied, "That's okay! People are important." That simple response—*people are important*—made Sara feel so good that she decided she wanted to be like that for others. "I thought, *Hey, I can do that*. It made me realize that I wasn't going to kill myself over handing in a fucking problem set if someone I care about needed me at that moment. The whole importance of grades just came crashing down. And my attitude became, *Hey, you didn't work out today, but you spent some time talking to a friend who is going through a hard thing, and that's valuable, and that makes you a good person, too.*"

Sara also began to learn more about her ancestry and culture. This happened senior year, when she became a resident of the Muwekma-Tah-Ruk dorm, which centers on the Native American community. "Since childhood I'd known that I was different, but I didn't understand how. I was raised really Catholic, so I was never in touch with my indigenous (Taíno) identity. But since I was a small child I've had an indigenous worldview that challenges settler colonial definitions of success. I remember being six or seven and having trouble with concepts like the human species supposedly being superior to other species, why this paper we call 'money' was valuable, and the concept of bodyguards—of someone's life actually considered more valuable than someone else's. I just thought I was this *weird thing* for feeling this way. The Muwekma-Tah-Ruk dorm community was like finally being home. Being around other people who value and have a deep sense of duty to their communities and history and ancestors was honestly the greatest thing that could have happened to me. Elementary number theory is interesting, but honoring the people who came before me is monumentally more important. I just need to be honoring me, too. I started owning my indigeneity, my Puerto Rican-ness. When people would say, *You're so exotic*, I started rejecting that bullshit. I'd say, *What do you mean exotic? Like a fucking bird?* I began to reject this exoticizing not only because it is fetishizing and demeaning, but also because it's a reduction of the ancestral strength and wisdom that has been given to me by those who came before me to just my physical being. That's when things took a turn for the better. Tapping into my indigeneity was a really wonderful thing. Muwekma changed my life."

I ask for Sara's advice on how a person can know when to get help. "Unfortunately, sometimes it comes to just hitting rock bottom," she tells me. "You need to hit a really low place or moment of really deep self-honesty before you can actually get better, because nobody can get better for you."

The once-and-forever math genius is now pursuing a PhD in education policy. Her methodology is to listen to people's stories by interviewing them. "I've completely gone away from math not because I don't like math—I love it—but because people are important and listening to people's stories matters. Epistemologically, people's different experiences are valid forms of data and valid forms of knowledge. It gets away from a positivist idea of *I have this hypothesis, let me test it out with numbers*. It's more *I have to be humble because I don't know, and I want to know*. It's a way of seeing knowledge not as a commodity but as a form of transformation. I shut up and listen."

While Sara hasn't had any disordered eating symptoms since the fall of 2011, she says her recovery isn't about never having to deal with these issues anymore; instead, it's about getting better at "summoning your defenses." Her first line of defense is sleep, which can be the first thing to fall by the wayside for anyone in graduate school. "There is no paper or exam that is going to make me lose my sleep. That alone is a huge percentage of the battle." But there are still times when the intrusive thoughts of extreme disgust with herself arise. "Like, you have a very urgent sense that something is going to explode if you don't address your huge thigh situation right now. But when you're managing it you're compassionate with yourself. *No, nothing is going to explode. I'm going to let the thought pass rather than act on it*. You push the thoughts away, and replace them with the commitment of *No, I must eat because I have to take care of my body and that is number one*. Anxiety and panic can only last for a certain amount of time. The body's pretty resilient. If something is giving me so much stress that I am picking at my hair, I'm mindful. I think, *Hey, your brain is doing this right now, and you do have ways of stopping it with your actions*. Then I get up, take a walk or go work out. My self-care is not perfect. Sometimes I go into spells when I'm picking at my hair. But then I come back to reality, go feed the cats, cuddle them, observe them and their life, their beautiful existence, and recognize that I'm just one being on this huge enormous planet."

Perhaps the most profound aspect of Sara's recovery is that she's at peace with her parents. She has learned, in essence, that forgiveness is not just "the right thing to do" but that it heals you. "I still grieve for sixteen-year-old me who has to hear those words about second place in the math Olympiad. But do I still get mad at my mom for it? No. My mother is going to be imperfect and that's okay. I'm not going to let that moment define her parent-ness for me because she's done so many other great things. And I also love my dad, even though he's had a lifelong substance abuse problem and he put us through things we should not have had to go through. He's been through a lot of pain in his life that he never got to process.

"I know I may never get that apology," she continues. "They may never know the ways they have hurt me unless I want to have that conversation with them. And since Dad has Parkinson's, and they went through Hurricane Maria, the earthquake, and COVID-19, maybe I shouldn't put that on them. And besides, you can't *make* someone understand, because a person can't learn out of someone else's head; they have to get there themselves."

By the end of a conversation that began talking about an eating disorder, Sara is now waxing eloquent on love, which at the end of the day is the root of her healing. "Loving my parents doesn't mean they get to treat me like shit or pretend stuff never happened. It's just accepting the fact that they have imperfections. Yes, they've hurt me. Yet, they've also done amazing things that have helped me be who I am now. If that's a form of forgiveness—thinking about a thing and not getting mad about it anymore—I have forgiven my mom. When it does come up and I have to grieve again, I'll go ahead and grieve again, and that's okay. The kind of pressure I've gone through comes with lifelong grief. Healing isn't linear. Some days you're going to be doing great, then you may fall behind a bit. It doesn't mean you're not still healing and growing."

MEET JEFF—Taking Good Care Through Acceptance of What You've Got

This is a story about having bipolar disorder.

"I don't want to project the message that I've got it all figured out," Jeff tells me. But as I listen, I think maybe he does have it figured out, to the extent any of us can. Jeff is a forty-seven-year-old conservative white man, a devout Christian, and a father of three. He lives in Northern Virginia, and has a diagnosis of bipolar disorder.

In June 1992, Jeff was eighteen and about to board a plane for the first time in his life. Neither of his parents had graduated from college, but they had seen the advantages available to those who had, and they'd impressed upon Jeff the need to go. Yet while Jeff was a gifted student, deciding on a path after high school had been somewhat of a struggle. "I was interested in myriad things but couldn't focus on any of them. I could've been that college student with six different majors and only a semester toward each of them." The military began to beckon. Jeff's father, both grandfathers, and one great-grandfather had all served in the U.S. military, and Jeff knew it would be an affordable way to get that college degree. He graduated from high school in

Sacramento, then spent a semester at a prep school followed by a semester at a junior college, all a part of the path to becoming a cadet at the U.S. Air Force Academy. Boarding the plane to Colorado Springs, Jeff was confident that he was headed not just to college but to a rewarding career as an officer in the U.S. Air Force. There was no Plan B.

Along the way, Jeff had fallen in love with Marianne, a girl he'd met at a yogurt shop while in high school. During his first semester at the Academy his friends were getting breakup letters left and right, but things with Marianne were going strong. When she joined his mom and sister on a visit to the Academy for Parents Weekend, Jeff surprised her by getting down on one knee and asking her to marry him. "Right now?" Marianne said, shocked. His answer was no—because the Academy didn't allow cadets to be married—but the intention was set. They survived the next three and a half years by writing letters stuffed with photos and spending a lot of money on what were called "long-distance phone calls" in the era before cell phones. Those phone calls were worth it. Jeff and Marianne got married ten days after his graduation. "From there it was, *Let's see what the Air Force is gonna do*, and I was going to walk along with that."

Jeff's first assignment was on a base in Wyoming where he guarded nuclear missiles and ran convoys with missile parts to make sure the missiles stayed active and alert. Marianne kept him grounded. "I won't soon forget when we showed up on that base for the first time. I was a lieutenant and got saluted as we entered. Marianne said, 'If you think I'm going to be this meek little officer's wife holding teas, playing Bunko, and putting on Christmas parties, that's not who you married.' Not that I was surprised. She raises my bar personally and professionally." I can hear in his voice that twenty-five years after he married her, he admires and adores Marianne, maybe more than ever. All these years later, Marianne doesn't recall having said any of this to Jeff. "But it's the way I remember it, and the memory reminds me of her strength and honesty. She may hold the same conviction today, but the words might be softer."

A few years later, Jeff was promoted to captain and earned a spot in the Air Force master's degree program, which he could undertake almost anywhere he liked. He and Marianne chose to move to the Washington, DC, area, where they could be near some of her family and Jeff could enroll in the criminology and criminal justice program at the University of Maryland. "That all went well," Jeff says. "Until it didn't."

In January 2000, Jeff was driving down the highway to meet a friend for lunch, when he blacked out. He woke up in Walter Reed National Military Medical Center and was told he'd had a manic episode. "That was the first time in my life where I didn't know what I was doing, and I didn't have the agency I needed to get myself through the situation." He was diagnosed with bipolar disorder and determined to be a "risk" since he was working in security. "The Air Force said, 'Thank you very much for your service. We'll hand you off to the Veterans Affairs Administration. You figure out what to do with yourself.'" He was twenty-six and Marianne was pregnant with their first child.

Marianne and Jeff wrote letters to senators and military officers explaining their situation in the hope that Jeff would be reinstated. Everyone responded the same way: *Sorry, I can't help you.* It seemed everything he'd been taught about how to succeed in life was no longer relevant. He started living in a state of bewilderment, loss of control, and anger. "I was mad at God," Jeff says. "I asked God, 'Why did you take me down this path if you were going to slam the door in my face?'"

They packed up their dog and cat and returned to Sacramento, where they hunkered down with relatives until they could get on their feet. Jeff took a job in the California Department of Justice. "I worked with some amazing people, but the bureaucracy was stifling and the work was unfulfilling." Their baby was born. His former compatriots in the Air Force were taking off in their careers, literally flying. Jeff witnessed them from afar and thought, *Those are my people.* He felt inadequate, ashamed, and maybe even judged.

"When you come of age with a military mindset, physical injuries are given a pass. You're told, 'Oh, you broke your arm, of course you get to take a break to heal that,'" Jeff says. "But if your brain's broken, that's on you." Back then, the Air Force offered minimal support for those who suffered with mental health issues, and the path to that assistance was unclear. This frustrated those who suffered, forcing them to develop more harmful coping mechanisms. "No one would ever say aloud, 'Go drink your brain away,' but there was that implicit understanding: *Do whatever you've got to do to make it through.*"

Jeff didn't use drugs or drink to shroud his bipolar disorder, but he walked a path familiar to all people in recovery. He took an honest inventory of his own self and his life, and came to terms with his "brokenness" while everyone else seemed so put together. Rather than catalog his losses he began to tally what he still had. He asked himself, *What can I be thankful for?* His family had stayed together, and he was grateful and determined not to squander that. He asked himself, *How can I make investments in the things that are still available to me?* He enrolled in an MBA degree night program, which would take five long years. "My wife and I had two more children in this span of time, by the way," Jeff said, with a smile in his voice, which I understood to mean, *It wasn't all bad.*

A new life philosophy began to take shape for Jeff even as the bipolar illness loomed like an ominous cloud. "The myth of American rugged individualism has cracks in its foundation. It makes you feel that you gotta be this self-made person who can stand up and say, *I did it all by myself.* But when you mess up, *It's all on you.* I came to realize that we as individuals don't have the power and agency to fix ourselves. After all, doctors go to other doctors to get better. We need other people, and that's okay." He continued, "Relationships are essential for living on this planet. To be connected is to be completely and totally your true, vulnerable self and be accepted, known, and loved for it. When you establish those connections, it feeds your sense of identity. It makes you understand that we were created for the purpose to love and be loved, and we were all given gifts and talents for the purpose of serving one another." Of all his relationships, his relationship with Jesus Christ is the most important one in his life. He especially admires Jesus' teaching that you must love God and love others as you love yourself. When you take honest inventory, Jeff explains to me, it's crucial to ask, *How can I help someone else today?*

It's been close to twenty-one years since Jeff's first manic episode. His children are teenagers. He created a rewarding career for himself as a Pentagon defense consultant first with the Air Force, then with the Marine Corps, and now with the Navy, where he advocates for funding that transforms naval logistics capabilities in support of maritime operations. He tells me that where he once dealt with "budget dust" (consulting on projects of less than $5 million) he now influences decisions on "budget chunks" ($100 million–$1 billion). His life feels deeply satisfying. Marianne, a kindergarten teacher, is still his rock. His children are his joy. His faith is strong. But the bipolar disorder is still eager to take over whenever he lets his guard down.

Of all the people I interviewed for this book, I've corresponded with Jeff the most, which feels odd and yet wonderful because we were complete strangers when he responded to a survey I conducted about adulting three years ago. What strikes me about Jeff is his ability to accept what he can't change while working hard to be in charge of what he can control. Which is not to say that to do so is easy. Jeff has had more bipolar episodes. The last two were in 2009 and 2018. Although I imagine that the details are raw and deeply private, at some point I feel I know him well enough to ask if he's willing to tell me about them because I think his story can help others. He agrees to share.

"I've been diagnosed with 'fast-cycling' bipolar one," he tells me. "I reach sustained manic highs with short, intermittent periods of depressive rest, then back to mania. My manic breaks have resulted from me not taking my meds (which, pre-diagnosis, I didn't realize I needed). There's a quickly sliding slope starting from forgetting to take meds as scheduled, to just thinking I can ration them to mitigate some of the side effects of weight gain and sleeping too much, to thinking I can manage the disorder by determining when to take them and when not to." (Do you see that Jeff's own mind gets in the way of his self-care? As the illness takes over he becomes unable to advocate for his own health.)

He can feel it coming. "My first indication of manic onset is reduced sleep. I normally sleep six to eight hours a day. If I find myself functioning on less sleep than that for a week or more, usually it's too late because I think I can manage it. My early manic episodes (pre-diagnosis) were marked by days of little to no sleep (two to three hours a day), unbalanced and pressing urges to get things done (work out, complete chores, finish tasks, etc.), and increased agitation and anger over inconsequential things. During mania, I am hyperaware of my surroundings and tend to overanalyze others' words and tone, and I get very frustrated with others who impede my desire to get things done. As the mania progresses, I become a flight risk. I've left my home, moving cars, hospitals, psychiatric facilities, and social gatherings. At times, I've shed clothing (sometimes, all of it). During my last major break, I was in Las Vegas to celebrate my manager's birthday. His celebration was on Saturday afternoon. I barely slept Thursday and Friday. By Saturday morning (predawn), I had left my hotel room, wandered through casinos until sunrise, purchased a bus ticket, rode to the airport, flew to Denver, lost my wallet, flew to DCA, then walked thirteen miles overnight toward home until an ambulance transported me to a hospital. Hopefully, that is my last break."

The disease takes its name from the fact that it presents as both mania *and* depression. So, after listening to this vivid description of mania, I ask Jeff about the other half: depression. "It gets centered on the shame and guilt of the destruction I've wrought with the mania. The loss of trust, shattered relationships, having to start from zero. Sometimes I'm an impatient individual yet wanting what I want on my terms. This disease is treatable, but you have to follow the path. At the crux is always I was not taking my medication as prescribed, because I thought I could handle it. That's the insidiousness of this disease. You go, *Oh, you're still fine, you don't need those meds*. That thought erodes the pharmaceutical foundation of keeping me in the sane box instead of the manic box. I can't control bipolar, so I have to take a drug, but I don't want the drug because some of those early manic symptoms feel good, such as increased productivity and energy. Bipolar says, *You don't need the drug*; then, bipolar takes me. Part of the depression results from knowing I can't control this. But most of it comes from the pain I've caused others."

He manages his relationships as best he can. "Bipolar makes others question me. *Is that just Jeff being excited, or is he off his medication?* I feel that extra critical lens applied to me around what I do, how I act, and how I speak. After an episode, this feeling of a critical lens on me happens for the next six months or so. Then, once I establish a new pattern, those concerns from others get less and less. It's my own fault. I eroded the trust that my wife and children placed on me to take my meds every day. We're going through counseling to make sure we do what we need to do to work on our relationship."

This is all really a lot. Jeff's situation—the very narrow ledge he must walk through life, never deviating from his meds ever, and the serious consequences that come if he steps off that ledge—seems a very challenging adult life to me. I've never been through something like this. I ask Jeff how he copes. "First, I'm a huge proponent of medication and counseling. Neuropsychiatry, psychology, and pharmacology have made huge strides over the past three decades in developing treatments for mental and behavior disorders like depression, anxiety, bipolar, etc. The bad news is that everybody reacts differently to medications and different counseling methods, so it may take time to find the right counselor, medication, and dosage. So, step one in recovery and maintenance is find your counselor, see them regularly, and take your meds as prescribed. *Do not* self-medicate with alcohol, cannabis, or other drugs of choice. Communication is key: be open with doctors and other care networks (counselors, colleagues, friends, family)."

The second thing Jeff does is surrender to the vulnerability. "Everything I've gone through prepared me for the next thing, and the next thing," Jeff says. "When you're obsessed with the power of the individual, then your vulnerability and lack of control seem like weaknesses. But I see strength in vulnerability. I may not know the whole plan, but in surrendering control to a God that loves us, there's a release. Twenty years after my first manic episode, through my church I am now a counselor for other people who have mood disorders, including bipolar, depression, anxiety, OCD, and other challenges." One of his daughters reminds him of his past self—early in high school she was very invested in following a traditional path to success by taking the "right" classes, going to the "right" college, and getting the "right" job. "I impress upon her that my current position has very little to do with the stress I put myself through in the first half of my life." His entire life changed on a dime, and he can't say what tomorrow holds. He wants his children to benefit from a lesson he learned the hard way.

"I was trying to do so much because that's what my identity was wrapped in. I've learned I have to do less so that I can be more, be the person God created me to be, not chase this endless loop of doing this *and* this *and* this *and* this *and* this. I'm not immune to the trappings of this world or the ethos of this culture that says you have to do more to be more. I have to come to terms with *Well, what does that look like now that I have to pull back and slow down?*"

I ask him how he's decided to dial down. "I think what I need to do is figure out what I've been designed to do. I like to write. I like to lead people. I like helping other people. So, I like helping to volunteer. Irony is I'm also a counselor for people who deal with bipolar and anxiety and depression. I can't heal myself so I help others to speak into my life. There's some vulnerability in saying I can't do it all. But that's okay. We weren't designed to do it all. We were designed to be great at a few things, good at some, and not that great at the rest. We were designed to be in a community of people to support each other. The travesty of the present is our family structures are being stressed and breaking down and more and more we don't know how to deal with one another, how to put phones down to have conversations, be present, be authentic and real with one another. We need to be able to support one another in this thing called life. We weren't designed to do it all by ourselves.

"I have so much to be thankful for, and I continue to count my blessings. Part of me still wishes that I could go back to my twenties and live without this disorder; however, I wouldn't be the person I am today. This is the proverbial thorn in my side—or head in my case! It's there to remind me that I am human and fallible. Bipolar disorder reminds me that I wasn't designed to live alone. That African proverb comes to mind: *If you want to go fast, go alone. If you want to go far, go together.* I want to go far. And I've sought out and surrounded myself with people who choose to walk with me."

IN SHORT: YOUR SITUATION IS VALID—OWN IT

If you want to take good care of your self—and you do, because that's what being an adult requires—then know yourself. Support that individual self as best you can while opening up to others, as appropriate. Despite what you do (and sometimes because of it) things can go terribly wrong in life, and it can be scary as hell when that happens. It's time to look at that possibility and what you can do about it.

Unpack and Reflect

- Do I feel like I know my situation in terms of my mental health, physical health, how my brain works, and the environments that challenge me? What more do I want to know in these areas?
- Looking at the "Self-Care Checklist," what are the things I'm good at when it comes to self-care? What things could I be better at?
- Who can I talk to about this stuff? Can I ask for help? Why or why not?
- What are examples of my resilience?

10

HOW TO COPE

(WHEN THE SHIT HITS THE FAN)

> Look for the helpers.
>
> —Fred Rogers

I hope nothing bad ever happens to you—but I've lived enough of life to know that you are unlikely to be spared. I can't predict which bad things will come your way, overwhelm you, and make you wonder whether you can go on. But my greatest wish is that if and when something terrible does happen, you will be able to get through it. This chapter is me holding your hand.

Not gonna lie, I am struggling somewhat myself right now. When I first conceived of this chapter, I was going to talk about what dying, death, and disaster feel like, how to cope with their immediate impact and then the longer grief that comes, and the lessons those agonies teach us. Then, in the middle of writing this book, COVID-19 came and brought a new set of reasons to feel scared, devastated, hopeless, angry, and changed. And, a few months into the pandemic, George Floyd was murdered at the knee of a Minneapolis police officer, and with his murder—which was, at the time, simply the latest murder of an unarmed Black person at the hands of law enforcement—came a greater reckoning with the racism deeply embedded in our society, which is its own ever-simmering disaster. Facing such sadness and uncertainty? It's a lot. But I'm going to do the best I can to process what's happening and press on in writing this book for you while being attentive to my own emotional needs. In some ways, that's the whole point of this chapter. So, let's do it.

But first, I want to give you a framework for understanding the process humans tend to go through when coping with a profound loss. It's known as the Five Stages of Grief, and it's the work of Elisabeth Kübler-Ross, who developed this concept back in 1969. It applies to any kind of serious loss you go through—things like death of a loved one, job loss, abuse, incarceration, a natural disaster, the end of a relationship, the loss of a home, being injured or getting a scary diagnosis, and so on. Any of these things can drag you down to that place where you wonder whether you can go on.

Dr. Kübler-Ross's five stages are referred to as "DABDA," owing to the first letters of each stage in the process: Denial, Anger, Bargaining, Depression, Acceptance.

1. *Denial.* You can't bring yourself to "believe" that the bad news is real. Another way to refer to this is being "in shock." The news seems not to have sunk in. You are going on with your life as if it has not happened. Or you're clinging to the idea that something has gone wrong. You feel confused. Or you are dealing only with the perfunctory tasks associated with it while not allowing yourself to *feel* any of it. You ruminate over alternative outcomes as if replaying them in your head might make them come about.

2. *Anger.* You start to feel it. This is not fair, and you are angry. You're trying to figure out who is to blame and why this happened. You yell, pout, slam things, are short with people, act out. You are frustrated, irritated, and angry.

3. *Bargaining.* You try to turn this thing around somehow to avoid the thing causing the grief. If you're responsible for the thing (e.g., you did something that resulted in your partner leaving you, cost you your job, or got you arrested) typically you're trying to make amends or you're pledging never to do this thing again. If you're more of the victim in the situation (e.g., you've been injured in an accident, you've received a scary diagnosis, you've been abused)

you're pledging to God or the universe that if you can just be spared this outcome, you will be a better person in some way so as to have deserved this mercy you're asking for.

4. *Depression.* Your pleas and bargaining have gone unheeded, and you fall into a deep funk over the way things are. You withdraw from others, you have little interest in the things around you, and you barely can go through the motions of life.

5. *Acceptance.* You accept that the thing has happened, that you cannot change it, but that you are still in charge of your actions and choices from here on out. You can explore options, put a plan in place, and move on.

Not everyone will go through all of the stages, and some stages can last moments while others last years. Just keep this framework in mind as part of your larger understanding that when the shit hits the fan you're going to go through a natural human emotional and psychological process, and after a loss or crisis, it's normal not to feel normal for a long while.

This chapter contains more stories than the others because it's the stories that show how a person gets through this stuff. I'll start by sharing some of the things I've been through, and then in the "Don't Just Take My Word for It" section you'll read about how other people have gotten through life's really bad spots, and I'm going to share a few bits of overarching advice in between. None of these stories may be about your specific situation, but the point is to take away lessons about how people process, cope, and move on, which tend to be, actually, pretty universal. Seeing how others have gotten through their serious struggles can give you ballast when you are going through your own hard times.

WHEN THE EARTH MOVED UNDER OUR FEET

It's the fall of 1989. I am twenty-one, freshly minted from college, and madly in love with Dan. We live together off campus in a place that, frankly, is more than we can afford. But I had persuaded Dan that we should live there anyway. (At this stage, I am years away from being financially responsible, and Dan is years away from standing up to me on such things.) I work at the Public Service Center on campus, where my job is to get undergraduates involved in community service opportunities. Dan, still a Stanford undergraduate, is in a metalsmith class as part of his product design major. For his final project of the fall term, he is designing our wedding rings and forging them in silver.

On Tuesday, October 17, 1989, I am at work in the rickety nineteenth-century house that holds the Public Service Center. Just one week prior, my boss had brought in painters to spruce up the dilapidated structure, and as they'd made their way up the stairs to the second floor where my office was located, I'd overheard one of them shout to the other, "This thing withstood the last big one but it's not gonna survive the next." (By "big one" they were referring to the 1906 earthquake, which devastated San Francisco.) At 5:04 p.m. on October 17, the 6.9 Loma Prieta earthquake hits the San Francisco Bay Area. I hurl myself over to the doorway of my office—said to be the safest spot—as the painter's words echo inside my mind. Trying to hold myself stable as the building jolts and rolls, I watch in horror as cracks zigzag across the freshly painted walls and a five-drawer vertical file cabinet flies across my office. While gripping the doorjamb and trying to stay on my feet, I look out into the hallway and lock eyes with my colleague Jeanne, who is holding on to her doorway eight feet away. Jeanne and I don't know each other well. She's maybe fifty to my twenty-one. But from that day forward I will feel close to her. We both know that there's a heavy clawfoot bathtub somewhere up above our heads on the condemned third floor. Our locked eyes said we weren't sure we were going to survive this thing.

Fifteen seconds after the quaking began, it stops. I have to find Dan. I have no luck with the office phone; it's dead. And the power is out. (Keep in mind that we are years away from cell phones, laptops, and Wi-Fi; at this time, email was the new technology for reaching people quickly, and you could only use it on your desktop, which was just called "the computer" and was plugged into a power outlet. And as I've said, the power is out.) I grab my things and make my way downstairs and out of the building, where I'm relieved to discover that all of my coworkers are accounted for and fine. As people mill about tallying what has happened—our building's brick chimney had come crashing to the ground, for example—I tell my colleagues that I need to go find Dan and I hop into my car. We live only two miles away. But within minutes cars are at a standstill. The traffic lights are out. Every driver has the same dazed look on their face. I find it a strange comfort to know that every one of us knows what the other has just experienced.

Dan had been doing homework in our apartment when the quake hit. He'd waited it out in the doorjamb, and when it was over he'd been relieved to see that only a stack of cassette tapes had fallen over. (This was a modern apartment complex of new construction, up to code, which is partly what made it so expensive to rent.) Having lived just two years in California, this is the first earthquake Dan has ever felt, so he has no basis for comparison. He finds himself wondering, *Was this a big one?* Something makes him think, *It might be.*

He tries to call me at work, but the phone is dead. He decides he has to come find me, and, guessing (rightly!) that the roads are either unsafe or jammed, he hops on his bike. Before leaving he tapes a cryptic hand-written note on the glass door of the lobby of our building that reads, "Julie, I'm biking to campus. Dan 5:15 p.m." He would later explain to me that he didn't want to put anything about the earthquake in the note, fearing that he'd look like he was overreacting. (Thirty years later, he says, *Why was I so worried about that???*) But he included the time so that I would know that it was written after the quake, and that he was fine.

It takes me close to an hour to drive the two miles home. I pull into the covered parking lot, where I see a crowd gathered on the lawn waiting for management to inspect the building and deem it safe for reentry. I stand around with clumps of strangers telling where we were when the quake hit and what it had felt like. I look around and see Dan's car in the lot but he's not here. I'm worried. Is he inside? Before long I see him biking toward us from down the street. My heart leaps with relief. We hug each other hard, and wipe away a few tears. Then we stand and make jokes with the one neighbor we recognize. Finally the building is "green tagged" and we're allowed to return. I don't see the reassuring note he'd left for me until we make our way back into the building.

The power is working inside our apartment. We try to call our parents who all live in the New York area, but the phone is still dead. We turn on the TV and sit shoulder to shoulder on the futon, our hands clasped tight. A newscaster announces, "People began laughing at first when they felt the first quake. And then people started screaming because it was so terrifying." I'd known that terror. And I was relieved to have some objective proof that I wasn't a baby for having been so scared. I did not want to return to that rickety old building known as my office.

Then comes the imagery. Billowing smoke. Houses in the Marina District sitting like a stack of crumbled Pringles. A section of the top level of the San Francisco Bay Bridge collapsed against the bottom level like the hypotenuse of a triangle. The two-tiered Nimitz Freeway in Oakland pancaked onto itself. The quake had occurred during rush hour. Thousands must have died. We keep trying the phone to get word to our parents. No luck.

A newswoman on our local ABC station named Anna Chavez is literally running onto the set and back off again to go get us more updates. After a few hours, our phone rings. It's one set of parents. We reassure them that we're fine and we call the others. In this pre-Internet world they might not have heard about the quake until their late evening news or in the newspaper the following morning, but as luck would have it the entire country had learned about our quake in real time, because it hit right before the start of Game Three of the World Series, which was being played in the San Francisco Giants' stadium, and everyone watching saw Candlestick Park shake.

Dan and I watch Anna Chavez and her colleagues for days. Anna hosts the 6 p.m. and 11 p.m. broadcasts. She delivers sobering updates yet comes across as someone who cares about all of us. I trust her. I open an email from my boss, which says we are putting together teams to go help out in Watsonville, a town closer to the epicenter that is home to many migrant farmworkers and has been hard hit. But I can't bring myself to do anything other than watch the news, eat, sleep, and hold on to Dan. As the week wears on, and the efforts turn from "search and rescue" (where they think they can still find people alive) to "recovery," I feel safe in my apartment with Dan and Anna Chavez. The thought of going back to work on Monday or going to help out in some other town frightens me.

When the body count is tallied, it is nothing short of a miracle that while over 3,700 people had been injured, only sixty-three had died. It's universally accepted that the death count was so low because it had been a "Battle of the Bay" World Series: The San Francisco Giants versus the Oakland A's. Everyone in the Bay Area is a fan of one team or the other. When the quake hit, these sports team allegiances meant that hundreds of thousands had left work early, and instead of being on the roads, they were either at Candlestick Park or relatively safe at home watching on TV.

Dan had come to college in California from Connecticut (a place with hurricanes and blizzards) and I was most recently from Wisconsin (a place with blizzards and tornadoes). These natural disasters are nothing to sneeze at. But unlike an earthquake, at least you can see them coming. For about a week in the middle of October in 1989, Dan and I did some serious reckoning over whether we were batshit crazy to want to call California our home. But it had already become our home. It was a place where we both felt more rooted and happy than we'd felt in any other place. We would decide to stay. I would go back to work. I would help out in Watsonville. The Bay Area would recover from the Loma Prieta earthquake. Life would go on.

Close to thirty years later, I'm in an airport in some city while on book tour with my memoir, *Real American*. I see a woman I recognize. She's a Latina, maybe ten to fifteen years older than me. I feel like I know her well, but I can't for the life of me figure out why. (I'm used to that happening all the time now. In my late forties the file cabinets in my brain started to feel really FULL.) I hunt around in my memory for who this woman can be and how I know her. Finally, it hits me. I can't remember her name, but I've placed the face.

I approach her. "Excuse me," I say, "but by any chance are you a news-caster in the Bay Area?" "Yes, I am. Or, I mean, I was," she replies, still kind. "I'm Anna Chavez." I get choked up, and while I know she might find this weird, I keep going. "You don't know me, but I just want to say that you were so reassuring during Loma Prieta. It was like you were holding me. I just want to thank you." Then she held my hand for real. Thanked me for thanking her. And with that she was gone.

OH BROTHER, OH FATHER, WHERE ART THOU?

Three months later, in January 1990, I got a handwritten letter in the mail. I'd been at an off-site retreat for work but came home at lunch to check on my fourteen-year-old niece, Mawiyah, who was visiting us for a few days and had come down with stomach flu. The letter came in a white business-sized envelope and the words on the front were written in my mother's very neat handwriting. I opened it in the front room where Mawiyah was propped up on the futon. The letter was addressed "Dear Children." It said that my father had prostate cancer, that it had metastasized (i.e., spread to other parts of his body), that it could not be cured, that he was dying, that all of us children were getting this letter at the same time, that we were not to call home, and that we were not to tell another soul except for our partners. As I read the letter, I moved to the bedroom and shut the door.

I am now twenty-two. Daddy is dying. My teenaged niece Mawiyah is staying with me and this is her Granddad we're talking about and I'm not allowed to tell her. Four of my five older siblings are also Daddy's children and are quite a bit older than me. I found a private moment later that day and called one of them, fighting back tears. This sibling told me I was being selfish in feeling this emotion, that I was crying for myself, not for Daddy. From their tone it was clear they were not willing to talk with me about it further. Years later I have come to know this sibling far better than I did then, and I can appreciate what they were able to give in that moment, and what they were not, and why. But at the time, I was twenty-two, losing Daddy, not allowed to call him or my mother, and a sibling had slammed a door in my face. I felt abandoned. And I had to put on a happy face for my niece.

Daddy, a man who had been a part of the effort to wipe smallpox from the planet by disseminating a vaccine, who had improved health conditions for marginalized people, particularly Native Americans and Blacks, during President Carter's administration, and who had looked after the health of the children of New York for Mayor Dinkins, was now dying of a disease he'd felt grow inside of him, a disease for which there was medicine, a treatment and cure, but whose symptoms he'd ignored. He'd gone for treatment only when it was really too late. I guess he did not trust that medicine would save him. Or maybe he was just fucking scared to confront what it feels like to be a dying person.

From my mother's account, I know that Daddy had seen too much pity in people's eyes over all those years of being a physician, and he didn't want people to look at him that way. When I was twenty-two, I resented Daddy's choice to ignore his growing, metastasizing pain, because if he'd just gone in for treatment we could have had so much more time with him. Yet a quarter century later as I face my own health issues, I can appreciate the reluctance to go get yourself looked at. And still, dear reader, I want you to go get yourself looked at if you sense you have a health issue dwelling inside you. (Pro tip: When you're giving advice to others, try to follow your own advice!)

Five months after the letter about Daddy arrives, in June 1990, Dan gets down on one knee on a stretch of beach in Northern California, asks me to marry him, and puts the ring he designed on my finger. I say a big emotional Yes. We start to plan a wedding, wondering aloud what Nana will do. She's Dan's grandmother, also a known racist who has made clear that she is unhappy that Dan and I are dating. We wonder whether she'll come to the wedding or whether she'll boycott, whether we should make a preemptive strike and not invite her, and whether anyone in Dan's family will stand up to her (and for us).

In August we are forced to part. I will be headed to law school after Dan graduates, and will spend his senior year doing an important law internship in Los Angeles, which will help me succeed in law school and maybe set me up for a job afterward. We visit as often as we can afford. In March 1991, my brother George, the eldest son, plans a first-ever vacation for the entire extended family. He's chosen a house in Northern California, northwest of Reno, next to a lake that has great fishing. Fishing is Daddy's passion. And even though we are not to talk about Daddy's health, we all know that this gathering is happening for that reason. Dan comes on the fishing trip, too. Although we are engaged to be married and living apart, my mother does not allow us to share a bedroom. We go for a drive, pull over at a rest stop, walk into the woods, and have sex while swatting away mosquitoes.

Dan graduates from college in June 1991. We move east for me to start law school at Harvard that fall. In August 1992, we get married in New York. The whole family attends, even Nana, who behaves graciously, which frankly I find amazing and wonderful. We have a honeymoon on St. John, U.S. Virgin Islands, where I go topless for the first and last time in my life.

I survive law school and even make a few friends. In my final year, I am elected to be one of four "class marshals." I take classes I love with my mentors Martha Minow (family law) and Charles Ogletree (criminal justice), among others. In early March 1994, when I am three months away from graduating and Dan and I are eating dinner, the phone rings. I answer, but intend to ask if we can call back after we finish eating. Both of my parents are on the line. "No," Daddy replies. "It's serious. We need to talk right now." I fear it's about Daddy. But no. It's about my older brother Stephen, who is dying of pneumonia in a Chicago hospital.

Of all my siblings (all much older than I am, all either the children of my mother or father but not both), I knew Stephen the best. When I was little, and he was in his twenties, he'd gone to law school in the city where my parents and I lived. He'd been the big brother who came to our home on weekends and goofed around with me. Usually he brought his girlfriend Marcia, who became my sister-in-law and whom I also adored. When I was in high school he and Marcia lived a couple hours away and they'd come and hang out every now and then. Sometimes I'd find Stephen snooping around in my room, reading stuff. It annoyed me, but not too much. I liked that he wanted to know more about me. Many years later I'd followed in Stephen's footsteps to law school, and he'd held me through some difficult moments as I bared my soul about race and social justice in the personal statement for my applications. Now, here he was, a member of the ACLU board in Chicago, advocating for marginalized people in that great city, yet also inexplicably on his deathbed with pneumonia at forty-three years of age. I was twenty-six.

I spoke with both Professor Ogletree and Professor Minow, two humans whose kindness I shall never forget—then flew to be by Stephen's side, as did everyone in my family. He lay in a hospital bed hooked up to machines and covered by a sheet through which I could see the outline of his bones. A ventilator was keeping him alive. When I had some time alone with him, his heart rate was jumpy as if he was agitated. I talked to him as if he was just a person, not a dying person, and told him stories about our times together. And I told him over and over again that I loved him so very much. His heart rate slowed and became steady, which I took to mean he felt at some peace hearing my words.

Dan and I returned to Massachusetts. I clamped blinders on my heart, and finished my final graduation requirement, known as the "third-year paper," a thesis-length piece of work meant to be worthy of publication. Stephen died two months later, in May. My blinders stayed tightly clamped through his funeral and graduation, through studying for and taking the bar exam, and through starting a new job as a corporate lawyer in California.

A year into that new job, when I was about to turn twenty-eight, Daddy was in the final moments of his long struggle with prostate cancer. My brothers and sister and I got called home on a Friday in early October 1995, late in the morning California time, and we drove or flew in from all over the U.S., my journey from San Francisco to Boston on to the puddle jumper plane to the small island of Martha's Vineyard being one of the longest. By early Saturday morning we had all arrived on the island and had made our way to their house in the middle of the woods. There were a dozen of us—my mother, we his children, our spouses and partners, and his grandchildren—and we gathered in the cool stillness of the room that had been Daddy's office but was now his dying place, kneeling shoulder to shoulder, lining the stiff hem of his hospital bed with a soft ribbon of family.

When I entered the room that Saturday morning, I saw Daddy in bed against the far wall looking more like ninety-three than his actual seventy-seven, shriveling before my eyes, almost entirely gray, this tall strong man who had once moved mountains, measles, smallpox, and bad people away; half the size I remembered. I gave him one last kiss, feeling the dryness of his lips, sensing the acrid smell of teeth, mouth, and tongue no longer brushed. "I'm here, Daddy. It's Julie," I bleated, like a small lamb. He couldn't talk or even smile, but his strong right arm lifted his hand a few inches off the bed, and for a long last moment I grasped those strong fingers that had once held my wobbly seat as I learned how to ride a bicycle.

In less than a half hour, the hospice nurse who had been keeping quiet in a corner stood and walked toward us, nodding her gentle, knowing gaze, telling us without language that he'd passed on. Then the weeping began, the mournful, awful wailing of survivors who could finally release what we'd been admonished to keep inside us for five years. The cries became a swell, a final song, a symphony of love for our husband, father, grandfather, father-in-law, and a song of anguish for ourselves. We were encouraged to leave the room so the nurse could clean the body and prepare it for its travel to a morgue and then on to a crematorium. We filed out one by one, and as I walked, eyes downcast, I passed the three-foot-tall statue from Mali we call "The Big Lady" that was standing near the door. I touched her shoulder as you touch the knob of a banister to steady yourself, or as you rub the knee of a famous bent-copper statue in a museum or stately entryway as a way of permanently recording that you were there.

HOW GRIEF SHOWS ITSELF

When Daddy died I'd just hit my one-year anniversary at the law firm—a beast that incessantly demanded to be fed with long hours of hard work. I took three weeks off to help my mom cope with all the banking and insurance paperwork associated with Daddy's death, but I knew I would one day have to go back to work. I returned in early November. I'd go in, and try to get stuff done, but mostly I was moving the piles of paperwork around on my desk. I'd take a long lunch. Avoid eye contact with partners. It was like I didn't know myself there anymore. I couldn't make a to-do list. Couldn't stick to it when I did manage to make one. My thinking was cloudy. I searched for some logical way to explain what was happening to me: *Maybe I partially suffocated myself with my pillow one night? Okay, yeah, that must be it.*

Over the holidays, my brother's widow, Marcia, called and asked how I was doing. This was odd. We'd been close since I was young, but we rarely spoke by phone. I told her I was fine but was having trouble focusing at work. She said she thought I was grieving, and asked if I'd gotten any grief counseling. (I hadn't. In those years, having been raised by people who didn't believe in therapy, well, I didn't believe in it, either.)

"Find a support group," Marcia urged. "Better yet," she said, "Dan is probably feeling at a loss for how to help you. Ask him to find you one." I went to Dan and relayed the conversation. This was pre-Google, so he paged through our local Yellow Pages, a thick book of listings of all businesses in our area code, arranged by category on thin sheets of yellow paper. He found a nonprofit grief counseling group one town over called Kara that offered group counseling in the evenings. It felt like he and Marcia were in cahoots to make me go and would not rest until I'd tried it once, so I just said, *Okay, FINE, I'll GO.* The next meeting was on January 3, at 7 p.m.

That night, I pull up to Kara, housed in a stately old mansion situated at the back of a big parking lot on a residential street. It's dark out by this time of day in January, and as I creep up to the foreboding front door it feels a little eerie. But there are a few lights on and as I go through the front door I see a group gathering around an oval table in a large conference room. I survey the scene. There are maybe ten or twelve people. All genders. All white. And at twenty-eight, I appear to be the youngest one there. The facilitator welcomes those of us who are new, and says we'll go around and share our names, whom we've lost, and how we are doing. I am relieved that she starts to the left of me and goes clockwise, which means I will go last.

I hear others relay who they are and that they've lost partners, siblings, parents, and friends. I hear stories about having a hard time at work, about not being able to focus, about not feeling like themselves. Some nod in recognition. When people break down, a box of tissues is passed. I begin to get that I probably had not suffocated myself in bed one night, but am, instead, experiencing a legitimate emotional process that has appreciable effects on the brain: GRIEF. I listen and listen and listen and listen some more. And when it is my turn I can finally open up about what is going on inside of me. That hour and a half in January 1996 spent with strangers sitting around a big table in a stately old building was the first time since Daddy died, since Stephen died, and since the Loma Prieta earthquake that I stopped trying to just plow ahead and perform the part of the person-who-had-all-her-shit-together, and instead slowed way down to let myself unpack and explore how I was doing. I decided that what I was going through mattered. That I mattered.

From that night on, I don't have to be dragged to Kara. The next session is two weeks later and it can't come fast enough. I even show up early, which is unusual for me. I start to get to know people a bit. It's a relief to hear their stories. The second session is another nourishing session. Two weeks later, Wednesday, January 31, I'm there again. But this time there are no lights on and not a single other car in the huge parking lot. Not even the facilitator is here? I check my watch—I'm a tad early, so everyone must be late? I check the front door and find it locked. I wait. Remember, this is pre–cell phones and pre-Google. I can't get answers right there on the spot. I wait some more. Finally at 7:12 it's clear that no one is coming. I get in my car and drive home.

Once home, I pull out what was known as "The Phone Book" or the White Pages, which is an alphabetical listing of the numbers for all residences and businesses in our area code (and is a companion to the Yellow Pages, the difference being its very thin pieces of paper are white). I find the number for Kara and get their voice mail. "Welcome to Kara Grief Counseling. Our drop-in adult counseling sessions are on the first and third Wednesdays of each month." I had my answer—they didn't meet *every other Wednesday* as I'd thought. The bad news was, this month had five Wednesdays so there was in fact no meeting that night. The good news was, the first Wednesday of February was only one week away. The great news was that I now knew that grief was a real thing and that I could cope with it by listening to others and by opening up about my own bewildering feelings, too. The greatest news was that although I was wandering around in a bleak and unfamiliar land, thanks to Kara, I knew I was no longer out there *alone*.

I went to Kara on the first and third Wednesdays without fail. Nothing was more important in my life at that time. At some point I start mentioning Stephen when I introduce myself, all the while wondering if his death "counted" since he had died two years earlier. It counted. I needed to process Stephen, and Daddy, and frankly, the earthquake when I had feared for my own life. I needed to validate it all. I stopped going to Kara when I felt like myself again, which was in August of that year. As I aged, I would learn that grief will be your constant silent companion until you begin talking to it and then at some point it will get up and walk quietly away.

FIND SOMEBODY TO LEAN ON

I've always made friends easily, and from my earliest years have counted on friends as a lifeline. As I mentioned in chapter 7, "Start Talking to Strangers," when I was less than two and we'd moved from a house in Nigeria to a huge high-rise apartment building in New York, I toddled over to my mother, who was standing at the kitchen sink, tugged on her apron, and said "friends, Mommy, friends." I needed my people, and I knew it.

Freshman year in college I sang the song "You've Got a Friend" at our dorm talent show. I wanted these new peers of mine to know that I could sing, yes, but I also wanted them to know I cared about people and would be there for them. I also hoped they would be there for me, too.

Losing my brother and father when I was in my twenties, I learned that grief is a language spoken only by the initiated. And that the loss of a loved one can be compounded by a second anguish—the distance of well-intended friends who either don't want to bring up your loss lest they "remind" you or who just don't know quite what to say. (Pro tip: A person dealing with a majorly bad situation is constantly thinking of it, unless they're in that first stage of grief, denial. And regardless of the stage of grief they are in, as the nonprofit OptionB counsels, one of the best questions you can ask someone in such a circumstance is, 'How are you doing, today?') Most of my friends didn't know about Stephen's death; it had happened so quickly and I had not been able to bear speaking of it given how many things I had to focus on in order to graduate from law school and start life as a lawyer. But when Daddy died, people knew. I received cards that read, "In deepest sympathy" and emails that said, "Let me know if there's anything I can do." The few who called asked, "How's your *mom* doing?" My heart wailed, *Ask me about me, please ask about me.* Then my head told my heart to stop being selfish: *Of course they're right to be most concerned about your grieving mom.* But I would've given anything for a few friends to ask, "How are *you* holding up? How are you coping? How are you doing, *today*?"

I picture grief as a vat full of tears hidden behind a wall. All we can see on our side of the wall is the spigot. Circumstances loosen the spigot and our tears flow, then we tighten it again to get on with our lives as custom and bosses demand. But when things remind us of our loved one—a song, a milestone, the birth of a grandchild they'll never know—the spigot loosens. It loosens and tightens, loosens and tightens, over months, years, even decades. None of us knows how big the vat of water is. How vast the grief. We need friends not to give us space, but to sit with us as we loosen the spigot.

I found one person who did just that during my months at Kara. Thane was a thirty-four-year-old gay white guy, just six years older than me, which made us the two young ones in the group. His amazing mother, Marilyn, had died shortly before Daddy. For seven months Thane and I sat with each other as the grief squeezed our hearts. Then we'd go back to our regularly scheduled lives, Thane as a program manager at a bio-tech company and me as a corporate lawyer. A quarter century later, we can still count on each other for a well-timed Facebook message on an important day, like "Your mom would be so proud of you" or "You know your dad is smiling." Thane is there for me unlike any other friend or family member has ever been, and I can't really explain why. I guess that as we huddled together against the howling grief we were more deeply open and vulnerable with each other, and we knew almost nothing else about each other's lives beyond the deaths and the grief, so the knowing was deep, specific, and intense. I saw this quote on a friend's Facebook recently: "Grief is just love with no place to go." I guess Thane and I had all this love with no place to go, so we gave it to each other. Our support of each other became a knitted blanket that held us close then and holds us close still.

ACCEPTING A NEW REALITY

You know how when the power goes out in your house, you know the power is out, yet out of habit, you flick on a light switch or try to use an appliance anyway? The part of your brain that knows how things should be hasn't caught up to the way things are.

The power going out is usually not a big deal, but it's a great example of how your brain can be slow to adjust to the new reality that you are experiencing when a disaster strikes, when someone has died or something scary has happened. During COVID, I received a lot of requests to speak to groups about one thing or another, and as each event approached, even though every single event was a virtual event that would require me to be sitting in my little backyard office looking at my laptop, I'd unconsciously picture myself walking up to a podium wherever the event would have been if there was no pandemic. I knew—of course, I knew—that I wasn't actually going to the physical site of the event. And yet somewhere inside my brain, I didn't know.

Part of getting through to the other side of bad things happening, of abrupt loss and change, is making your brain conceive of what's happened, and then learning to accept it. You gotta tell yourself, *No, it's a pandemic. I can't travel there.* Or, you think about seeing your friend at a reunion and have to remind yourself, *No, remember, they died.* My brother George went through a terrible tragedy in 1991. His house burned down in a firestorm that swept through the Oakland and Berkeley hills. A few years later I asked him, "Can I borrow your tent?" "I don't have a tent," he replied with a smile. "Yes, you do," I insisted. "No, I don't *have* a tent," he again replied, still smiling but insistent. "Come on, George. Yes, you do, you know, the one we borrowed a few years ago?" He answered again. When I finally got it, I felt like an insensitive idiot. George had lost everything in the fire except his wife and daughter and the few things they could cram into their cars. Everything. His mind had adjusted to the reality of all he'd lost, but mine had not.

The main underpinning of this book is that to be an adult you have to develop agency and resilience to make your way forward. (Agency is knowing that you can do the task in front of you, having that sense of "I can/will," and resilience is knowing that you can bounce back from whatever comes, having the sense of "I can cope.") But no matter how much agency and resilience you may or may not have, they exist within a larger context of life. And in that context *you are not in charge of most things.* (Say that again with me now!) But here's the thing: even when you can't control what is happening, you can control how you respond.

Alcoholics Anonymous, Narcotics Anonymous, Overeaters Anonymous, and other "Twelve-Step" addiction-support programs each consider philosopher Richard Niebuhr's Serenity Prayer to be the bedrock of their work. It goes like this:

God, grant me the serenity to accept the things I cannot change,
the courage to change the things I can,
and the wisdom to know the difference.

You don't have to be an addict, or believe in a higher power, to deploy this simple but profound piece of advice about how even in the face of life's greatest challenges we can still move forward.

MAKING MEANING FROM IT

My dear friend Adina Glickman, whom we met in chapter 9, "Take Good Care," in the section on resilience, worked at Stanford helping students overcome the various obstacles that get in the way of strong academic performance, such as anxiety, procrastination, and even adequate study skills. She's now in private practice as an academic, life, and career coach. She reminds me that resilience develops big-time when the shit hits the fan. "The more you experience, the better you get at knowing how to pick up the pieces. The next time someone is dying, or you're in an accident, or there's a disaster, you'll draw upon the reserves in your mind and your heart and your spirit. *Okay, I've had something like this happen before*, you'll think. You'll reassure yourself that you are stronger than you were the first time something bad happened to you, and you actually will be stronger."

When it comes to pure tragedy, Adina's view is that we can survive what has happened by "making meaning" of it. This notion of making meaning comes from the field of positive psychology, a relatively new approach to understanding the human psyche that looks not at what is wrong with us but at the good things in the human experience to figure out how to develop wellness and well-being. Adina says attaching meaning to the bad things that happen is not about thinking "things happen for a reason" or "it was meant to be this way" but about asking yourself, "What will I do with this rough experience so I can move forward?" Maybe you learn something. Maybe you change your life in some important way. Maybe you just allow yourself to feel the tremendous gratitude for the thing or person you've lost.

At this point, I go, *Yeah, yeah, yeah. But what if the thing is really shitty, like a friend dies. Then what?* Adina recommends "turning back to your own self," asking, "'What is my trajectory, what is the purpose of my life? The purpose of my life isn't just to grieve. It's to grow, flourish, create, and give. And the purpose of my friend's life who died doesn't get to be fulfilled and that's the end of that road, but the purpose of my life is to honor, love, grieve, and live my life.' We want there to be neatness but life is not neat, it's very messy."

Then she tells me about a friend who lost her father suddenly to a heart attack when she was just twenty-four. "My friend would say that this terrible loss created in her a capacity for grief that she's actually made good use of. After her father died, she struggled with infertility for seven years, and she grieved every loss, every miscarriage, and every failed IVF. She connected those griefs to what she had experienced at twenty-four. It was like, *I have some experience with grief, I know what that's supposed to be like, I have a reference point. It sucks, but I can do something with this grief now.* She ended up with three daughters, now grown, not from IVF, but conceived the old-fashioned way, and is a fertility advocate now. Her father's death made her grow a muscle she could make use of."

TWELVE STEPS TO SURVIVING WHEN THE SHIT HITS THE FAN

You've lost your job. Someone is abusing you. Someone you love is badly hurt or dying. You're going to jail. You have been injured or get a scary diagnosis. All of your plans have been upended by a pandemic. Your home was destroyed in a natural disaster. Your relationship is ending, and not in a "conscious uncoupling" kind of way but in a way that is very painful. These are examples of things that qualify as the shit hitting the fan. The key here is to figure out what has happened or is happening, get some immediate support, make a plan forward, and get to the other side. Or as Winston Churchill once said, "When you're going through hell, keep going."

1. *Call someone.* Fred Rogers, quoted at the top of the chapter, hosted a public television show for pre-K children called *Mister Rogers' Neighborhood*, which debuted in the United States in 1968, the year I turned one, and lasted for more than thirty years. Every Gen Xer

and some Millennials were raised with this guy. Mister Rogers told us that when bad things happened we should "look for the helpers," and that's a key piece of wisdom about living through bad stuff that I want to pass on to you. (This would be in the immediate moment when the bad thing is happening. Right then, look for the people who are already helping or whose kind look on their face says they are willing to help you.)

Even if it's the middle of the night, call someone. Other people will be able to think more clearly about what is happening. You may even be "in shock," which we say to mean "unable to accurately or deeply/fully process what is going on." Although part of being in shock is not being able to realize you're in shock—that awareness will dawn on you after the fact. So, at times like this you need someone you know you can trust to step in and support your thinking and decision-making. When I was in my early thirties, my dear college classmate Jim found out that his wife was cheating on him. We hadn't seen each other in a few years, but that didn't matter. The bond was there. He called me. I went to his place to hold him, bear witness to his pain, help him process aloud what had happened, and help him think through what to do next.

2. *Record what is happening.* You're going to get facts and advice from those around you as this is happening. If you're losing your job, it's your boss and your HR manager. If it's medical, it's a health care professional. If it's a natural disaster, it's public safety workers, neighbors, and insurance agents. If you're being hurt by someone, it's a social worker, nurse, nonprofit worker, or bystander. If someone's been in an accident, it's law enforcement and witnesses. Take notes. Write down the date and time, the name and position of the person who's telling you the information and how to contact them, and the information itself. You're developing a record that will be an important source of information for you when weeks later your memory of the specifics is hazy. I saw a cyclist get hit by a car when crossing a street. He was okay but we called 911 and waited until help arrived. I provided my name and phone number

so if and when he needed an eyewitness testimony he could find me. And his lawyer did in fact call me months later.

3. *Ask for support.* You will most likely need assistance—with the thing itself or with the regular things of life that you have no ability to handle while you're dealing with the bigger thing. People can't support you if they don't know what you are experiencing. So, choose the group of people that's right for you and let them know what is going on. Depending on what it is, you may want to cast a wide net or keep things held closely to your vest. All of that is up to you. But don't try to go it alone. We've talked about your trusted others. This is what they're for.

4. *Accept the support you are offered.* When people get wind that something has happened they often say, "Let me know if there's anything I can do." It's a very kind intention, but it's often frustrating for the recipient because it's now on you to think of how this other person can help. Of course, if something comes to mind when they say this, then speak up (*I need someone to pick up family at the airport; I need dinner for my family for the next few weeks; I need the laundry done; I can't be alone—can you sleep at my house?*). The better helper is the one who offers you something specific: *I will cover your shift. I will pick up your kids. I will take care of these tasks for you. I will bring you some meals.* And when that person appears and offers help, if you could in fact use the help, let them help you. (Pro tip: You are not obligated to accept. Unfortunately, some people do like to feed off other people's pain or will try to insert themselves in your life at this time because they want to be closer to you. Your Spidey sense will be telling you if you want to accept help from this person or if that somehow makes things worse, or if it's something you really DON'T need, or might even find annoying. Trust your gut here.)

5. *Keep an ongoing to-do list.* You are emotionally compromised and perhaps in a daze. And you may be for some while. Do not expect

that your brain—which is already struggling to comprehend this big change—will remember all the things you need to take care of. Write them down. Trusted others can help you figure out what should be on that list and can regularly review it with you. This is a companion to the record you're keeping of all the information that is coming your way.

6. *Do your research.* If it's a pandemic, read regular news about it and understand what you need to do to keep yourself and your loved ones safe. If you have a diagnosis, consume all the information the Internet will share with you about it. If someone is actively dying or has died, lean in to the doctors, authorities, and family members who know the most and ask questions. If it's a natural disaster, read, watch, or listen to the updates, go to the community info sessions, read up on how insurance companies handle this stuff. This information gathering may be the thing that most makes you want to curl up in a ball and have your parent or parent stand-in handle it for you. And while you do want to be sure to take care of your psychological and emotional health (see item 8 on this list), the act of gathering information is also when and how you will begin to own the situation. Becoming your own little expert on something is actually empowering. Then you become the person who can say to friends a year or two later, *Yeah, that happened to me, let me share with you what I learned.*

7. *Figure out what you CAN do.* My daughter, Avery, was eighteen and enjoying her freshman year of college with the freedom to do as she pleased when the pandemic forced her to come back home. Her spring break got extended from one week to two, and then college went virtual for the remainder of the semester. At this point, life for Avery became a fishbowl with her parents, older brother, and grandmother seemingly peering in from all sides. She'd worked so hard to get up and out of our town and our house, and now she was sucked back into it again with a laptop in

her bedroom as her only portal to her studies, to her friends and mentors, and to her LIFE. Almost all of her clothes and belongings were still back at her school, which would not permit her to retrieve them and took months to send them to her. That is a first-world privileged problem to be sure, but it was nevertheless probably the biggest upheaval at that point in her life. A trauma.

Avery took me out for a scenic drive on Mother's Day that year. It was my first time going anywhere since we'd started sheltering in place. As familiar vistas gave way to the unfamiliar and a larger horizon opened up in front of us, I said to her, "Maybe we need to stop dwelling on what we CAN'T do, and start thinking about what we CAN do." In July, as she watched her school and so many others twist and turn over whether to bring students back into the classrooms and the dorms, and over how and which students to welcome and which to keep away, this kid of mine decided that what she most needed was a HOME that she could put her belongings in, that no one could take away. She rented an apartment with a roommate near campus, arranged the utilities and Internet, got rental insurance, and bought a used scooter that she paid for partially with her savings (we helped). Her university could decide to shut its doors completely if it needs to, but Avery decided that as long as she is in charge of where she lives, she'll be all right.

8. *Seek resources and supports.* After the acute thing or news is behind you—you're away from your abuser; you've had your last day at work; your loved one has died; you are living with a scary diagnosis; your relationship has ended; you're rebuilding the thing that was wrecked—you're ready to get some counseling to help you process what happened and think through its impact on you and what you'll do next. You need to talk through what happened, otherwise it will always reside in your psyche as a trauma that can then impact future relationships, future decision-making, and your ability to regulate your emotions around others. A great resource for coping and developing the

resilience that will help you move on is the website OptionB.org, based on the book by the same name written by Facebook COO Sheryl Sandberg and her coauthor Adam Grant following the tragic sudden death of Sheryl's husband.

9. *Learn your lessons.* If the thing happened to you out of no fault of your own (say you got a scary diagnosis, a natural disaster hit, a loved one died) the lessons will come later; there will be things you come to appreciate more than before, strength you didn't realize you had. If you actively did the thing that landed you in this heap of trouble (say you committed a crime, did a bad thing, took a stupid risk), on top of the lessons noted above, you will also need to take time to process what you did that you probably shouldn't have done, and what you're going to do differently should you find yourself in a similar situation in the future. My friend Lisa, whom we'll hear more from shortly, is an alcoholic, and years into recovery she sometimes still wants that drink. One key lesson she has learned and repeatedly reminds herself of is: "I don't need to make matters worse *today*."

10. *Do the ongoing recovery work.* This is my nod of deep respect to the millions who struggle with alcoholism and other forms of addiction and are doing the recovery work. In the stories section of this chapter you'll read about Lisa, who found the ongoing support of Alcoholics Anonymous to be the only thing that reliably gets her through really tough times. If you are an addict, a twelve-step program—AA or one of its brother and sister programs, such as Narcotics Anonymous, Overeaters Anonymous, and Gamblers Anonymous—might be the way to go for you. You'll be in community with others who can help you feel seen and can remind you how to use the steps and help you get your life back together again.

11. *Prune the toxicity and get rooted in something new.* My dear friend Donnovan (whom we met in chapter 3, "You're Not Perfect," and

chapter 9, "Take Good Care") advises that in times of great strug-gle, "We learn that our time is limited, so being picky about who we give our time to is essential. Prune toxic people and situations from your life and surround yourself with people who energize, support, and challenge you (in good ways), and who inspire you to do the same for them, whether romantically, platonically, or professionally. Learning to prioritize one's time this way is one of the keys to fulfillment." This doesn't mean shutting down or clos-ing off the world, Donnovan notes. It's about developing healthy boundaries so that you can have more energy to give to the things that matter more to you.

When recovering from a bad situation, it can also help to find something new to devote your time and energy to. A hobby that you enjoy that you want to get better at. That skill or language you've always said you wanted to learn. Deepening some rela-tionships. Use your sharpened perspective on what really mat-ters in life to drive toward something that creates more meaning and enjoyment for you. Remember Ashley from chapter 7, "Start Talking to Strangers," whose mother died when she was twenty-four? Her decision to join The Dinner Party, the organization for people in their twenties and thirties who are grieving the loss of a loved one, was a vehicle that helped her move on from this trauma.

12. *Help others.* Perhaps the best thing you can do when you come out of something terrible is to commit to being there for others. A friend of Dan's named Richard lost his daughter in a kayaking accident—something they had always enjoyed doing together—when she was in her twenties. It has been years since the accident, but Richard is no less distraught about it. When I ask him how he is, he says, "I'm alive today," and he means it. He's saying he's mak-ing the choice to live, today, when there is the constant thought "If I just leap, she'll be there." Richard plows his grief into nurturing others who are grieving. He's a counselor at Kara, the grief coun-seling organization where I sought help way back when, which

also offers one-on-one support in addition to the group session I was a part of. When you understand the experience of searing emotional pain, you can be of profound use to others. And, doing for others will help you feel purposeful and good about yourself. But keep in mind, you don't have to become a counselor or therapist or a volunteer in order to help others. Just keeping track of all that research you did and of the lessons you learned the hard way means you can be there for the next person who goes through the awful something. It's an awesome feeling to be a trusted other for someone else.

My friend Donnovan is also a volunteer counselor at Kara. When he was thirty-nine, his youngest daughter, Micah Mei, died suddenly, when she was not yet two. I've known Donnovan since we were eighteen, and I've always known him to care deeply for others. But it seems to me that in enduring what is called "The Worst Loss," he has become even more compassionate toward the suffering of others. He has a practice of keeping track of the dates on which friends' loved ones died. "Each week, I turn the page on my little green checkbook calendar—contacting those who have lost a loved one. Each time, creating the time and the space for remembering."

DON'T JUST TAKE MY WORD FOR IT

MEET CASEY—Rebuilding His Life After Prison

On June 17, 2014, Casey was a seventeen-year-old high school graduate who was madly in love with his girlfriend, Hailey. "She and I were sitting by a river, smoking marijuana, and having one of those open, vulnerable conversations. We got into a pretty heavy conversation about her past drug use and my past drug use. And at one point she looked at me and said as genuinely as possible that she had gotten clean before, and gotten reconnected with her family, and it was the happiest time of her life, and she didn't know how she'd gotten back to this point. I just looked at her and felt myself trying to say, *That's what we're going to do from now on. We're going to put this all down. Let's do that.* But the words were just holed up at the bottom of my throat and wouldn't come out."

Three days later, Casey's world came crashing down. He was arrested for distribution of cocaine and spent the next year of his life in prison in Walker County, Georgia, near the border with Tennessee. Hailey was with him that day, and the last time he saw her she was handcuffed with her head between her knees, sobbing. This isn't the circumstance many associate with a kid like Casey, who is white, upper middle class, and grew up "in an excellent household with nothing but love and support and care" on the outskirts of metro Atlanta. I met him through his mother. He was journaling while incarcerated and was looking for someone to give him some feedback on his writing and I agreed to be a resource for him. Now, five years after he and I first connected, he's out of prison and we're talking on the phone about what he went through.

Casey tells me he never fit in at his "preppy" high school. "It was a high-income area. A lot of parents were CEOs of companies. Kids referred to their homes as mansions. They wore nice clothes, were very into sports, seemed to subscribe to a very fixed identity. Everybody drove a Jeep or truck with nothing to haul. It was a very pre-fraternity, pre-sorority lifestyle, which came with a certain stigma toward others. Me myself I could never grasp it. That's how I found myself bouncing around the outskirts of that, trying to figure out how and where I fit in. I was someone in search of myself. Bounced from the nerd crowd to the music crowd to the sports crowd to the drug and less-than-positive-role-model crowd. But didn't really feel like I truly connected or belonged in any of them. My life always felt like a catch-up. It was a chase to find myself somewhere when I felt so lost. I dealt with a lot of really deep downs."

Casey's family had money; that wasn't the source of his struggle. "Looking back on it, a lot of things boiled down to an insecurity with women. I felt like I was always good *enough* for something, or to be a part of something, but I was never just good, or the best, or never fit in well." He had a relationship the first year and a half of high school with a girl who went to another school. "Because of her I felt that that particular insecurity of being just good *enough* was handled, because I had someone who cared about me."

By senior year Casey's life "revolved around drugs," including using and dealing cocaine, marijuana, and mushrooms. He met Hailey that spring. She went to a different high school but they had a friend in common, and one day in March of senior year they were all together on the lake. "She and I ended up sitting and talking on the beach until three a.m. It was beautiful, and connected, and emotional, and from that day on we were just inseparable. She was one of the first people that checked all the boxes for me. I found her very attractive. But also from that initial communication with her, based on whatever we were talking about at the very beginning—how great it was to be out of high school, or what our plans were, or what have you—I felt that emotional intimacy, that openness. I felt that I could trust her to have that openly deep emotional conversation from the very beginning. I've always defined myself as a hyper-emotional person. I think deeply, feel deeply, love deeply. She's one of the first people I found who was receptive to that. It didn't freak her out, scare her, or push her away." Hailey's life revolved around drugs, too, and it was a big component of their relationship.

"More than likely what we were talking about was just fear. We were just about to graduate from high school. I was at that point selling a lot of drugs. I had plans to go to college and to be something, but I couldn't put my finger on what that was. I didn't know what I wanted to do, what I was going to become, and who I would be sharing that next journey with. While everyone else had that glorious release of graduating high school and throwing your cap up, I didn't really feel that, because my life was in a chokehold by the drugs that I was doing and selling and this false persona that I had assumed myself into. I was able to break down that barrier of the drug dealer persona with Hailey, and what was left was somebody who didn't know who he was or what he wanted."

Hours before Casey got busted, he'd taken Hailey to get her ears pierced. Then they went to a strip-mall parking lot where Casey sold cocaine to one of his regular customers: a friend's father who was fifty years old. On this particular day the man was wearing a wire and seconds after exiting the man's car Casey was surrounded by DEA agents. He took a plea deal that came with a seven-year sentence of which he would serve two years, which would further be reduced to one year because he was in a first-time-offender program. Days before his eighteenth birthday he was booked into Walker State Prison, a multicultural though largely white facility about a three-hour drive from home. "I was terrified of what would happen to me."

I ask Casey how he coped on the inside. "I made up fantasies about getting out. I remember calling my mom and screaming on the phone with her about Hailey, and where she was, and how I wanted to talk to her. When I look back today, through the entirety of the prison sentence, I was enveloped in Hailey. She was my source of hope and inspiration to get out and do better. It was much easier to deal with all these scary feelings of being in an adult penitentiary by packaging that into the feeling of losing a woman and wanting her back."

A man named Scott befriended Casey, and within the context of abject fear and bewilderment at what was happening, Casey felt he could trust Scott. "I think he had a son the same age as me who had been in trouble before. I have a really big thing with eyes. The look in Scott's eyes and how genuinely he cared when he was taking me under his wing, reassured me. He helped me formulate a plan and derive a sense of hope out of this craziness."

Casey began writing letters to Hailey's mother in the hope that Hailey would end up receiving them. "I wrote letter after letter after letter. Eventually, Hailey's mother wrote back and said she was sharing it all with Hailey. That was enough to get me through another four or five months. Hailey's mother had mentioned how beautifully she thought I wrote and that I should do that for myself as well. That inspired me to write my own journey."

And this is where my story intersects with Casey's. One day Casey might want to apply to community college, and these introspective essays he was writing might help. I was reading his drafts and giving him feedback. "We had community meetings, just like in *Orange Is the New Black*," Casey remembers. "One day about nine or ten months into my sentence, little eighteen-year-old Casey decides to get up in front of three hundred prisoners and read this paper that he rewrote fifty-five times about what he thought it was to be a man. I remember at that point standing as absolutely vulnerable as I could be. You could hear a pin drop in that room as I was reading. When I finished, three hundred prisoners gave me a standing ovation. I stood in front of that podium and bawled my eyes out in front of these people. That led me into a journey of wanting to help these other people."

I'm struck by the implicit lesson here. Take your suffering, be vulnerable and humble about it, and turn it into something where you can be of service to others.

"All kinds of guys wanted to tell their story. Some came up to me boldly.

Others came in such a shy manner they couldn't even talk. But they wanted to do the same thing. They wanted to put their life story on a piece of paper. A lot of them didn't have the same upbringing I did. Many of them couldn't read or write. I had them put as many notes and thoughts and things together as they could. A lot of times it was fifteen pieces of scattered notes on pieces of paper and I would put that together on a single page or two pages and tell their story based on what they told me. I remember hearing them on the phone reading these papers to their wife or their kids or their mother. Or having someone else read it for them. I remember them bawling and the people on the other side of the phone crying. It was very, very impactful to be in such a dark place and fashion some sort of light out of that. When I was in prison, there was fear and there was depression and every negative emotion that you can think of, but helping those men to get their stories on paper? That was everything."

Originally Casey's plan was to write a book that would include all these people's stories once he got out. He hasn't done that so far. But he still might.

Casey got out of prison in August 2015, shortly after he turned nineteen. His parents' connections enabled him to quickly get a part-time job at the marina where his parents kept their boat. When the summer season dwindled he prepared to enroll in the spring semester at Kennesaw State University, just north of Atlanta, with a major in journalism.

Things went downhill fast. "I had just been through this huge very scary and emotional thing, and I was sitting in freshman classes with people acting like freshmen do, talking about who can buy them alcohol and things. And even though my prison journey was different from most people, I still had that defensiveness, that hardness inside of me. I wasn't able to connect with anyone." His housing situation wasn't great, either. He didn't get on-campus housing and ended up in an off-campus apartment with men in their thirties and forties as roommates. "I didn't have a college experience." Now twenty-four, I can hear in his voice that he so deeply wanted to connect with people and couldn't. "I was back to that high school me. I wanted to be a normal college kid, whatever that meant. Drink and party and be carefree like the rest of them. I did slip here and there with alcohol. Ended up getting a DUI because of that. Spiraled out of control." Casey lasted about two semesters at Kennesaw, "and then couldn't do it anymore."

A friend got him a sales associate position at Sprint, a role he was very good at, and he was soon made a manager. "At that point in my life I had this force behind me. I had been through the whole prison thing and I didn't make it in college, so I had this ambition to make something of myself. I wanted to overcome. A less flattering way to look at it is I wanted to prove to everyone who saw me fall that I could be as successful as the people who didn't go through that. Even today a part of me is driven by that. I want to be great, and I'm grinding for it."

He hit a glass ceiling at Sprint and it was time to move on. He applied for several high-paying "dream jobs" at banks. On paper the banks were interested in him, and he did very well in the interviews. But it seems his felony conviction caught up with him. (Even though as a first-offender his records are to be sealed, the banks seem to have found out.) So, after a year he moved to his current position at an optical retailer. "I wanted a company where I could climb the corporate ladder if I was willing to do the work. I got here and I fell in love with optics. I manufacture, cut, and inspect pairs of glasses, assess patient needs and things like that. I'm a pharmacist of the glasses world. I've really latched onto it."

And Casey is still, as he puts it, "grinding and trying to come up in the company." On top of being an optician and manager, he's a nationally certified dispenser of glasses. "I purchased a program that walked me through the certification. It's volumes of information. I bought the textbooks, read them, and studied, studied, studied, then went online and took the test." There's a tone to his voice that is deeper than excitement: it's satisfaction.

Casey supports himself, lives with his best friend (a guy he met while working the job at the marina), and things are "stronger than they've ever been" with his parents. He's not in therapy. "It didn't quite take for me. I wasn't as open and honest as I need to be." But he is religious. He's gone from a childhood of Catholic-on-Sundays to "jailhouse religion," which he describes as "you've never believed in God but now you open a Bible and start praying as a coping mechanism when you're in prison." Since his release, he's been baptized into Christianity.

He doesn't have a significant other. "I was in a relationship when I got out, but it was toxic. Right now, it's important that I continue to build myself. Without solidifying who I am and what I want and what direction I want to take, all of those insecurities (the feelings of hopelessness, loss, and depression) will resurface. If I'm not sure of myself, that insecurity gets projected on someone else and that's not fair to either of us. My difficult realization is that it's not the right time for me to be in relationship until I can build something meaningful within myself."

Casey observes others in order to learn more about how to move forward in life the way he wants to. On a recent night at 11 p.m. he got a Snapchat message from someone in his old high school crowd who was "drunk as can be" and begging Casey to come see him in the city. "I would be damned if I was going anywhere, because I have a job and responsibilities," Casey says. He woke up the next morning to a text saying the kid got a DUI. "I am at a very interesting vantage point, where I can have intellectual conversations with successful adults and see what steps they're taking. I can also see the people I've left behind who are in the vicious toxic cycle I was able to break free from. I can see what decisions I'm supposed to make and which ones I'm not supposed to make. Keeping an eye on that is key. I can have a bad day at work—and I know one person will bitch and whine about having a bad day whereas someone else will say I had a stressful day but I was able to get a lot done. Just knowing of that shift of attitude shows me I can formulate a path for myself."

He continues, "If I was talking to my eighteen-year-old self I would warn him that perspective is very easy to lose. I would say I felt so lost that I didn't know what turn to take or what step to make next, and eventually things became a lot more clear, but what I had to do was do what I know is right. I had to start to formulate a life for myself. Start building myself in whatever manner gave me an identity. I was lost for so long. I had to close the door on the spiral of drinking and drugs that made me feel so good and allowed me to overcome my insecurities, but during all that time I was stagnant. Being able to take some responsibility myself was the way forward, even if it was just cleaning the house or paying a bill. Piece by piece I was able to construct a life and when I had some semblance of structure, I could sit down and say, I know what I can do next, but what do I *want* next? For someone who was lost for so long, setting that intention is very important."

I tell Casey that it sounds like he finally knows who he is, and that I'm happy for him. "Sometimes you have to go through hell to know who you are. I feel I embody that daily."

MEET AMEERA—Surviving the Death of Friends, and Cancer

Life taught Ameera to hate her birthday—twice. She grew up in a Chicago suburb as the youngest of three children of Pakistani Muslim immigrants. Her family had a hardscrabble start in America, but by the time Ameera came along, they were leading a middle-class life. On the night of her seventeenth birthday, the celebration turned to tragedy when two of her friends died in a car crash. Then on her twenty-fifth birthday, she felt a lump in her breast, which turned out to be cancer. These experiences gave her two options: "Wallow or grow." I met Ameera through her older brother, a physician in my town who admires how his little sister dealt with so much adversity at a relatively young age. When he heard about this book he encouraged me to hear her story. I was delighted when Ameera agreed to speak with me.

The car crash "changed everything." She takes me through the events of that night so that I can better understand. "It was August 15, 2010. We went home from the Cheesecake Factory. None of us drank or anything like that. The friends I lost were two guys. One was my first crush. His sister called me that night, asking 'Where's my brother, he's not back yet.' I said, 'Maybe he's at the gym?' She called back two hours later hysterical. 'The car flipped over. He burned. He died.' I went to my sister's room, broke down, called my parents, called my brother. That feeling in your stomach when something bad happens? I had that for months afterward. I haven't even had those feelings with cancer. It was waking up every day and thinking, *Oh my god, is this real?* In hindsight, no one understood what I was going through. I wish my parents had given me someone to talk through the trauma with, but I had to navigate it by myself. I had guilt. It was *my* birthday they were driving back from. I was dealing with the *why* and *what if* piece. Going through such a big loss and coming up with answers on my own, I remember thinking, *This has made me so much more mature than my other friends or than how I was before.* It's really what started my becoming an adult process."

There was more. Shortly after losing her friends, Ameera's mom developed breast cancer (which she would survive). Then a few months later, a beloved uncle died of cancer. "These crises were a back-to-back kind of thing. I'd always thought that problems like death and cancer were adult problems. But once you go through them you realize: *Maybe I am an adult* and *I'm going to have these problems come up* and *How do I deal with it.*" These life events forced Ameera to ask bigger questions sooner than she otherwise might have. Questions like, *What am I supposed to be doing?* and *Why do things happen?*

Ameera went off to college at the University of Illinois Urbana-Champaign with these questions in mind, and she majored in psychology. She'd always been into makeup and beauty, so when she was nineteen and a sophomore, she began blogging and posting photographs with simple captions on Instagram, like, "I did this makeup today." It was the early days of Instagram. She started getting noticed by brands, bloggers, and other artists. "But I didn't want to be another beauty blogger." So, she titled her blog *Beauty Beneath* and began to write about deeper issues such as colorism, weight, and how women judge one another about wearing too much makeup or not enough. She reached twenty thousand followers, and got invited to events hosted by Lancôme, Chanel, and other beauty brands. She knew that to get to the next step she needed to "put her whole life out there" because "people want to feel like your friend, and the bloggers you like the best are the ones you feel you know intimately."

She began getting sucked into the virtual world. She calls it "curating your life to be what people want to see, and doing things just to get a picture." She'd imagined that she'd like it if people recognized her in public but when they did, it actually made her feel a bit uncomfortable. One day while still in college, she was having a conversation with her brother about her long-term goals, and realized that she wanted to become a therapist. Then she started to worry that her blogging persona might get in the way of that. "If someone found my Instagram and blog they might not take me seriously or might be hesitant to come to me. I decided I didn't want my whole life to be on the Internet. It was too much. I wanted privacy back." She wrote a message to her following, then took her account private. She wanted to continue writing but didn't know how.

Ameera graduated from college in 2015, and in 2017 she began a master's program in clinical psychology at the Chicago School of Professional Psychology. At midnight on August 15, 2018, her twenty-fifth birthday, she felt a lump in her breast. Her mom, having recently beaten back breast cancer herself, came over right away and confirmed that it was indeed a lump. They called Ameera's brother, the doctor, on the phone, and he said it was probably just a fibroadenoma. Ameera got a doctor's appointment the next day and was reassured that there was a 90 percent chance it was nothing, but they would biopsy it just in case. "Everyone was wrong," she tells me.

The biopsy showed she "only" had DCIS (ductal carcinoma in situ), which is called pre-breast cancer, and "Stage Zero." It's not nothing, but it is the kind of news you want when you find a lump in your breast. Her doctor said, "Time is not of the essence." Still, Ameera asked for a second opinion, which turned out to be lifesaving. The second doctor determined she'd been incorrectly biopsied. That she was *not* at stage zero. That her cancer could be aggressive. "I freaked out. How is one doctor saying something so different from the other?" Her surgeon removed the lump and biopsied the lymph node; the biopsy showed the cancer was Stage 2B and invasive. "It went from nothing to a big something. Now time *was* of the essence." She had to worry about her receptor status with the hormones estrogen, progesterone, and HER2. Being positive on any of these means your cancer is going to grow more slowly, but she was "what's called a 'stage-two triple negative'—negative on all three receptors—which meant an eighty percent five-year prognosis. It kept getting worse and worse and worse."

Her physician brother pushed for full-body scans for Ameera—to get a look at everything—something doctors don't like to do because it tends to cause patients anxiety. "We did it for peace of mind, and we were able to confirm that it was just *that* tumor and *that* lymph node." The only treatment for triple negative was aggressive chemo. "The chance of recurrence is big in the first three years, so you have to have a lot of monitoring. After three years, you're someone regular with breast cancer, and after five years you're a normal person." I was talking to her about six months into all of this, when she was focused on doing a "cold-capping" technique to try to save her hair, and soldiering on to complete her master's degree.

Ameera realized that losing her friends in that horrific crash eight years earlier was helping her handle the "why is this happening/why me" aspect of her cancer diagnosis. "I hate when people say, *What's meant to be happens*, or *This is your fate*. Being able to say that to someone is a privilege. I really don't like that answer. I tried to find another logic to make myself feel better.

"Life isn't fair," she tells me. I tell her I agree. "You're put in a situation because if there is something you're longing for, whether to be a stronger person, smarter person, whatever it is, you're not going to get it handed to you; you're going to have to go through something to make yourself be like that. The takeaway from my friends passing away was being able to learn how to cope. I've always wanted to have more purpose or meaning to my life. So, I hope when I'm on the other end of the cancer, I'll have reached some sort of perspective or meaning. The biggest thing for me is having a positive impact on the world. My friends impacted me. Their deaths taught me to value life more. Maybe I can impact others going through adverse experiences because they've seen me go through it or read my blog or talked to me, or because getting through cancer made me a better therapist. I'll have that in my tool belt."

You don't expect a twenty-five-year-old to get cancer, and when you're the person having that unique experience it "makes things more scary," says Ameera. Along the way she was comforted by reading other people's cancer experiences. "Whether they're similar or different, reading them makes you feel, *Okay, I'm not the only one* and *you'll get through this.* It's not like, *It's not a big deal, it happens to everyone,* but just to feel that other people have made it through makes things easier."

She resumed blogging to be that person who can help others feel less alone. "I started a new blog called *Every Day's Ameeracle,* where I decided to be open about my cancer experience. It's been rewarding in a lot of ways. People will say they learned something, or that it helps them feel connection." Her new blog got a lot more traffic than the first one ever did and was shared all over the world. "People are more interested in what I have to say. I have a different kind of following." As she approached her first chemo treatment, she tweeted Mindy Kaling from *The Office* and *The Mindy Project* and got an extremely kind and supportive reply that made her day.

Ameera has gained a lifetime of perspective. "People who've had cancer can tell you what matters and what to focus on. We can say, *Your boyfriend of two months dumping you is not going to make or break your life. There are other things to focus on. If you want that certain job, do it.* You know what matters. Having cancer has been a lot but it's not all bad. You appreciate normalcy more. I can look back and appreciate being with family, going to college, traveling to Europe with my friends. If you don't have the sad moments, you don't really know what the happy moments feel like. When I hear my friends say, 'Oh my gosh, this sucks, I wish I could die,' I cringe. My taste buds got messed up, and I couldn't imagine what it would be like to be normal and eat normal food. And then I got better, and I had Pizza Hut, and it tasted normal, and I am like, *This is amazing.*"

Experience has revealed her friends' true colors. "Some have been great while others have not. Usually I would be bothered by the latter," Ameera says, which is another example of gaining perspective. "You realize that everyone's a little bit selfish. The majority of my friends have stepped up or gone above and beyond. Some come over and take naps with me! But a handful have been disappointing. People say, 'Let me know if you need anything,' but if you actually let them know, they'd probably have an excuse for why they couldn't help you. The day I was diagnosed, I texted a friend from college whom I'd known for seven years. She replied, 'That sucks. Did you start treatment?' I didn't hear from her for a month, and then finally she texted, 'How are things?' And I said, 'I was wondering where you have been.' And she said, 'Just because you are vocal about your problems doesn't mean other people don't have things going on in their life. Other people have problems too.' I said, 'I hope you're getting the support you need, and I hope you talk to people about it.' And I never heard from her again."

Having had her own disappointment with a few friends, she's more ready to show up for others in a manner that helps rather than harms. "I'm able to sense when something could be wrong, then kind of acting on it." She's learned that people don't want to hear "I understand" or "Oh my gosh, I can imagine," and that it's better to say, "I don't understand, I can't imagine. But I will listen and try to understand what you have to say." She says she's become far more able to intuit the needs of others. "In general, with friends and family I've become hyperaware of what's going on with them, and I'm the one they'll call if something is wrong. I'm always trying to help people talk through things. If I hadn't gone through any of my experiences, I wouldn't have that perspective. Everyone is different. But having perspective gives you the knowledge on how to comfort others."

I really relate to this. After losing my brother Stephen and Daddy within a span of eighteen months when I was in my mid to late twenties, I learned the language of grief. Ever since then I've been determined to show up for any friend who has just lost someone, because I'm able to ask, *How are you doing?* and really wait on that answer.

So, in that spirit of asking the tougher questions and being willing to hear tough answers, I ask Ameera how her cancer battle is going. "It's been hard, but it hasn't been earth-shattering. For instance, the chemo hasn't been as bad as I expected based on the movies! It's an hour or two at the hospital. The hardest thing has been losing my hair. Not for aesthetic reasons, but hair is a big security blanket. I'm doing this process called 'cold-capping,' putting ice packs on my scalp before and after chemo, to try to save my hair, so I stay at the hospital much longer than I would otherwise."

I ask her what's been shitty about all this. "At twenty-five, I don't think I should be going through something like this. Twenty-five is out of college, exploring, having an opportunity to travel, and time to relax. I'm limited. I can't travel. I'm tied to something and can only move limitedly. Literally and figuratively." I ask what she means. "Literally, I'm not allowed to go anywhere because I'm immuno-compromised. I can't go on a plane, can't go to a place with lots of germs because I'll get sick, my white blood count will go low, then I can't get chemo. Figuratively I'm stuck in that I can't really plan anything. People will sit and imagine what they're going to do. Not that I'm not going to have opportunities in the future but I don't have the mental bandwidth to focus on anything beyond the cancer and my work and my internship. There is no room for other imagining. It's only been five months and I can't really imagine a life without cancer."

I ask her what she's learned, and am not surprised to hear an answer filled with agency and resilience. "You need to be your own advocate in terms of your experience with doctors. Not that you can't trust them, not that they don't have your best interests at heart, but I have done as much research as I could without having gone to med school. I've read three-hundred-page studies. Everything you can find on the Internet. Whenever I meet with doctors, they laugh because I already know everything. If you're going through something medically, you should know it as much as you can.

"No one is going to know you best besides yourself. If you have an instinct or a gut feeling, there's a reason you're having it. Explore why you're having it. Figure out why. Ever since I found that lump, I one hundred percent knew something was really wrong, that I was going to be having chemo, and that I would have to freeze my eggs. You need to be confident in learning the truth about what you think because you don't want to find something out in ten years that *oh shit*, you could have dealt with back then when it was manageable and now it's too late. You'd rather be wrong about something and have done everything to find out that truth than to find out your gut was right after it's too late. This applies to everything. Like starting a career and you think, *Oh, you know, I have this idea, but I'm not going to do it because it's stupid*, then someone else does it and then it's too late for you. Carpe diem. If you need to do something, you need to do it now."

When we spoke, Ameera was in her second-to-last semester of her master's program in clinical psychology. She'd told her faculty, "I'm not going to stop my life until I need to." She missed a lot of class because of chemo but she was getting through. "I'm doing as much as I can and taking time off as needed." Her best friend got married days after Ameera first felt the lump in her breast. "I still danced at her wedding, still enjoyed it ninety percent as much as I would have had I not been going through the cancer thing. I thought, *My best friend is only going through this once. I don't want to regret the experience in the future, thinking, man, I was so bummed out.*

"I'm letting cancer take up a lot of my life, but I don't want to let it take up more than it needs to. I'm living my life as best I can." Her boyfriend has been amazing. She met him on "Minder" (Muslim Tinder) three years before her diagnosis, and he lives in California near her brother. "After my mom, he has been my biggest support. We talk twenty-four/seven. We FaceTime. We text. He's a very big piece of helping me feel normal. Recently, he was here for three days, and I literally forgot I was sick. He doesn't smother me or constantly ask how I am, but he's mindful of what's going on. All we did was sit and watch movies and eat food. He's not pushing me to do things, but he's not treating me like I'm on my deathbed, either."

I ask her what "normal" now feels like. "I can't travel. I'm losing my hair—even with cold-capping it's like sixty percent gone. I think I'll be hesitant to go out to nice dinners. Beyond that I'm still planning to be a full-time student, and I can miss class as needed. Even going to work, going to the mall, watching a movie and stuff makes me feel more normal. Very normal things are my favorite things these days. Eating pizza, things that other people would think are boring, I just love that stuff now. It's a privilege to be able to be bored and have nothing going on."

I'm pleased to say that although the shit most definitely hit the fan for Ameera, life goes on. When I checked in with her closer to the publication of the book I got this response: "Life is good. I'm officially one and a half years cancer free, thank God. My hair's grown into a bob. I've lost my chemo weight. I got my master's (on time) last year after completing treatment. I'm working as a licensed professional counselor, which has been fun. Life is very different than when we last spoke!" Rounding the bend to her twenty-eighth birthday, Ameera can both celebrate the joy of another year spent on earth and the miracle of modern medicine while working through the lingering sadness of that day.

MEET LISA—Coping by Working the Program and Achieving Sobriety

I want to give you a heads-up that this story refers to sexual abuse and life-threatening physical violence.

On the Fourth of July last year, a high school classmate named Lisa (not her real name) posted on Facebook that it was the twentieth anniversary of when her boyfriend tried to kill her. I reached out. It had been over thirty-five years since we'd last seen each other. We were never good friends, but we were in choir together throughout high school and I'd always liked her and found her to be kind.

Lisa is a fifty-three-year-old white woman who was born and raised in Wisconsin and has lived there for most of her life. At forty-nine she earned a master's in marriage and family therapy from Edgewood College, in Madison, and she now works as a therapist in Washington State. While Lisa has always been that person to whom others turned for emotional support with their trauma, it's her own story of trauma that I'm focusing on here. She's had the shit hit the fan in every sense of that word and has not just survived but thrived.

I could fill an entire book with the abuse Lisa suffered: at the hands of immediate family members before she even started kindergarten, and from boyfriends, strangers, and husbands. I cannot do justice to her experiences or her pain in the space available here. But to give you context for what will ultimately lead to her sobriety, which is the focus of this piece, here are some brief details about Lisa's life.

The second-youngest of six children, Lisa was abused and practically discarded by her parents early in life. "I walked many blocks to and from my mother's best friend's house when I was four and wondered, *Why didn't anyone care where I was?* I had lot of shame around that. My siblings and I were afraid of our father but were never there for each other. We just disassociated and fended for ourselves." She was stealing alcohol from her parents' liquor cabinet regularly by age ten. "I liked it because it hurt when it went down." At twelve she was raped by an older boy she thought was her friend. At fourteen when she told her mother she wanted to kill herself, "She got my dad's hunting pistol, stuck it into my face, and said, 'Get dressed and go to school.' I remember telling myself it was not safe to have feelings anymore. I just shut down." She began doing drugs and having sex with older men. Senior year, she transferred to an alternative school after getting arrested and publicly humiliated at our school. When administrators at this new school called her mom in for a conference to discuss the fact that Lisa wanted to go into a drug treatment program, her mother grabbed her afterward and said, "Don't ever embarrass me like that again."

"I had been through so much by the time I was seventeen I just vowed I would never treat another person the way that I've been treated. I can sense when somebody doesn't feel good. I would go to the underdog, to the person who had been beat up. I was always that person." This gives me so much to reflect on. In high school, I'd see Lisa in that small group of students who smoked cigarettes outside the main entrance, and we always made eye contact and said hi to one another. But I had no idea she was going through any kind of trauma. I was not, I realize, her friend.

Lisa would be flung out into the seas of life without so much as a sail or a rudder. She would have three husbands, all addicts in one form or another, in addition to that boyfriend who tried to kill her whom I read about on Facebook decades later. She would be diagnosed with three autoimmune diseases and be given medication for one of them, which she'd be deathly allergic to and which would bring her to within inches of her life. She would have three wonderful sons, one of whom would die tragically from asthma when he was eleven. "This was the worst thing that ever happened to me," she tells me, against the backdrop of an unyielding amount of trauma across the span of her years.

And in the middle of all this she would be a kind friend to other struggling young people, and become a regular at Al-Anon (the organization for friends and family of alcoholics), and support her family financially, and be a loving mother to her kids, and lend a supportive ear to strangers at the bus stop, and fend off abusers, and enter a relationship that was healthy, and graduate from college at thirty-nine, with honors, and become a teacher for struggling kids who needed "the resource room." When life was hard, she would go back to drinking, until it finally dawned on her that she was an alcoholic, too.

"I was going to Al-Anon regularly and was asked to be a speaker at a combined AA/Al-Anon meeting where there are always a lot of couples in the audience." She clarifies that in many couples the man is the alcoholic in AA, and the woman is in Al-Anon to deal with what it's like to be married to an alcoholic. "So, I'm telling my story, and I'm staring down at these couples, and in the middle of my speech I realize, *I'm telling the story of an AA person not an Al-Anon person.*" I don't get what she means, and I ask her to break it down for me. "I'm talking to them about my codependency, my addiction to addicts, how I get obsessed with their behavior and what they're doing. Then I find myself talking about my drinking and how my drinking had played a role in all of those relationships. And it came to me quite apparently, as I'm staring down at a lot of couples there—the men in AA, the females in Al-Anon—that I can't stay married for the life of me, I'm totally broke, I'm living with my mother of all people, I'm basically homeless, my life is going nowhere, and I'm disabled. That's where I had the bright light shining moment."

She could now say, "I'm an alcoholic." After the speech she had what she describes as a complete mental breakdown. "It was, *Oh my god, what am I doing to myself? I should not be drinking!* I remembered what it was like when I was sober and in school, and things were going well for me. I crawled to an AA meeting in my community. They welcomed me. They said, 'We're here for you, we know you're an alcoholic, welcome home.'"

Thanks to the people in the AA community, who are like family to her, Lisa would find her way to a feeling of safety and surety she had basically never known. She was about to reach her eleventh-year anniversary of sobriety when she and I talked on the phone.

"I'm an alcoholic. Alcohol and other drugs were my solution. When life gets really hard that's what I use to disassociate. To cope. There've been many times in the last eleven years where I've felt emotions I did not want to feel. But I'm very resilient, and I have a lot of faith, a belief that everything always works out the way it is supposed to, and that everything serves a purpose. Even when the worst thing that could ever happen to a person happened, the death of my child, that's when I devoted my life to service. There's nothing to be afraid of now. Each day really is a gift. I know it sounds corny but I don't push away the negative anymore. I embrace all parts of life. If I were to take away any part of my life, I wouldn't have the full life that I actually got to experience."

Lisa's not just *in* AA. She became an integral part of her clubhouse. For years she'd be the one to set up gatherings, buy the supplies, and make a Thanksgiving meal for fifty to sixty people. I ask her how she's doing now, amid COVID-19. "I'm eleven years sober yet I'm going to three meetings a day. That's what's so crazy about this disease. Once it's part of you, it has you. Jails, institutions, or death is how this disease ends—I lost a lot of friends just last year. Or sobriety. I want to die sober and I want to enjoy my life. Every time

I was drinking I was not enjoying my life. Every time my life was shit, I had been drinking. So, I go to a lot of meetings. Every day it's a seven thirty a.m. Al-Anon meeting, an Adult Children of Alcoholics (ACA) meeting at noon, and AA meetings at five thirty p.m. Every day. I go with a mask or via Zoom. Every day it's, *I don't need to make matters worse TODAY.*" (Yes, she's the friend who uttered this wisdom I quoted earlier!)

I tell her that people reading this might see a bit of themselves in her story and ask if she can share what an AA meeting feels like. "For years, people have told you to go to AA or ACA or Al-Anon and you just avoided it. But one day you wake up and decide that something's gotta give. It takes a lot of courage to be in the parking lot, get out of your car, and walk through that front door. You don't know if they're going to want to change you, if the people are depressed, if they're scary, if they're going to judge you, if there's something wrong with you. But if you're going to a meeting, you're not coming in on a high note. Something in your life is bad. The meeting is a door to hope, and it's often the last door on the block. So, you take that chance and you walk through that door and you meet people who have similar experiences to you, who offer friendship and compassion and brutal honesty about their experience, and that's inspiring. Twelve-step groups are the most real and inspiring people on the planet. If you want to get someone's truth you go there. You can take all the shame you've ever felt and dump it in the big spot in the middle of the chairs and leave it there. Those people are my family. My chosen tribe."

MEET ANTHONY—Healing Through a Profound Change in Perspective

Anthony is a fifty-four-year-old African American man from Stamford, Connecticut. He went to Tufts University and earned a master's in African studies at UCLA. He offers yoga to people from all walks of life. But little in his first eighteen years would have predicted the healed and healing life he lives today.

When Anthony was six months old, his mother took him to Mississippi and asked her parents to raise him. They did so until Anthony's grandmother got sick. Anthony was about five when his mother took him back up to Connecticut, but she was not able to provide him with much care. He was informally taken in by the family who lived next door, called the Harrises. First it was day care with the Harrises. Then day care turned into spending nights, which turned into staying for the weekend. Within months, Anthony became a ward of the state, which had declared him "neglected and homeless." The Harrises became his foster family. "I used to read to my older foster cousin when I was as young as six years old. He was really impressed with me. When I got to school, I was an A student, precocious. But I was diagnosed as ADHD and considered 'bad.' Mrs. Harris told the school, 'If he's bad in school call me, and when he comes home I'll whup his ass.'"

Coming up through elementary school and then up through junior high, Anthony watched his foster cousin graduate from Stamford High, yet the kid could barely read or write his name. "He was a nice guy. A state champion wrestler, three or four years in a row. Gregarious. They just passed him through. I looked at this and thought, *That's not the school I want to go to.*"

Anthony's caseworker was "a well-intentioned white woman" who visited him weekly. "When I was in eighth grade, I told her, 'Miss Moretti, I want to go to a private school.' She said, 'Oh, Anthony, foster children don't go to private schools.' I knew what she meant. She meant, *You little poor black boy, that's not for you. No one's expecting much of you.* My foster mother was illiterate. I knew no one else who could get me to a private school. But I knew this white woman could get me to the door. I had to educate her and position her to help me. My expectations for myself were much greater than her expectations for me."

Anthony was on a mission. "Every time she would come to the house, I would make the same statement. Finally, she got really upset and decided to show me how I was going to fail at achieving that dream. She did some research and came back with a list of ten schools. We discussed the pros and cons of each: Exeter, Andover, Hotchkiss… boarding and day schools. After going over the pros and cons of each, I said, 'Considering my circumstances, I don't want to go away. What do you think is the best considering my circumstances?'" Miss Moretti chose a local day school called King School for Anthony.

Anthony says, "If I wrote a book about the nice white people in my life, it reads like a horror story. Nice white people were telling me, 'This is your place.' Luckily, I never knew my place. Miss Moretti made me an appointment at King School, then she picked me up and drove me over there. I met the assistant headmaster, Mr. Draper. I knew I was dazzling him and his colleagues—this little black boy who was stringing together sentences where the noun and verb agreed. They waived the fee for the entrance exam and I passed with flying colors. They said, 'We're willing to give him a ninety-percent scholarship for four years, but the state has to come up with the remaining ten percent.' Well, the state didn't want to be upstaged by the school so they agreed to pay the ten percent each year. I ended up going to King School. Don't let anyone tell you who you are—you have to have a bigger idea of who you are than how society sees you. That was a pivotal experience."

After he graduated from this prep school, Anthony enrolled at Tufts University in Medford, Massachusetts. "At the prep school, I was used to being the big fish in the small pond. Knew how to kick these white boys' asses on the football field and in the classroom. Won the scholar-athlete award at King." He expected life to open up in front of him at Tufts. Instead, wherever he went—whether to class, to a party, or down the street to buy some food—all eyes were on him. And one night all hell broke loose. "Tufts let me know, *We don't care about how smart you think you are or how fast you are, you are a Nigger in our book. You can sit your ass down on that bench, and whatever you think you are good at we are going to take that from you.* Tufts had me questioning my humanity and my right to *be*. It came to a head when I was at a frat party and a fight broke out and someone called the cops. Within minutes, I was surrounded by eight police cars with guns drawn ready to shoot me on campus. That was the nadir of my experience at Tufts."

That experience broke Anthony. Fortunately, he was about to find a helper. "There was a Black woman professor of political science named Pearl T. Robinson. She saw me as a walking time bomb because I was so enraged by the way Tufts was treating me and by the way all of the racism in America was treating me, and she asked me to come to her office. When I walked in she asked a question that changed the course of my life: 'Have you ever thought about going to Africa?' It was such a powerful question coming from a woman I had great respect for that it interrupted my pattern of anger. The world just *stopped*. I asked her to repeat herself. She did. In that moment, I saw my whole life. I realized I had to get out of Tufts, out of Boston, out of Massachusetts, out of the East Coast, out of America, cuz I was *done*. I was ready to blow some shit up."

I know from my own experience as a Black American (who began life radically more privileged than Anthony) that many of us hail Africa as our motherland, locate her in our DNA, write of her in our narratives, dream of her in our dreams, that we drape Ghanaian kente cloth in our cultural rituals, and that

Africa sits out there as a beacon, beckoning, even if we're not really sure why. Among other reasons, it feels like a place where our skin color is not a stamp of inferiority. Anthony says he had to ask himself, "Where is Africa really?" And "How do I really get there?" Professor Robinson suggested a few summer programs he might apply to. He was accepted by Operations Crossroads Africa Inc., to go build a school in Kenya. "I had to raise three thousand two hundred and fifty dollars to go. I said to my friend Jeff, 'Let me get five dollars from you. I'm going to Africa.' He said, 'Where's your passport?' I didn't even realize I needed a passport. I took care of that. Raised the money no problem. Fellow college students kicked in. Adults. Churches. I held bake sales. Did car washes. You name it. My biggest donation came from a man named Mr. Hubbard, the father of one of the few other Black kids in my prep school, a man for whom I had tremendous respect. He apologized before he gave it to me, saying that he didn't have much money at the time. It was five hundred dollars. Obviously, I never forgot that. I went to Kenya, and turned twenty-two the summer I was there. It was the first major paradigm shift in my life."

Professor Robinson sensed that spending meaningful time on the continent of Africa might teach Anthony to love himself as a Black man. The professor was right.

Anthony's summer in the east African country Kenya was life-changing in the truest sense of the phrase. "Living in that Kenyan village, I was able to see myself and my potential and what I could be in the world completely differently. One young man spoke five languages, yet he looked up to me. Almost worshipped me. Called me his brother. He said, 'You come from this great country, America. Please tell me, my brother, how many languages do you speak?' I realized, *Wow, I'm the dumbest person in this village. I look good on paper, but I've been sold a bill of goods. I sipped the Kool-Aid.* I realized I was inadequate. I wanted to be a Renaissance man, but I was so far from being a Renaissance man. I sat down and wrote my life manifesto in that village. I was going to be multilingual, travel the world, and truly educate myself."

His time in Kenya was a major next step in Anthony's journey to transcend what America had in mind for him as a poor Black male child. "In addition to getting properly educated, I also wanted to heal myself from this anger and this rage. I'd been going two hundred and fifty miles per hour, and the wall was coming. I had to do something to prevent a collision. Living in this village, I was getting loved every single day. They opened my heart up. One day I was walking hand in hand with a grown man toward a meeting of the men in the village. It really made me uncomfortable. So, I feigned like there was a mosquito on my shoulder and I pulled away. He let me do that. Then he reached out and took my hand again. I felt, *Okay, I'm really uncomfortable with this, but you're in a different country, so just hold his hand, relax, no one's going to kiss you or have sex with you, just go with this.* We got to our final destination, this little place where the brothers would hang out. There was a tattered Ping-Pong table. A small light. I saw how they interact with each other, touching each other, so happy to see each other. I was like, *Wow, this is how they live.* It scared the shit out of me. But after two weeks I couldn't wait for my brother to come get my hand and just love me. I realized these people have a joie de vivre, they had a love that was oozing out of them every single day. They did not tire of me; they just loved me and loved me. I realized that's how I want to live. I want that in my life. I can see it, I can feel it, I can touch it. I realized I couldn't have that and be convicted in my rage. I had been wanting to destroy Tufts and America, but I realized I cannot have the joy and happiness AND the rage at the same time. I knew I had to get rid of the rage. I didn't know how, but I had to find a way. Realizing these brothers loved me unconditionally changed me profoundly."

Anthony graduated from Tufts with a degree in English literature, moved to DC, and landed a dream job at Africare, which does grassroots work in forty countries in Africa. They sent him back to Africa, first on a bunch of short-term assignments, then, after going to France to learn French, he landed a long-term gig: two and a half years in Niger. "Wherever I went was to heal," Anthony remembers. "The work was just my Trojan horse to get me there. In Niger, in the middle of the Sahara Desert, I met a one-hundred-and-five-year-old Sufi monk and learned how to breathe and meditate and find my center. I sat in a mud hut for two and a half years. I saw what was essential to live. I learned how to slow down and move with the rhythm of Mother Nature. That was the crux."

Anthony's job in Niger was to oversee a four-million-dollar USAID project focused on reclaiming natural resources that benefited ten thousand people in the surrounding villages. There in the desert, a lack of water wasn't the problem; the problem was how to get to it. In many areas the water table was a mere two meters below the surface of the sand. With the right equipment, farmers could locate the water and grow crops. In just one year, a place could go from arid to green, with crops of onion and millet. "Every day, I woke at about four thirty a.m. in my hut, which was the last hut in the village. I'd hop on my horse. Ride out in the desert a little bit. Come on back, sit down, and just watch the sunrise." By 7 a.m., it was too hot to be outside. He worked in the Africare office in the village when he had to, but mostly he worked in his hut, which was naturally kept cool by its "semi-dure" exterior (a mixture of cement, sand, straw, and cow dung). "I was entrusted with four million dollars. I would get tranches from headquarters saying we need another two hundred and fifty thousand dollars, and here's what we're going to do with it during the next six months. The buck stopped with me." He spent his days doling out food, water, horses, camels, trucks, gas, money, and supplies. "I made sure there was no embezzlement or misappropriation. People with a little power and say were used to taking advantage of the projects. Used to getting a little extra gas. I was like, *No, we're not going to sacrifice this whole village because you're accustomed to getting extra.* I took it very personally." As a little personal side project, Anthony used his own funds to make sure the kids in all of these villages had a decent school setup. "I got notebooks, pencils, and chalk to every classroom. Refurbished blackboards with cement, cow shit, and sand, and painted them black. I said that any teacher that was teaching would be supplied with food."

When sunset came each day, Anthony shut the work down and brought himself back to his center. He listened to Miles Davis on his boom box, which he powered with batteries. He listened to the tam-tams of the village. "The night was magnificent. With no electricity and few vehicles there was no pollution. The full moon in the desert was otherworldly. It just lit up the sand. I saw the stars. I saw the divots in the moon. I was at one with the universe. I would be in my little hut chilling out, and God would just whisper, *Hey Anth, come on out, man, and see what I did to the sky.*"

Six years after Anthony left Niger, his village got electricity. "I ended up going to ten countries in Africa. Also, spent four years in Asia, mostly Japan, China, Korea, and Vietnam. I traveled the world, healing myself, sitting at the feet of enlightened beings, peering in on longevity from cultures of antiquity. I came to appreciate that the experience I'd had in Kenya was something my brothers needed in the States. I knew I needed to bring this back to my brothers in America. For years this was in the back of my mind."

Unlike most people I've interviewed for this book, I happen to be speaking with Anthony in person. He's in my backyard, sitting in a wooden chair by my firepit. He looks at me with the piercing eyes of a human who is centered and clear, who knows himself and can really see himself, so isn't afraid to look others dead in the eye. I find it refreshing. It's an invitation to know and be known. He leaves me with this: "Don't let anyone tell you who you are—you have to have a bigger idea of who you are than how society sees you. My experience of systemic and interpersonal racism at Tufts almost killed me. At that time, I vowed I would dedicate my life to destroying universities like Tufts. Instead I went to Africa and Asia and sat at the feet of masters. Thirty years of self-reflection, healing, and transformation taught me this: it's not about Tufts and the like, it's about me. I learned how to access and consciously claim my power, keep my sanity and health, and hell, even thrive in the eye of the storm."

We'll hear what Anthony would go on to do with his life in chapter 12, "Unleash Your Superpowers."

IN SHORT: YOU WILL BE OKAY

Great pain comes for everyone at one time or another. So, if the shit hasn't hit your fan yet, it will. And if it already has? It probably will again. You may be sucked down into the bowels of hell. You might even get yourself into that pit through choices of your own. But you are more capable than you know. You have it in you to get up out of there and keep going. And to become a fuller version of yourself than you were before—more knowing, more empathetic, more resilient. And strong.

You want to be that fuller version of yourself, and the world wants that for you, too. The world is after all simply a collection of people doing their thing. And the world community would benefit from more of us having the wherewithal and inclination to look beyond ourselves and to ask, *How can I be of use? How can I make things better, for others?* Some say the very definition of adulthood is knowing that you have to care about more than just yourself. That's the part of adulthood where we're headed next.

Unpack and Reflect

- Who do I admire because of what they've been through?
- What are the toughest experiences I've ever personally dealt with?

What did I learn from them? How am I different because of those experiences?

- Think about a challenge you're experiencing right now, and what it means you CAN'T do. Reframe it and ask yourself: What CAN I do?
- When times have been really rough, who were the "trusted others" who were there for me? For whom am I a "trusted other"?

11

MAKE THINGS BETTER

(FROM YOUR TOWN TO THE WORLD BEYOND, WHY YOU SHOULD TRY)

The world is so fucked right now we don't have time for everyone to become perfect before they jump in and help.

—Jameela Jamil, actor

I thought I lived in a society. And I thought the definition of "society" was something to the effect of *individuals who come together for the common good.* So, in the months in which COVID-19 raged on in the United States while the rest of the world seemed to have been able to get it under better control, I was questioning what it even means to live in a society. Or whether the United States of America qualifies as one.

Clarice Cho is a twenty-six-year-old hand-lettering artist who doubles as my social media manager and executive assistant. In the spring of 2020, she and I were on our regular weekly call and we were talking about what it means to live in a society, within the context of the pandemic, and she shared her vantage point as a Chinese American on the fundamental differences between the two cultures. "In Chinese culture, it's collective over individual. That can be bad: Communism has notable drawbacks. But America is a selfish place in contrast. It's *I individually matter more than the good of the whole, so I'm not gonna wear a mask because I don't want to.*" Listening to Clarice I found myself wondering whether I was willing to trade a democratic society for a communist one in order to stop the spread of a deadly virus. This was a really depressing conversation.

As I was writing this book, we could very plainly see individualism eclipsing the needs of the collective whole in America—hundreds of thousands of people were dying from a virus that some other societies had managed to contain, and the economy was shrinking because people couldn't work, and people were losing their jobs and getting evicted from their homes, and on top of all that, unarmed Black people were being maimed and killed by law enforcement, and protesters were being assaulted by law enforcement for exercising their First Amendment rights, and on top of that the climate was clapping back, and on top of that we couldn't even count on the simple gift of a stranger smiling at us in a grocery store because their face was shrouded by a mask—so, all in all, I found it challenging to try to project confidence in these pages about *your* ability to make things better.

But nobody's here on this planet but us. A scary, shitty time that challenges our faith in humans and in society is precisely the time to dig deep and figure out how to make a massive positive shift. Never in my lifetime had this been more clear or true that while I was writing this book. In July 2020, President Obama delivered the eulogy for Congressman John Lewis—the legendary Black congressman, originally from Alabama, who represented Atlanta, who at age twenty-five was beaten by police while marching for civil rights in Selma, and who famously urged people to get into "good trouble." In his eulogy for Lewis, Obama urged us to "take up the unfinished work of the last generation." Wow, so much is unfinished. Much may never *be* finished, because in the sweeping symphony of human existence there is always another page to turn. But today, not tomorrow, we can see that things can and must be done to make things better. This book is called *Your Turn*, and that phrase is nowhere more urgent than in this chapter.

Believe me, I know the gall it takes for anyone older than you to say any of this. As I write this, young people across the nation are trying to lead us out of the bad situations that people in the Gen X, Baby Boomer, and so-called Greatest generations have failed to fix, or outright created. Please know that I'm not presuming to know more than you or anyone in your generation about the imperative to make things better. As I offer the simple point that people can, do, and must work to make things better, I speak with a large dose of humility on behalf of the older generations who have failed you.

YES, YOU SHOULD TRY

Somewhere deep inside of me I feel a connection to all other humans as if they are my own kin. I can't explain it better than that. (I know I'm not the only person who feels this way, but I also know that not everyone does.) I feel a physical unease at the thought of any of us not making it, not being okay, being left by the side of the road as the rest of humanity progresses forward. And although I know that with over seven billion of us on the planet—a population facing huge threats like climate change, systemic racialized violence, widening income inequality, hunger, and disease—it is impossible to ensure we all make it, I do believe quite strongly that those of us who have more in this life, whether it be education, access to opportunity, money, influence, ability, or time, should step in to try to help those who have less of those things.

This may seem like liberal garbage to you. You may believe it's on each individual to make whatever they can of their lives, period. That's fine. I'm not here to tell you what to believe. Remember, nobody has the right to tell you what to do with this one precious life of yours. My message in this chapter is simply this: regardless of your political persuasion or philosophical ideology, the world (or just your little corner of it) could really use your help. Even Ayn Rand, the paragon of Liberalism and Objectivism, whose philosophy boils down to *We have no obligation to others and we should serve our own self*, has said, "There is nothing wrong in helping other people, if and when they are worthy of the help and you can afford to help them."

Besides, even if you have zero feeling of duty or obligation to others, you should try to make things better in the world because doing so is good for *you*. Some call this "enlightened self-interest." In his book *Being Mortal: Medicine and What Matters in the End*, physician and author Atul Gawande cites the Harvard philosopher Josiah Royce in explaining that in order for us to feel at the end of our lives that our own life has been worthwhile, we need to seek a cause beyond ourselves to focus on. "The cause could be large (family, country, principle) or small (a building project, the care of a pet). The important thing was that, in ascribing value to the cause and seeing it as worth making sacrifices for, we give our lives meaning."

If you have enough privilege to be reading this book, there are people who could use your help and causes that could benefit from your hard work, time, dollars, and/or heart. I hope you'll find something beyond yourself to believe in. And I hope you'll give it your all.

FIND YOUR WHY

When I first read the 1973 U.S. Supreme Court decision in *San Antonio Independent School District v. Rodriguez*, I cried. I was an eighteen-year-old college freshman taking a political science class in which this case had been assigned. The original lawsuit had been filed by working-class parents who argued that Texas had a history of giving more money to the public schools in wealthier towns and less money to the public schools in poorer towns. The Supreme Court held that, while the facts were true, the U.S. Constitution doesn't regard education as a "fundamental right" (which would then necessitate giving it greater protection), and just because the funding scheme devised by Texas had a disparate impact on poor kids it doesn't mean it violates the Constitution's "equal protection clause" because wealth is not a "protected class" (which, if it was, would merit greater scrutiny into the potential unfairness). Reading and rereading this case, which emanated from Texas but described a reality in most of the fifty states, I thought to myself, *This is not how I want my country to be.* The amount of funds given to a public school district impacts among other things the quality of the teachers hired to teach there, the number of kids in each classroom, the types of courses taught, the resources and opportunities available in the school, and the quality of the building itself. I was sitting there in my dorm room at my elite university thinking, *If they give fewer dollars to the schools for the kids who already started life with less, how are those kids ever going to be able to compete? How is that fair?*

The *San Antonio v. Rodriguez* lawsuit was the reason I went to law school. The reason I marched and voted for more funding for California's public schools over the years. The reason I served on the board of a non-profit that helped low-income students of color get extra enrichment so that they could get to and graduate from a four-year college. I am hardly the only person to feel this way about *San Antonio v. Rodriguez* and its impact across many states. The case is regarded by many as being one of the worst Supreme Court decisions in the modern era, one that played a major role in creating the unequal public school systems that exist today. Even though I don't focus on this issue for a living, I know I will always look for ways to fight against the systemic unfairness in how public schools are funded in my region. That sadness is in my bones.

Growing up you may have heard the phrase "find your passion," a term I feel is wildly overused in childhood. Parents, teachers, and other adults might have urged you to "find your passion" not because they wanted you to have a happy and meaningful life (I mean, they might) but because they wanted you to impress others such as college admission deans with that passion. They were well meaning, but in the thirty-plus years I've been an adult, most of the people I've come to know hadn't found their passion by age eighteen, no matter what they said in their college essay. In this chapter I'm urging you to think about the causes that matter to you so much that you feel the commitment in your bones, and you want to put your time, effort, dollars, and heart into this thing even if the whole world just laughs at you. In fact as I mentioned in chapter 5, "Stop Pleasing Others," when something matters deep within you it doesn't matter if the world ridicules you. You'll just laugh back and say, *Fuck that. This matters to me and I'm going to try to help this cause anyway.*

So, instead of "find your passion" I prefer the language Ananda used in chapter 3, "You're Not Perfect," abut "finding your why." Ananda's story illustrated that when you know your "why"—that is, you know the values that underpin your actions—then your behaviors, choices, and decisions are made based on those values, instead of on any number of other things that might sway your mind. You gotta know your why. It could be anything. One way to get at it is to ask yourself, *What are the causes or issues that make me say to myself "Wow, that just isn't right"?*

Try not to be dissuaded by the sheer number of problems that need addressing or the seemingly intractable nature of so many of them. I'll admit that while I am quite ready and eager to help a specific person who has a specific hurt, I've tended to be skeptical about the utility of trying to step up and fix a portion of "the system" unless I can fix the *entire* system. Like, what point is there in serving food at this one soup kitchen when millions of people are going hungry? What good does it do to make things better in this one little school or classroom when millions of children don't have access to a decent education? My despair at not being able to fix *all* of it has sometimes prevented me from seeing the good I can nevertheless achieve by jumping in to try to help fix *some* of it. But I mean, did I think I was actually going to end hunger, or improve all of public education? Maybe? (Can you see the bit of narcissism embedded in that ideal, like, *With over 7 billion people on the planet I AM THE ONE WHO WILL SAVE US ALL?* Naw dawg. You won't. I won't. Brahma, Buddha, Jesus, Mary, Moses, Muhammad, Shiva, Vishnu, and the world's most amazing secular humanist are not the standard we're supposed to try to hold ourselves to.)

Making things better doesn't have to be at the scale of leading all of your people out of bondage into the Promised Land. A whole bunch of us making some tiny portion of the world better is actually feasible, however, and in the aggregate, all of us together can effect positive change on a grand scale. Future generations are counting on us to try. And remember, it makes *you* feel good when you're making those efforts.

THE POWER OF OUTSIDE-THE-BOX THINKING

There are infinite ways in which you can make things better. You can make things better by changing how you use your time, how you spend your money, how you make decisions, and/or how you live your life. You can devote an entire career to serving others. For example: teachers, nurses, EMTs, and firefighters go to work every day to try to improve someone else's life. Or you can volunteer for a cause once a week, or once a month. You can investigate problems. You can design and develop solutions. You can start a whole new industry or a whole new way of doing a very old thing. You can plant trees, clean the air, and purify the water. You can create a business that makes the world better based on how you source your materials or how you treat your employees, or based on what you sell. You can run for local, regional, statewide, or national office. You can march in the streets. You can heal the sick and provide comfort to those who are hurting. You can create words, imagery, or sound that moves others and compels them to act in better ways. You can speak up for those who need an advocate. You can go after the bad guys. You can prevent cruelty to other living beings. You can completely change up your way of life so as to be an example to others. You can donate a little money here and there, you can encourage others to do the same, and you can leave an organization a portion of your money when you die. You can respect those who are dying by volunteering with the organization No One Dies Alone.

You can help everyone simply feel welcome. Imagine how isolating it is if you can't play at a public playground because you or your family member is one of the one-in-four people with a visible or invisible disability that means typical playgrounds are inaccessible. My friends Jill Asher and Olenka Villarreal made fixing this their "why." They're the cofounders of Magical Bridge Foundation and Playgrounds, which proves that playgrounds can and must be designed and built with "every-BODY" in mind. Says Jill, "Children and adults with physical disabilities can spin on our inclusive carousel, where they roll on and feel the joys of swirling with everyone else. They can go down our roller slide and scoot over and wait with dignity while their wheelchair is retrieved. People with physical disabilities can also play on our two-story treehouse, swing in our bucket swings, and sway in our sway boat. There are also retreat opportunities for those with autism or sensory challenges, and the laser harp is programmed with gentle sounds that are pleasing to those who have sensory overload." Olenka and Jill and their team have built a dozen of these playgrounds around the world, including one in my town, which happens to be where they also live. When I went to the opening and watched everybody out there simply enjoying themselves on a lovely day, my heart swelled with happiness. It is indeed "magical."

Regardless of how or how much you do to make things better, I promise you this: if you take the skills and talents innate in you, and pay attention to the ways you like being in the world and to the environments in which you thrive, you can use those raw materials to make a difference. And to make things radically better, don't keep doing things the way they've always been done. Think outside the box. Think *around* the problem. Come at the issue from a completely different angle like Jill and Olenka did. That's how we get to interesting and innovative solutions. The next three sections present three fantastic examples.

GETTING COMPANIES TO DE-EMPHASIZE PROFITS AND RE-EMPHASIZE PEOPLE

"Social impact organization" is a newish term for companies that want their main purpose to be doing good in and for the world. The ride-share company Lyft is an example. It might appear that Lyft's founders acted from a place of *This is crazy. There's too much traffic. Too many single-occupancy vehicles. You should connect with your neighbor while you get from here to there.* "But they were interested in so much more," says Joan Hanawi, Lyft's social impact manager. I love Lyft, and often choose it as a commuting option. But I'll confess I had no idea they wanted to have a positive impact on the world; I thought they were just driving paying customers from here to there. Joan schools me. "If you want to participate in our democracy, you need to show up at a polling location, so we will offer free rides to the polls. If you are trying to move forward in life, we offer rides to job interviews, job trainings, and the first few weeks of work. And we know that often food deserts and transportation deserts are overlapping. If you're trying to just get food on the table, we can get you a free ride to a grocery store." This is what Joan came to Lyft to do. "I got to build their social impact strategy from the ground up. I got to be the one asking questions like, *How do we redefine the transportation industry so that we're caring about the people we serve and making sure we can expand transportation access to those who need it most?* And, *Where does transportation have the opportunity to make a unique difference?*" Not a bad gig for a twenty-eight-year-old.

Now, in contrast to the phrase "social impact organization," when we think of the word *company* we tend to think "an enterprise that maximizes profits above all else." Since profit is tallied only after all expenses have been paid, many companies take the approach of minimizing employee pay and benefits—a huge portion of any company's expenses—in order to maximize profit. Walmart, the world's biggest non-governmental employer, is a good example. It got called out for its paltry wages and benefits some years ago.

But not every company needed a course correction as badly as Walmart did. Not every for-profit company thinks maximizing profits is the sole reason for its existence or the greatest measure of its success. A growing number of for-profit companies choose instead to focus on their mission and vision and putting their employees first by offering competitive wages, great benefits, a positive work environment, and settling in for the long haul. Yet they still manage to be profitable. How do they do it?

Let me back up and say that I learned about all of this completely randomly at one of my book events in Idaho. I was having coffee with the couple who had spearheaded my visit to Ketchum, and the husband in the pair, Dave Whorton, started talking about this concept of "Evergreen companies," which he obviously cared deeply about. I thought, *Hey wait, what?* And as I listened more I found myself thinking, *Young adults need to know about this.* So, I was grateful that Dave was able to spend a bit more time with me to teach me about how Evergreen companies differ from traditional for-profit businesses, so that I could share this information with you. Let me also back up and say I'm not trying to tell you where to work. I'm trying to show you that even within systems we think of as entrenched in their ways (as we often feel when it comes to "corporate America"), a mindset as seemingly foundational as "profit at all costs" can be discarded and replaced by a more humane and enjoyable way of doing business that can be sustained, scaled up, and celebrated (as I'm doing here)!

So, here's what I learned from Dave, who is an entrepreneur, business leader, former venture capitalist, and the founder of Tugboat Institute, whose mission statement says, "We believe in the vital importance of humans coming together to create and grow enduring, private businesses that make a dent in the universe." Sounds pretty cool, right? Tugboat Institute started paying attention to the fact that a set of companies have always done right by their employees, always had a great purpose, always been a leader in their respective markets, and have not sold out to the idea of growth or profit at all costs. Dave and his team created the term "Evergreen companies" to describe these existing companies, of which there are hundreds if not thousands around the world. Dave says the first thing that makes Evergreen companies different is that they're all privately held and intend to stay that way (this means they don't have outside investors breathing down their neck to force them to go public or get acquired in order to return a huge profit to the investors). In a way, the leaders of Evergreen companies invest in creating a workplace of satisfied employees who can be confident they'll have a job for the long term if they want it and who deliver great goods and services to the market, instead of investing in the remote possibility of a big payoff that will make them hugely rich one day. As the leading evangelist for the Evergreen company concept, Dave actively teaches CEOs and entrepreneurs about the idea, and encourages them to join the cause.

You may think that a CEO is supposed to want to sell their company to a bigger company or to take their company public; that's been the popular thing to do since the first "dot com" bubble of the late 1990s, which began the new era of entrepreneurs and their employees becoming millionaires overnight if a company was sold or went public. But there's a huge downside in seeing a company not as a collection of people who make great products and services and that could last forever but simply as another commodity to be sold. When a company heads down that path, they often lose control of their mission and decision-making authority to the investors who are hungry for a huge payout. Those companies are "built to sell, not to last," says Dave.

Dave tells me that in contrast, Evergreen companies remain "private, purpose-driven companies designed and run to grow and scale for 100 years or more, guided by these 'Evergreen 7P Principles': purpose, perseverance, people first, private, profit, paced growth, and pragmatic innovation." He says, "I can say without hesitation that the Evergreen path is a better path for human beings and our society—and an antidote to the get-big-fast-at-all-costs playbook and mentality that has permeated business since Netscape's explosive public offering in 1997." It's not that Evergreen companies don't need outside investors in all cases; a few do. But, Evergreen leaders "understand that building a great business takes time and means treating employees fairly, serving customers well, reinventing oneself and one's business, and sharing in the success. So, Evergreen leaders will only take on investors who will allow them to stay private forever, sharing in long-term owner distributions of excess cash."

As I've said, there are hundreds if not thousands of Evergreen companies in the world; here is a small subset of those whose brands you may have heard of *and* which have made it onto one of the *Forbes* "Best Employers" lists (which ranks all the large and medium-sized public and private companies in America based on employee satisfaction, which I think is an important metric for you to pay attention to, too).

COMPANY AND HEADQUARTERS	INDUSTRY	*FORBES* BEST EMPLOYERS LIST RANKINGS
Trader Joe's Monrovia, CA	Food markets	#1 large employer (2019); #2 for new grads (2020); #2 in Illinois (2020); #8 in Texas (2020); #15 in New York (2020); #77 in California (2020)
SC Johnson Racine, WI	Packaged goods	#8 large employer (2019)
Wegman's Rochester, NY	Food markets	#19 large employer (2019); #95 for new grads; #2 in Maryland (2020); #5 in New York (2020); #12 in Pennsylvania (2020); #22 in Virginia (2020)
In-N-Out Baldwin Park, CA	Restaurants	#28 large employer (2019); #29 for new grads (2019); #2 in California (2020)
Edward Jones St. Louis, MO	Investment management	#43 for new grads (2020); #113 large employer (2019); #8 in Iowa (2020); #10 in Missouri (2020); #14 in Michigan (2020); #20 in Texas (2020); #31 in Florida (2020)
Mars & Co. McLean, VA	Retail food	#84 for new grads (2019); #166 large employer (2019); #3 in New Jersey (2020); #18 in Georgia (2020); #28 in Illinois (2020)
Fidelity Boston, MA	Investment management	#99 for new grads (2020); #121 large employer (2019); #3 in Rhode Island (2020); #8 in New Hampshire (2020); #40 in Massachusetts (2020); #51 in Texas (2020); #82 in New York (2020)
SAS Institute Cary, NC	Information technology	#227 overall
Enterprise Holdings St. Louis, MO	Rental cars and trucks	#225 for new grads (2020); #19 in Kentucky (2020); #37 in North Carolina (2020); #47 in Indiana (2020); #69 in Missouri (2020); #93 in Ohio (2020)
Panda Express Glendale, CA	Restaurants	#490 large employer (2019)

Clase Azul Tequila San Francisco, CA	Alcoholic beverages	Top 25 Small Giants (2020)
SmugMug Mountain View, CA	Photo-sharing platform	Top 25 Small Giants (2020)
SRC Holdings Springfield, MO	Manufacturing	America's Best Small Companies (2017)

Note: Other Evergreen companies you may have heard of but that are too small to be included in a *Forbes* survey include Patagonia (outdoor apparel), Clif Bar (health bars), Radio Flyer (toys), the San Francisco 49ers (professional football), Chobani (yogurt), and Stella & Dot (jewelry and accessories).

I'm not trying to tell you where to work. If you're headed to the for-profit world, do your research, and know that it's possible to find companies that create and sell great products and services while also offering collaboration, mentors, and good pay and benefits. All told, these companies are making the world a better place, and you can join them. And hey, if you're an entrepreneur, you could even create an Evergreen company of your own. If you want to learn more about the concept, check out Dave Whorton's Tugboat Institute (tugboatinstitute.com).

GETTING COWS TO BURP OUT LESS METHANE GAS

Methane gas is a problem because it traps heat in the air and is a major contributor to global warming. Cows burp out a tremendous amount of it (and a lot comes out as farts, too). A few years back, an Australian scientist named Rob Kinley was on Prince Edward Island, off the coast of Nova Scotia. As the story goes, he noticed some cows grazing near the seashore. And he noticed that those cows seemed to be healthier than those who could not forage near the algae. He returned to Australia, trained his eye on whether eating seaweed could be good for cows, and discovered that cows that eat a particular strain of red seaweed—*Asparagopsis taxiformis*—are both healthier and burp less methane gas into the air. The basic thing happening here is that the bacteria in a cow's stomach naturally produce methane, and there's a natural antibacterial chemical within the seaweed that suppresses the activity that produces the methane. End result: far less methane and also healthier cows!

Kinley wrote up his research and joined a small community of other scientists who were interested in this subject. But at the time, these studies were little noticed outside of the research community. Enter Joan Salwen, a former Accenture partner, who comes upon Kinley's research and shares it with some of her friends, including Mike Bracco, a former banker and investor who is also *my* friend. "Joan and I and the others all looked at each other," Mike tells me, "and we said, 'It sounds too good to be true. No one seems to have picked up on it, and so it's probably not replicable.' But then we looked at each other and said, 'But if it *is* true, the potential for impact on the world is too big to NOT follow up.'" So, Joan, with the support of her cow-council friends, set about to find out more about it.

Their first step was to find donors to fund more research, which would ultimately cost almost a million dollars. Their second step was to find scientists who would conduct their own independent studies. Scientists at the University of California, Davis, which has one of the nation's top agriculture programs, agreed to participate. The UC Davis scientists came back with news that shocked them all: *Asparagopsis taxiformis*, delivered to cows in the form of a supplement shaken onto their feed like you would shake salt on food, reduced methane emissions from the cows by 75 to 80 percent. And it didn't hurt the cows, and it didn't change the flavor of the milk or meat that came from the cows. Now this team had to figure out how to grow, harvest, and market this special red seaweed at scale, and get it into the stomachs of cows. And to make any of that happen they had to get more people to care.

They got more people to care by telling a good story, which goes something like this: *Did you know that there are one hundred million cows in the United States, more or less (both dairy cows and beef cattle) and approximately one hundred million families? So, the simple way to think about how many cows we have here in the United States is to imagine every family having one cow. Now when it comes to methane production, each cow produces about as much greenhouse gas emissions in a year as are produced by one gas-powered car. Feeding one cow this supplement is the same as converting one car to electric power.*

But is this *really* a big opportunity at a macro scale? Mike says, "Well, let's think about how much energy, time, and focus goes into adopting electric vehicles. The U.S. projects that through persuasive marketing and government incentives, twenty to thirty percent of gas-powered cars will be replaced by electric vehicles between now and 2050. If we take the environmental benefit of all of those cars coming off the road through 2050, we can achieve the same thing by feeding one third of the cows in the U.S. this supplement. And we can achieve it within three to five years. It's just not that hard. All you do is shake a little bit of this special salt, this special seaweed flake on their food, and it dramatically reduces the methane. The scale of the benefit for this is massive relative to many other environmental initiatives that are funded. And did I mention there are one billion cows worldwide?"

With those kinds of stories and data, Joan Salwen, Mike Bracco, and Matt Rothe were able to secure venture funding to make this research into a thing. They created a company called Blue Ocean Barns (blueoceanbarns.com), which continues to work closely with the original scientists in Australia. (I'm delighted to hear this, partly because the scientific community and media tend to be biased toward science produced out of the United States and Europe—boo!—which may be why the Australian research was not making much headway in the first place.) Through various partnerships between scientists and nongovernmental entities, they're pulling together a confederation that will bring this product to market as quickly and as effectively as possible. Before COVID-19 the plan was for the red seaweed to be ready to be used by dairy farmers and cattle ranchers quite soon.

I tell Mike that this sounds great, but I have to ask about the larger concern shared by many that we shouldn't be slaughtering cows for their meat, or drinking their milk for that matter. "Yes. But for the time being people love cheese, milk, and beef, and we're not as a country transitioning quickly away from that. Even if this is an interim alternative while we create alternative meats and plant-based substitutes, it's worth it." I also want to know about potential harm to the environment by growing more of this seaweed and feeding it to cows. "This is what's called the 'life-cycle analysis,'" Mike tells me. "Seaweed aquaculture is considered environmentally beneficial generally speaking, because it sequesters carbon and prevents ocean acidification." In short, it seems fine.

Now, you might already have heard something about changing cows' digestion to save the planet, because Burger King did a huge ad in the summer of 2020 featuring a kid wearing a white cowboy hat, strumming a small guitar, and yodeling (yes, yodeling!) about how cows that eat lemongrass fart less. All true, and all good. (Note: Lemongrass impacts what happens in a cow's intestines whereas red seaweed impacts what happens in a cow's tummy, hence the different types of, um, emissions.) But, as Mike tells me, the lemongrass only reduces cow emissions by about one third whereas the red seaweed reduces cow emissions by as much as 80 percent. And when it comes to the existential threat of climate change, it's gotta be "Go big or go home." Mike says, "Burger King tried to make a big splash. Tried to say, 'Hey, we're the first ones to bring it to market.' The lesson was that it's not enough to have a good idea. You have to get it to the place where it's easy for other people to understand and adopt it. It has to be cost effective. You have to answer how is a farmer going to get this to their cows? And who is going to pay for it?" Blue Ocean Barns has already fielded interest from a number of well-known companies that use a lot of milk in their products and see this innovation as a way to help meet their corporate climate change and sustainability goals. Maybe McDonald's will get on board as well and we'll be treated to a whole new set of fast-food wars.

In the meantime, Mike tells me that *Asparagopsis taxiformis* is not unfamiliar to humans. "It's not your typical kelp, or the type of seaweed you'd use for sushi, but it's not rare, either. This same seaweed is actually used in poke bowls. Native Hawaiians have collected it out of the ocean, dried it, and used it as a seasoning with poke for generations." See how looking at old stuff in new ways can make all the difference? Sadly, there's no evidence that *Asparagopsis taxiformis* prevents human burps. But read on for an example of how simple changes to the daily life of humans are most certainly making things better!

GUARANTEEING A BASIC INCOME TO EACH CITIZEN

"The issue with economic insecurity, the issue with poverty, the issue with folks not having a lot of money isn't because folks themselves are deficient or that they don't know how to use money. The issue is that *they don't have money*. And especially in this moment where I just read that Jeff Bezos made thirteen billion dollars *yesterday*, there's no excuse then for people to be hungry, for people to be stressed about rent, and for us not to provide just an income floor for everyone in our country." These are the words of Michael Tubbs, spoken on a *CBS This Morning* podcast I happened to be listening to in the summer of 2020. Tubbs is the thirty-one-year-old mayor of Stockton, California, the youngest mayor in Stockton history, its first Black mayor, and probably the most improbable person you'd ever expect to be mayor of Stockton or any other city. And Mayor Tubbs is a leading proponent of the concept of "universal basic income," also known as "guaranteed income."

Mayor Tubbs was born in Stockton to a teenage mother and an incarcerated father. Statistically speaking he was not expected to thrive. But his mother, grandmother, and extended family loved him fiercely and made sure he worked hard in school. And did he. He became a student of mine at Stanford. We met during his freshman year when he entered the contest to speak at our campus church for our annual Founder's Day ceremony. We selected him for that honor. And I remember feeling chills run up my arms as I heard him deliver his speech from the pulpit because he sounded like a civil rights leader from days gone by. During his sophomore year I had him in a seminar I was co-teaching on race and the law. Admission was competitive and Tubbs was one of only two sophomores we took. (The rest were juniors or seniors.) Late in his junior year, he applied to be the student speaker at opening convocation, which is the main university ceremony for all new students and their families held each fall, second in size only to commencement. He was selected for that honor, too. And he stood on that stage and told the audience of close to five thousand people that he hadn't even attended opening convocation in his own freshman year because, at the time, he wasn't feeling very sure that he yet belonged at Stanford. In the spring of his senior year, instead of partying with his friends he was running for city council in Stockton. Once again, Tubbs got what he had worked hard for.

Mayor Tubbs told *CBS This Morning* that universal basic income is "an idea as old as this country. Thomas Paine was talking about this in the late 1700s. Dr. King was calling for this in a moment similar to this one with massive civil unrest, in 1967, in his book *Where Do We Go from Here*. And essentially the idea is that it is a public benefit given to everyone, that's regular, monthly, and it's cash with no restrictions. And the point is to allow people to build economic resilience, to allow folks to have a floor so when pandemics like COVID-19 happen or when other economically destructive events happen, people have the resources to shelter in place, to provide for themselves and their families."

Mayor Tubbs and his team decided to study the concept of a universal basic income in Stockton through a pilot project. One hundred twenty-five Stockton residents at or below the town's median income were randomly selected to receive a monthly outlay of $500 for eighteen months, which was extended by six months to help people get through the pandemic. Stockton is in good company in this effort to explore universal basic income. A 2019 Democratic presidential candidate, Andrew Yang, became hugely popular with his promise to give all Americans $1,000 a month if elected president. Milton Friedman, a libertarian economist now deceased, had endorsed the idea. So does Facebook founder Mark Zuckerberg. And although it was touted as a way to share the state's riches, as opposed to helping those on the bottom, back in the early 1980s, the state of Alaska created the Alaska Permanent Fund, which pays all residents (including children; excluding the incarcerated) an annual dividend from its oil and gas revenues, which hit a high of $2,072 per year in 2015 and was $992 in 2020. Curiously, research on Alaska's most recent disbursement showed a 14 percent increase in substance-abuse incidents the day after the payout was made, which was said to be offset by an 8 percent decrease in property crime. "Crime-related concerns of a universal cash transfer program may be unwarranted." Research has also shown that the Alaska dividend "had no effect on employment" and that Alaskans use the extra money to fund everything from stocking up for the harsh winter to paying down student loans to visiting family in the Lower Forty-Eight. The Stockton pilot similarly seems to be refuting concerns that a universal basic income rewards laziness and disincentivizes people from working. In Stockton, one recipient used the money for dentures, to feel comfortable smiling once again. Another used it to take a day off work to interview for a better job (which would have been impossible for someone who would otherwise be living paycheck-to-paycheck and working a job with no paid leave time).

As for how universal basic income is paid for, that's all a question of a community's priorities. Whether to increase funding for the police or create a universal income for citizens is a choice. Whether to pay for national defense or great public schools is a choice. And it doesn't have to be all or nothing. In explaining how universal income is paid for, Mayor Tubbs points to the bailouts of big companies when the pandemic hit, and to the already immense Pentagon budget. "There are ways to pay for things if we really want to, and if we have the political will to do so."

According to a 2020 *Vox* article that surveyed studies of basic income schemes around the globe, the upside of a basic guaranteed income extends beyond what people are able to buy with the money. A basic guaranteed income seems to change how people *feel*. "The evidence so far suggests that getting a basic income tends to boost happiness, health, school attendance, and trust in social institutions, while reducing crime." Dan Price, a CEO in Seattle and founder of Gravity Payments, has his own spin on this issue. He read that having more money leads to more happiness up to an annual salary of seventy thousand dollars (after which additional salary dollars do not boost happiness). So, he ensured that all of his employees had salaries of at least seventy thousand dollars and he took a 90 percent pay cut himself to help pay for it. Not only did happiness rise, but profits rose, too. Looking after everyone's needs makes things better.

Mayor Michael Tubbs tends to make shit happen. So, I'll be closely watching for the studies about his universal basic income pilot, and where he decides to go from there. He's also piloting guaranteed college scholarships for worthy high school grads in his city. If you're interested in learning more about his personal and political journey, check out the HBO special *Stockton on My Mind*, which came out in 2020. Tubbs was an unexpected baby and he's an unexpected mayor. I think the lesson here is that unexpected sometimes leads to a winning formula.

FIVE STEPS YOU CAN TAKE TO MAKE THINGS BETTER

You don't have to make every playground accessible, fundamentally change corporate America, stop all cows from pumping methane into the air, or convince your city to offer everyone a universal basic income in order to make things better. I put those ideas on the page simply because I find them exciting and inspiring. *You do you.* But here are some baseline behaviors you can activate in order to get better at making things better:

1. *Register to vote, and vote.* This is a democracy (or at least it's trying to be) and as the nonprofit, nonpartisan League of Women Voters says in its motto, "Democracy is not a spectator sport!" Get registered in your state and commit that you will always vote no matter what. In my dream world, voting would be automatically open to you once you hit the legal age, but for the time being each state has its own rules and regulations on who can vote, how far in advance of an election you need to register, how to register, and how, where, and when to vote. Be aware that depending on where you live and who you are, your local leaders may be trying to make it harder for you to vote so you may need to go the extra mile. Do it. Sometimes major elections come down to a few hundred votes (see *Gore v. Bush* in 2000), so don't ever fall into the trap of thinking, *Eh, it doesn't matter.* It does. And if you're voting by mail be sure to get that ballot posted well in time for it to arrive by Election Day.

2. *Read the news regularly.* (And by "read" I mean "watch and/or listen to," if television, radio, or podcasts are your preferred thing.) You're probably also getting a lot of news through your social media accounts and/or YouTube. If you're getting your news primarily this way, be sure to read the underlying piece rather than just relying upon an influencer's view of things. Also be aware that reading the news an influencer or friend posts, or that an algorithm has recommended for you, basically filters all the news down to stuff you already care about. Challenge yourself to widen your blinders and take in more information, otherwise you're going to exist inside a bubble where everyone says the same thing all the time and you may soon start believing falsehoods. Widen your blinders not just topically, but geographically; you want to be up on the main issues in your city, region, state, and nation, and in our world. Local news can seem so irrelevant when the world is on fire, but your local officials have a lot of say over the quality of life and economic prosperity in your town and region (à la Mayor

Michael Tubbs of Stockton, California), in addition to how polic-
ing happens and who gets indicted for what. So you need to pay
attention to what your city council is up to, and your school board
as well, if education is an interest for you. Read your town's local
paper or newsletter, if it has one. For a great roundup of national
and international news I recommend a weekly magazine called
The Week (on Instagram: @theweekmag; on Twitter: @TheWeek),
which does a great job of canvassing major stories in our nation
and from around the world and presenting those stories from both
liberal and conservative perspectives. Another great resource is the
online magazine *AllSides* (allsides.com), which is committed to
presenting left, center, right, and underrepresented viewpoints on
every major topic in a pretty user-friendly way.

3. *Be aware of bias and don't believe the lies.* Journalists go to journalism school for a reason. There, they learn how to ensure that
information asserted as fact is verified by multiple sources. But
with the creation of the Internet, social media, and the smart-
phone, for the first time in human history, anyone with a phone
can have an opinion and with the press of a few buttons share it
with anyone in the world. This feels like and in some ways is the
democratization of information. Yet it also means there's a lot of
unverified crap out there posing as news. And even major, verified
news sources tend to have a bent. The *New York Times* feels liberal.
The *Wall Street Journal* feels conservative. Anything written by a
human is subject to bias (and hey, anything written by a bot is
subject to the biases of the person who created the bot). In short,
you need to be wary about sources of information. Ask yourself,
Who benefits when the story is told this way? Seek to understand
the other point of view within reason. Exercise your analytical
reasoning to determine what's fact, what's opinion, and what's
outright fiction. And when it comes to whether something is real
or fake, do your research. I've been that person who posted stuff
and then discovered it's fake. (So embarrassing!) If it can happen
to me it can happen to you! These experiences have taught me
to fact-check first. I like *PolitiFact* (politifact.com; @PolitiFact), a

nonprofit newsroom "that believes in facts" and has a "Truth-O-Meter" graphic that shows you whether something is true, mostly true, half true, mostly false, false, or a lie (which they call "pants on fire"). I also go to *Snopes* for the same purpose (snopes.com; Instagram: @snopesdotcom; Twitter: @snopes).

4. *Engage your friends, family, and neighbors.* Whether you're thinking about an issue related to your lived experience, or a topic you learned about in school or from the news, or something supported by someone you respect dearly, or an issue being debated by your city council (like universal basic income), bring a beginner's mind, humility, and curiosity. Learn from those who have been working on that issue for years before you. Learn what didn't work and what does work. Use your voice, time, hard work, influence, and/or money to make that thing better. When you catch up with an old friend or a family member you don't speak with much, talk about a few of the issues that are stirring within you. When we think critically, act responsibly, engage in our communities, and get involved civically, we help make things better.

5. *Stop saying you'll do it and just do it.* Don't be that person who says what they're gonna do. Let your friends and family wake up one day and discover you've gone and done it. This was me with respect to the migrant children our federal government had taken from their parents and locked up in cages. For a full *year* I'd been saying with my friends, "That's so terrible. I can't believe this is happening. We should do something." For a whole damn year. Finally, in June 2019, when yet another article had come out in the paper about the atrocious conditions the kids were living in, I knew that my complacent days were up. I went to Walmart and bought a megaphone. I told the cashier, "I'm going down to Texas to stand up for those migrant kids." And she blinked at me twice and handed me a twenty-dollar bill from her own pocket, and said, "God bless you." Then I went to Office Depot for the poster board, markers, tape, batteries, a clipboard, paper, pens, water, and a couple plastic bins to hold all of this stuff in. I told the cashier there what I was doing, and he said, "I have

to ask my manager for permission to hug you." Then he asked me if he could hug me. And I said yes. Then I took my Jeep Wrangler to my mechanic and said I was headed to Texas (a seventeen-hour drive), and they said I was overdue for new tires, so I raced over to a tire shop to get some new ones. There was a huge backlog. I was told it might be a few days before they could get to me. I thanked the guy for his time and then told him my story. "I'm going to drive this thing down to Texas and try to draw more attention to what's happening to those kids." He just looked at me. Looked down at his stack of orders. Told me my car was next in line.

I knew I couldn't do much for the migrant kids. But my "Caravan to Clint" drew some pretty decent media attention and a whole lot of people jumped on board and met me there. We stood on street corners in El Paso. Stood outside the federal buildings in El Paso and Clint. Donations poured in and we split them between a shelter in El Paso and a shelter in Juárez, Mexico, which we walked across the border to get to. Every night ended with a candlelight vigil where the kids were being held. Someone had the great idea to sing a lullaby in Spanish through the fence. In my bones those kids are my kin, and I needed to do my part, however small, to show them they are not forgotten.

DON'T JUST TAKE MY WORD FOR IT

MEET ANGELINA—Making Things Better by Being an Upstander for Women

When Angelina Cardona Keeley was twenty-eight she became a contestant on season thirty-seven of *Survivor* (*David vs. Goliath*), which aired in 2018. Despite refusing to kowtow to the producers' stereotypes about how young female contestants should behave and be portrayed, and despite emerging as one of the show's most strategic and outspoken female contestants—which means "bossy" in the minds of some—she nevertheless made it to the final vote. While things did not go her way, she was able to achieve things arguably more important than a million-dollar payout. I have her on the phone to dig into that story.

Angelina comes from Sparks, Nevada, where her father manages a local store. Her ancestors were from Mexico, El Salvador, Spain, and Portugal. Her parents divorced when she was young, and her mom went on to become an elementary school teacher after putting herself through college part-time at night. Both were very hardworking people. It was a huge deal for them all when Angelina got a full scholarship to Stanford. And that's how she and I met.

"Everything in college was eye-opening," says Angelina. She was being exposed to the significant impediments women face in life, things like rape culture, sexual assault, the wage gap, and the workplace glass ceiling, which she studied in the classroom and drew attention to as an activist in the student community. "These issues lit me up," she says. In her senior year she served as Stanford's student body president, having run on a platform of ending sexual assault and relationship abuse. Yet even as she served in that role she was stalked by a fellow student whose behavior went from inappropriate to concerning to threatening. "I was twenty. Trying to be a good leader. I felt so bombarded. Stripped of my sense of safety." When she called the police, the officer asked her, *What do you think you are doing that might be making him behave this way toward you?* She pushed past this victim-blaming mindset, went for a permanent restraining order, represented herself in court, and won. After graduating from college, she created anti-bystander training for college campuses. "We need to empower people to understand that they have a role when it comes to these issues. That it's not just victims and perpetrators but the world they exist in. What we do to enable rape culture, and what we can do to change that."

She began to see herself as a women's rights activist, and set her sights on making an impact in that capacity. She admired Shirley Chisholm, the first Black woman to run for president of the United States, and Teach for America founder Wendy Kopp, who had written about how to improve public school teaching for her senior thesis in college, then grew that idea to scale by creating a nonprofit organization. The next step for Angelina was an MBA, which she earned at Yale, where she focused on gender equality in leadership and the workplace. "I'd come to realize there's no silver bullet to changing gender inequality but what gets us closer to it is having women in decision-making positions across all industries."

For her capstone project at Yale she produced a daylong conference for a hundred high school girls from the surrounding New Haven, Connecticut, community—girls who were mostly of color and mostly working class—that would expose them in a hands-on way to what it takes to be a CEO, elected leader, scientist, and engineer, all fields in which women are underrepresented. The day ended with everyone packed in a classroom—the girls, the volunteers, a number of professors, the girls' parents, and many of Angelina's classmates—to listen to a local congresswoman deliver the last big inspiring talk. Then Angelina was to close the conference with her own remarks. But as she stood at the podium and began to speak she was flooded with all of the positive energy she could feel in the room. "What's the word for when your heart feels full?" she asks me. Instead of closing out the conference with her own words, she passed the mic to any of the girls who wanted to come up and share whatever was on their minds. "Almost every single girl found the courage to get up and share something very personal about themselves. A hope or dream that they had. We went way over time. It showed me the power of what we did that day, the power they have to encourage each other and feel empowered by that camaraderie. I realized there's a secret sauce, some magic here that I need to bring along." As she looks back on that day, on how she felt and on what seemed to happen for those one hundred girls, she says that other than her wedding day and the day her daughter was born, it was the happiest day of her life.

With Wendy Kopp's strategy for building Teach for America in mind, and a picture of Shirley Chisholm on her wall, Angelina began thinking about creating a nonprofit organization that would help thousands of girls envision a much bigger future for themselves. She would center it around being a "future student body president," since that was the path she knew well. Her hunch was that early leadership mattered in the life of a girl. But before any of that could get off the ground, she was a working-class kid who knew that dreams have a hard time igniting without capital. "I realized I need to build my own safety net." And with her newly minted MBA degree in hand, she went off to the corporate world.

Angelina joined the consulting firm Deloitte, in its San Francisco and then Costa Mesa, California, offices, where her job was to help companies solve problems and address their strategic needs. She had fantastic colleagues and earned the kind of money that would set herself up for a much easier life than she'd had growing up. But early on, something felt off. "I'm Catholic. I believe in God. I believe we have a purpose and a plan and unique gifts that we can give to the world. I'd be doing spreadsheets and marketing materials for my clients during the day, but I knew the work was not my heart's work. At night I'd try to quench that part of myself by doing little extracurricular things on the issues that matter most to me, such as helping a client study why there aren't more women in mergers and acquisitions work." Months of feeling successful but uneasy turned into years.

I get it. I went into corporate law instead of being a lawyer for systemically underserved and marginalized people (which was the reason I had gone to law school). And that's how I learned the hard way that if you're trying to make things better in the world you'll fall short if you relegate that work to the margins of your life by doing it late at night after your regular job. Angelina felt, "It's really hard to break out of the status quo, especially when you're making a great paycheck, have good relationships there, feel some degree of comfort, and you fear the unknown. It wasn't until I had a real pause from the status quo that I could say, *Okay, I need to make a change.*" That pause was being on *Survivor*, which was the adventure of a lifetime and an unexpected dive right into the gender dynamics that concerned her.

The *Survivor* producers were putting together the *David vs. Goliath* season, which would pit people perceived as strong against those perceived as weak. They wanted the cast to include Ivy League–educated women who were attractive and outspoken. Someone gave them Angelina's name, and based on the little they could tell about her from her social media they knew they wanted her. The idea of fierce competition and the prospect of a decent amount of winnings was insanely appealing to Angelina (every contestant wins some amount of money—maybe the earnings could help seed the girls' empowerment nonprofit she dreamed of creating). But her application came to a standstill. She would learn that in *Survivor*, as in the reality TV genre more broadly, the whole point is to showcase sex, conflict, or comedy, so the producers typically refuse to cast a twentysomething woman who is in a serious relationship because that woman won't be flirty, sexual, or have the potential for what is known in the industry as a "showmance." Angelina had just married the love of her life, Austin, who is an officer in the Marine Corps. "They were like, 'I'm sorry, the casting director won't take you further because you're married.' I was like, 'That's bullshit. That's a narrow way of looking at it.' But whatever, I keep living, right?"

But the casting agent who had first found Angelina kept pushing for her to be cast on the show. With mere weeks to go before *David vs. Goliath* was set to film, the casting agent circumvented the usual process to show Angelina's video and application to the show's host, showrunner, and executive producer, Jeff Probst. The agent told Probst, "This is your Goliath. This is the person who is going to complete this cast. You want her on your tribe." Jeff agreed. They raced to put Angelina through the battery of examinations, personality tests, and interviews to which all finalists are subjected. "I was just myself through it all. Jeff gave me a big thumbs-up and a wink. I got the call two days later. I was like, *I'm going to starve and I'm not very athletic right now, but I'm going to do this.* I have a very strong spontaneous streak, I love adventure, and I'm *very* competitive. My bosses were fine with me taking a leave. That whole package, on top of potentially winning money, was too appealing to say no to. I had this hope that maybe I would say or do something that would push the envelope a bit, on TV, or with the producers, to bring my values to bear." Three weeks later she was stranded with a bunch of strangers on a beach in Fiji, where she was about to become a women's rights activist.

Angelina ended up making some of the most strategic moves *Survivor* had ever seen from a female-identified contestant, including creating a contro-versial fake immunity idol and by bargaining with Probst for more rice for her desperately hungry tribe in exchange for giving up immunity for herself. The bargain was made, and Angelina survived the subsequent vote. The commu-nity of *Survivor* fans known as the "fandom" refers to Angelina as the "Feminist Queen." They praise her for raising gender dynamics in her confessionals (the every-other-day private sessions between a contestant and a producer, many of which get aired). And they credit her with pushing the show in a direction where gender and gender dynamics are talked about much more openly.

For example, Angelina openly addressed a common workplace dynamic that had made its way onto the sands of *Survivor*—she suggested to her tribe that they vote out a powerful member who would be a threat down the road, but her idea was overlooked. Yet when a male contestant brought up the same idea it was received positively. "That's a universal experience for women. We put ideas out there and then someone else runs with it." These are "seemingly inconsequential things," she tells me. But I know as well as she does that in the aggregate they matter. "*Survivor* has a viewership of seven million; hopefully some of it stuck with the audience, like, 'Oh, I see myself in her,' or 'I get what she's saying,' or 'It's causing me to look at things differently than I may have.'"

In the very first episode, Angelina spoke with a producer on camera about the gender dynamics associated with hidden immunity idols. (Idols can protect a contestant from being voted out of the game.) She noted that the idols play a big role in a contestant's ability to advance in the game, yet 85 percent of the time are found by men. The show aired this observation. What she also said to the producer (which wasn't aired) was, "Well, why does that happen? What are the underlying circumstances? What role do women have at camp? What's expected of them? How do we perceive aggressive game play differently in women versus men? It's a reflection of the world we live in." Since Angelina's season aired, women contestants on the show seem more motivated to search for hidden idols and to be more aggressive in their actions and language, and there's been a spike in the number of women who have found idols. Many fans point to Angelina's influence as the reason for this increase.

And she took on sexual harassment, which had been happening for years on *Survivor* but had not gotten the attention it deserved. Female-identified contestants going as far back as Ghandia, in season five (2002), have reported unwelcome physical touch. Sue, a popular player from season one (2000), was brought back as an "All-Star" for season eight (2004), but she quit in the middle of the game after a male contestant rubbed his naked body against her during a competition. Those seasons occurred well before the #MeToo movement, when women were less likely to be taken seriously even by other women when they spoke out about sexual harassment, and they were often blamed or ridiculed for doing so. While Angelina did not personally experience sexual harassment on the show, her willingness to be outspoken about the experience of women in season thirty-seven (2018) helped move the dial on the producers' response to sexual harassment in later seasons.

Angelina finished her season in third place, for which she received $85,000 as well as the deep satisfaction that she had helped improve the *Survivor* experience for other women, and had inspired at least some viewers to change their attitudes and behaviors. Season thirty-seven is considered one of the top five *Survivor* seasons of all time, and Angelina's refusal to let things go unsaid is a part of why that is so.

When I watched the season myself, I found myself cheering Angelina on. Not just because I know and love her, but because she was kicking ass as a smart and strong young woman who was also, yes, beautiful. My daughter, Avery, then eighteen, had started watching *Survivor*'s earliest seasons, and I encouraged her to jump ahead to this one, to see Angelina. In classic mother-daughter fashion Avery resisted my suggestion. (It's like I'm the *last* person who can recommend something to her; I get it.) But I'm confident that if and when Avery ever does watch season thirty-seven, she'll see herself in Angelina and will be rooting for Angelina, too.

Jeff Probst is also rooting for Angelina. In a December 2018 interview with *Entertainment Weekly* published days before the finale in Angelina's season would be broadcast, Probst was asked if there was one person he'd like to see play again and he named Angelina. "The truth about *Survivor* is that we want our casting to mirror what is happening in our culture. And as a dad to a daughter, what excites me more than anything is the rise we are seeing in the power of women. For years, strong women have been judged differently than men—in life and on *Survivor*. And strangely, for years it has been hard for us to find women who were as 'memorable' as men. But what has been happening is the female voice is growing stronger with every passing day, and we want that voice represented on our show. Angelina is polarizing. Some people criticize her for being 'too much,' but she is playing a strong game and making big moves and not backing down from anyone. I like that. We need that. When a man does it, he is rewarded. It shouldn't be any different when a woman does it. Angelina would get my vote."

Angelina's impact lives on. In season thirty-nine (2019), a male contestant touched a number of female contestants inappropriately. But this time, the producers talked with both him and the complaining parties off camera. This time, the producers gave him a warning. And this time, when he continued to behave inappropriately, he was asked to leave the show. Angelina watched this unfold on-screen, and penned an op-ed for *Time.com* in which she urged Jeff Probst to speak about the situation at the finale and explain how the producers could handle such situations differently next time. By the time the live reunion finale show came around, Jeff Probst did in fact address the matter head on, using some of Angelina's suggestions. "He owned it, he apologized, he gave the victim her own time to speak about it, and he told her that they should have been better about supporting her at the time. There was no brushing the harassment under the rug."

Angelina changed *Survivor*, but *Survivor* changed Angelina as well. Being far removed from her regular life reminded her that she wasn't on this earth to help corporations solve problems and develop strategic plans. Alone on the sands of Fiji she reignited her plan to start a nonprofit to develop young women into leaders, which she would begin by winning some money from the show so she could support herself.

"In the two months of living on a beach in Fiji and playing this crazy-ass game, you're completely isolated, you don't know what's happening in the news, and you finally have a break. I had been running, running, running since I was thirteen: AP classes, volunteer, do this, do that, nonstop. But in the game, you're sitting alone with just the clothes on your back. You're dirty. You smell terrible. You have nothing in your stomach. And you're looking at the most gorgeous sunset of your life. It forced a pause in my life that I've never experienced before. A fellow contestant realized, *I gotta propose to my girlfriend*. For me it was like, *Okay, what am I scared of?* I was scared of not making money, not having security, not having a glamorous job, and of making a choice that people might not understand. Another gift of *Survivor* was that it broke me of perfectionism that I didn't even know I suffered from. I almost didn't want to go on the show because I felt, *Oh no, I won't be able to wear makeup. I'll look fat on TV, or haggard and tired*. I've worn makeup every day of my life because I feel like I always have to be put together. It caused me to question, *Where does that come from? Why am I scared of being vulnerable?* You go into confessionals with producers for forty-five to sixty minutes every other day, and they really dig into your soul. A couple of producers were like, *I notice you really don't like not having it all together, and not being in control and not doing or saying the right thing*, and it was a mirror for me and I was like, *Oh wow, they're right. I almost didn't play this game because I was worried about looking imperfect on TV. But look, I threw myself into the fire and I have no choice but to be imperfect, and my hair is going to grow on my arms and face, and boy, will it, because I'm a Latina, and my makeup will wash off the first day after I jump into the ocean when Jeff says, 'Go.'* The through line there was when I was looking at my life. It was, *You know what, it's okay to not make a salary for a year, to take the winnings and use it to support myself. It's okay to take a risk and have a job not everyone understands or they think is just volunteering*. It allowed me to give myself permission to try and fail and not be perfect, and that was important because you just can't have those fears as an entrepreneur. It was very freeing for me."

Angelina registered her nonprofit for girls' empowerment in July 2018 and set out to build an organization. "Now I had to do my research. What does it look like to empower young women to get into political leadership? How does it manifest itself? Who else is doing this work? I spent a lot of the fall of 2018 doing that legwork in preparation for a January 2019 launch. I found research that shows that when students run for office in middle and high school they are seven times more likely to run for adult politics. I conducted a nationwide study on why high school young women don't run for office. I found that a few organizations were encouraging young women to run for school leadership, but they do so by hosting expensive conferences, which are cost-prohibitive for so many girls. So, my solution is an online learning platform I call a 'campaign school' that empowers young women to get into school politics and teaches them how to do it."

She launched a pilot campaign school in a high school in Stockton, California in February 2020, right before giving birth to her daughter, Sophia, and right before COVID-19 hit. A grant promised by a foundation dried up due to the pandemic. She got a cease-and-desist letter from an organization that was already using the name she'd chosen for her organization. Now thirty-one years old, she's at a crossroads in her attempt to create better life paths for young women. "It's scary. I have to raise more resources but there are very few gender-equity philanthropic dollars out there. I need to make money for my family. I have to change the name. On top of that we don't have any childcare. COVID is happening. Just because you take the jump to your dreams doesn't mean everything is perfect. But I've been scared and out of my comfort zone before with *Survivor*. I've learned that when you get to the other side, you almost always realize you were able to conquer something you didn't think you could so you feel more confident in conquering the next mountain. This non-profit to help girls become leaders is my other baby. The pandemic validated the virtual learning environment for our campaign school and taught us a lot about what works and doesn't. I believe in it more than anything. This is the direction in which I'm headed."

MEET LYDIA—Making Things Better for Sick, Mad, Disabled, and Neurodivergent People

Lydia X. Z. Brown is known as the "Human LinkedIn." They know people everywhere they go. They also know the best Ethiopian restaurant in any region in America. "It's my most favorite food in the entire world. If I'm going to spend money in this capitalist system, it's going to be on Ethiopian Black woman-owned businesses."

I'm speaking with Lydia at dinnertime their time, and I keep overhearing asides between Lydia and their roommate about the meal Lydia prepared, which they are now both eating: a tuna tomato sauce pasta recipe handed down by Lydia's mother. I'm a fast typist but Lydia blows away every other interviewee when it comes to the speed of their thoughts. Or perhaps it's just that every single thing that they said was captivating, and I didn't want to miss a single word.

Lydia is a twenty-seven-year-old queer, nonbinary trans East Asian person who is multiply disabled and neurodivergent, and who as an infant was transracially and transnationally adopted from China by an evangelical white couple who raised Lydia in the Boston area. Lydia is married and owns a house near DC. However, at least for now, their spouse lives in New England and Lydia lives with a roommate due to jobs and life amid COVID-19.

Lydia is a lawyer who advocates for humans whose needs are overlooked, mocked, or trampled upon. They graduated from Georgetown University in 2015 with an Arabic major and psychology minor, "because I hate myself and hate being happy." I hear Lydia's sardonic tone, and I smile while continuing my furious typing. They went straight to law school at Northeastern University, which they call "hell," so I ask them why they chose law in the first place. "I went to law school because I hate myself and hate having free time." I push harder. Why this graduate degree? "I went to law school because I'm squeamish and afraid of blood. And I could have gone to biz school, but I suck at math." I'm a former lawyer who knows that it's possible to be drawn to law itself, not just as a way *not* to pursue other things. I push again and get the answer I'm looking for.

"I realized toward the end of college that I'd spent the last several years doing an enormous amount of disability advocacy and activism work on my campus in DC and in my home state of Massachusetts. It occurred to me that I could get a PhD in my area of academic interest: Islamic studies covering South Asian Sufi music and poetry, which I love. Or, I could go get a set of practical tools to be more useful to communities I belong to and strive to be in solidarity with. I don't think lawyers or the legal system will save the day because the system is made from colonialism and white supremacy. Yet a bar license gives me the ability to wield certain tactics to support harm reduction and help pave the way and support the work of those who are on the ground building the world and future we want to live in. I had the ability to do law and the ability to acquire that form of social privilege that many in my community could not do due to disability, class, and race. I went to law school because I believe every single one of us has a moral obligation to do what we can to make things better."

This is why I'm talking to Lydia.

Over the last decade, Lydia's work has centered on "issues of interpersonal and state violence that target disabled people at the margins of the margins. Especially disabled people living at the intersections of disability, race, class, gender, sexuality, language, and nation. And that type of violence often takes place in the home, in schools, in nursing homes, in psych wards, in long-term residential institutions, in jails, in prisons, and by police." Even as Lydia unspools their tale of selfless, philosophically grounded, driven efforts to help others, they sprinkle "because I hate myself" into our conversation a number of times. I point that out, and Lydia lets me know that sprinkling a joke or a wry comment into conversation a number of times is an autistic thing. I pause to take note of that. But I'm also interested in any potential truth in the underlying joke. "Do you really hate yourself?" I ask. "For me being a multiply marginalized person in the world means I'm taught to be ashamed of multiple things that make up who I am. It's very hard to exist when you are disabled, openly queer and trans, and a person of color. I don't actually hate myself except when in a severe bout of depression, but..."

This is also why I'm talking to Lydia.

There's been a velocity to Lydia's sense of purpose in the world from a very young age that takes my breath away. Here's what I mean. As a high school student in Massachusetts, Lydia wrote disability rights legislation and pushed for its passage. While in college they started the blog *AutisticHoya*, which got a lot of attention (and still does) and led to invitations to speak to various groups around the country. While in college they also became one of the youngest governor appointees to a state disability council. In their first year of law school, they were the youngest person nationwide to ever be appointed to a state developmental disability council. In their second and third years of law school they were an adjunct professor down the road at Tufts University's Experimental College, where they taught a course on disability theory, policy, and social movements. In the summer after law school graduation, "instead of

sitting down to quietly study for the bar exam and block out human contact"
(which is precisely what I did), Lydia spent weeks traveling to Alabama, Washington State, and Colorado to lead workshops on disability justice, intersec-
tionality, and youth empowerment for disabled people of all ages and service
providers. Lydia fell asleep during the second and final day of the Maryland bar
exam, had to be woken by a proctor, and still passed.

Upon graduating from law school, Lydia had a fellowship through the Justice Catalyst Foundation at the Bazelon Center for Mental Health Law in DC,
which was Lydia's first-ever salaried job. There, Lydia supported Maryland
children with learning, developmental, or mental health disabilities—most of
them also Black or brown—who had been denied support for their disabilities
at school and were facing disproportionate and adverse discipline including
expulsion. The Bazelon Center would get referrals from parents and sometimes from the students themselves. Lydia would respond and do their best to
be of use, which in and of itself is service because many such calls for help
just go unanswered.

"Lawyers can't take most of the cases they get called about, either because
there is no real case, or because they don't have the resources to, or because
it's not their practice area. I was part of a group that would take referrals from
parents who called about issues affecting their disabled children. I would volunteer to take some of the cases, meet with the student and their family and
interview them about what happened, what help they were looking for, and
what they wanted to accomplish at the end of the day. I would work with my
supervisor, an education and disability rights lawyer, to set strategy and create
an action plan. I'd bring it back to the student and family and say, 'Here's what
we can help with, and what we can't help with,' and oftentimes even more than
trying to provide legal representation I wanted to be as supportive as I could
emotionally. The student and family had probably been told no over and over
again for racist, classist, ableist reasons. Educators and administrators tend
to see disabled kids as too burdensome, too overwhelming, too much effort,
or they don't believe you, like, 'Bye.' That's frustrating and demoralizing. So, I
also performed the more traditional role of a lawyer, that of counselor. Even
if I couldn't do much from a legal standpoint, I wanted them to know that I at
least believed them. They would at least feel listened to and supported when
and where it matters."

I ask what came of that work. "Most important was that for most of the

students that I was working with I might have been one of the only openly disabled adults they might ever meet who was proud to be disabled and working
in a profession (law) that most disabled people were told they could never go
into." I ask Lydia how they knew their involvement mattered to the students. "I
wanted anyone I worked with to set the terms of our relationship and boundaries. When I talked with students about what was going on at school, what
they were struggling with, either directly related to their disability or how they
were treated, I made it really clear that I was on their side. I might say, 'Wow,
that sounds awful. Some of the things you're talking about I also know from
personal experience.' But I did not experience all the same things. I'm a light-
skinned POC. I certainly did not face the same racism. So then I'd let them
know that in other ways I've experienced some of the same things: not being
believed by teachers, being relentlessly bullied by fellow students. I was even
falsely accused in high school of planning a school shooting. I remember one
high schooler who was clearly very happy to know that there was an adult
not just on their side but with a shared sentiment of *Wow, fuck these ableist
assholes*. That meant a lot."

I ask Lydia for the best example of how they serve disabled students. "It's
hard to come up with one thing. A lot of people try to tell hero martyr stories.
That's not how I see myself or who I want to be. People come in with the mindset of *File a lawsuit and save the day*, but that's not how our profoundly white
supremacist, ableist, and patriarchal legal system works. You lose more than
you win. Yet everyone you work with is a human being. They are the agents
and narrators of their own story, not me. At end of the day it wasn't *Did I win
this?* but *Did I do right by the people who asked me to work with them?*" I ask
Lydia how one knows whether we've done right by someone. "You can work to
hold yourself accountable to the communities and people you work alongside.
When you are not directly affected by the thing, you can work to be accountable to those who are. You can be honest about the risk you take, about what's
comfortable and not comfortable, and the personal and structural reasons you
take certain risks or don't. Nothing that I do is ever linear or able to be applied
universally to anything beyond extremely broad principles. To work toward justice, to show radical love or radical care is highly contextual and situational
and relational as well. I'll show up at five a.m. because someone in crisis called.
From the psych ward. From jail. If they're about to be evicted. If they're being
walked out by a sheriff's deputy. I've driven across state lines. Driven eighteen

hours in two days." Some of Lydia's clients got in trouble at school for defending themselves against bullies or for engaging in friendly activities. "I'm the one who shows up cuz that's what we do for each other. We show up."

Lydia's fellowship at the Bazelon Center lasted a year. When that fellowship ended in the fall of 2019, Lydia joined a Georgetown Law think tank called the Institute for Technology Law and Policy, where they co-led a research project on disability rights and algorithmic fairness and justice, i.e., how automated decision making (AI) harmfully affects disabled people. In January 2020, they became an adjunct professor in the Georgetown Disability Studies program. Then, in the middle of March 2020, their boss at the think tank called them into her office and informed them that she had taken a new job as CEO at a major civil rights organization in DC and wanted to move the research project on AI over to the new organization. She wanted to bring Lydia along, too. This meant a new workplace and new colleagues for Lydia, although the work would be the same. Lydia accepted the opportunity. "Three days after that, we all went into quarantine, so I didn't have time to emotionally process it."

Lydia is also director of policy, advocacy, and external affairs at a nonprofit called the Autistic Women and Nonbinary Network. And Lydia founded and directs the Fund for Community Reparations for Autistic People of Color's Interdependence, Survival, and Empowerment, a redistributive justice and mutual aid project. In its two years of existence, the fund has given out over $50,000 to several hundred people in microgrants ranging from $100 to $500. "We help people pay for therapy, rent, get art supplies, escape abusers, keep the lights on, pay for childcare, anything under the sun that is not illegal or violent." Lydia seeded the fund with a $7,500 award they received from the American Association of People with Disabilities for being an "emerging leader," and the ongoing revenue to support the fund largely comes from small individual donations. Given all Lydia is up to, they are frequently interviewed by the media, where they are often not given proper attribution for their expertise. "They'll say, 'As blogger Lydia Brown says…' or they'll intro me as 'Lydia X. Z. Brown, a well-known blogger.' Yet blogging is not my profession nor my job title, and it's not the majority of work that I've done. A nondisabled white man doing this work would be called an attorney. This mislabeling is racialized, gendered, and disability code language."

It's clear that Lydia is thriving professionally. They are thriving in their personal life, too. "My spouse and I are both openly disabled, openly queer, openly trans activists and lawyers who have both been working on the same issues for ten years, and none of that is how we met. They had a really good friend in college who was part of a writers' program I was also in, who knew both of us. That friend said, 'You're both super nerdy geeky people. You should get to know each other.' And we did. And we slowly became extremely close friends and fell in love with each other."

Lydia also has a strong set of close friends whom they call their chosen family. "I think of them as my sisters, brothers, siblings and my cousins, and we have a familial relationship even though we live often in different locations. They are people that I trust with my life. Just as much family as the people who raised me. They're family differently—not more or less, just different. Even if we don't talk for weeks or months, we're still close deeply and emotionally and would be there for each other in a heartbeat. Most of my friends aren't friends with each other. Some of them are. They're not a cohesive group amongst themselves. I've always wished for that but never experienced it."

We're touching upon family now, so I feel I can go there. I ask Lydia about their parents, whose evangelical Christian beliefs may make it hard for them to accept Lydia for who Lydia is. "They're my family of origin. And very much a part of my life. My parents belong to a fundamentalist Christian church and raised me Evangelical. Dad has Southern Methodist roots. Mom is Roman Catholic. I am not at all what they expected. One of the proudest and happiest moments of my entire life, after years of them struggling to accept my sexuality, my gender, and my partner as my partner, was the day my parents drove nine hours on a highway to be at my wedding, where they served as ushers and gave a blessing and a toast."

This is also why I'm talking to Lydia. I feel like I'm speaking with a person who, if we could all just pause for a moment and listen deeply to, could unlock the door to a happier and more just future for us all.

I end the conversation by asking Lydia what their professional goal or purpose is. "I never know how to answer that question. Part of it is a sense of nihilism and impostor syndrome where I feel everything is useless, pointless, and worthless, and find it gross and disturbing that people pay me to do the work that I do because working for justice isn't something we should be paid to do. And at the same time in a capitalist society we need money in order to eat. Nonprofit organizations rely on conditions of injustice and inequality; if injustices went away they would cease to exist. Without mass incarceration we wouldn't need public defenders. If we didn't have hunger we wouldn't need housing nonprofits. They perpetuate the injustices they are fighting against. I don't want to describe my future as a 'career' or 'work' because I don't want to be defined by my labor or productivity, or to define it as a function of something that should be eradicated. I want to end white supremacy and ableism. If I play some small role in collectively making that happen then what I do won't exist anymore and there's nothing I'd like more. I want to do what I'm able to do and hope that things don't get horrifically worse."

MEET HANNAH—Making Things Better by Giving Something Up

Hannah is a twenty-eight-year-old upper-middle-class white woman. She graduated from New York University (NYU) with a self-designed major in film, television, and finance, and now works for the National Basketball Association (NBA) in their global partnerships division. Half her life ago, when she was fourteen, she convinced her parents to sell their Atlanta home and donate the proceeds to people who were in need. I've got her on the phone to understand what prompted that decision, what came of it, and any lessons she learned that might be useful to others.

Hannah grew up in Atlanta with her mom, dad, and younger brother. Her mother was a partner with the consulting firm Accenture, mentored with Big Brothers/Big Sisters in her spare time, and went on to cofound and teach at a leading private girls school in Atlanta. Hannah's father was a journalist at the *Wall Street Journal,* a consultant for the U.S. Olympic Committee, and a volunteer with Habitat for Humanity. For as far back as Hannah can remember, her family lived a very comfortable upper-middle-class life. Unlike most of the women in her neighborhood, Hannah's mom worked outside the home. When Hannah was seven, they moved to a house her mother had had her eyes on for years, located on a neighboring street—a historic three-story six-thousand-square-foot home with five bedrooms, eight fireplaces, a chef's kitchen, and a working elevator. It was her mother's hard-earned dream house.

One day when Hannah was fourteen, her dad was driving her home from a sleepover and they had the experience that would change their family's life. "We stopped at a very familiar stoplight about a mile from our home. I looked to my left and saw a very typical scene in Atlanta, a man with a sign that read 'homeless hungry please help.' As I'm looking at him, a beautiful black Mercedes pulls up on my right. I have a freakout. It's kind of all hitting me at once.

I said, 'Dad, if that man,' pointing to the Mercedes, 'didn't have such a nice car, this man,' pointing to the homeless man, 'could have a meal.' Dad said, 'If *we* didn't have such a nice car, then that man could have a meal.' At dinner that night I said, 'I really want to be a family that doesn't just talk about things but *does* things.' My mom explained that we write nice checks at Christmas, and she reminded me that I volunteer at a food bank, and that Dad was on the board of Habitat for Humanity for Atlanta. I said, 'It's not enough.' Mom said, 'What do you want to do, sell our house?' I said, 'Yes.' My dad and brother practically passed out."

Hannah's feelings about income inequality date back to memories of being a little kid visiting Habitat for Humanity houses with her dad. When a house is completed and is being handed over to its owner, Hannah's dad often attends the dedication ceremony and when Hannah and her brother were little they would go with him. "I grew up going to these Habitat for Humanity sites with my dad pretty regularly and we'd play with the kids who were receiving the house. I remember one time when I was eight and my brother was six, my dad was dedicating a house to a mom in East Atlanta. He'd become very close with the mom, and he was getting teary. We didn't really care that much about the dedication, though. There was a basketball hoop across the street and my brother and I played with the woman's kids. A boy and a girl, just like us. We were just being kids and shooting around together. I remember afterward getting in the car to go home and my dad asked if we'd had fun with the kids. And we said, 'Oh yeah, yeah, yeah, that was great.' And he said, 'Oh, well, the woman getting the house is a single mom and is raising the kids by herself. They have a really different upbringing than you do.' But we had had a great time with the kids as if we'd had the same upbringing as them. It was a learning experience that ingrained in us that everyone is equal. Maybe that's part of why I was so angry as I began to see injustices. Looking back on this Habitat situation I don't remember thinking these kids are Black and I'm white. I just remember thinking they had grown up 'differently from me.' And for me, at that time, that meant money."

I can imagine that many kids raise outlandish ideas at the dinner table. But for some reason, Hannah's parents took fourteen-year-old Hannah seriously when she said they needed to sell their house and donate the proceeds to those in need. Their home, as Hannah has described it to me, "had chandeliers in every room, space we didn't need, a whole floor we never even used." So,

I can perhaps reasonably surmise that Hannah's parents also sensed some-where inside of them that they were leading a life of excess, and that they genuinely wanted to do something about it. I'll fast-forward and tell you that their generosity most definitely helped people. Thousands of people. And Han-nah and her parents grew a lot, too. But I'm unpacking the story a bit because when we think about "making things better" I think the most interesting bits are "better for whom?" and "what constitutes 'better?'" and "who decides?"

Selling one house and buying another smaller and cheaper house in the same neighborhood would turn out to be relatively easy for Hannah's family. They put their house on the market and while waiting for it to sell they bought a new house a few streets away. (Being able to own two homes at once is a further example of the family's financial privilege.) They ended up netting a $800,000 surplus, and every Sunday morning for months on end, Hannah, her brother, her mom, and her dad talked about where to donate their money. "We wanted to be really thoughtful about it. We'd talk about the big problems of the world. 'Which is more important to you, climate change or homelessness in the U.S.?' And we'd listen to each other and write it all down on a whiteboard. After we'd had a lot of these sessions, we started narrowing it down to wanting to do something that would help eradicate hunger and poverty. We knew we wanted to make sure that the money that we were pledging was going to go a long way. So, we decided to focus our efforts outside the U.S. for a variety of rea-sons, particularly because there was less of a safety net elsewhere. So, then it was, 'What areas of the world most interest you? Are you interested in Asia? Africa?'" Hannah describes her role in this process as "the big dreamer with the irrational idea," and her twelve-year-old brother Joe was "the skeptic who frequently asked, 'Why are we doing this again?'" Joe's role was important. He forced them to remember, refine, and defend what they were doing. "He kept us in check. He would poke at what I was saying. 'Why is it important that it's our *house*? Why can't it be something else?'" When he was thirteen Joe made a video in which he states somewhat sardonically, "One day my sister got out-raged about hunger and now we're selling our house."

Hannah and her family chose to donate their money to a New York non-profit organization called the Hunger Project, whose mission is to bring about "the sustainable end of world hunger." With their $800,000 donation Han-nah's family could sponsor two Hunger Project "epicenters" in Ghana, which are community empowerment hubs uniting thousands of people in dozens of villages around key community resources such as a health clinic, a bank, and a food storage facility. The epicenter is led by a community board at least half of whose members have to be women, and the Hunger Project expects that after a maximum of eight years of working within the "epicenter" model, a community will be "sustainably self-reliant." The community-led nature of this epicenter concept was appealing to Hannah. "I didn't want to give people things that they weren't going to use. You read about Westerners coming and building wells and the wells break and nobody uses it, or they didn't use it in the first place. We wanted to be sure we were doing something that these communities wanted and cared about, rather than have them feel that white people are coming in and telling us what we need. That's what I liked about the Hunger Project. They try to empower communities from within so they can help get themselves into a better situation." One of the two epicenters Hannah's family supported ended up being extremely successful because of the tremendous buy-in of the local people. The second needed a bit more help but is definitely on its way.

Hannah and her family adapted easily to their smaller house, which, though half the size of the other house was still plenty big and had cost close to a million dollars. Hannah went to the same school, she had the same friends, and she didn't talk much about what the family had done. In many respects, despite being the catalyst for a rather monumental set of decisions, little in Hannah's life seemed to have changed. But then the family began to get some unwanted attention. "I didn't talk about it with my friends, but I know that they talked about it. I know that people around me talked about it. I remember my friend telling me that they'd been talking about it in the student lounge one day. Someone had said that they didn't like that I was asking people to donate money. But we'd never asked anyone for money. Part of me thinks that since I didn't talk about it, I couldn't really control the narrative. People came up with their own stories."

Her parents, on the other hand, felt they had to proactively explain to friends, family, and colleagues what was going on. "There was a lot of judgment. I remember my mom saying she had lost a friendship over it. My parents selling an expensive home and donating half the proceeds had brought to light some differences that made my mom's friend uncomfortable. Her friend had said, 'That's just not my reality.' When we told our best family friends that we were moving, they said, 'But you're moving farther away from us,' even though it was just three blocks. There were a lot of weird reactions. People didn't know how to handle it. They were really uncomfortable."

Complete strangers had their opinions as well. Hannah and her dad had gone on to write a book about their experience called *The Power of Half*. This led to an appearance on the *Today* show, a write-up in the *New York Times*, and mentions in many other newspapers and magazines. In some places the family was being praised and lauded for their sacrifice. In others they were being criticized. And since Hannah was the one who sparked the whole idea in the first place, she was often the one in the crosshairs.

"Yeah, we paid a price. The *Today* show segment ended up on YouTube. Some of the comments were pretty scathing. One was about hoping that I got raped and died. For my mom that was pretty jarring—that someone could watch this video and want that for her daughter. There were a lot of negative comments, especially after we wrote the book. They said we were doing it the wrong way. That we were acting like we wanted other people to sell their houses. And people were also really upset that we didn't give the money in the United States. I think that really rubbed people the wrong way. That was just something we had to deal with. A lot of people were really inspired, and a lot of people needed to speak out.

"I have a lot of guilt about how we structured the book. The end of each chapter is 'Hannah's Take,' and it's the actionable items portion where you can take what's in the book and put it into practice in your own life. It gave people the wrong idea, that we were encouraging people to do something bold to make the world a better place. But I wanted people to come to that conclusion themselves, and only if they want to. I never wanted anyone to feel that I was asking them to give up anything. I got the reputation of not wanting people to have nice things, that they should feel the injustice of hunger and it should hurt and they should make some kind of sacrifice and that they should give everything away. We were just sharing our story. And our book ends with a 'Call to Action,' and now I feel a little bit uneasy about that, because I wish we had just stuck to the story. I think then people could take a look at their lives on their own time and make their own decisions about what they wanted to do. That's how I feel now. If our family selling our house inspires you to take a look at your life and make a change, I love that. But if it doesn't that's totally fine, too. This was just about what we did and how it affected my family. It's not about anybody else. What haunts me the most is I don't want anybody to think I have a judgment on the way that they're living when I don't."

I ask Hannah about how she thinks about the problems of hunger and poverty now that she's an adult. "I'm still outraged about the same things. But I've grown up a little. As a fourteen-year-old I felt I could do something about hunger. Now as a twenty-eight-year-old I feel like I can do less about it, and that one fourteen-year-old selling their house isn't going to solve the problem. I realize that voting and getting the right people in office is important. That's stuff that as a fourteen-year-old I wasn't thinking about. I'm trying to not make such a grand gesture. My goal is to do little things that one person can do." The idea of giving away half of something became her family's metric. "Give half the time you spend watching TV. Half the money you typically spend eating out each week. I still try to live by that. You can only really sell your house once. So, now I give away half my clothes once a year." Hannah also participates in the NBA Cares program at work, through which she mentors a bilingual child. Hannah continues to look for ways to make things better.

I find myself feeling a bit of awe that Hannah's family would go from talking the talk to profoundly walking the walk. I don't live in a six-thousand-square-foot house, but I do live in a very expensive part of the country and we could sell our house and do a helluva lot with those proceeds. And I'm very concerned about income inequality. So, why am I not doing what Hannah and her family did? What would it take for me to walk that walk?

I can't help but be reminded of my trip to Clint, Texas, in the summer of 2019, which I mentioned earlier in this chapter. For a year I'd been feeling distraught every time I read another story about how migrant kids were being separated from their parents and kept in squalid conditions in Clint. On the one hand, after a year of bellyaching about the situation I'm proud of myself for dropping everything to drive down to Texas to spend five days protesting in the hot sun for the purpose of drawing attention to what was happening. We did in fact get a lot of media attention, which added a bit of fuel to the already raging fire. At the tail end of the week, national-level politicians were flying in to give speeches and participate in rallies. But as to our small piece of it, I'd done nothing to prepare the community for our visit, and had done nothing to prepare myself and the random set of wonderful folks who joined me for how to make meaningful connections with the leaders and regular folk in Clint and El Paso. We drove for seventeen hours, we raised some hell for five days, and we drove home. The effort was not sustainable. Other than a few new friendships, the impact of our efforts has blown away like dust on a summer night in El Paso, which fills me with sadness and regret, and it forces me to ask, *For whom did I do this? For whom did I make things better?* Perhaps I helped those kids in some small way. But perhaps I did it to help myself—to make myself feel that I was *doing something* even if I wasn't really doing much, in the long run, for the migrant kids.

When we're trying to make things better we need to be courageous and ask ourselves these tough questions. If the thing we did ended up being *all* about us, if we ended up harming instead of helping, that's problematic, of course. Rarely is it crystal clear. Hannah and her family definitely made a sustainable positive difference in the lives of thousands of Ghanaians by donating sizable funds to support the Hunger Project's work. And I also know from the lessons I took home with me from my trip to Clint, Texas, that *the experience in and of itself had to have changed Hannah's family, too.* And changing yourself may not be what you set out to do when you're trying to make a situation better for others, but it's nevertheless an important and valid dividend. Here I'm alluding again to the words from Atul Gawande's book *Being Mortal,* which I quoted in the first couple pages of this chapter: having a cause outside our own selves gives *our* life meaning.

So, I end my conversation with Hannah by leaning in to the ways in which she and her family may have been changed by this whole experience. And I'm delighted by what I hear. "To me this is the absolute most important part. We'd been very distant as a family. But in doing this we learned so much about each other. I'm obviously so grateful that we were able to do this and have an impact on the communities in Ghana. But I got to know my family. What values they have. We began having a different level of communication that we hadn't had before and it completely changed us. We were all in this together. My parents said, 'Every person in this family has an equal vote on what we're going to do with this money. It's not a hierarchy.' It bled into everyday decisions among us, and it helped me understand that my parents were really empowering us. I noticed myself being so much more open about all aspects of my life with my family because they understood me on a different level. Issues with friends. Anything that as a teenager I was dealing with. Instead of being an angsty teenager hermit sulking in my room I felt like I could open up. I started trusting them. We got to know each other on a different level than we had before. I am forever grateful for that."

Of all the relationship changes afoot in the family, the relationship between Hannah and her mother had perhaps the biggest improvement. "Mom and I used to have a pretty strained relationship. She was put into an interesting position as a mother, because she had just become a partner at Accenture when I was ten or so and was very indebted to her career. I remember her telling me that she was one of the only working moms in my neighborhood. Her college friends would tell us that she used to be very outgoing, wild, and funny, the life of the party. But that was not my experience. My experience was that she was very rigid, detail-oriented, and a serious rules follower, and she seemed to expect specific things from me that I could not give her because I was more of a free spirit and defiant and didn't want to listen to the rules. My dad was a free spirit, easygoing, chill, with the sense of humor of an eighth grader, which I think made my mom feel like she needed to be the bad guy. So, we had a very strained relationship. I was very defiant. I feel so bad now that she had to deal with me. This decision to sell the house and donate the proceeds broke down some of those walls between us. I started to understand who my mom was as a person, not just this image she was needing to project of us as a family. So, it's my relationship with my mom that changed most. I got to know her differently. We were able to open up to each other and not feel such a strain in our relationship, instead of me being bad and she had to punish me."

I feel for this mother. I also fear that in some ways I *am* this mother. While the dynamics and personalities in my family are different from those of Hannah's, like Hannah's mom I'm trying to be the successful professional woman in the house while also being there for my children and seeing them for who they fully are. I am at times anxious and therefore controlling, and overly sensitive and therefore defensive. In contrast, Dan is mellow and easygoing, almost always. I envy the more easygoing relationship Dan seems to have with Sawyer and Avery. I am working to heal these old wounds within me and to bring that healthier self into our home and into my relationships with my family.

So I'm incredibly happy for Hannah's mom, and for Hannah, that they found a way to make things better between them. The house they sold was Hannah's mom's dream house, the culmination, I imagine, of years of tremendous work and sacrifice and time away from family. It looks like she gave that up because her then fourteen-year-old daughter had a pretty important concern that was very much worth listening to. Hours after ending my phone call with Hannah, I text her back. I have to.

ME: Have you and your mom ever talked about the fact that your relationship is improved? Or is it more just implicitly understood between you, or perhaps even not understood implicitly between you but it's definitely clear in your own heart?

HANNAH: We have talked about it many times, especially in the past couple of years. I realize now that the main emotion I felt toward her through our project was admiration. The way she listened to me, led our family through our Sunday meetings, and ultimately helped us all come to the conclusion that the Hunger Project was the right fit was not lost on me. She listened to my idea and was my partner in convincing my brother and dad. I really respected that.

ME: Aw jeez I'm tearing up. I kinda sorta in some ways am that mom in my family.

HANNAH: It makes me emotional too!

ME: She sold that house to get closer to you, kid.

HANNAH: Absolutely.

IN SHORT: YOU CAN MAKE SUCH A DIFFERENCE IF YOU TRY

So much ails our society and planet. You are coming of age in a time of scarcity and turmoil. Yet you have so much capability baked into you. Don't be daunted by what you *can't* do. Think about what you *can* do, and what you may be *uniquely suited* to do. Start. No matter who you are, or where you're coming from, there are three things that you have access to at all times that will help you succeed. It's a very human form of magic and it's what we're exploring next.

Unpack and Reflect

- Who do I admire for the way they make their part of the world a better place?
- What types of injustice do I feel in my bones? What is my "why"?
- How do I show up for issues I care about? What can I do to make community or civic involvement a bigger part of my life?
- How do I try to motivate others to make things better?

12

UNLEASH YOUR SUPERPOWERS
(MINDFULNESS, KINDNESS, AND GRATITUDE)

We're all just walking each other home.

–Ram Dass, author of *Be Here Now*

Ram Dass—born Richard Alpert—came into this world during the Great Depression ninety years ago. His parents raised him in the Boston area, where he attended the finest schools. He attended Tufts University, where he was drawn to the study of psychology. He went on to get a master's degree in psychology from Wesleyan and his PhD from Stanford, where his doctoral thesis explored "achievement anxiety." He joined the faculty at Harvard and rose to prominence in his field. In the early 1960s he became interested in how individuals could expand their minds through the use of psychedelic drugs. With his friend and colleague Timothy Leary, he conducted a handful of research projects on the subject. Soon after the research came to light, both Alpert and Leary were asked to leave Harvard. His exploration about how humans can achieve higher-level consciousness not just with psychedelics but with a spiritual practice and greater awareness led him to India, where, in the year of my birth, 1967, he changed his name to Ram Dass.

This chapter is not about drugs, or God, or mysticism. But the quote that opens it—*We're all just walking each other home*—is the explanation of the purpose of our human existence that makes the most sense to me. These words resonate inside my mind like a language I once knew well but can no longer speak. In quoting to you this concept I find so capti-vating, I simply thought it best to share that the guy who uttered it was also deeply into LSD for a while.

This chapter IS about some fucking awesome powers that lie within you: Mindfulness, Kindness, and Gratitude. Powers that are neither enhanced nor decreased by your degree of schooling, socioeconomic status, sexual orientation, race, ethnicity, religion, age, gender, abilities, neurological situation, relationship status, job, ancestry, or how you were parented. Each of these three powers has a switch that you can always flick on. (I kid you not, always.) When you summon any of them, you instantly transform the experience you're having and that of others around you. All you need to do is decide that you want to use them. That's it. Like the day Clark Kent said, *Hey, I got this cape. Maybe I should use it.* The more you use each power, and create an awareness around using each of the pow-ers, the stronger each power gets. To facilitate that happening, throughout this chapter I'm going to refer to jotting things down. All of this should be kept in the same general space, perhaps a diary, perhaps an electronic document. You decide. I'm going to refer to this place as "your journal." Once you get really good at using these powers, your life becomes your most favorite playlist on repeat with the people you love most jamming along with you. Let's go!

MINDFULNESS: KNOW THYSELF AND DEPLOY THYSELF WITH INTENTION

I was introduced to mindfulness in 2007, when I wasn't getting along so great with some of my Stanford colleagues. I was all but forced to work with an executive coach whose job was to help me understand how I was coming across to others. That executive coach, Maryellen Myers, taught me mindfulness. At first, the process was clunky and strange—I'll explain it to you in a second—but after a few years it became easy, and these fourteen years later it is as natural to me as breathing.

Mindfulness is a process of paying close attention to what's going on within your body and mind. The concept goes far back in time, and it's informing folks in the twenty-first century most notably through the writings of Jon Kabat-Zinn, a longtime professor at the University of Massachusetts, now retired. Right off the bat I want to be clear that mindfulness isn't about being self-absorbed. Mindfulness is the opposite; it's actually about knowing yourself well enough in each moment so that you are able to let the self go and be present to whatever is happening around you.

Being mindful feels like I've given my spirit or soul or innermost most eternal and enduring self (concepts that to me are interchangeable) the ability to speak to me about what's going on for me in the moment, and to help me ascertain what I need to say or do in that moment in order to act consistently with my values, not lose my shit, and not hurt other people. It allows me to behave up front in the manner of my choosing instead of behaving more impulsively or even recklessly, which might then require me to circle back with an apology.

That sounds pretty good, right?

YOUR ROAD MAP TO MINDFUL TOWN

With a shout-out to my incredible coach Maryellen Myers, who introduced me to the concept of mindfulness and helped me be much more functional in the workplace and in my personal life and in just being a fucking human (and whom, as I've said previously, will surely be one of the people I picture when I die, if there's any truth to that concept), here's my take on how mindfulness works. This is just *my* interpretation and a glimpse into *my* practice, based on what I've learned from others. (Pro tip: To really get with the program I encourage you to read Kabat-Zinn and other authors, some of whom you'll find listed in Appendix II: Resources.) Please know that it took me many years to get to mindfulness as an ingrained instinct so that I don't even need to think about it. So, don't expect it to happen quickly. But this is a road map for how to get to mindful. I hope it's enough to get you curious about unleashing this superpower.

1. *Get quiet.* Until mindfulness becomes so practiced for you that it is simply part of your way of being, you're not going to be able to make it happen if there's noise around you. So, go to a place where you can sit or lie comfortably for a minute or two with

few distractions. This whole thing is about your mind, and your mind will not get the attention it needs if other things are going on. See how meta this gets?

2. *Notice your thoughts.* What comes up for you is not random shit, it's the stuff that is literally *on your mind.* It matters, by definition, to YOU. Pay attention to the topics that come up. Notice them. Say to yourself, "I'm thinking about X; I'm worried about Y; I'm feeling Z." Be kind to yourself as you notice your thoughts. You are taking an interest in you, and you're rooting for you. So, no judgment. Just notice it, name it, and you'll find that the thought quiets down. (If it doesn't quiet down easily, you might have to say to yourself something like, "Yep, yep, I hear that, it's a big concern.") In noticing the thing, you're reassuring your mind that you know it's a thing. (Note, this may be sounding a lot like meditation to you, and the two concepts are definitely related. There's even a thing called "mindfulness meditation." The major difference is that in meditation you're trying to quiet your thoughts and clear your mind, but in mindfulness you're noticing your thoughts and you're curious about them. Both meditation and mindfulness are sharpening your mental focus but with different outcomes.)

3. *Take an inventory of your body.* Slowly scan your mind across every part of your body. Let this entity that carries you through life—your body in its separate parts—feel seen. Is there pain or discomfort or a sense of lacking or excess anywhere? Notice, acknowledge, but don't judge. This body is YOU. Noticing different parts of your body and how you feel about them will in time turn into a practice of greater self-love, which is a little off topic, but worth pointing out as a dividend of developing a mindfulness practice.

4. *Jot it down.* So, you can't do this in the moment obviously. But right after being mindful, which has taken you maybe a couple minutes, get out your journal and jot down what came up for

you. Over time, having kept track of what you noticed in your mind and body, you'll have a record of your thoughts and things that are making you feel discomfort, which in turn will deepen your practice.

5. *Practice all of the above daily.* It takes weeks for something to become habit (and we're just talking habit here, not a mindfulness instinct, which, as I've said, took me *years*). So, stay at it. You're trying to get to a place where you no longer have to *make yourself* do it, because it has become part of your routine, and better yet, because you enjoy it.

6. *Take it on the road.* Once you think you know what mindfulness is, and you've done it a few times just with yourself, you're ready to level up and take your mindfulness on the road. This could be in your house with roommates or family, to work or school, and to all kinds of random interactions with strangers where you're going to try to notice what's happening in your mind and your body as you interact with other humans and the broader world. *Yikes?* Or, how 'bout *Whee!!*

7. *Notice what's coming up for you.* You could be anywhere that humans are saying stuff or things are happening: in a meeting, at the grocery store, talking to a friend, driving past an intersection, in book club, at the gym. Your body sends you signals before your brain can interpret and give language to what's going on. Your mouth might be dry. Your palms might be sweaty. Your voice might be changing pitch. Your stomach may be jumbly. Your knee may be jiggling. Your teeth may be biting your cheek. Your hands may be pulling at your hair. Your heart may be beating rapidly. You may feel a little disoriented, even dizzy. You may feel like you want to explode. Each of these things is an example of your body trying to tell you that everything is not as it should be. It's telling you that you're scared, mad, or ashamed. (A mindfulness practice will also allow you to notice the good feelings that come up, too, like if you're

incredibly excited, energized, and happy, and all of that's great; I'm focusing here on the more problematic feelings that arise and that I want to help you gain control over.). Notice it all. Tell yourself, *Aha, my voice sounds really deep right now* (or whatever your body is doing).

8. *Seek to know the underlying trigger and the feeling that causes the trigger.* Ask yourself what was said, what you saw, or what had happened *right before your body reacted* in whatever way it did. You're searching for what *triggered* your body's reaction. Your mind with its memory and language will tell you the answer. Once you have that information (e.g., *I saw X happen; That person said or did Y*), ask yourself, *And how do I feel about that?* or *And why does that concern me?* If possible in the moment, quickly jot down what you noticed, what you think the trigger was, and why you think it impacts you. Just create a little shorthand for yourself. Put more of it into your journal later. You are a complex human being. You've had thousands of experiences, some of which have made you relaxed, satisfied, peaceful, others that have made you afraid, mad, or ashamed. You've learned how to respond to those things. Through mindfulness you're learning to unpack all of that, understand it, so that you can be more in charge of what you do next.

9. *Move from having reflexes to having chosen responses.* You will get to a point where the trigger can happen but it no longer speaks for you. Your mindfulness practice allows you to say, *Ah yes, I'm feeling defensive because it sounds like they are questioning my smarts.* Or *Okay, I have a lot to say about this, I really need to jump in here no matter who else is speaking.* Just slowing it down that much then allows you to have control over what you do next. Without mindfulness what you do next is reflex. If it's a good thing, you might interrupt, overtake the conversation, stop listening to others, and just let your enthusiasm carry you along. If it's a bad thing, you yell, you get snarky, you scuttle out of there,

you escalate your rhetoric, you punch someone. With mindfulness, you ask yourself, *Do I want to respond and if so how? Is my
response an action or set of words or is my action to not respond
right now?*

10. *Practice, practice, practice.* Over time, with practice, you'll get
    good at letting mindfulness run in the background like your
    Internet browser. It's like you become your own Google. You
    engage it by searching, "Hmm, what's happening for me right
    now?" and up pops an answer. Once you enjoy mindfulness, i.e.,
    you don't have to "make yourself" do it, you intentionally turn
    to it as a way to help yourself understand what's going on around
    you or cope with how you do you. After some time you won't
    have to think about doing it anymore. It will have moved from
    an "I should" to an "I am" or even to an "I." You may have to take
    a leap of faith in reading this because you're not there yet. But
    do it. It'll be worth it. Mindfulness—an awareness of your own
    mind—is a tool that is always inside you. You're just locating, pol-
    ishing, sharpening, and using it. With more and more use, it'll
    always be there at the top of your tool kit. One day you'll be able
    to summon it with mere thoughts, like Thor and his hammer.

KINDNESS: DO UNTO OTHERS AS YOU WOULD HAVE OTHERS DO UNTO YOU

It's hard to describe kindness without using the word *kind*. ("Do kind
things"; "Be kind to others"—these are not helpful definitions!) So, what
IS kindness? What does it mean to be kind and do kind things? Believe
it or not when trying to define *kindness* there's an analog to obscenity—
stay with me—which the U.S. Supreme Court had to try to define back
in 1964. In the case *Jacobellis v. Ohio* the justices were reviewing a case
about pornography and they had to decide if what they were looking
at was "speech" protected by the first amendment or "obscenity," which
could be censored. Justice Potter Stewart said: "I shall not today attempt
further to define the kinds of material I understand to be embraced

within that shorthand description ["hard-core pornography"], and per-haps I could never succeed in intelligibly doing so. But *I know it when I see it*, and the motion picture involved in this case is not that."

I think it's the same with kindness. You know it when you see it. So, we'll get down to examples. (Note, in this chapter I'm focusing on kind things you can do *right now for another human near you.* You can also do kind things of a larger scope such as volunteering for a cause or donating to a cause, but the focus of this chapter is on using your kindness superpower to unleash what you as an individual can do for another individual in the moment.) Before we get to examples though, why does kindness even matter?

Pope Francis says our existence is interdependent, almost like our purpose is to be here for each other: "Rivers do not drink their own water; trees do not eat their own fruit; the sun does not shine on itself and flowers do not spread their fragrance for themselves. Living for oth-ers is a rule of nature. We are all born to help each other. No matter how difficult it is . . . Life is good when you are happy; but much better when others are happy because of you."

There are seven billion of us on the third rock from the sun and sometimes our days are rough. We have heavy burdens, hurts, needs, and small things that just make us sigh or ask, *why?* When aided in these moments by another human, or even an intuitive animal, kindness lifts the actual burden, and also lifts our heart. We think to ourselves, *Okay, I was treated kindly, and that is a sign that the world is good, and I can keep going on my journey because of this knowledge.* And then the magic kicks in: When treated kindly we are more likely to be kind to someone else. And then the super-duper magic kicks in: Anyone who witnessed the kind act exchanged between us and someone else is more likely to be kind to a third someone else. And the cosmic wonder of it all is that you being kind to someone else can even make YOU feel better. Being kind to someone else lifts YOUR spirits. Pulls YOU out of a sad state. Kindness is a magic elixir with exponential power.

In chaos theory, it's said that an infinitesimal thing like a butterfly fluttering its wings can, weeks later, cause a tornado somewhere else very far away. The "butterfly effect" also applies to kindness. As I type these words, there's a stranger in Portland, Oregon, named Nan who has just sent me another postcard. Their postcards come to my P.O. box—my publicly available address—so it doesn't feel creepy. This is the sixth I've received. The handwriting is a big flowing cursive. They seem to be writing because they care about me. Their second postcard had two flying bumblebees on the front and on the other side it said, "I wish you time in the zone—writing flows, delight follows & you like reading what you wrote. Sincerely, Nan." All this from a stranger!

Nan's postcards make me feel cared for. And make me ask, *When was the last time I was this kind to someone?* I decided to write Nan back. I found a little card that read "You Made My Day" and on the inside I wrote, "Just want you to know I'm getting your postcards and they make my day. Thank you for thinking of me. I appreciate it! Julie." It's not lost on me that Nan's postcard had a drawing of not just busy bees, but of bees beating their wings in flight! Butterfly effect!

One day Dan put a question out on Facebook: what's one word you'd use to describe me? (Brave soul!) It didn't take long for a flood of responses to come in from friends who knew him from across the span of his beautiful life. The word they overwhelmingly used: KIND. Let me give you a glimpse of how kindness shows up in the form of my man Dan. It was a Saturday morning in late April, about six weeks into the pandemic. We were still in bed. But I'd been awake for awhile, arms outstretched to the bedside table so I could attend to the various bits of work that come through my phone. Dan could probably feel the stress slaking off me. He rolled toward me, pressed his face into my back, and said, "What can I do to make today better for you?" This is what makes me want to go back in a time capsule and tell my twenty-year-old self, *Yup, him, for sure.*

In the coming months, I gave a bunch of virtual talks to school communities where parents who were struggling with the duration of the pandemic were hungry for guidance. *What guidance could I offer?* I wondered. I mean, I was winging the whole pandemic thing, too. But these were people who'd invited me to speak under different circumstances about either overparenting or race, and now they were turning to me again, so I wanted to try to be of use. I had to come up with *something* by way of wisdom. I developed a list called "Ten Steps for Sheltering in Place Without Losing Your Mind," and in and among my suggestions about how to hold their shit together I mentioned that morning in bed with Dan. I spoke for thirty-five to forty minutes, and then the moderator asked the questions that had been rolling in as I'd talked. The first question was, "How can I find my own Dan?" Apparently, this question had been asked by many.

I think the better question is *How can I be like Dan?* That's what this chapter is for.

HOW TO BE LIKE DAN (AKA GET YOUR KINDNESS ON)

Kindness isn't hard. You just have to want to do it. And when you want to, you'll notice opportunities to be kind everywhere. (Of course, there are always causes to donate to, or to volunteer for. But as I said earlier, I'm focusing on kindness at the level of individual to individual here.) You can offer kindness: In your home. As you walk down the street. In a store. At your school. In your workplace. In your car. To your self. And the more you do it, the more natural it gets, and the more good vibes you'll get from doing it. So, it'll just grow and grow like a muscle within you. Imagine you being the butterfly that beats their wings with kindness, and sets in motion a tornado of profound life-changing kindness for the entire world. Here are some suggestions based on the things I see and do in my own life. Note, kindness works for all: loved ones, acquaintances, and strangers (and it's often hardest for us to offer it to loved ones, so pay attention to that).

1. *Ask your partner, friend, or coworker, "What can I do to make today better for you?"* In other words, be like Dan. Ask this question, and—this is key—be willing to do what they say, within reason. They might come back with an existential "fix the world" but if they do, don't be daunted, just press back with "How could I make your part of the world better, today?" It blows people's mind just to be ASKED. In Jane McGonigal's book *SuperBetter*, which we discussed in chapter 9, "Take Good Care," she writes that research shows that it powerfully boosts someone's mood if we say to them, "On a scale of 1 to 10 how's your day going?" And then no matter what number they give (call it "X") ask them, "Is there anything I can do to move it from X to X+1?" We have

tremendous power to help our fellow humans by offering kindness. Give this one a try.

2. *Greet new people.* Whether it's your apartment building, dog park, office, job site, school, or support group, there's a newcomer and they're hoping someone kind will notice them and take an interest in their existence. Exchange names. Say something like, "If you need help figuring things out, let me know." Exchange whatever contact information is appropriate for your age and situation. We are a human community. YOU are someone else's entryway into a new part of the human community. It's a beautiful act of kindness to simply notice someone. Don't be creepy now; try to take your cues from them. But there's never harm in dropping a random act of kindness and moving on. My social media manager, Clarice Cho, is a twenty-six-year-old pandemic-era transplant to Brooklyn, and she decided it was the perfect time to adopt a puppy after wanting one for her whole life. When Klaus, jet-black and all of seven inches tall, had some trouble with potty training, a kind neighbor helped out. "I ran into the same guy two days in a row. He goes, 'Hey, we've seen this dog before, what's his name?' Before long he's giving me advice on a patch of grass around the corner where all the dogs pee. And Klaus peed! A couple days later I went to the magic grassy spot and saw that same neighbor, who greeted me with a smile and checked in on Klaus's progress. I'm no longer just a face in the crowd."

3. *When a stranger is lost, help them find their way.* Now here I mean *lost* lost, like I don't know where I am (which happens far less often than it used to since most of us have GPS in our pocket and car, but still. I mean if someone is lost today it means they're *really* lost). One of the things I loved most about working on a college campus was helping visitors who were visibly lost. I'd see people look around at buildings, look back down at a piece of paper or their phone, look back up again (this is the telltale sign of "visibly lost") and I'd walk over and say, "Hi, it looks like you might be looking for something. Can I help?" Now, BEWARE:

your tone must be helpful and polite. Legions of people who don't "look like they belong" on the basis of skin color or perceived class have been sternly asked CAN I *HELP* YOU (which is code for "What the fuck are you doing here?"). Don't ask it like that. Ask with a genuine motive in your heart of serving the other person. Your entire purpose is to be *kind*.

4. *When someone can't find a grocery item, tell them where it is.* This is a variant on the above, with a twist. At the holidays, I like to put on my Santa hat when I go to the Safeway. I get what I need, but I also roam around looking for those who are confused and lost. Because often at the holidays the regular shopper is at home cooking or baking so the partner or child or other loved one of the regular shopper is now in the aisles of the Safeway with a list. Take a gander. Listen a little. They're probably muttering to themselves about the thing they can't find. Say, "Hey, are you looking for gluten-free pasta? It's in aisle 9!" Then smile and keep going. Bonus points if you're not sure where the gluten-free pasta is, and you race over to aisle 9 to double check, you find it, race back to the person, catch your breath, and then say casually, "Hey, are you looking for gluten-free pasta? It's in aisle 9!"

5. *When someone drops something, run over there and pick it up and hand it back to them.* Forgive the non-pandemically-conscious nature of this, but assuming it's safe to be within six feet of a stranger, when they drop something run over there if you're able and hand it to them. Note: This has ramifications around skin color—if you're white, do not shriek if a dark-skinned person is helping you. And if you do shriek, go work off your shame by paying that act of kindness forward by helping a dark-skinned person. I have a friend, Black and male, who ran after a white lady after she dropped something out of her purse and he was trying to get it back to her. It was a terrifying encounter for him. But my heart loves that he did it even against the racialized backdrop that makes that encounter so fraught. Acts of kindness offered across various lines of identity should help us bridge our many misunderstandings.

6. *Pay someone's tab.* With that story of my Black friend and the white stranger in mind, here's a story of my own. I was on a writing retreat in a small town on the California coast and went into the little grocery store for provisions. I was in line behind a white woman who was buying wine, cigarettes, and aspirin. Her credit card was declined. Twice. She let me go ahead of her and started fumbling around in her purse. When the cashier was ringing me up I nodded my head in the direction of the woman and drew a line in the air with my finger around her stuff. I was trying to say, *I'll pay for her stuff, too.* The cashier raised their eyebrows at me. I nodded my head and pointed at her stuff again. When I was done the lady said, "I'm just going to go out to my car because I probably have some cash there." I said to her, "Naw, you're good." She said, "What?" I said, "I took care of it for you." She said, "You didn't have to do that!" I said, "I know, but I wanted to. I know what it's like to want an aspirin, a cigarette, and a glass of wine. Just pay it forward." Secretly, I hope she'll realize that not only was she helped but she was HELPED BY A BLACK WOMAN. No lie, I hope she'll cross some cultural lines—whatever that may mean for her—when she pays it forward. While we're on the subject of picking up a stranger's tab some other ideas for where to do this include at a drive-thru, a coffee shop, or a highway toll booth. Driving can be stressful. You can make someone's day!

7. *Know whether to fix it or listen.* I'm pivoting now toward ways of being kind that are more subtle than the above. Sometimes when people complain about a problem, they want help with the solution. And sometimes when they complain they want to just get it off their chest and be listened to. Responding in the right way in the given situation is an act of kindness. Responding in the wrong way can really annoy the person. I'm a fixer, and I often annoy the heck out of my daughter, Avery, when she just wants to be able to vent and be listened to. I've learned that it's helpful to empathize and then ask what she needs. Like this: "I'm so sorry this happened to you. That's frustrating. Are you looking for ideas or do you just want to vent?" Showing up in the manner

that is right for your loved one (regardless of what you'd want if you were in their shoes) is a huge act of kindness.

8. *Be an ally.* When you see someone with less power than you having a difficult time, step up and use your power to help. In 2017, I was traveling in South Carolina for my book tour and was accompanied by my friend Jay-Marie, who is trans. Some locals invited us to a Ranky Tanky concert at the Dock Street Theatre, said to be the first building in the thirteen original colonies built to be a theater. Jay-Marie went to use the women's restroom, which was at the end of the crowded plush lobby, and I noticed them get some looks as they went through the restroom door. I thought to myself, *They'll be fine.* Then I said to myself, *You know what? I need to be sure, and THEY need to know I'm thinking of them.* I went into the restroom and announced loudly, "Hey, J, I'm here." From within a stall, I heard a confident "Thanks." This can happen anywhere. In a park where someone is getting picked on. In a subway when the cops have been called, and they're talking to the person you know is not the wrongdoer. Being an ally takes bravery, but the more privilege and power you have the more it needs to be used. Your kindness here is in noticing that someone might need help, an advocate, or a witness in a situation. Take up your kindness and your bravery. Someone will be glad you did.

9. *Talk to a teenager.* Teens writ large have a reputation for moodiness, aloofness, and poor judgment. Part of that is our perception, part of that is hormones, and part of that is the way they get shit on by society. Teens are some of the most highly scrutinized yet under-seen humans we've got. So, the next time you see a teen you know (a younger sibling or family member, a neighbor, a friend's kid, a kid you're mentoring), look them in the eye and say, "Hey, great to see you, how ARE you?" If you know something about their interests, bring it up: "Hey, how are those guitar lessons you were telling me about when I saw you last?" If you're close enough to inquire into their personal life without it being awkward ask, "Is there anyone special in your life I should know

about?" (Note the language is deliberately nongendered.) Resist asking about college, grades, or standardized tests. Resist mentioning the stress of being a teen. Just lean in to their humanness. Showing a teen that you know they exist and you care about them as they are is a tremendous act of kindness.

10. *Listen to a senior's stories.* I may find it easy to roam through a store in a Santa hat helping strangers but I'm hardly the paragon of kindness, and often I find it hard to be kindest to my own loved ones. Sad but true. And I'm admitting this to you because maybe you're this way, too. Take my mom, with whom I've shared an address as an adult for twenty years. She's eighty-two now. And like anyone at her age and stage of life, she likes to tell stories, and sometimes I feel the need to tell her, "Yep, I know, you've told me this before." Boo, me! We should be listening to our elders, not dismissing them. If you're lucky enough to have a living grandparent, call them up or go over to their house and say you want to hear some of their favorite stories. You might have heard them a dozen times before. That doesn't matter. This isn't about you at all, remember. You're doing an act of kindness for *them.* And for someone whose memory about yesterday may not be so sharp, but whose memory of the 1940s, '50s, and '60s is crystal clear, ask and listen. Don't be bad like me and tell them "You've already told me this." Leaning in and listening is not only an act of kindness, it's an act of respect. And you just might learn something. If you don't have a relative who is elderly, maybe you have an elderly neighbor? Or perhaps your community has an elder care facility and they need volunteer visitors? Slowing down to sit closely and listen well to someone who has triple or quadruple your life's worth of stories inside of them is an act of kindness.

11. *Let someone's needs tag along with your own.* Here I'm thinking you're going to the grocery store or doing an errand in town later today. Write a note to your neighbor asking if you can pick anything up for them and tuck it into their door. A new couple moved onto our street last week (amid the pandemic) and I saw

them in their driveway as I was driving out to the store. I pulled over, introduced myself from a safe distance, chitchatted a bit, and then I said, "Hey, I'm headed to Walgreens, do you need anything?" I'm telling you, they beamed like, *Oh my gosh, someone nice lives here.* And I was beaming inside, too, feeling, *Hey, look how KIND I am!* No, they didn't need anything but I think all three of us were glad I asked.

12. *Be an elf.* I love the thought of a person never even seeing my face, just feeling like, *Wow, someone I don't even know took care of that for me.* One year, at the holidays, our family paid the layaway tab at Target for three families, which I knew was helping some kids experience Santa Claus. I realize my privilege is showing. If you're privileged financially, too, you can use your money to create acts of kindness. And not just at the holidays. And if you aren't especially privileged financially? There are all kinds of elfin things you can do for free. Plow the snow from a neighbor's path early one morning. Bring your neighbor's newspaper to their door or bring their garbage bins in. Put some beautiful ornaments on the tree in the yard of a family that is suffering during the holidays. They won't know who did it, but they'll be blown away that someone cared.

In your journal, note the kind things you noticed yourself doing and how you felt while doing those things and after. By taking note, you're drawing greater mental awareness to the acts and to their effects on you. Over time you'll have made them simply a part of your instincts. Kind will simply be how you ARE.

BE GRATEFUL FOR ALL YOU'VE BEEN GIVEN

If mindfulness is awareness, and kindness is a thing you do for others, then the third of your superpowers—gratitude—is a mashup: an awareness of the good things that have happened to *you*. This is deceptively simple. It's not just about saying thank you frequently and appreciating what you have. It's about developing a practice of noticing and

expressing what you're grateful for. Research shows that paying attention to what you're grateful for helps you draw more of those things into
your life going forward. It's kind of like when you learn a new word and
suddenly you see it everywhere—it's not that that word has never been
in your environment before, it's just that you're noticing it. Gratitude
works the same way. The more you notice yourself feeling grateful, the
more things you are likely to feel grateful for. And here's where that
journal I'm encouraging you to keep is key: over time you will have a
record of what you're grateful for and you'll be able to track the growth
of gratitude and abundance in your life. And you'll be more satisfied
with the life you lead. *What?* Yeah.

Aesop said (or, at least, a whole lot of gift cards quote him as saying)
that "gratitude makes what you have enough." In a world of tremendous
inequality, I'm struck by the studies that show that happiness is not a
function of how *much* you have, but of how much you appreciate what
you *do* have. In our early twenty-first-century existence, capitalism has
disassociated us from our value as living, breathing beings, as if the size
of our bank accounts measured our worth as people. As my friend and
coach Mary Ruth Quinn has taught me, we humans have meandered
off our path, and we need to get back to our own voices and values.
Noticing what we're grateful for helps us get back on our paths and feel
content with where we are. Parenting author Sarah MacLaughlin (*Raising Humans with Heart: Not a How-To Manual*) writes, "Gratitude . . . is
about accepting *what is*." Giving gratitude means experiencing more *awe*.

Gratitude is also humility, a recognition that you are not just here
with your self-made badass self, but rather, you are a collection of atoms
and molecules born of other people. You've had opportunity that was,
yes, sometimes earned but often given, and you are standing on the
shoulders of those who came before and did the best they could. It's
an acknowledgment that you are not alone in this life but are part of a
cosmos, a connected community of intertwined beings whose actions
impact one another. Each time someone comes to one of my talks I feel
humble. I try to convey it to my audiences. I say, "I'm really honored that
you decided to take a chance that a couple hours with me tonight might
be worth your while. I'm going to try to make good use of your time."
And I mean it.

WHAT DO YOU HAVE TO BE GRATEFUL FOR?

Often when we offer gratitude or say grace we talk about big things like "my life, my health, my partner, the food on the table." Those things are so important to recognize. Yet gratitude seems to provide an even richer sense of well-being when we express thanks for smaller, more specific things instead of larger, more abstract ones. So, get that journal, and start keeping a gratitude list along with the things you're jotting down about mindfulness and kindness. And, as with mindfulness and kindness, recognizing what you're grateful for will benefit you personally. When you look back on your day and acknowledge the small good things that happened along the way, your psyche will feel, *Wow, it was a pretty great day.* What might you be grateful for? Here are some things to notice:

1. *Your existence.* The older you get the more you'll realize you're grateful that you woke up today and that you're in decent health. If you've had health issues, you get this, or if someone you know is suffering, you get this. Every single day that you're physically and mentally stable and well is a gift. Cherish it. Express gratitude for it.

2. *The existence of your people.* If you live with other humans, don't be ships passing in the night. Whether it's lovers, roommates, housemates, or family, take whomever you live with and pause for six seconds to put your hands on their shoulder and look them in the eye and just smile. We are all so busy, but the humans we've conjoined our lives with can form our closest relationships. Relationships are like plants; they wither or thrive. Pause your hectic life and appreciate your people.

3. *The specific things loved ones and colleagues do for you.* With a loved one, instead of saying, "I love you," say, "I love *when* you . . ." or "I love *how* you . . ." and name something very specific that they just did. (You may remember that in chapter 7, "Start Talking to Strangers," I shared some love notes that Dan and I have exchanged over the years as a way to express our gratitude to each other and keep this relationship burning.) With coworkers,

instead of saying, "It's great working with you," say, "You're a great colleague because . . ." or "I appreciate when you . . ." and then list something very specific. This will make the person feel good, and the specificity will make it much more likely that you're going to see this same awesome stuff from them again.

4. *The things a delivery person or service worker brings you.* They didn't make the pizza, or whatever's in that UPS box, and they didn't cause the Internet outage or flatten the tire on your car. They're just trying to give you what you need, solve your problem, make you happy. Go beyond "Thanks" to "Thank.You. So.Very.Much!" Extra points for a wide grin that shows your teeth. Extra points for eye contact. (And if eye contact is hard for you, or you have social anxiety, then extra points for trying this at all!)

5. *The work of a person whose advice or expertise you rely upon.* Your doctor, teacher, dentist, carpenter, plumber—these are all folks you can't do without. After a physical exam, thank your doctor for their expertise. After a course wraps up, thank your teacher for how they conducted the class. After your plumber fixes that leak, thank them for coming out to help you late at night. Everyone craves appreciation. Even the people you *think* don't need it, do. Your gratitude will send them off to the next patient, student, client, or customer better prepared to encounter the next set of challenges. By expressing gratitude, you are paving the way for everyone to have a better experience.

6. *The qualities of an opponent.* This one's hard for me. Between my lawyer personality and my Lythcott personality I've had a lot of training in how to prove my point, and a lot less training in how to be congenial. You are much more likely to be heard making whatever point you're trying to make if you begin by expressing genuine gratitude for something the other person has said or how they said it or who they are in the community or the family or the house or the organization.

7. *The experience of having the right of way.* A lot of folks are accustomed to being deferred to as they walk the path of life (due to class/caste, race, gender, and social position). But none of us is better than any other person, and *anyone* who steps to the side as you walk by, lets you go first, or holds a door open for you deserves a sincere *thank you.* You may not even *notice* that you're accepting all of this deference. Notice. Ask yourself about the systemic sociocultural causes of why this is happening. And in the immediate term, for the love of God, say, "Thank you." Whether the person is being paid to do this or not, thank them.

8. *The material things you have.* If you have a roof over your head that's paid for or that you can pay for without too much stress, speak your gratitude out loud. Same with food and the other basics of life. When the pandemic hit I found my focus narrowing from what I hoped to save up for and have one day—say, in the form of a second house on the coast—and got a whole lot more appreciative for the house I do have, in which I've raised two kids with my husband and mother and which keeps us warm and safe and dry. I've written this book for you from my tiny office in our backyard, and every time I'm done for the night and I flick off the heater or the fan (depending on the season), turn off the light, and come back into our house, I am so grateful that we bought this little shed for me. I wrote my first book in our bedroom!

9. *The small things, whenever they happen.* A card that comes by snail mail is such a gift these days. So, be like Nan, my very kind pen pal in Portland. Buy or make some cards that you can just randomly send or deliver. Drop a note to a local bookseller who is devoted to your community, to a tireless public servant who is fighting for an issue you care about, to a person who was kind to you when you were having a tough time. Often we say, "Oh, I should really reach out to this person." Then months pass. It's okay. Forget how many months (or years) it's been and do it NOW. Turn your *oughts* and

shoulds into *ams* and *ares*. And know that your act of gratitude will make someone's day.

10. *Nature.* I'm not an outdoorsy person, but after being cooped up for two straight months during the pandemic, when my daughter, Avery, took me on a scenic drive for Mother's Day, I couldn't get over the majesty of the redwoods and the hills and the sun starting to set through the trees. Be grateful for a view. Clean air if you've got it. A park. A pretty street. A patch of garden. The birds that come to your feeder. The potatoes, beans, peppers, tomatoes, mint, and basil in your garden. Be grateful even for the rhubarb in its ginormous glory. It's trying to make it in this world just like you.

PUTTING YOUR POWERS TOGETHER

Dan, Mom, and I bought a home together over twenty years ago. This means I'm both mother and daughter (and wife and self and other identities) all under the same roof. I find the three-generational mother-daughter dynamic to be particularly instructive, and something that allows me to practice mindfulness, kindness, and gratitude all in one conversation sometimes. For example, when Avery went off to start her second year of college, amid the pandemic, she called home one night incredibly frustrated about how to get to all of her online classes, register her moped with the DMV, put in a repair order with her landlord, and buy enough food for the week. Like any parent, I wanted to help my baby and as I've already shared with you, I have a tendency to want to fix rather than listen. So I started to give her advice. She just sighed and said, "Mom, I *know* those things. I'm just telling you that I'm frustrated that I have to deal with all of it." I feel so bad when I do this. I'm trying to help, not harm. Much to her credit, Avery is kind to me as she gives me this feedback. My kids teach me so much!

Well, the very next day, I'm having my morning coffee with my mother (which as you know is a practice I adopted during the pandemic) and I start to tell her how completely stressed I am about writing this book you're reading while giving talks to various groups, and all the things I have left to do by a certain deadline, and what my editor is expecting. And my mom starts asking me what I'm prioritizing and suggesting what I might do differently. I feel frustrated. My mindfulness practice kicks in. While my mother continues to offer advice, my mindfulness practice tells me what is happening for me: that I am feeling judged and fixed instead of held and heard. So, instead of flying off the handle at my mom I'm able to speak kindly to her about the fact that I just want to vent. But I also use gratitude to express to my mom that I appreciate that she's trying to help. Mindfulness also tells me, *This is exactly how Avery must have felt talking with you last night.* After I talk with my mom, I text Avery and say, "I'm so sorry I tried to fix things last night. I love you and I'm sorry you're struggling. I'm here for you and I know you can do this." This is an act of kindness. I get a huge "Awww, thanks, Mom" with some emojis in return. Then, I sit quietly with myself and my thoughts for a few moments and thank God, the universe, and everybody else who runs this show for being in a position where I can be both mother and daughter at once and have each role inform the other. Mindfulness, kindness, and gratitude all showed up for me that morning over coffee with my mom. All three tools were polished sharp in my tool kit, and as a result, I was mindful, kind, and grateful with my mom. And I was able to repair things with Avery, too. Calmness descended all around me. I felt like calling my coach Maryellen to say, "Look what I just did!" It's hard work being a human in community with other humans. But when we deploy these three superpowers, we become the very best version of ourselves and we can be an unstoppable force for good.

DON'T JUST TAKE MY WORD FOR IT

MEET ORLY—Creating Kindness from the Inside Out

When she was just four years old, Orly Wahba had a deep sense that she was supposed to do something to bring people together in the world. "I felt it in my bones. My dad has always been a dreamer in the most positive sense, and when I was little he instilled in me that God is big and anything I want to achieve is possible." Orly is now one of the world's leading voices on the value of spreading kindness. Dan used to be on the board of her kindness nonprofit, Life Vest Inside, which is how I know her. I'm on the phone with her to try to understand how kindness became her central focus. As with all things worth doing, it wasn't easy.

Orly is a thirty-eight-year-old Jewish woman who was born and raised in Brooklyn, New York. Her mom is a Sephardic Jew who was born in Egypt and came to the United States when she was six. Her father, also Sephardic, was raised in Israel and came to the States after serving four years in the Israeli army. Her parents met at sixteen and twenty-three, got married a few years later, and had five children of whom Orly is the middle child. Her mom was a housewife who "did everything for us," and her father's work created a comfortable middle-class life for them all. The family consider themselves "modern Orthodox," which means they keep the Sabbath and keep kosher. "And we were very spiritual and closely connected to God." Growing up, Orly attended Yeshiva of Flatbush, a Jewish school where half of the day is taught in English, and half in Hebrew. Then, in the deep of the night when Orly was fifteen, a fire raged through their house, in which her father's business was also located. Her parents tried to salvage whatever they could but emerged from the rubble "blackened and broken." In the ensuing years the family would move from place to place, living with relatives for a time, moving, moving again, with some staying here and some staying there all over the greater New York area. They would not be back together under one roof again for six years. Their quality of life declined. In talking with Orly on the phone at her home in Jerusalem these many years later, I get a clear sense that this fire demarcated a "before" and an "after" in her young life.

"I've had a close relationship with God since I was a little kid," she tells me. "I didn't understand where animosity came from. It hurt me. I felt it really deeply. And I didn't understand why our differences caused so many issues. Bringing people together was just a part of me. I knew I had to be a part of the solution. I knew I was meant to do *something* that would bring people together. I didn't know how or when, but I knew my why. As a kid talking about changing the world, people look at you like you're nuts. As an adult they think you're even more nuts. *Oh yeah, YOU'RE going to change the world. Yeah, yeah, yeah. You're so naïve.*"

Orly went from being a shy but happy little kid to a kid with low self-esteem. "When you're told you can't do something long enough, you come to believe it.

I didn't like going to school. Learning was very difficult for me." In third grade she was taken out of the regular class and put in a classroom for struggling kids. This new teacher shared a poem called "Thinking" by Walter D. Wintle, which is about the fact that if you think you can't do something, well, you can't. Orly read and reread the poem countless times. It seemed like it had been written for her. "Because of the kindness of a teacher who didn't give up on me, suddenly learning became easy. In a short period of time I went from being on the bottom of my class to excelling in school." But middle school brought a new set of challenges. "In seventh grade, every friend turned on me. They wouldn't let me sit with them and made plans behind my back. I felt I didn't belong so I didn't want to be there. I went to the nurse every day." High school was not much better. "Now you're trying to figure out who you are amidst everyone telling you who you should be." Orly loved doing kind things for people. "If you missed school, I was the kid copying notes and giving them to you. I got a sense of real fulfillment from doing stuff like that." But this kindness tended to be one-way.

Then sophomore year her house caught fire. "We were physically all okay, but overnight my family lost everything. And it does something to you when your safe haven goes up in smoke. The proof of your existence—all of your baby pictures and videos—is gone. It does something to you when you see your parents break down crying. I felt, *They're going through enough; I can't be a burden on them*. I hid my feelings from them. I hid my feelings from my friends, too, because they were fifteen and going through their own stuff. So, I acted like everything was good. I would make jokes, like, *Yeah, my house burned down*. But things were going south. My dad lost his business. I would pretend that everything was good but everything was wrong. One night, I went to bed, and the way I see it is that I didn't wake up the next morning. I had fallen into a dark depression, a suicidal darkness. I didn't go to school for a few months. Every day I just alternated between sleeping and crying. The thing that hurt me most was that not one person came to visit. Not one person picked up the phone. I was angry at everyone. My friends. My family. God. Angry at myself. I wouldn't talk to anybody but I was screaming at God. I wondered, *If I wasn't here tomorrow, would it matter*? The answer seemed to be no."

After several months Orly's parents forced her to go back to yeshiva to complete her sophomore year. "You didn't want to talk to me. I didn't want to talk to you. I was morbid. My academics fell apart. One morning before school I was washing my face. I looked up at myself in the bathroom mirror and I didn't see that four-year-old kid who'd dreamed of changing the world anymore. She was no longer in there. It scared me. I didn't know how I was going to pick myself up. But I said to myself, *This can't be my end.* I made a promise to myself to be there for people the way I wished people had been there for me, to see people the way I wished someone had seen me. That promise woke me up and guided me forward. The next few years I walked alone. It was a great gift. I was no longer looking to impress others. I now had a chance to fall in love with me for me." It seems to me that what happened was that Orly decided that she mattered to *herself.*

High school wore on. These were years in which she describes herself as "quiet and shy." She'd been too afraid to raise her hand in class. But one day, on a school seminar during her senior year, she took a risk. "We were sitting in a circle talking about overcoming obstacles. I had something to offer, and I felt compelled to share, so I raised my hand. I was no longer focused on *What am I doing, and how is it impressing others?* I shared about the fire and the hardships of sophomore year. This was the first time I'd spoken aloud about any of it. These kids I used to be so intimidated by were listening to me. Asking *me* for advice. The more I gave to others by way of advice or help, the more I healed. I became obsessed and in love with this concept of giving."

But Orly had always been a giver, so I ask her what changed. She explains that the difference is in *why* you're doing the giving. "I hadn't realized that there are two forms of giving: giving from a place of weakness and giving from a place of strength. Giving from weakness feels like you're making a sacrifice. Perhaps you're doing it because you're insecure or trying to impress someone or to get them to like you. That's what I'd been doing for so many years. You can feel depleted by that kind of giving, and you may come to resent that giving. On the other hand, giving from a place of strength is like a candle that lights another but retains its flame. It's powerful and it's positive. You can give to others freely without being depleted because you're doing it from a place of abundant self-love."

Orly had known as a four-year-old that she was on the planet to be a force for good, and in her senior year of high school, she finally began learning how to go about doing it. She did it by reframing her sense of service and of whom she was serving. "I learned that we have to see ourselves as part of the puzzle. That creating kindness is really about preventing unkindness. And preventing unkindness starts with how we see ourselves, to first and fore-most look inward and love who you are. If a person doesn't respect and honor themselves, they can't give respect and honor to another. But when you love yourself with all your flaws and mistakes, you can be open to loving others for who they are and what they believe. The Bible says love your neighbor as yourself. The loving-our-neighbor part is easy. The hard part for many of us is loving ourselves."

Orly's example of how we can have a hard time loving our neighbor if we don't love ourselves is religious intolerance. "Where does religious animosity come from? It comes from a person who doesn't feel strong enough in their own beliefs, which makes them very fearful that another person will come along and influence them. And so they feel the need to force their beliefs down everyone else's throat. But if they truly love and believe in their own ideals, then they can be open to the fact that the other person has their story just as they have their story. For example, I come from a very traditional Jewish home. I'm very connected spiritually, and I'm very comfortable in what I believe. But I have friends from all different beliefs—Muslim, Hindu, Christian, atheist—and I have enough space in my heart to love them all. There are no superfluous people in the world—it's not like God said, *Oops, I made an extra person*. We each bring something to the table. That's where respect comes into place. Like in an orchestra. Every instrument plays in a different way and sometimes some are louder and sometimes others are louder but each contributes to the beauty of the symphony. You get to a place where you understand the individuality of every person, and also the universality of us all connected."

Her second example is the value of inclusivity and how it can be turned against itself. "People are so focused on inclusivity that you try to become so inclusive you become exclusive. The true meaning of inclusivity is that you may not believe what I believe, you may actually hate what I believe, but you're okay with the fact that I'm going to share my perspective and it's different and that's okay. We all leave our own mark. We need to recognize the individuality of every person. We need to be okay with the fact that people are just going to be different from us. That even though you're sure your way is completely right, it's all right for this other person to think otherwise. It doesn't make them less of a person. We have to love them in spite of our differences."

Back to Orly's story. She graduated from high school and went off to Brooklyn College, where she earned degrees in film production and English.

In her free time, she directed plays and did loads of community service work, including tutoring kids. After college, she became a substitute teacher at Yeshiva of Flatbush in Brooklyn. She was good at it. When a full-time teaching spot opened up they offered it to her, and also asked her to direct the musical theater program. This was 2004–2005. "Teaching is about inspiring students to see the beauty in themselves so they can begin to see the beauty in others. If we can instill self-love in children, they will have a lot more room in their heart to love others and embrace others fully. That's how we will be able to heal and repair the world."

After many years of teaching kids about loving themselves so they could love others, Orly created a visual metaphor around the concept—the idea of each of us being buoyed by a life vest we have inside of us, which in turn allows us to help others. Then, with her background in film production she created a film centered around this metaphor that would demonstrate the ability of kindness to go from one person to the next to the next and to come back to the person who set it in motion. The film, just under six minutes, shot with one camera, all continual action, begins with a construction worker wearing his tell-tale orange vest who sees a kid fall off a skateboard and comes to the kid's aid. The kid then helps an old lady cross the street. The old lady gives change to someone trying to feed a parking meter. And so on. After kindness has exchanged hands maybe thirteen times, the film ends with the same construction worker, still in his orange vest, being handed a glass of water by a waitress who has seen how hard he's been working.

"In September of 2010, I was standing on a street in Red Bank, about to finally make this short film I'd been working on all summer. I looked up and said, 'God, I have no idea where you're taking me, but I have a feeling in my heart that something I am doing here today will change the course of my life.' I didn't know what it was. I didn't know if my film was going to reach anybody. But it was imbued with a tremendous amount of meaning." The four-year-old Orly who sensed she was here on the planet to bring people together was about to be vindicated. She took what she initially thought would be a one-year leave from her teaching job to make the dream come true. "I put my all into the film. I created the nonprofit Life Vest Inside and invested all of my savings in it. Everyone thought I was nuts. 'What are you doing?' 'How do you think you're going to make an impact?' So many people discouraged me. But it was a calling in my heart and there was no option. I knew I had to answer the call."

In October 2011, Orly posted her film *Kindness Boomerang* (you can find it on YouTube). Within a couple months the film went viral globally. She wrote a book, *Kindness Boomerang: How to Save the World (and Yourself) Through 365 Daily Acts*. She sparked a kindness revolution. "It has been incredibly humbling because I know it has zero to do with me. I'm just being a conduit for good, bringing that good through me. Each of us can be that conduit if we allow ourselves to be it. So many good things can flow through us. I'm seeing it more and more and more, people sharing those same words of kindness in different languages. I started seeing shifts all over the world."

As a beacon for kindness Orly also must serve as its guardian. "There are those that have taken it to mean something different, who are using it as marketing or a catchphrase without understanding its meaning. It's sad to see. If people are going to talk about kindness but only reserve it for those they believe deserve it, that's not kindness. Kindness does not see race or religion. You don't just check kindness off your to-do list and think, *I'm good to go*. Kindness is a lens through which you look at the world. It's not an action that you do on Monday from five to six p.m. We need to see ourselves as part of a puzzle. Our choices matter. To get to the point of actually living a kind life we have to do the inner work, which is hard. We have to stop and stare at ourselves in the mirror and ask ourselves difficult questions, like *Who am I? What do I stand for? What do I represent? What are the characteristics and values that are dear to me? How do I want to be known? How do I treat others?*" Orly says it's very easy for us to spot unkindness in others. But it's very difficult to look at it within ourselves. "We don't want to feel that guilt. But once you see it you have a responsibility to do something about it. You can't change another person's belief system. All you can be responsible for is to live *you* the best you can."

Orly's nonprofit, Life Vest Inside, and its flagship product the *Kindness Boomerang* film are now close to ten years old. The film has been viewed over a hundred million times. Orly remains a full-time volunteer with the organization "to inspire all people to live a life of kindness" while doing other work for pay on the side. In addition to the inspiring film, Life Vest Inside also offers leadership training, a kindness curriculum for schoolchildren, and international events like Dance for Kindness, which brings people all over the world to do the same dance on the same day. The goal is to empower as many people as possible to recognize that your greatest strength is right there inside of you.

COVID-19 became an important reminder of what matters most for Orly, who says, "When people weren't allowed to go out, and everything stopped, there was a silence, a silence like an enormous mirror. It showed us we're great at doing the busy work, but we need to do the inner work. The most important work is the work of the heart."

MEET ANTHONY (AGAIN)—Tapping the Strength of His Mind as a Superpower

We're back with Anthony, the Black man who had police draw guns on him in college, whom we met in chapter 10, "How to Cope." You'll recall that he went to the continent of Africa at the strong urging of a Black faculty mentor, where he regained (or, perhaps, developed for the first time) an abiding self-love, a sense of his power in the world, and a road map for how to help others.

Anthony returned to the U.S. and went to graduate school at UCLA for African studies and anthropology. "My plan was to get the PhD and become a professor. But by the time I was coming up on my master's, half of the psychology department were my holistic healing and well-being clients. Here's how that started: I was getting up at five a.m. to do my breathing. A friend was really down and had pain in her body, so I shared with her how to breathe and do bodywork. That is, *You're not thinking about your dissertation right. It's affecting your breathing and your posture. Breathe like this, lie down like this, sleep like this. These are pressure points in your body to be mindful of.* It's all about thinking, breathing, moving. I told her, 'How you're coming at your life is off. Understand that.'" He explains that this is the same thinking pattern he himself had experienced at Tufts. "How I was thinking about Tufts University was off. How I was being treated there was making me angry, which was affecting my breathing, which was affecting my physiology, which was affecting my endocrine system." The friend told another colleague. And so on. "I had about eight graduate students knocking on my door, asking if I could help them. They encouraged me to get out of academia and follow a career in natural health and healing. I thought about it."

An anthropology professor had befriended Anthony and become his mentor. He'd given Anthony office space and some extra funding. Then the university decided to move the anthropology department to a brand-new building and merge it with professors from a different department. "I was in the new office by myself early one morning, doing a little meditation, and I hear some-one rattling keys at the door. I knew it wasn't my mentor, Professor Hammond. He was away. I thought, *Okay, I'm going to meet another professor today.* I came out of my meditation and turned around and looked at this short, fat, bald white man. He looked at me and spurted, 'You must be in the wrong office.' If I'd been an undergrad at Tufts, I'd still be cursing him. But by then I had done so much work on myself. I thought to myself, *This environment is new to all of us, and he goes to the assumption that I don't belong.* He turned out to be right. I didn't belong. I decided, *I am in the wrong place because I'm not going through the gauntlet of old white men to get my PhD in anthropology.* In undergrad, I didn't know how to choose my battles, so I fought every single one. But now as a PhD student, I gracefully bowed out and started my business in natural health and healing."

I ask Anthony for more detail on that very pivotal interaction. Having been the Black person in the historically white, elite university context for much of my career, I know the sting of these presumptions of unbelonging in such spaces. I've certainly felt demeaned in those moments. You feel you've made it, and in an instant you're brought to your knees. Was Anthony really above it all? Did he really just gracefully bow out? Is mindfulness that magical?

"What I mean is, I responded instead of being reactive. 'No,' I told him, 'I do belong here. I'm the mentee of Professor Hammond. My name is Anthony.'" In other words, Anthony made nice with the white person, which made it easy for the white person, and also for himself. I get it. I've done that in my own town here in Silicon Valley where I've knocked on the door of a mutual friend and been met with the same reaction Anthony got from the anthropology profes-sor. "Yes," Anthony says, hearing my brief tale. "I smoothed it over as we always do." But it was more than that. Different. And better. It wasn't about appeasing the racism, it was about getting where he needed to get, which was out of there, safely. Doing what he needed to do in order to be in charge of himself and further his goals. That's mindfulness. "Had I been the angry Black man, we know how that would've turned out. I know how to play the game, but I just choose not to. I extricate myself from situations. I'm a yoga practitioner now working with executives, professional athletes, youth at risk, and incarcerated youth and adults." Anthony doesn't get held back by the bullshit of others. He keeps going. And he does that by being mindful 110 percent of the time.

"I had to make a decision. Am I going to go through the gauntlet of old white men and get this PhD? Or do I decide not to take on this battle? By now, at UCLA, I realized I don't have to go this way. There are other ways I can travel the world and support myself. And if I AM going to go through the gauntlet, I'm going to saunter through, unlike the way I did it at Tufts where instead of sauntering I would ball my fist up and fight it, fists raised, go toe-to-toe in every lecture, be more prepared, and fight fight fight fight. My thinking about it now is completely different. I've developed the tools to deal with the old white men. It's a mindset. Very concretely: anger is like short shallow breathing. Let's change the breathing pattern, and then we can change the thoughts. There's nobody having anxiety attacks that are doing deep abdominal breathing. Heat in your lower belly changes the thoughts. You can't have a panic attack while you are breathing in your lower belly."

He walks me through another interaction where he is mindful about what is going on for him, and fiercely clear in expressing himself to those around him. "I was the token at my prep school. I wanted to be there, and they wanted me for diversity. Everyone got what they wanted. Now, forty years later, as a yoga practitioner, I hear from white folks who want someone with more 'authentic experience' to work in their yoga studios. And I say, 'I can come work with you guys. I can come as a teacher. But to come as the Black guy who rubber-stamps what you're doing? NO. I'm not going to come rubber-stamp your feeling good while you're not really doing the work and while you're gentrifying the community without a word."

I ask Anthony what he means by "gentrifying the community without a word." He explains that "gentrification can be humane if you say, 'We're gentrifying. Bringing in a bigger economic base. Let's be better at it. Let's not treat people as less than human.' But if you're acting like it's not happening, and you're holier than thou, that's horseshit. I met an aboriginal person in Vietnam who cautioned people, 'Don't show up like the great white hunter who looks around and acts like he owns every fucking thing.' The great white hunter is the person who moves onto a street with Miles Davis living next door and complains about the noise."

So, Anthony tells clients, "If you want to work with me, we have a program and process we can take you through, with love. It'll make you uncomfortable and you should be uncomfortable. You should look at your shit and want better for yourself and for the community that you're in. If you're a white man going to an Indian reservation and you're feeling comfortable, you're not doing the work. They're making you feel comfortable. No, you should feel uncomfortable, period. Everyone adjusting to you does not equal you doing the work.'"

I ask him what he says to with people who have the opposite need, who don't have a sense of having any innate power.

"First, disabuse yourself of what you've been taught. Attack your belief system. For example, I spoke to a bunch of foster kids who were moping around and feeling bad about themselves. I came in and turned that upside down. I said, 'Hi. I'm a foster kid. Let's talk about who has a compelling story.'" Anthony asked for a show of hands and invited kids to share their stories with him and each other. "Then I told the kids about me, and how being a foster child is what got me to a prep school. How I'm sure my social worker Ms. Moretti points to me to this day, because she became part of that compelling story. 'You are in the best position to tell a compelling story,' I told these kids. 'The middle-class A student may have a harder time going to college because you're out here grinding and doing your work and people want to be a part of your story.' You can see the lights go on. I tell the kids, 'Tell stories of transformation. They can feel your story.'"

I ask him about his long-held commitment to bringing his story of personal transformation on the continent of Africa back to Black men in the United States.

"It goes like this. If I can't take you to the desert, I'm going to take the desert to you in the power of the story I tell. I've sat on death row with brothers. 'I'm not scared of you,' I tell them. Silence breaks people down, so I start by not saying anything for five minutes. Then I say, 'Brother, I'm from the same side of the street as you. Let's look at where you are. Why are you here? Who is doing the thinking *for* you?' Had I believed Ms. Moretti when she said, 'Oh Anthony, private school is not for you, you're just a little poor black boy in the hood,' where would I be?' But I didn't believe that. I'm interrupting your belief system—first and foremost, that's universal—that you don't matter. 'Who says that? Who? Who?' I tell them, 'I demand a recount.' I tell these guys that the frog drowning in the well doesn't know it's in the well. You need to put yourself proximate to people outside of your realm of consciousness. You will never grow or transform if you stay within your current realm of consciousness. I want to make you uncomfortable, breathe with that; that is what will transform your life, expand your consciousness. I'm going to challenge you." I ask him how an incarcerated person can be in proximity to people outside their realm of consciousness. "I tell them, 'Read every book on this bookshelf. Read Malcolm X. Read the dictionary. Learning new words expands your consciousness.'"

He continues.

"The transformation comes in the great questions, not the answers. If you don't have a question, go think about that. I owe that knowledge to Professor Pearl T. Robinson at Tufts. She asked me the question that blew my wig off. 'Have you ever thought about going to Africa?' I had to stop my anger. I had to stop everything. I had to look at this woman I had great respect for and say, 'What did you just ask me?' I had to bow down. *Whoa.* 'Have you thought about going to Africa?' That's a question. I had to grapple with that question. I knew right there that that's what I gotta do. It changed my life. Saved my life. Transformed my life."

While Anthony takes his yoga practice to incarcerated persons and foster kids, a number of Anthony's yoga clients are wealthy; this is how he earns a living. I ask him how his message goes over with the privileged people. How he connects to them. "I went to school with those people. At prep school I was these kids' mother and father because they did not get that love. These were the most lonely and dejected kids. All they had was money. Even though I was from the hood, I came to understand them very well."

"I tell them, 'DuBois talks about "double consciousness," which is being able to code-switch. We understand the Black world, and we understand the white world. I did cross-cultural sensitivity workshops for white women who want to do good by going into these incarceration centers with Black men. First and foremost, I have to make them feel comfortable in order to get into their psyche and their heart. I brought my passport with me and told them how my story began, not even knowing I'd need a passport, and that since then I've filled three passports. I told them that when I went to Somalia as a Black man and pulled out that American passport, I was no longer a brother, I was an American. This was during the incident that inspired the film *Black Hawk Down* and there were Somali people ready to shoot me in the airport. On the one hand, I am a brother. I'm not making the decision to destroy their country. But on the other hand, when the American citizens are evacuated I can pull that card, I can use that privilege. Even though I am not treated as an American here in America, around the world I've been able to use my American passport and my Blackness to get into places. Then I said to these women in the sensitivity workshops, 'Put your hands up. Look at your palm. Turn and look at the back of your hand.' I said, 'That's your passport. That's your privilege. Understand your privilege.' I talked about me being in the Kenyan village with the kid asking how many languages I speak, and him speaking five languages and writing his second book at fifteen. I told them that kid made me feel angry at my prep school and my university. I'd thought I was a little different, better, and that kind of seeped into me. As my foster mother would say, 'You was smelling your piss.' I realized this privilege really made me inadequate if I wanted to be a real Renaissance man, a real traveled professional.

"When I'm working with CEOs of major corporations, these trust fund babies, I tell them, 'You have to understand that your privilege is a blind spot. You realize you're not qualified to be here. I'm not going to tell you that but I'm going to put everything in your path where you come to that self-realization. Your being a privileged white man is really a disadvantage vis-à-vis people who are well traveled, and have knowledge from all over the world. Your privilege has its shortcomings. It has failed you, because no one has challenged you.' I tell them, 'I know you. I went to school with you. I know how to make you feel comfortable. I know how to take off all your clothes without you even knowing, and you look up and say, "I'm naked," and I say, "Exactly." When we're here in your mansion, where you're having a retreat for your team, Imma let you be the man. I'm never gonna disparage you in front of your peers and staff. But when we come back to this house after the retreat is over I'm gonna fucking give it to you. I'm going to tell you the things you need to know.' We had a four-hour session. This person changed so much. Literally went to work the next day and he was asking people kindly, 'How are you? You should go home.' A friend said to him, 'Who the fuck *are* you?' I get them to where they can see themselves. You gotta deal with personal pain points, places of insecurity, especially if they're in a position of power. If you alleviate them, then they can be interested in others. Whereas misery loves company. They feel, 'If I'm miserable, I'm gonna try to make you miserable. If I'm happy, I'm trying to make you happy.'"

The aspect of Anthony's work that is about teaching mindfulness to wealthy people enables him to pay his bills. But teaching mindfulness to incarcerated youth and adults is pure service. "They've grown up with 'kill or be killed.' My work is about helping these brothers experience unconditional love by another brother." The ultimate in mindfulness, and kindness, and gratitude. The ultimate in paying it forward. And in being.

IN SHORT: EVERYTHING YOU NEED IS WITHIN YOU

Each of these practices—mindfulness, kindness, and gratitude—can turn a shitty day completely around for you. You can use them to make someone else's day better, too. With effort, you can hone each one of these practices into instinct so that each becomes natural, like breathing. They are your sword and shield, your cape and hammer, your magic. Unleash them. They will not let you down.

I was telling Dan that I had quoted Ram Dass at the start of this chapter for his "why" of human existence: "We're all just walking each other home." I said to Dan, "I mean, it doesn't actually work because the minute you get to the first person's house, then that person would have to turn around and walk the second person to their house, and no one would actually get home, but I just love the idea of that mutual obligation to each other, that we would do that for each other, if somehow we could." Dan held my eyes in silence. "It's not the house," he told me. "The walk itself is home." Tears began streaming down my face.

The walk is home.

You have no idea what will happen on this walk, in this life, on this journey. But it is yours. You are capable. And the time is now. Our final chapter looks at confronting what's next, with all the potions, tools, tips, and resources you've assembled up to this point. Shall we?

Unpack and Reflect

- Who do I know that best embodies these superpowers? What can I learn from them?
- When I'm mindful, what comes up for me? What do I notice by way of recurring feelings?
- What acts of kindness do I enjoy doing?
- What am I grateful for right now, specifically?

13

ABOVE ALL ELSE, KEEP GOING

I'm gonna take my horse to the old town road
I'm gonna ride 'til I can't no more

—Lil Nas X

Some will say it's a very rough time to be making your way into adult life. A global pandemic and political unrest shed light on the tremendous systemic inequities already affecting opportunities and quality of life among Americans and around the world. Your plans may have been completely upended. It may be hard for you to find any work (let alone meaningful work) while the economy is recovering. If you're thinking, *This isn't how it was supposed to happen*, you're right.

But these are not the worst of times. Your ancestors endured war and the threat of war, a lack of food and shelter, violence, legal discrimination, and other types of pain. You come from people who survived long enough to give you life. Take in that sweet thought for a moment.

And now it's your turn. You were born for this.

You will meet moments of raucous laughter, ecstasy, and wonder as an adult. You will meet moments of despair, ruin, and failure. Much is out of your control. The only thing you are in charge of is yourself, though even that self can be unwieldy at times. But nature finds a way, as my son, Sawyer, likes to say. And even though he is fighting anxiety every day, I can envision a time when he is able to be at peace with his fears and, therefore, able to make his way. And I see that for you, too.

THIRTEEN STEPS FOR ADULTING

These steps are going to read as very familiar but I want to set them in one handy place for you. They come from the chapter headings of this book, but if you look at them all together you'll see that they provide a road map to becoming an adult.

1. Decide that you want to become an adult.
2. Know that you can fend for yourself, and commit to doing it.
3. Focus not on being perfect, but on continually learning and growing.
4. Construct your good character.
5. Figure out who you are and what you want to do with this life.
6. Look at places where you're stuck and work on them.
7. Build good relationships with other humans.
8. Be responsible with your money.
9. Take good care of your body and mind.
10. Trust that you can and will survive the terrible things that may happen.
11. Make things better in the world, somehow.
12. Be mindful, kind, and grateful whenever possible.
13. Keep going.

DON'T JUST TAKE MY WORD FOR IT

This chapter ends with just one story.

MEET SHAUN—HANDLING LIFE ONE STEP AT A TIME

In photos and over the phone, my Australian friend Shaun comes across as a happy-go-lucky dude. When he invited me to be on his parenting podcast, I said yes, partly because I'm interested in visiting new places (even if only virtually) and partly because so few men are writing and podcasting in the parenting space. I am always interested in different perspectives. Over the course of two hours together, Shaun and I click. I particularly love the tenderness in his voice when he speaks about his two-and-a-half-year-old son, Oscar. I find his observations and philosophy about childrearing to be on point, and also deeply grounded and utterly without ego, which is the thing that tanks so much of modern parenting. At the end of the call, I tell Shaun that while I don't want to come across as paternalistic, I want to compliment him on having developed such deep maturity at a relatively young age. "What are you, thirty-one?" I ask. He laughs. "I'm twenty-four." This means Oscar was born when Shaun was twenty-one. Now I am really intrigued. A few weeks later, we are back on the phone, and I am interviewing him for this book.

I'm ending this book with Shaun's story not because I think you're going to have a child one day and need to know how to deal. (You may or may not have children; it's largely up to you and your ability, physically and financially, to honor whatever you decide.) But because there's nothing like a baby to grow you up *real fast*. If buying a houseplant is a small step toward adulting, and getting a dog is a large stride, then having a baby is a giant leap that comes with a prayer that you're going to get enough stuff right—because it's a *kid*. "Reflecting on it makes me emotional," Shaun tells me. "Having Oscar has changed my life in massive ways. It was definitely unexpected when it happened this early on in my life. With that being said, I always wanted to be a dad. It's just that the reasons have changed."

Shaun met Oscar's mother, Jess, when he was nineteen and she was twenty. He'd just made a move to the big city, Perth, on the western coast of Australia, and after months of putting off finding a new dentist he finally made himself do it. There he was, enduring the awkwardness of lying back in the chair and having people stare down at him, when he saw a beautiful set of blue eyes, belonging to Jess, the dental assistant. "We just locked eyes for some reason. It didn't feel awkward or uncomfortable. Without her even having to say a word, I felt a softness there. I felt connected. We get so caught up thinking about what we need to be *doing* or *fixing*, but in that moment the feeling of softness was almost a feeling of simply *being*. It was like a sigh of ease."

You may recall that my beloved Dan and I began dating at nineteen and twenty. So, this conversation with a stranger named Shaun who is less than half my age takes me right back to 1988. I can't help but notice the joy I feel repeatedly at having found a person to stand shoulder to shoulder with in this one precious life.

When the dental appointment was over, Shaun and Jess lingered and made small talk. He didn't want the conversation to end and even considered booking another dreaded appointment just to see her again. But it didn't come to that. A week later, Jess made the move via Facebook. A month later they were dating. A year and a half later, in January 2017, they found out Jess was pregnant with Oscar.

But let's go back a second.

Shaun grew up as the eldest of three boys in a home with an alcoholic father. He tried to be there for his mother when things were bad, while protecting his brothers. After graduating from high school, he went straight into the working world, where he started out stocking shelves for liquor and convenience stores and "digging big holes" for a pool installer. Pretty quickly, though, he realized that as a lifetime lover of "sport" (as sports are called in Australia), he ought to try to find work in that field. He did a yearlong course that offered a diploma in "sport development," which led to a job with a cricket organization. His next job was with the Western Australian Football Commission, where his role was to promote the game of Australian-rules football throughout schools, community centers, and after-school programs, "basically trying to engage kids in the sport and provide them a place to be able to improve their health, make friends, and become lifelong lovers of the game." From there, he started a coaching business where he provides one-on-one support to athletes.

In January 2017, Shaun had just turned twenty-one and was living the life. His coaching business was going strong just from word-of-mouth referrals. He had a cool apartment in the city and hung out a couple of nights a week with friends and colleagues. And he and Jess had started living together. One Saturday, they went out on the town with another couple for a long summer evening (January is summer in Australia). "We had a really nice dinner. Went to a couple of bars. One of my mates from the football club had just found out that he was going to be a dad with a partner that he'd been off and on with. He had a reputation for being a bit of a Casanova, so I'll be honest, we laughed to ourselves and thought, *How's he going to be a dad?*"

Jess wasn't feeling very well that night. The next day, she was worse and stayed in bed all day. On Monday, she was still quite sick and got a doctor's appointment for that afternoon. Shaun didn't go with her because he had coaching clients. Besides, they both thought it was just a stomach bug. Midway through a coaching session, Shaun's phone vibrated with a heap of texts, and he "had this weird feeling." When the coaching session finished, he looked at his phone and the texts were all from Jess saying, "Can you come home, please?" "I call. No answer. At this stage I'm thinking, *Do I cancel my next session?* I try to call again. No answer. Again. No answer. Finally, she picks up the phone. Just silence. 'Are you there?' I say. 'Hello?' I just hear quiet sobbing. And it hits me like a steam train. 'Are you pregnant?' I ask her. It's this somber 'YES.' I freeze. I feel anxiety, excitement, love, and fear all in one. 'I'm on my way home,' I tell her. I hang up the phone. Start driving. I have this overwhelming feeling of *I'm going to be a dad with the woman I love and want to be with for the rest of my life, like how awesome is this?* I've got my pedal to the metal, trying to channel my inner Dom Toretto, from *Fast and Furious*, when this other thought hits me. *Wait. What if Jess doesn't want to have this baby? What if she doesn't want to have it with me?* We hadn't had this conversation yet. I called my mom. 'Mum, I've got something to tell you.' She goes, 'Jess is pregnant, isn't she?' Then she tells me, 'Shaun, if you want to support her, simply be with her.' I run up the stairs, nearly run through the front door, give Jess the biggest hug that we've ever had. And even though I have the urge to start talking and figuring it out and doing something, I have my Mum's advice, 'Simply be with her,' front of mind. So, I just wait. And listen. Turns out she had the exact same feeling as me: stoked to be a mum and to be a parent with me. But she was also scared that this would be holding me back in some way whether in my career or whatever, and she was scared about her career, too. We talked forever. We decided we wanted to take that next step in our journey together."

Life was about to get crazier. They'd gone to tell Jess's parents the news, both of whom were very supportive, and while they were there Shaun got an offer for his dream job, with a company in a small country town called Broome, a three-day drive north of Perth. He'd be working with fifteen- to nineteen-year-old aspiring professional athletes, most of whom were from indigenous communities. "It was something I'd put in for a couple months before, and had been working really hard for. But I had no inkling that I'd even have a chance. Jess walked into the room, and I had a blank look on my face. I was honest with her. Told her it sounds like such an awesome opportunity, but is it even worth considering in light of everything?" These two twentysomethings had just found out they were going to be parents, and then, in the same breath, had to decide whether to move fifteen hundred miles away from their own parents so that Shaun could take this new job.

Talk about terrifying.

Talk about adulting!

After thinking on it for a week, Shaun accepted the job. All went well. Oscar was born and spent the first eighteen months of his life up in Broome, which was, by all accounts, a wonderful place for the three of them. I ask Shaun how he and Jess decided to move to Broome, which was perhaps the riskiest decision so far in their young lives. "I believe in following your heart, not your head, as often as possible," Shaun tells me. "I felt the pull toward the opportunity, and Jess reciprocated that. The idea of getting out of the city and living that country/regional life had appealed to me for a long time. And at the end of the day, as much as I believe it takes a village to raise a child and that parental support is amazing to have, I thought taking on this sort of move will either make us or break us. And I don't know why, but I wanted to run toward that opportunity to grow in one way or another. There were so many challenges in our time up in Broome. We learned so much more about each other than we would have had we stayed in Perth. We had the space and time to *be*." And by "be" Shaun doesn't mean "chill out and do nothing," but rather, "lean in to discovering who we are." This is big.

Of course, I can't help but be super curious about this move to Broome. As a fifty-three-year-old woman of color, I'm picturing this (at the time) twenty-one-year-old white dude who thinks he can just head out to the hinterlands of Australia to coach indigenous kids. I ask him about his cultural readiness for the job. I like his answer. "I'd always felt an interest in learning about the oldest culture on this planet. The indigenous people in Broome have over sixty-five thousand years of rich beautiful history. I was never going to learn like that in a city like Perth. The opportunity was to build relationships with communities, remote schools, and the countrymen and -women throughout these areas, in order to help their young people. We wanted to prepare them athletically, but also prepare them for a potential move to what we call 'the Big Smoke,' which is a term for a large city like Perth or Sydney or Melbourne."

I ask him what's been hardest about parenting so far, and learn that it centers around his father's alcoholism. "I told him, 'Dad, I'm not going to have my family around that type of behavior.'" His father promised he wouldn't go back to drinking again because of Oscar, and, at first, he made good on that promise. "He has been there for us and for Oscar in many ways. He's an awesome granddad, and Oscar loves him." But after a time, Shaun's father went down that path of alcoholism again, and Shaun had to draw the line. "We don't have any contact with him right now." Shaun was 100 percent clear that he wasn't going to let the very things he had witnessed as a child infect Oscar's upbringing, but admits, "It's hard." That's the thing with adulting—it's on you, which can feel like an imperative you'd just as soon opt out of in favor of being cared for by someone else. But it can and should also feel like an invitation to be the person in charge, the one who sets the rules and boundaries you want to live your life by. This is what I mean by the terror and joy of fending for yourself.

"I'm clear that the environment you create and the associations you put time and energy into can be either evolutionary or detrimental," he tells me. "Family or not, I don't want to put time and energy into relationships that are detrimental. If I can feel my best self around someone and we're on the same page, that's awesome. If we don't align, that's okay because there are plenty of relationships in life, and I'll just not put my time and energy into that one."

Shaun and Jess are two youngish people who grew up in the working and middle classes and now have a child, unexpectedly. So, I want to know how things are going financially. "I've never taken my eye off making sure that we are not just stable but thriving." Jess is the manager of a very successful cosmetic dental practice. "I'm so proud of her," Shaun tells me. And he expanded his athletic coaching business to include life coaching and podcasting (which is how we met), and all of that is going well. He tells me that he and Jess ate up the advice in the financial planning book *The Barefoot Investor* by Scott Pape, which Shaun recommends "to any young person in any country because it provides step-by-step insights and lessons into how to set up these autopilot financial systems that allow you to not think about finances as much." This book taught them how to set aside money for the future and for Oscar. But Shaun also says that in a very philosophical sense they value time over money "because time is finite." They take turns looking after Oscar when he is not at a childcare center, "which he loves." Shaun's mother and Jess's parents are close enough to spend a lot of time with their grandson. And Shaun and Jess prioritize their relationships and continual learning over everything else.

I ask him what being a parent has taught him about himself. "I was and still am very ambitious, whether personally, spiritually, or professionally. I'd always thought of myself as being considerate, but becoming a parent put me on my ass in a lot of ways. It forced me to think beyond my self-interest to thinking about Oscar and Jess much more often, and about the implications of my behaviors and actions on them." I ask for examples. "Well, I actually didn't know that babies didn't sleep the way that we do from the start, which was a learning curve. Then I just assumed, to be honest, that Jess as the mum would be doing most of the wakeups during the night. It wasn't a belief that she *should*. I just thought that's how it *was*. My curiosity into how it all works led to a lot of conversations with Jess. I learned that the mindset of *I can do everything that I want to do the way I was doing it before* would be to neglect my role and lead to burnout for Jess. Oscar was bottle-fed from quite early on, for all kinds of reasons, so I was able to start getting up during the night for however long it took to feed him, burp him, change him, to give Jess time to rest."

Shaun says this is an example of how he constantly asks *why* and brings "a tidal wave of curiosity to *everything*" (which often annoyed his teachers, family, and colleagues). "But it's why I'm living an extraordinary life." He says, "Becoming a parent helped me to take other people's perspectives into account in the workplace. I'm more patient. A better listener. And a much better friend. What hasn't changed is my ambition. The constructs that have been set up in our Western society around you go from school to university or from school to a job, then you get a house, have a family, get married. That whole structure. I'm not against it because I'm following it in some ways, but I'm following it in my own way, and that fills me up with pride. Who knows? Oscar might not be taking notice of how I'm trying to do things, but I hope a sliver gets through, a sliver of the idea that you're your own person, that there's no set way to do things. We might have to do things differently tomorrow. Follow your dreams and live life in your way."

Shaun is especially curious about what he can learn from Oscar. "Before having Oscar, I thought of parenting as guiding a child and teaching them all these different things about life, and a part of me still believes that. But there's a part now that wholeheartedly believes that Oscar has come into my life and into Jess's life to teach us a lot more than we will ever teach him. He has simply come through us, not from us, and I just arrived in this life twenty-one years before he did. There are times and moments day to day where he's teaching me more than I could ever teach him, I think."

IN SHORT: CONTINUING ON IN THE FACE OF LIFE'S CHALLENGES MAKES YOU FEEL *ALIVE*

When I give talks on my first book (*How to Raise an Adult*, on the harm of overparenting), I tell parents that when we do too much stuff for our kids instead of teaching them to do things for themselves, we deprive them of this chance to *be* that Shaun says he felt when he and Jess made the big move to Broome. What I mean by "being" is the task of learning to be a human, which is not something anyone can handle for you. You have to do it yourself. You have to want to. You have to learn how. And you have to *have to*—meaning life has to throw you that "tag, you're it" wrench. Having baby Oscar was Shaun's "tag, you're it" moment, but it doesn't have to be a baby. It can be anything. It can be something as existentially big as heeding the barbaric yawp from within you that urges you to choose an option others don't understand. It can be as practical as handling things when your moving van catches fire. Listen to Shaun retell this stage of his life. Hear the various pieces of uncertainty combusting in his brain, which then forged themselves into a decision, a commitment, a willingness to go for it and learn from it, whatever it may turn out to be. To *be*. It's not just the question; it's the whole damn point.

Unpack and Reflect

- You've learned a lot about yourself while reading this book. Ask yourself: With whom do I feel safe talking about this stuff? With whom am I afraid to discuss this stuff, and why?
- Look back over your young adulthood. What are the big things you've learned so far about yourself and your way of being in the world? What can you be proud of? Is there anyone you want to thank for helping you so far?
- Look ahead. What are three specific things you want to work on in order to continue to learn and grow? Who will you ask for guidance and assistance here?
- What do you think you want from this one wild and precious life of yours? What are you going to do in order to make it happen?

APPENDIX:

RESOURCES

FENDING

- Watch YouTube videos on life skills called "Dad, How Do I?" with over three million subscribers

WHAT TO DO FOR WORK

- Read *You Can Do Anything: The Surprising Power of a "Useless" Liberal Arts Education*, by George Anders
- Read *When to Jump: If the Job You Have Isn't the Life You Want*, by Mike Lewis
- Google "best cities for young people" for updated information on the places that offer the job opportunities, cost of living, and lifestyle most suited to people your age
- Check out *Forbes* data on best employers sliced and diced in all kinds of ways: https://www.forbes.com/best-employers

THE VALUE OF HUMAN CONNECTION

- Read *Friendship: The Evolution, Biology, and Extraordinary Power of Life's Fundamental Bond*, by Lydia Denworth
- Read *Social: Why Our Brains Are Wired to Connect*, by Matt Lieberman

GETTING UNSTUCK

- Read *Maybe You Should Talk to Someone: A Therapist, HER Therapist, and Our Lives Revealed*, by psychotherapist Lori Gottlieb, our resident guru in chapter 6, "Get Out of Neutral"

- Check out Adina Glickman, whom we met in chapter 9, "Take Good Care," and chapter 10, "How to Cope," and who is a certified academic, life, and career coach. You can book her here: https://www.adinaglickman.com/recent-grads

- Check out Lexi Butler, who spoke about how to hustle in chapter 6, "Get Out of Neutral," and offers career coaching. You can book her here: http://naturallylexi.com/

MANAGING YOUR MONEY

- Check out Denae Hannah, the storyteller we met in chapter 8, "Money Matters," who got out of debt and became a financial counselor. You can book her here: https://www.wealthydenae.com/. In addition, she recommends these resources:
  - Financial literacy for college students: https://mindovermoney.stanford.edu/
  - National financial resource lists and virtual financial counseling: https://mytrustplus.org/
  - Locate your local Financial Empowerment Center: https://fecpublic.org/
  - K–12 financial literacy: https://www.councilforeconed.org/
  - Find an Accredited Financial Counselor®: https://www.afcpe.org/find-an-afcpe-certified-professional/
  - Find a Certified Financial Planner™ (there are pro bono options): https://www.plannersearch.org/

- Read *Rich Dad, Poor Dad: What the Rich Teach Their Kids About Money That the Poor and Middle Class Do Not!,* by Robert T. Kiyosaki

- Read *The Barefoot Investor: The Only Money Guide You'll Ever Need*, by Scott Pape

- Read *I Will Teach You to Be Rich: No Guilt. No Excuses. No BS. Just a 6-Week Program That Works*, by Ramit Sethi

- Read *You Are a Badass at Making Money: Master the Mindset of Wealth*, by Jen Sincero

OWNING YOUR SITUATION

- Read *Normal Sucks: How to Live, Learn, and Thrive Outside the Lines*, by Jonathan Mooney

DEALING WITH ANXIETY

This list of "the best anxiety support groups of 2020" is offered by Verywell Mind (https://www.verywellmind.com/), an online resource affiliated with the Cleveland Clinic, one of the top hospitals in the United States:

- **Best Overall:** Turn2Me (https://turn2me.ie/)
- **Best Free Screening Tools:** Mental Health America (https://www.inspire.com/groups/mental-health-america/topic/anxiety-and-phobias)
- **Best Informational Site:** Anxiety and Depression Association of America (https://adaa.org/adaa-online-support-group)
- **Best for Free One-on-One Support:** 7 Cups (https://www.7cups.com/)
- **Best Peer-to-Peer Support Group:** The Tribe (https://support.therapytribe.com/anxiety-support-group/)
- **Most Active Anxiety Forum:** Daily Strength (https://www.dailystrength.org/group/anxiety)
- **Best for Joining Multiple Support Groups:** SupportGroups.com (https://www.supportgroups.com/)

MINDFULNESS

- Read *Wherever You Go, There You Are: Mindfulness Meditation in Everyday Life*, by Jon Kabat-Zinn
- Read *Full Catastrophe Living: Using the Wisdom of Your Body and Mind to Face Stress, Pain, and Illness*, by Jon Kabat-Zinn
- Read *Peace Is Every Step: The Path of Mindfulness in Everyday Life*, by Thich Nhat Hanh
- Read *Mindfulness: Finding Peace in a Frantic World*, by Mark Williams and Danny Penman

COMMITMENT TO INCLUSION
IN *YOUR TURN: HOW TO BE AN ADULT*
BY JULIE LYTHCOTT-HAIMS

As a Black, biracial, queer person, I know that representation matters. As an author, I want to do my part to bring an anti-racist, decolonized, and inclusive approach to publishing.

Too many authors, editors, and publishers across every genre embed characters and narratives with unnamed whiteness and other characteristics considered "the norm," and only identify race and other characteristics when those identities deviate from this assumed norm. In nonfiction in particular, often a topic is investigated and elucidated from the perspective of white, middle-class, straight people without making such assumptions plain. Yet the human population is richly diverse, and none of us wants to feel ignored or othered on the page. We all yearn to be included.

Inclusion is the act of creating environments in which any individual or group can be and feel welcomed, respected, supported, and valued so that they are able to participate as their full, authentic selves. This is the experience I want readers to have whenever they read one of my books.

I hope that *Your Turn* demonstrates that it is both valuable and feasible to craft a text that imagines all readers. I've attempted to do so through my narrative choices. I've also incorporated perspectives of people who, in the aggregate, reflect the rich diversity of our human community here in the United States. For example, in *Your Turn* there are:

- people from across the gender spectrum
- people from a myriad of racial and ethnic backgrounds
- people from across the sexual orientation spectrum
- poor, working-class, middle-class, upper-middle-class, and wealthy people
- neurodivergent, neurodiverse, and neurotypical people
- minimally educated, moderately educated, and highly educated people
- immigrants and the children of immigrants
- single people and people with partners

- people with mental health challenges
- people with disabilities
- people with disease
- people with addictions and people raised by addicts
- people who were fostered or adopted as children
- people who have struggled with fertility
- people who have had interactions with law enforcement, including incarceration
- liberals and conservatives
- Christians, Jews, Muslims, atheists, and Hindus
- people who have served in the military
- critics of capitalism and beneficiaries of it
- elected officials
- people who are estranged from family and people who are close to family
- people from all over the United States
- artists, actors, engineers, students, doctors, lawyers, teachers, directors, businesspeople, entrepreneurs, professors, dog owners, vegans, tech people, military consultants, public speakers, philanthropists, therapists, reality TV stars, nonprofit founders and workers, educators, outside-the-box thinkers, marketers, dancers, mentors of first-generation college students, financial consultants, writers, activists, Lyft drivers, designers, health and wellness practitioners, bankers, rock climbers, UPS drivers, eyeglass makers, athletic coaches, higher ed administrators, and parents

By putting these people on the page with equal dignity, all are "normalized"; none are outliers or "others." I included a profile of a Black male college student who was surrounded by police officers with guns drawn following a brawl at a fraternity party because who he became following the incident speaks directly to our present moment. Its inclusion as one of the many stories in the book illustrates that, unfortunately, this too is normal.

To do the work of ensuring that all lives, in fact, *do* matter, we must intentionally bring those who have been kept in the margins onto the center of the page.

Julie

ACKNOWLEDGMENTS

I'm fortunate that so many folx held my hand, hugged me hard, pushed me from behind, pulled me through, cheered, and gnashed their teeth right along with me as I wrote this book. They include:

The one and only editor I've ever had: Barbara ("Favorite Editor") Jones, from whom I've learned to know my voice, my authority, and my right to tell it my way. Thank you for teaching me that I can yell and cry without fear of losing you. Thank you for patting my hand, wiping my face, hugging my brain, and rubbing my heart. I trust you.

All the folks at Henry Holt and Company, St. Martin's Press, and Macmillan, who keep believing in my books and making my work theirs and their work mine: Scottie Bowditch, Janel Brown, Allison Carney, Amy Einhorn, Pat Eisemann, Rebecca Lang, Ruby Rose Lee, Jason Liebman, Caitlin O'Shaughnessy, Jason Reigal, Maggie Richards, Kenn Russell, Nicolette Seeback, Christopher Sergio, Catryn Silbersack, and Kelly S. Too.

My literary agent: Kimberly Witherspoon, who fills my tank, points me in the right direction, and puts up guardrails before I go careening off of the side of the road. And all the folks on her team at InkWell Management, including Alexis Hurley, Maria Whelan, Jessie Thorsted, and Nathaniel Jacks.

The amazing folks at Hella Social Impact: Stefania Pomponi, Lynn Johnson, Edita Rodriguez, and Ashley Keeler, and Yona Deshommes of Riverchild Media, all of whom helped make this book go deeply into the right places.

My colleagues in the Parenting Squad, the Silicon Guild, and TheLi.st who are there with advice and solace as I navigate the worlds of book publishing and public speaking.

Amanda Hall, Jean Forstner, and their wonderful teams at Kepler's Books and Magazines, and Kepler's Literary Foundation.

My dedicated team: Clarice Cho, Catherine Hay, and Jeanette Miller, for your diligence, integrity, patience, and zeal.

I also want to pay deep respect to the guests whose stories complete these chapters—Akshay, Alex, Ameera, Ananda, Angelina, Anthony, Ashley, Ben, Casey, Denae, Elena, Hannah, Hugo, Irshad, Jamie, Jeff, Jim, Joe, Kirstin, Kristine, Kyle, Levi, Lisa, Lydia, Michael, Oliver, Orly, Sara, Shaun, Stefania, Tone, Wesley, and Zuri, and to the dozen others with whom I spoke but who are not in the book. You've demonstrated that so much good can come from being vulnerable and I am humbled by the trust you placed in me. To Leigh Marshall, who worked tirelessly to help me locate, interview, and write about these folx.

To all who strengthen these pages with their insight and candor: Chris Andrews, Jill Asher, Marcia Baczynski, Kanesha Baynard, Christina Blacken, Mike Bracco, Kris Brockmann, Lexi Butler, Clarice Cho, Richard Dweck, Amanda Gelender, Adina Glickman, Lori Gottlieb, Joan Hanawi, Joe Holtgreive, Carrie Kholi-Murchison, Jane McGonigal, Sally Mentzer, Debbie Reber, Emma Seppälä, Rachel Simmons, Michael Tubbs, Olenka Villarreal, Dave Whorton, and last but never least, Donnovan Somera Yisrael.

To my former colleagues and students at Stanford, with and for whom I developed a pedagogy of seeing young people as they are and helping them elicit truths about themselves so as to make good choices about the way forward. My decade as a freshman dean forms the basis for the guidance I offer in this book. It was such a joy to dip back into those memories and to find you there. Special thanks to Bill Burnett and Dave Evans at the d.school for seeing synergy between their work and mine and for bringing me onto the teaching team for the undergraduate course Designing Your Life.

And finally, on the personal side, I feel deep gratitude to my ancestors, who lived long enough to birth the people who birthed me and whose spirit infuses me with gratitude, purpose, determination, joy, and liberation, and to the Lythcotts, Snookeses, Forresters, Averys, McDaniels, Wirthensohns, Sobomehins, Williamses, Haimses, Hermans, Jacksons, Handlers, Lonczaks, Benders, Scorses, Wests, and Ruprachts: Thank you, fam, for your love and support. Thank you also to the friends who check in, offer support when times are rough, celebrate when stuff goes right, and hold me accountable to my own dreams: Elizabeth Arata, Jessica Armstrong, Neha Bagchi, Amy Bender, Mike Brody, Susie Brubaker-Cole, Deborah Golder, Deb Gruenfeld, Diane Hunter, Susan Ito, Eric Jackson, Lindsay Kafka, Lee

Daniel Kravetz, Thane Kreiner, Megan Maxwell, Victoria Osman, Nicole Sanchez, Erika Schillinger, Paul Solorzano, Luke Taylor, Randy Weiner, and Andy Weis. Special thanks to Jazmin Quill, my almost sister, who took me to the strawberry farm where the Pacific meets the land to sort out why I could not write this book. To Michal Pasternak, who took me on long walks to unwind the spool of adulting and help me think about how to weave it up into something coherent and useful to others. To Mary Obelnicki for pushing me to see the parts of the human experience that are not well understood. To the seers who speak for the universe and tell me to keep going: Jeanette Smith-Laws, Maryellen Myers, and Mary Ruth Quinn. To George and Jean Lythcott, and Dan Lythcott-Haims, for being my first experiences with unconditional love. To Lucille Clifton, whose poetry made me feel that if she was possible and her words were possible, then maybe I, too, was possible. To those who follow and support my work and who cheered me on when I struggled. To a stranger named Nan in Portland whose postcards of encouragement became a highlight of the final months of writing this book.

And finally, to Jean Lythcott, my mother, whom I am coming to understand and adore more with each passing day, and with whom I hope to write a book one day.

To Avery Lythcott-Haims and Sawyer Lythcott-Haims, my favorite young adults, from whom I learn constantly, who lent a few aspects of their journey to these pages, and for whom I most want to get this book right. And to their friends: Carla Kong, Nico Diaz-Wahl, Zachary Englhardt, Thomas Price, and Desmond Alioshin, who allowed me to bounce definitions of adulthood off of them.

And for Dan Lythcott-Haims, the best thing that's ever happened to me, who held me in 2012 as I sobbed and said, "I think I might want to try to do something with my writing," and who has beamed with love as I've delivered three books since. Baby, you're still the one. There's no one I'd rather be an adult with.

INDEX

ABOUT THE AUTHOR

Julie Lythcott-Haims is the *New York Times* bestselling author of *How to Raise an Adult*, *Real American*, and *Your Turn*. She holds a BA from Stanford, a JD from Harvard Law School, and an MFA from California College of the Arts. She resides in the Bay Area with her partner, their two itinerant young adults, and her mother.